CONTRACT LAW OF THE INTERNAL MARKET

CONTRACT LAW OF THE INTERNAL MARKET

Stephen Weatherill

intersentia
Cambridge – Antwerp – Portland

Intersentia Ltd
Sheraton House | Castle Park
Cambridge | CB3 0AX | United Kingdom
Tel.: +44 1223 370 170 | Fax: +44 1223 370 169
Email: mail@intersentia.co.uk
www.intersentia.com | www.intersentia.co.uk

Distribution for the UK and Ireland:
NBN International
Airport Business Centre, 10 Thornbury Road
Plymouth, PL6 7 PP
United Kingdom
Tel.: +44 1752 202 301 | Fax: +44 1752 202 331
Email: orders@nbninternational.com

Distribution for Europe and all other countries:
Intersentia Publishing nv
Groenstraat 31
2640 Mortsel
Belgium
Tel.: +32 3 680 15 50 | Fax: +32 3 658 71 21
Email: mail@intersentia.be

Distribution for the USA and Canada:
International Specialized Book Services
920 NE 58th Ave. Suite 300
Portland, OR 97213
USA
Tel.: +1 800 944 6190 (toll free) | Fax: +1 503 280 8832
Email: info@isbs.com

ISBN 978-1-78068-240-2
D/2016/7849/98
NUR 822

British Library Cataloguing in Publication Data. A catalogue record for this book is available from the British Library.

PREFACE

Two principal ambitions have animated the writing of this book on *Contract Law of the Internal Market.*

The first ambition is to demonstrate to contract lawyers that there are constitutional limits to the role of the EU in acting in the field, but that full appreciation of the nature of those limits, and the consequences they entail for the shaping of an EU contribution to the making of contract law in Europe, requires awareness of a complex interaction of often ambiguous constitutional rules, often politically inconsistent institutional rhythms and often evasive judicial pronouncements. A contract lawyer today needs also to be an EU lawyer.

The second ambition is to demonstrate to EU lawyers that the intervention of the EU in contract law – through judicial application of the free movement and competition rules and through legislative harmonisation – is not simply a niche area that has grown erratically but ultimately remains on the edges of the EU's core public law activities, but rather that the rise of EU contract law asks some vividly important questions about the principle and practice of conferred competence and about the choice of priorities in market regulation as protective instincts and deregulatory impulses collide. This has long been visible in the field of consumer contract law and labour market regulation, but the adjustments made by the Treaty of Lisbon, especially but not only the grant of binding effect to the Charter, have sharpened the interest. An EU lawyer today does not need to be a contract lawyer, but he or she could learn a lot from appreciating the contract law of the internal market.

I have been writing in this area for almost twenty years and I am very pleased to have had the opportunity to bring together my thoughts in this book. Contract law in the EU is largely, though not exclusively, driven by the pursuit of the internal market and this exposes it to the accusation that the EU *diminishes* a proper understanding of the place of contract law. The thematic argument that forms the core of the book is that it is important in understanding the EU's impact on contracts and contract law that the EU has only a limited competence, but that, largely in consequence on the generous scope of the internal market as a concept, those limits are less of a restraint than may initially be supposed and that, moreover, pursuit of (in short) social justice within contract law is a lot less constitutionally elusive than is sometimes claimed. I don't want to dismiss the allegation that the EU has an internal market bias, but I do want to insist that the internal market is built on a more stable and rich foundation than mere deregulation. There is, as this book shows, contractual autonomy that is regulated within the EU, by free movement law, by competition law, by the Charter and through the process of re-regulatory legislative harmonisation and anti-discrimination law more generally. That is my understanding of *Contract Law of the Internal Market.*

I have enjoyed working with Intersentia and I am grateful to them for offering me very good support, from start to finish.

The book states the law as at 30 April 2016.

CONTENTS

TABLE OF CASES: ALPHABETICAL

Foto-Frost v HZA Lübeck-Ost, C-314/85 [1987] ECR I-4199 ... 53, 63, 64

TABLE OF CASES: CHRONOLOGICAL

CHAPTER 1
THE LANDSCAPE OF CONTRACT LAW IN THE EU

1.1. CONTRACTS AND CONTRACT LAW

A contract sets out the terms on which the parties agree. The contract is typically an exchange of promises. It may be very simple and the transaction may be immediate – an agreement to pay a price in return for a bar of chocolate. It may be very complicated and may envisage a long-term relationship between the contracting parties – supply of goods or services or a combination of both over a period, with payment due in instalments as the work progresses. But the basic common idea is that the parties enter into a contract in order to benefit from it. They should both be better off as a result of the exchange envisaged by the contract.

It follows that contract *law* has the function of facilitating and protecting the process of exchange. Contract law stipulates the form in which promises should be made in order to be treated as legally enforceable. It then ensures that promises are kept and, where they are not, it stipulates appropriate sanctions. Legal enforceability serves to grant confidence to those entering into contracts that their expectations will be met, which is of particular importance where the planned deal envisages a long-term relationship between the contracting parties. The law therefore promotes freedom to participate in exchange. It encourages parties to sign up to deals because they know they will be reliably performed and, if they are not, sanctions will be imposed. Contract law provides certainty and predictability.

So contracts and contract law are central to the market economy. More generally the decision whether to enter into a contract or not and, if so, with whom is an expression of personal autonomy and individual freedom. There is a political context. Sometimes, however, an agreement may be entered into without the necessary element of freedom or full understanding. Contract law may therefore perform the function of stopping agreements being used for purposes for which they are not intended by both parties. Rules allowing the review of contracts entered into under duress or as a result of fraud come into play here. So too, stretching more broadly beyond practices as pernicious as duress or fraud, the law intervenes in some circumstances where one party might not be fully able to grasp what is on offer, which is especially pertinent in the case of contracts entered into by parties holding unequal economic power. For example this may cover the prohibition of the use of unfair terms where intransparency and asymmetry of information may contaminate any sense of true negotiation. The law addresses imbalances which lead to agreements that are not motivated by genuine agreement between the parties, and thereby frees space for more truly consensual practices. Furthermore, want of alternatives may defeat the weaker party's capacity to object even where that party might be capable of understanding the disadvantages of concluding an agreement. Review of oppressive terms that would not have been accepted in a more competitive market might be considered necessary. More generally still, where necessities such as water and energy are involved, and especially where choice between suppliers is constrained, there is a case for requiring supply on defined terms rather than leaving the matter for negotiation. There is a political context, and it pushes beyond autonomy and freedom. This points to a still broader regulatory dimension to contract law, whereby the context within contractual negotiation is defined and sometimes confined by particular interventions into the structure of the market. So, for example, conclusion of an enforceable contract to supply financial services to a consumer typically involves compliance with a number of formal requirements, such as provision in advance of stipulated information. The aim is to regulate the market in order to make it more transparent, better understood by the consumer and so more competitive. Sometimes the supplier may enter the market in order to offer goods and services only provided it meets particular preconditions. Professional qualifications are of this type: regulation precludes someone offering their services as doctor or a lawyer without having met certain defined requirements. This environment of regulated contractual autonomy is today wide-ranging. Advertising is a means to alert consumers to what is on offer and thereby to induce them to enter into contracts, but it is common to find rules which restrict the permitted scope of advertising to that which is fair and decent and which accordingly impinge on the freedom of contracting. There are also broader social standards which are translated into legal rules – obligations not to discriminate on particular grounds (such as race or gender or sexual orientation) may affect freedom to choose whether to enter into a contract and how to perform the agreed promises. In this sense protection and even promotion of certain socially desirable norms, most of all that of equality, becomes part of the landscape of contract law. Once again and afresh contract law's political context is revealed.

So contract law is composed of rules that facilitate exchange between private parties, rules which provide certain mandatory requirements that must be met as a precondition to releasing the enforceability of agreements (which embraces both terms enforceable irrespective of agreement and terms that may not be enforced despite apparent agreement), and it stretches more broadly to encompass 'regulatory contract law', which covers rules which frame the circumstances in which contracting may occur. There are evident tensions here between a strain that would champion private autonomy and a strain that would mandate protection of vulnerable groups liable to be exploited by an unregulated unleash of market freedom. These, moreover, are neither watertight nor static categories. 'Contract law' is rich and varied, it is part of a complex social order and it has come a long way from a nineteenth-century vision of commercial dealing between men of equal social and economic status who are able to look after their own affairs.

1.2. CONTRACTS AND CONTRACT LAW IN EUROPE

In Europe contract law and contract regulation have typically developed at national level. The chosen patterns vary between different jurisdictions in Europe.

Most systems are based on codification, which itself commonly has a cultural and political significance that transcends its economic function. The adoption of a uniform system of private law within a defined territory may act in itself as a proclamation of the significance of that territory as a nation characterised by its own distinct identity, of which a *Code Civil* or a *Bürgerliches Gesetzbuch* not only forms part but also helps to constitute. In England the common law provides the main part of contract law, although the United Kingdom provides an example of a State where more than one system of contract law prevails, since English and Scots law are different. A great deal more could be said about the cultures, traditions and forms of contract law, but for the purposes of this book one simple and plain fact provides the background: in Europe there is diversity among systems of contract law and contract regulation.

The European Union has no objection in principle to difference. However, difference which obstructs the construction of the internal market, to which the European Union is constitutionally committed by Article 3(3) TEU, is a matter with which the European Union is required to engage.

1.3. CONTRACTS AND CONTRACT LAW IN THE EUROPEAN UNION

In all its activities the EU is tethered to the principle of conferral. Article 5 TEU declares that this means 'the Union shall act only within the limits of the competences conferred upon it by the Member States in the Treaties to attain the objectives set out therein'. This logically means, as confirmed by Article 5 TEU, that competences 'not conferred upon the Union in the Treaties remain with the Member States'. The EU may act *only* in the areas in which the Member States, ratifying the Treaties in accordance with their domestic constitutional requirements, have given it a mandate. This *matters* because it represents the source of EU's claim to exercise power on a legitimate basis. Contract lawyers, like any other kind of lawyers, need to be aware that when they encounter the EU they are dealing with a legal order that is able to deliver no more than its founding Treaties permit. This is the constitutional constraint.

There is no competence to be found in the Treaties which confers any general authorisation on the EU to operate in the field of contract law. In fact they are almost entirely bare of references to contract or contracts, and the few explicit references that are made are fleeting and tangential. This is explained in more detail in Chapter 3.3.

However, although the European Union has no general competence conferred by its founding Treaties to legislate in the field of contract law, it reaches contracts, contract law and contract regulation primarily through its mission to create and maintain an internal market stretching across the territory of all 28 Member States. The EU is committed by Article 3(3) TEU to the creation of an internal market which, according to the definition provided by Article 26(2) TFEU, 'shall comprise an area without internal frontiers in which the free movement of goods, persons, services and capital is ensured'. This project of economic integration has enjoyed enduring prominence as the EU's most visible transformative feat over the sixty-year period in which it has expanded both geographically, from six west European States to 28 States stretching from the Atlantic Ocean to the shores of the Black Sea, and functionally, as its competences and objectives have been widened at times of periodic revision of the Treaties. The main point which animates the exploration conducted in this book is that the road to the EU's influence on contracts, contract law and contract regulation runs primarily through the internal market. The EU's contract law is principally the *contract law of the internal market*. Exactly what this means is the subject matter of this book.

1.4. THE CONTRACT LAW OF THE INTERNAL MARKET

Contract law of the internal market engages, first, the review of contracts, of *national* contract law and of national regulatory initiatives that restrict contractual autonomy more generally; and second, the partial or total replacement of national contract law and contract regulation by *EU* contract law and contract regulation.

Contracts and national contract law may be subject to review where they collide with the project of establishing an internal market. This is the subject of examination in Chapter 2. So contracts may be controlled by, and require justification in the light of, (some but not all of) the Treaty provisions on free movement. National contract law may be checked against the standards demanded by the Treaty in so far as it acts as an obstacle to inter-State trade. The Treaty provisions on competition law add to the control of contractual autonomy in order to promote the achievement of the objectives of the internal market. More broadly still, and stretching even beyond the internal market, anti-discrimination law and the application of constitutional principles to contract law impose certain constraints on private autonomy. The European Commission is responsible for the enforcement of the competition rules; the Court of Justice in Luxembourg provides authoritative interpretation of both the free movement and the competition rules. But the constitutional genius of EU law, which distinguishes it from orthodox international law, is that it demands that these rules are *also* subject to direct application by national courts in the Member States in everyday legal proceedings. EU law is capable of direct effect before national courts and, in the event of conflict, it prevails over national law.

These rules exert relatively little impact on contract law as *narrowly* understood. Rules on formation, validity, breach and remedies are, as a general observation, not normally of a type that cause obstruction to the patterns of cross-border trade which are the lifeblood of the internal market. Mostly this is *national* law. Chapter 2 explores this more fully. It shows how national measures of market regulation which are not themselves tied to contracts or contract law may fall to be challenged where they obstruct the free movement of goods, persons or services between Member States. This broader landscape of 'regulatory contract law' is affected to a significant degree by EU law. An obstruction to inter-State trade in goods or services within the meaning of internal market law may stand only if justified. Where there is no justification and the national rules must be set aside in so far as inter-State trade is concerned, the result is a diminution in public regulation and an enhanced space for the *contractual* autonomy of traders and buyers within the internal market. Contractual freedom is the converse of prohibiting obstacles to inter-State trade. Free movement law promotes freedom of contract – it opens up and protects a wider terrain of contractual autonomy within the internal market.

The second dimension of contract law in the internal market concerns the replacement of national contract law by *EU* contract law. This is primarily the role of legislative harmonisation. Its constitutional foundations, most of all the role of Article 114 TFEU, are examined in Chapter 3 and the thematic patterns that characterise the EU's legislative *acquis* are explored in Chapter 4. Chapter 5 considers attempts to provoke more critical scrutiny of the EU's pretensions. The basic model of harmonisation holds that the EU sets regulatory standards in replacement for diverse national choices, thereby to open up scope for freedom of contracting within the internal market on the terms set (in common) by the EU. The replacement may be partial or total (Chapter 6), but the orthodox governing rationale for EU intervention of this type holds that diversity among national contract law regimes causes obstructions to and distortions within the EU's internal market law, and so the EU should intervene to replace national regimes with a single EU regime. This then provides a common foundation for economic activity in the EU's internal market, but it also involves a choice made at EU level about what shall be the content of that common EU contract law regime. Since national systems, in their diverse ways, seek not only to promote contractual freedom but also typically to compensate for the existing inequalities which hamper the weaker party's access to genuine autonomy of decision-making, so too must the EU, in adopting harmonised standards, reflect the choices made at national level about the proper intensity of the regulation of the market. Harmonisation of contract law and contract regulation facilitates trade and protects contracting parties within the internal market – this is the EU's brand of regulatory contract law. Harmonisation transplants to EU level the need to take a stance on the proper scope and limits of contractual autonomy.

Harmonisation of laws contributes to the transformation of fragmented national markets into a single EU market, and it is one concrete example of how such a deregulatory project entails also a commitment to regulation and a consequent need to make an intensely political choice among available techniques of regulation. Harmonisation serves to open up opportunities for cross-border contracting, while at the same time it regulates its boundaries.

This is the contract law of the internal market. It is admittedly a patchwork. Private parties make contracts; States make contract law. The EU, driven by the commitment to the internal market, affects contracts and contract law both by reviewing them as obstacles to inter-State trade and by adopting its own harmonised regulatory standards. The pattern is not always easy to discern or explain, and the EU does not possess anything resembling a systematic programme of contract law, but inspection of the EU's role reveals an intense and increasing narrative of co-existence, reinforcement and overlap between EU and national level. This is a multi-level system. There is today no contract law of a Member State; there are instead contract laws in a Member State. And a major influence in the emergence of that plurality is the contract law of the internal market.

1.5. THE CHALLENGE OF THE CONTRACT LAW OF THE INTERNAL MARKET

Although the pursuit of the internal market is the constitutional motivation for the majority of the EU's influence on contracts and contract law, this is not to say that it is an exclusively deregulatory exercise. This is the basis on which to engage with the serious allegation that the EU infects contract law not only with a fragmenting dynamic that breaks open the cherished systematic coherence of national private law, but also that it injects a market-orientation into contract law which corrodes or even eliminates the distributive and/or protective concerns that have been developed over time (and often after arduous struggle) within national contract law. The claim made in this book is that even within the internal market project the wide scope of the EU's conferred competence is accompanied by an openness to selecting a protective quality for the rules. The EU is not constitutionally unsympathetic to important protective aspects of regulatory contract law developed at national level. Quite the reverse – both constitutionally and in the practical elaboration of the legislative *acquis* the EU acts as a force which restrains the aggressive deployment of private economic power.

EU law is about promoting contractual autonomy in the internal market, but also about restricting its exercise. There are choices which EU law removes from the autonomy of contracting parties. The EU's Charter of Fundamental Rights, which acquired binding force in 2009 as a result of the entry into force of the amending Treaty of Lisbon, provides a frame. Articles 16 and 17 of the Charter are the most obvious sources of challenge to the regulatory ambition pursued by the EU in the name of harmonisation. Article 16 states that '[t]he freedom to conduct a business in accordance with Union law and national laws and practices is recognised' and Article 17, the *Right to property*, declares in its first sentence that '[e]veryone has the right to own, use, dispose of and bequeath his or her lawfully acquired possessions'. This is, in short, favourable to contractual autonomy. So it is open to commercial operators to complain that regulatory burdens imposed by national or EU measures are in violation of these Charter protections. This suggests a *constitutionalised* protection of private economic interests from public regulation. But Articles 16 and 17 co-exist with other Charter rights and principles that favour intervention in the public interest. Article 35 on public health, Article 37 on environmental protection and Article 38 on consumer protection speak to and stand for the virtue of confining market freedom in order to achieve broader goals in the collective interest. They assert respect for values that generate the adoption of restrictions on contractual autonomy introduced at national level and at EU level. Article 17 of the Charter itself concedes that '[t]he use of property may be regulated by law in so far as is necessary for the general interest', while, more broadly, Article 52(1) admits of limitation on the exercise of the rights and freedoms recognised by this Charter as 'provided for by law', on condition that such limitation shall respect the essence of those rights and freedoms and shall be made only where necessary.

What matters is exactly how judicial and legislative choices about competing priorities are made. The Charter, in fact, captures the very debate about the virtue and vice of contractual autonomy that has dominated thinking at national level for many decades, and transplants it to EU level, without resolving it in favour of any particular set of values. In the EU, that debate takes place against the background of the limits of conferred competence – as the Charter itself makes expressly clear in its Article 51(2). But the internal market as an empowering legal concept tugs ever wider the scope of that conferred competence. Contract law might appear to be a matter of little concern to the EU and instead a matter of national responsibility. But the internal market is the functional competence that *opens up* contract law to the EU – to authorise it to review national contracts and contract law and to create harmonised EU contract law.

They key point to grasp is that the Treaty provisions on free movement, competition and harmonisation have a profound effect on contracts and contract law without at all making that explicit on their face. This is the connection to the insight, stretching beyond contract law and in fact a structurally central feature of the entire EU system, that the EU has a wider role than may be anticipated from a purely textual reading of the Treaties, most of all because of its functionally wide mandate to act in furtherance of the internal market project.

1.6. THE AMBITIONS OF THIS BOOK

As already summarised in the Preface, I have two principal ambitions in writing this book.

The first ambition is to demonstrate to contract lawyers that there are constitutional limits to the role of the EU in acting in the field, but that full appreciation of the nature of those limits, and the consequences they entail for the shaping of an EU contribution to the making of contract law in Europe, requires awareness of a complex interaction of often ambiguous constitutional rules, often politically inconsistent institutional rhythms and often evasive judicial pronouncements. In short, the allegation that the EU has an internal market bias that tends to impoverish the accumulated tradition and culture of national contract law is not without foundation, but there is a great deal more to the inquiry than simply deregulatory thirst.

The second ambition is to demonstrate to EU lawyers that the intervention of the EU in contract law – through judicial application of the free movement and competition rules and through legislative harmonisation – is not simply a niche area that has grown erratically but ultimately remains on the edges of the EU's core public law activities, but rather that the rise of EU contract law asks some vividly important questions about the principle and practice of conferred competence and about the choice of priorities in market regulation as protective instincts and deregulatory impulses collide. This has long been visible in the field of consumer contract law and labour market regulation, but the adjustments made by the Treaty of Lisbon, especially but not only the grant of binding effect to the Charter, have sharpened the interest.

Contract law in the EU is largely driven by the pursuit of the internal market and this exposes it to the accusation that the EU *diminishes* a proper understanding of the place of contract law. The thematic argument that will form the core of the book is that it is important in understanding the EU's impact on contracts and contract law that the EU has only a limited competence, but that, largely in consequence of the generous scope of the internal market as a concept, those limits are less of a restraint than may initially be supposed and that, moreover, pursuit of (in short) social justice within contract law is less constitutionally elusive than is often alleged.

CHAPTER 2
CONTRACTUAL AUTONOMY AND NATIONAL CONTRACT LAW IN THE INTERNAL MARKET

2.1. PRIMARY LAW AS A BASIS FOR INTERVENTION IN CONTRACTS AND CONTRACT LAW

The theme which binds together the material traversed in this chapter is that EU internal market law acts as a restraint on contractual autonomy and on national contract law. It is *primary* EU law – the provisions of the Treaty and those of the Charter of Fundamental Rights – that is the subject of inquiry. There are measures of secondary legislation, mostly Directives, which are relevant to choice of a contracting partner and to contractual enforceability, such as those concerning equality and those concerning protection of weaker parties such as consumers and workers, and these will be mentioned in this chapter and examined more fully in those that follow. But Directives can be amended or withdrawn. They represent a political consensus assembled through the EU legislative process at a particular time that may not endure. As a matter of constitutional hierarchy, primary law – the Treaty and the Charter – is different. It may not be altered save in the exceptional circumstances which apply at times of Treaty revision, requiring unanimous support of the Member States and performed according to the procedures laid down by the Treaties and mandated by national constitutional law.[1] Change of this type happens relatively irregularly and when it does happen, it is almost unknown for protection granted by EU law to be withdrawn. So the relevant rules of primary law are entrenched to a high degree. Moreover, Directives are limited in their impact on domestic legal proceedings. Where a Member State fails correctly to implement a Directive, the Directive is denied horizontal direct effect in legal proceedings before a national court – it may not be relied on as source of protective rights by a private party, including a contracting party, against another private party.[2] No such principled

1 Art. 48 TEU.

2 Case C-91/92, *Dori v Recreb* [1994] ECR I-3325; Case C-192/94, *El Corte Inglés v Cristina Blasquez Rivero* [1996] ECR I-1281; Case C-80/06, *Carp Snc v Ecorad* [2007] ECR I-4473; Case

constraint attaches to primary law, and indeed key Treaty provisions associated with free movement, competition and equal pay are capable of horizontal direct effect, as will be explained in this chapter.

Therefore primary law – the Treaty and the Charter – constitutes the foundation of the EU legal order, and the concern of this chapter is to show how the relevant provisions surround and constrain contractual autonomy and contract law. The issue, then, is constitutionalised protection of values under EU law and their application to contracts and to contract law. This concerns mostly the values of the internal market, although reference will also be made to more recently emerging values of non-discrimination and equality which operate beyond the sphere of the market.

At least three distinct models may be envisaged. First, EU law may be relied on directly to provide the basis for a claim against a contracting partner or even in certain circumstances to require that a party enter into a contract. Second, EU law may be relied on to exclude or to block the application of a rule that would otherwise apply to the advantage of a contracting partner. Third, and the least direct but potentially the most wide-ranging variant, EU law might exert an indirect effect, via interpretation of existing legal texts in the light of primary law. On this model public authorities, including courts, are placed under an obligation to perform their duties with respect for the protection of (in particular) fundamental rights, which in this way 'radiate' across all areas of law including contract law.

All these three models are visible in EU law. But there is no systematic constitutional protection of values which extends into contract law. The EU's influence is more fragmented than that. But, using the platform of the internal market in particular but also principles of non-discrimination and equality more generally, EU law acts as a restraint on contractual autonomy and national contract law.

2.2. THE FUNCTIONAL BREADTH OF FREE MOVEMENT LAW

The Treaty rules on free movement are written with extraordinary breadth. They are not focused on contracts or on contract law at all. This is not how they are structured. They are functionally oriented. They are targeted at the construction and maintenance of an internal market for the EU. Working back from that objective, *any* practices fall within the scope of the Treaty provisions on free movement, irrespective of their form, intent or classification under national law, provided only that they obstruct in some way the achievement of the EU's

C-555/07, *Kücükdeveci* [2010] ECR I-365; Case C-508/14, *Česky telekomunikačni* judgment of 6 October 2015.

internal market. This is how and why free movement law reaches contracts and contract law – not because the Treaty offers any embroidered explanation of the place of contractual autonomy within EU law, but rather because contracts and contract law may collide with the impetus to create an internal market.

So EU free movement law restrains the application of contracts and national rules of contract law. Where they impede inter-State trade, they must be justified. The principal focus of inquiry is Article 34 TFEU, concerning the free movement of goods, Article 39 TFEU on the free movement of workers, Article 45 TFEU on the right of establishment (the free movement of natural and legal persons) and Article 49 TFEU governing the free movement of services. Restrictions on cross-border trade are also capable of being treated as limitations on the freedom to choose an occupation, the freedom to conduct a business and the right to property which are contained in Articles 15, 16 and 17 of the Charter of Fundamental Rights, but the Court has taken the view that the Charter does not add anything to the law beyond the pre-existing control exercised by the free movement rules.[3] The several Treaty provisions on free movement are not interpreted in a precisely congruent manner, as will be explained, but what unites them far exceeds what divides them, and all of them are foundation stones of the liberalisation of inter-State trade pursued by the EU's internal market project.

The analysis that follows is built on a separation into three distinct issues which is useful for the purposes of exposition, but it is not one that is dictated by the functionally driven Treaty provisions. Free movement law applies where there is an obstruction to the completion of the market: it is effect-based, and it is not organised according to the particular type of national practice under review. That noted, the three dimensions of free movement law which now fall for consideration are, first, its control of contracts (section 2.3), second, its control of rules of national contract law narrowly understood (section 2.4) and, third, review of rules of broader 'regulatory contract law' applied at national level (section 2.5).

2.3. CONTRACTS AND FREE MOVEMENT

All the provisions of the TFEU which deal with free movement apply to the acts of public authorities in the Member States. This covers legislative and administrative acts, but is perfectly conceivable that a public authority which uses its purchasing power to conclude contracts that discriminate in favour of local suppliers could be condemned for action that tends to reinforce the

---

[3] See Case C-390/12, *Pfleger* judgment of 30 April 2014 (Art. 56 TFEU); Case C-98/14, *Berlington Hungary* judgment of 11 June 2015 (Art. 56 TFEU); Case C-367/12, *Sokoll-Seebacher* judgment of 13 February 2014 (Art. 49 TFEU).

fragmentation of the market along national lines, in violation of the free movement rules.[4]

There is no reason in principle why the Treaty rules governing free movement should not also affect contracts agreed between *private* parties. After all, if two private parties agree on a course of action that will block inter-State trade or otherwise cause a compartmentalisation of national markets within the wider EU, then the result is damage to the internal market. And the internal market is the jewel which the free movement rules are designed to protect.

However, contracts between private parties are caught only where they concern persons or services, not where they concern goods. This is not dictated by the Treaty. It is the result of the interpretation placed on the personal scope of the Treaty provisions on free movement by the Court of Justice.

The Court's interpretation means that a contract struck by private parties concerning goods is no business of free movement law (but, as explained in section 2.7 below, it will be a concern of the competition rules). Just briefly, over thirty years ago, the Court hinted at a different solution. In *Dansk Supermarked v Imerco* it stated that 'it is impossible in any circumstances for agreements between individuals to derogate from the mandatory provisions of the Treaty on the free movement of goods'.[5] But this dictum has been completely ignored in the case law since and, in any event, the context in which the Court made this remark involved a Danish law that impeded cross-border trade – clearly an act of a public authority. The Court's more consistent view is that expressed in *Sapod Audic*, in which the Court insisted that an obligation arising out of a private contract cannot be regarded as a barrier to trade for the purposes of (what is now) Article 34 TFEU 'since it was not imposed by a Member State but agreed between individuals'.[6] In support of this proposition the Court reached back as far as one of its landmark rulings on the free movement of goods, the classic *Dassonville* ruling of 1974, in which it confined the reach of the law governing the free movement of goods to trading rules 'enacted by Member States'.[7] Perhaps this approach is rooted in a reluctance to use free movement law to disturb private autonomy, but the Court has never articulated it in these terms.

The particular case of contracts is simply one manifestation of the Court's consistent refusal to interpret Article 34 TFEU to impose obligations on private parties. *Schmidberger v Austria* involved private parties obstructing the passage of goods through the Brenner Pass in protest at the environmental damage done by such traffic.[8] The Court found that Article 34 TFEU was in principle apt to form the basis for review of the Austrian public authorities' failure to

---

4 e.g. Case 45/87, *Commission v Ireland* [1988] ECR 4929; Case C-243/89, *Commission v Denmark* [1993] ECR I-3353.

5 Case 58/80 [1981] ECR 181, para. 17.

6 Case C-159/00 [2002] ECR I-5031, para. 74.

7 Case 8/74, *Dassonville* [1974] ECR 837, para. 5.

8 Case C-112/00, *Schmidberger v Austria* [2003] ECR I-5659.

intervene to suppress the protests, but Article 34 TFEU would not apply directly to the private parties themselves. The Grand Chamber took the same approach in *Alands Vinkraft AB* in which it cited *Schmidberger* in treating inaction by public authorities rather than private actions as the true target of Article 34.[9] Admittedly there are cases that tug at the borderline. In *Fra.bo SpA* the Court held that a private law entity was held to be subject to obligations arising under Article 34 TFEU, but closer inspection reveals that it was a private law entity *in form* only. Its functions included a quasi-regulatory power conferred by the (German) state to certify whether the products in question, copper fittings designed to join together pipes, should be admitted to the German market.[10] It is well established that Article 34 applies to the activities of a private company where it is backed by public funding and its mission is dictated by the State.[11] Article 34's irrelevance to 'true' private parties is not challenged by *Fra.bo*.

Private practices that interfere with cross-border trade in goods have always been treated as the province of the Treaty rules on competition law alone. This is perfectly clear and firmly established. The problem, however, is that the Court takes a quite different view of private practices that interfere with cross-border trade in persons and services. Such contracts and other arrangements are assessed from the perspective of both competition law and free movement law.

Walrave and Koch v UCI, a decision of the Court in 1974, provides a powerful starting point.[12] The Court was asked to consider the governing rules of an international sport (cycling) federation. Such bodies are typically powerful and, in order to ensure sport is played everywhere according to common rules, they tend to be monopoly regulators, but they do not normally hold the status of a public authority. The Court however brought their practices within the scope of EU law. It concluded that the prohibition of discrimination based on nationality pursuant to (what were then) Articles 7, 48 and 59 EEC, now after amendment Articles 18, 39 and 56 TFEU, 'does not only apply to the action of public authorities but extends likewise to rules of any other nature aimed at regulating in a collective manner gainful employment and the provision of services'.[13] The Court provided two principal reasons for this finding. The first: the Treaty objective of tackling obstacles to inter-State trade would be 'compromised if the abolition of barriers of national origin could be neutralized by obstacles resulting from the exercise of their legal autonomy by associations or organizations which do not come under public law'.[14] The second: given the diversity between Member States on the scope of and relationship between public regulation and

9 Case C-573/12 judgment of 1 July 2014.
10 Case C-171/11, *Fra.bo SpA* judgment of 12 July 2012.
11 e.g. Case 249/81, *Commission v Ireland* [1982] ECR 4005. See also P. Oliver, 'L'Article 34 TFUE peut-il avoir un effet direct horizontal?' (2014) 50 *Cahiers de Droit Européen* 77.
12 Case 36/74, *Walrave and Koch v UCI* [1974] ECR 1405.
13 Para. 17.
14 Para. 18.

private agreements, limiting the Treaty provisions 'to acts of a public authority would risk creating inequality in their application'.[15]

This is logical and it is forceful. Both arguments – which one may usefully label an 'effectiveness' rationale and an 'equality' rationale respectively – carry weight. The Court has embraced this as its orthodox approach to the personal scope of the Treaty provisions dealing with the free movement of persons and services. So, following this approach, in *Bosman* it allowed a private party, a footballer, to rely on EU law to attack the practices of the private bodies that organise the sport in so far as they caused obstacles to inter-State trade and discrimination on ground of nationality.[16] The same reasoning led it to subject trade unions to obligations imposed by the Treaty rules on free movement. In *Viking Line* it stated that Article 43 EC, which is now Article 49 TFEU, 'is to be interpreted as meaning that, in principle, collective action initiated by a trade union or a group of trade unions against an undertaking in order to induce that undertaking to enter into a collective agreement, the terms of which are liable to deter it from exercising freedom of establishment, is not excluded from the scope of that article'.[17] So collective labour action fell to be tested against EU free movement law in so far as its exercise obstructed cross-border corporate mobility. This meant that it was put to the test of justification mandated by EU law.

So Articles 45, 49 and 56 TFEU provide a basis for review of not only the actions of public authorities but also the rules of private bodies that regulate in a collective manner employment, self-employment and the provision of services. The Court has gone still further on occasion. In *Angonese* it ruled that 'the prohibition of discrimination on grounds of nationality laid down in Article 48 of the Treaty [now Article 39 TFEU] must be regarded as applying to private persons as well'.[18] It did not confine this to a case where *collective* action was taken by private parties. This appears to mean that unilateral action by a private employer or service provider may be controlled under the Treaty provisions on free movement.[19] However, the Court has not routinely adopted this formula. Unless and until it does it would be premature to assume that EU law definitely goes so far. In fact, pending judicial clarification, the assumption that it does *not* is probably safer.

In sum, private practices that interfere with cross-border trade in goods have always been treated as the preserve of the Treaty rules on competition law, in contrast to private practices affecting people and services, which are assessed from the perspective of both competition law and free movement law.

---

15 Para. 19.

16 Case C-415/93, *URBSFA v Bosman* [1995] ECR I-4921.

17 Case C-438/05, *Viking Line* [2007] ECR I-10779, para. 55; see also Case C-341/05, *Laval* [2007] ECR I-11767, para. 98.

18 Case C-281/98, *Angonese* [2000] ECR I-4139, para. 36.

19 See also Case C-94/07, *Andrea Raccanelli* [2008] ECR I-5939; Case C-379/09, *Maurits Casteels v British Airways* judgment of 10 March 2011.

This is the law! Yet it is hard to understand it. A convergent approach to the personal scope of *all* the freedoms is perfectly feasible in principle and in practice. The most obvious point is that the 'effectiveness' and the 'equality' rationales explained above as the key contributions of *Walrave and Koch* seem in principle capable of application with as much force to the free movement of goods as they do to the free movement of persons. Yet the Court has never relied on them in cases concerning goods, and it has never attempted to explain why they have no purchase in that context.

There are three obviously possible models for a convergent approach to the personal scope of the freedoms: first, the subjection of private parties to obligations to respect the demands of the internal market in all circumstances, including bilateral contracting; second, the application of free movement law to private parties only where they act collectively; or third, a complete immunity for private parties and a preference to focus free movement law on public authorities alone. Another possible way to slice the cake would be to confine the application of free movement law to private parties to instances of direct discrimination on grounds of nationality, while adopting a broader restriction-based approach to supervision of public authorities. Choosing among these models would involve some sort of assessment of the strength of the Court's predilection for, on the one hand, the 'effectiveness' and 'equality' rationales, which militate in favour of the first or perhaps second of the three possible common solutions (and no limitation to discriminatory practices only), and, on the other, respect for private autonomy, which would push in favour of the retreat sounded by the third possible common solution (or, less decisively, the first or second softened by a discrimination-only proviso). The several possible models have been subject to assessment.[20] Within this inquiry lurk profoundly intriguing questions about whether, and if so to what extent, constitutional or public law values should govern private autonomy and contractual freedom.[21] But the current inconsistent system applicable to the personal scope of EU free movement law, whereby some freedoms have a broader personal scope than others and yet in circumstances where no attempt is made to explain why, is very hard to defend. In conclusion, one can only concede with a sense of limp regret that the absence of convergence between the several Treaty freedoms in the matter of their personal scope now seems ingrained in internal market law.

---

20 Cf. e.g. (with different views) S. Prechal and S. De Vries, 'Seamless web of judicial protection in the internal market' (2009) 34 *European Law Review* 5; P. Müller-Graff, 'Die horizontale Direktwirkung der Grundfreiheiten' (2014) 49 *Europarecht* 3; G. Davies, 'Freedom of Movement, Horizontal Effect and Freedom of Contract' (2012) 20 *European Review of Private Law* 805; R. Van Leeuwen, 'Private Regulation and Public Responsibility in the Internal Market' (2014) 33 *Yearbook of European Law* 277; R. Babayev, 'Contractual Discretion and the Limits of Free Movement Law' (2015) 23 *European Review of Private Law* 875.

21 This theme is elucidated with flair by H. Schepel, 'Freedom of Contract in Free Movement Law: Balancing Rights and Principles in European Public and Private Law' (2013) 21 *European Review of Private Law* 1211.

2.4. CONTRACT LAW NARROWLY UNDERSTOOD AND FREE MOVEMENT

The law of the EU's internal market does not command review of all national measures that restrain the exercise of commercial freedom. That would be to go too far and, in strict constitutional terms, it would negate the promise made by Article 5 TEU that the EU's competences are limited to those conferred on it by its founding Treaties. EU internal market law bites, and puts national measures to the test, only where they contradict the demands of the project to construct and maintain the internal market which is mandated by Article 3(3) TEU and Article 26 TFEU. Put another way, EU law does not object to mere difference between national laws – it objects to such difference where that damages the internal market. This applies to review of contracts and contract law as it does to anything else.

Rules of contract law narrowly understood will commonly not cause harm to the internal market and so will not be subject to review in the light of the Treaty rules on free movement. Rules on matters such as validity and breach will typically apply equally in law and in fact to all economic operators and to the goods and services they supply without reference to their origin. Such rules structure the way contracts are made and enforced, and in this sense they affect commercial freedom, but that is not enough to trigger the application of free movement law. Free movement law applies where national practices exert a particular effect on *cross-border* trade pattern – where they obstruct the EU's internal market. Most rules of contract law narrowly understood do not do so.

For the EU law specialist the previous paragraph induces a headache. The Court has long struggled to articulate a legally precise test apt to separate legal rules that need to be checked in the light of internal market law from those that can be left untouched as expressions of local regulatory autonomy. The landmark ruling is that in *Keck and Mithouard*.[22] This ruling was in essence a retreat by the Court from a brief period in which it had adopted a troublingly wide approach to the scope of free movement law, to the detriment of both local regulatory autonomy and its own legitimacy. *Keck and Mithouard* was a correction of this exorbitant tendency. In it the Court displayed a much keener anxiety to insist that free movement law requires the existence of a genuine connection between the challenged national measure and the process of market integration. A national measure which constitutes a restriction on commercial freedom, but which applies equally in law and in fact to all operators, may affect the market – but it will typically not affect the making of the EU's internal market. This is – in short – the type of rule which the Court in *Keck and Mithouard* intended to place beyond the reach of the law governing the free movement of goods.

22 Cases C-267/91 and C-268/91 [1993] ECR I-6097.

And although the Court has never explicitly applied *Keck and Mithouard* to the free movement of persons and services, it has developed functionally similar tests which place limits on the potential of those Treaty provisions to intervene in national regulatory autonomy where no prejudice to the internal market is shown to follow.[23]

The case law in which the Court has been asked to sharpen its understanding of the applicable test is abundant; so is the academic literature which has commented on and criticised the Court's contortions. The full breadth of this debate, which is tangential to contract law, lies beyond the scope of this book.[24] For present purposes, the point of *Keck and Mithouard* is that it provides a basis for treating most national rules of contract law narrowly understood as immune from challenge pursuant to free movement law and instead as expressions of local regulatory autonomy.

An example from the field of contract law is offered by *Alsthom Atlantique SA v Sulzer*.[25] The French Code Civil provides that '[t]he vendor shall be liable for any latent defects, even if he is unaware of those defects, unless he stipulates that he shall not be liable.' This is plainly important in determining the allocation of risk under a contract. The proceedings at stake involved a claim by the buyer, Alsthom, for payment of costs incurred to remedy latent defects in engines for use in cruise ships sold to it by Sulzer. Sulzer argued that French law on the point differed from that found in other Member States and that 'such case-law may distort competition and hinder the free movement of goods'.[26] So this was an instance of a litigant relying on EU law in an attempt to defeat the detrimental consequences dictated by national law. But the attempt failed. The Court pointed out that the relevant rules of French law 'applied without distinction to all commercial relations governed by French law' and that they did not have as their 'specific object or effect the restriction of patterns of exports thereby favouring domestic production or the domestic market'.[27] It added too that parties to an international contract of sale enjoy the freedom to determine the law applicable to their contractual relations and 'can thus avoid being subject to French law'.[28] The relevant rules were mandatory, but avoidable by choice in the context of this commercial contract. EU free movement law did not help Sulzer. Similarly in

---

23 e.g. Case C-190/98, *Volker Graf v Filzmoser Maschinenbau* [2000] ECR I-493; Joined Cases C-544/03 and C-545/03, *Mobistar* and *Belgacom Mobile* [2005] ECR I-7723.

24 Cf. e.g. S Enchelmaier, 'The Awkward Selling of a Good Idea, or a Traditionalist Interpretation of Keck' (2003) 22 *Yearbook of European Law* 249; J. Snell. 'The Notion of Market Access: a Concept or a Slogan?' (2010) 47 *Common Market Law Review* 437; S. Weatherill, 'The Internal Market as a Legal Concept' in L. Azoulai and M. Cremona (eds.), *Collected Courses of the Academy of European Law*, Vol. XXV, OUP, Oxford forthcoming.

25 Case C-339/89 [1991] ECR I-107.

26 Para. 5.

27 Para. 15.

28 Para. 15.

CMC Motorradcenter the Court decided that free movement law, today Article 34 TFEU, did not preclude a rule established in the courts of a Member State from imposing an obligation to provide information prior to contract.[29] The Court observed that the obligation under German law to provide information prior to contract applies 'without distinction, at least as regards products coming from the Community, to all contractual relationships covered by that law and that its purpose is not to regulate trade'.[30] The latter point about purpose is irrelevant, because the application of free movement law depends on a national measure's effect on the market, not the intent motivating it. But the former point, that the rule was unassociated with origin or nationality, is decisive to take it outwith the scope of free movement law.

Both cases pre-date the Court's ruling in *Keck and Mithouard*.[31] But they find functionally comparable means to achieve a result which insulates local regulatory choices which do not harm the functioning of the internal market from review in the name of free movement. Both rulings deserve to be understood as having partially paved the way to the fundamental re-orientation of free movement law effected by the Court in *Keck and Mithouard*.[32] Both would be decided in the same way today, and both judgments could easily be re-written in the light of *Keck and Mithouard* so that the national rules at stake would be treated as applicable equally in law and in fact to all operators, and so untouched by Article 34. So, in this vein, as a general observation national rules of contract law that lack the necessary connection with the project of market integration are untouched by free movement law.

This does not mean that all national contract law of this type is inevitably walled off from Article 34. Any taint of discrimination in favour of traders from the regulating Member State at the expense of those from other Member States would readily bring EU law into play. So too a refusal in the legal order of one Member State to recognise contractual rights or obligations created according to the law of another Member State could feasibly amount to an impediment to inter-State trade,[33] although this area brings to mind more readily the instruments adopted under what is now Article 81 TFEU governing the law applicable to contractual obligations and recognition and enforcement of judgments.[34] Moreover, review in the light of the impact on the internal

---

29 Case C-93/92, *CMC Motorradcenter* [1993] ECR I-5009.

30 Para. 10.

31 Cases C-267/91 and C-268/91 [1993] ECR I-6097.

32 Cases C-267/91 and C-268/91 [1993] ECR I-6097. Cf. P. Nebbia, 'Internal Market and the Harmonisation of European Contract Law' in T. Tridimas and P. Nebbia (eds.), *European Union Law for the Twenty-First Century: Rethinking the New Legal Order*, Vol. 2, Hart Publishing, Oxford 2004.

33 e.g., in relation to property law, E.-M. Kieninger, 'Securities in movable property within the Common Market' (1996) 4 *European Review of Private Law* 41.

34 Reg. 593/2008 [2008] OJ L177/6; Reg. 1215/2012 [2012] OJ L351/1, replacing Reg. 44/2001 [2001] OJ L12/1.

market would be plausible if one tweaked the facts of *Alsthom Atlantique SA v Sulzer* to involve mandatory rules of contract law which could *not* be avoided by a choice of law clause. This might count as a barrier to inter-State trade which would therefore require justification.[35] And more broadly restrictions affecting the opportunity to conclude a contract may be caught: so for example in *Citroën Belux* a Belgian rule forbidding the offer of comprehensive insurance for six months in combination with the purchase of a Citroën vehicle was treated as an obstacle to inter-State trade (albeit one shown to be justified since it protected consumers from confusion about what was on offer).[36] Careful case-by-case and fact-sensitive analysis is required, but as a general observation only where national contract law is shown to operate in a manner hostile to the process of market integration is EU law governing free movement engaged. Put another way, free movement law is not directed at challenging diversity between national measures *per se*.[37] There is space for national contract law which is not imperilled by the Treaty rules governing free movement.

2.5. REGULATORY CONTRACT LAW AND FREE MOVEMENT

The previous section examined contract law narrowly understood and concluded that it will usually not count as a restriction on inter-State trade. The picture is different where a wider understanding of contract law is adopted. The concern here is with rules that do not directly address contractual validity and breach, but rather with rules which structure and constrain the circumstances in which commercial activity may proceed in order ultimately to result in the conclusion of a contract. At stake are, for example, rules that stipulate the composition or packaging of products or rules that confine the style of advertising that may permissibly be used. This is typically treated as public law or as a species of administrative regulation, but in order to express the idea that it is regulation of the market which has the effect of limiting and channelling the autonomy of private parties, it may usefully also be labelled 'regulatory contract law'. Member States have typically made very different choices about the style and intensity of such intervention in the market, and this area, in contrast to that explored in the previous section, is one where national choices frequently cause direct obstacles to inter-State trade. If a product

35 Cf. M. Hesselink, 'Non-Mandatory Rules in European Contract Law' (2005) 1 *European Review of Contract Law* 44, 74–76; A. Hartkamp, 'EU Law and General Contract Law' in A. Hartkamp et al. (eds.), *The Influence of EU Law on National Private Law*, Kluwer, Deventer 2014, pp. 401–464, at pp. 404–412.

36 Case C-265/12 judgment of 18 July 2013.

37 S. Weatherill, 'Diversity between national laws in the internal market' in U. Drobnig, H.J. Snijders and E.-J. Zippro (eds.), *Divergences of Property Law. An obstacle to the internal market?*, Sellier, Munich 2006, pp. 131–150.

or service exported to another Member State runs up against rules defining its permitted shape or content which are different from, and more restrictive than, those of its home Member State, then those rules will exclude the product or service from the target market. Cross-border trade is thwarted: the exporter's opportunity to enter into contracts with consumers in the target State is denied.

The *Cassis de Dijon* case – more properly, *Rewe-Zentrale AG v Bundesmonopolverwaltung für Branntwein* – is a landmark case in EU internal market law, and it captures perfectly what is at stake.[38] Its importance lies in the fact that it was the first time that the Court fully elucidated how Article 34 TFEU controls local regulatory autonomy in setting technical standards in so far as it may impede the construction of the internal market. And it set a path from which the Court has never deviated.

Cassis de Dijon is a blackcurrant fruit liqueur made in France with an alcohol content of between 15 and 20%. Germany, in contrast to France, required that such products should have a minimum alcohol content of 25%. The litigation arose because in consequence the product could not be sold in Germany, since it did not comply with German law. Free movement across borders and the opportunity to contract with German consumers was impeded. The critical point was that Germany did not discriminate on the basis of origin in the application of its rules. A German-made product with the same relatively low level of alcohol as the French-made product would equally have been excluded from the German market. Product composition, not origin, was decisive. The point, then, was that a fragmentation of the internal market along national lines was caused by the fact that German product standards were *different* from French standards.

The Court ruled that because such regulatory diversity damaged the internal market by reducing scope for private contracting, Germany could apply its rules to exclude products made according to different standards in another Member State only on condition that it could show a justification for the rules in the general interest. In this way EU law puts trade-restrictive rules of this type to the test: Germany may not simply hand importers its rulebook and require them to comply with it; it must demonstrate why compliance with its rulebook is sufficiently important to override the interest in promoting cross-border competition and consumer choice in the internal market.

Germany could not justify its rules. In fact it put forward fatuous and feeble attempts to do so. The claim that public health policy required the suppression of *weak* alcoholic drink because it might induce tolerance in drinkers and lure them towards stronger stuff was treated with polite derision by the Court. The German market was already home to 'an extremely wide range of weakly or moderately alcoholic products' and in any event products with a high alcohol content may be and are consumed in a diluted form.[39] The slightly more coherent claim that

[38] Case 120/78, *Rewe-Zentrale AG v Bundesmonopolverwaltung für Branntwein* [1979] ECR 649.
[39] Para. 11.

consumers needed protection from the risk of buying a product with which they were unfamiliar and which might not be to their taste was met by pointing that this might justify an obligation to label a product to inform the consumer of its contents, but that the imposition of a prohibition on liqueurs that were made according to a slightly different recipe from that expected by German consumers went too far. So its rules stipulating minimum alcohol requirements were incompatible with EU free movement law and could not be applied to exclude the French-made goods from the German market. The ruling is of immense significance to the structure of the internal market. By reading free movement law – for the Court has not confined its '*Cassis* approach' to goods alone[40] – in a way that is not limited to an attack on *discriminatory* national measures, it sharpens the deregulatory cutting edge of free movement law as applied by the judiciary. Legislative harmonisation is required to advance the internal market only where national measures survive the cut of free movement law because they are shown to protect an interest that is sufficiently serious to override the market-making impetus. It is certainly not unknown for an adequate justification to be shown for national measures that restrict inter-State trade. Such cases have tended to involve genuine threats of harm to the consumer's health or economic interests[41] or, more broadly, to matters such as the protection of the environment.[42] On occasion still more sensitive issues have arisen. In *Omega Spielhallen* intervention by the public authorities in Germany based on protection of human dignity prevented a British supplier of a 'Laserdrome' (simulated killing) game from offering such services to German buyers.[43] The German order, the Court noted, 'is capable of restricting the future development of contractual relations'.[44] However, the Court, treating the protection of human dignity as a value recognised by EU law, held that the restriction on trade was justified.[45] In *Ilonka Sayn-Wittgenstein v Landeshauptmann von Wien* an Austrian law dating from 1919 prohibiting use of noble titles prevented the applicant from using the much fuller and grander version of her name that she used in Germany when she did business in Germany, but the Court treated this restriction sympathetically as a means to promote the equality of citizens before the law.[46] In this way concern for fundamental rights becomes part of internal

40 e.g. Case C-76/90, *Manfred Säger v Dennemeyer & Co. Ltd* [1991] ECR I-4221.

41 e.g. (health) Case 53/80, *Eyssen* [1981] ECR 409; (economic interests) Case 382/87, *Buet* [1989] ECR 1235; Case C-265/12, *Citroën Belux* judgment of 18 July 2013.

42 e.g. Case 302/86, *Commission v Denmark* [1988] ECR 4607; Case C-379/98, *Preussen Elektra* [2001] ECR I-2099; Case C-573/12, *Ålands Vindkraft* judgment of 1 July 2014.

43 Case C-36/02, *Omega Spielhallen* [2004] ECR I-9609.

44 Para. 21.

45 Article 1 of the Charter now identifies human dignity as 'inviolable'.

46 Case C-208/09 [2010] ECR I-13693. The Court referred to Art. 20 Charter. See also Case C-391/09, *Runevic-Vardyn* [2011] ECR I-3787; Case C-202/11, *Anton Las* judgment of 16 April 2013.

market law.[47] The Court's copybook is not spotless – its cramped approach to the justification of industrial action which restricts inter-State trade in *Viking Line* has properly been criticised as insufficiently attentive to values loaded not only into national and international law but also EU law itself[48] – but cases of this type, in which politically and socially sensitive matters are put to the test, are in any event not the norm. Most of the Court's diet is made up of demolition of wholly spurious attempts by Member States to justify protectionist or at best merely anachronistic measures. *Cassis* itself is a perfect and typical example and for every *Omega Spielhallen*, where sensitivity is required, there are a hundred cases in which the Court is asked to believe absurd claims that, for example, the marketing of cheese requires strict rules on minimum fat content,[49] that 'shallots' must be reproduced directly from bulbs and cannot be applied to seedling vegetables[50] and that advertising medical and surgical treatments should be prohibited on national television networks but at the same time permitted on local television networks.[51] Most of all, *Cassis de Dijon* stands for a preference for autonomy in the market, expressed by allowing room for consumer choice about what to buy, ahead of plain daft and indefensible public regulation, and this priority is displaced only where exceptionally national rules put to the test are shown to be justified. Dual regulation of a product or service by both home and host State is excluded in the absence of justification – as is well illustrated by *Cassis* itself.

The German rule was treated as a restraint on the free movement of goods and at the same time as a restraint on contractual freedom and opportunity. This use of free movement law to liberate contractual autonomy within the internal market from the oppressive effect of composition or packaging requirements under national law is also well illustrated by *Walter Rau v de Smedt*.[52] The case concerned Belgian rules which required that margarine be packed in cube-shaped blocks. This had the effect of excluding imports from States where different packaging rules prevailed or, at least, it forced them to create a special extra production run apt to comply with Belgium's peculiarities, with consequent

47 S. Weatherill, 'Economic Rights and Fundamental Rights' in S. De Vries, U. Bernitz and S. Weatherill (eds.), *The Protection of Fundamental Rights in the EU after Lisbon*, Hart Publishing/Institute of European and Comparative Law, Oxford 2013, Ch. 1, pp. 11–36.

48 Case C-438/05, *Viking Line* [2007] ECR I-10779. See e.g. L. Azoulai, 'The Court of Justice and the Social Market Economy: the emergence of an ideal and the conditions for its realisation' (2008) 45 *Common Market Law Review* 1335; D. Ashiagbor, 'Unravelling the Liberal Bargain: Labour and Social Welfare Law in the Context of EU Market Integration' (2013) 19 *European Law Journal* 303; and on how the Court's approach could (and should) change, S. Weatherill, '*Viking* and *Laval*: The EU Internal Market Perspective' in M. Freedland and J. Prassl (eds.), *EU Law in the Member States: Viking, Laval and Beyond*, Hart Publishing, Oxford 2014, Ch. 2, pp. 23–40.

49 Case 286/86, *Deserbais* [1988] ECR 4907.

50 Case C-147/04, *de Groot* [2006] ECR I-245.

51 Case C-500/06, *Corporación Dermoestética SA* [2008] ECR I-5785.

52 Case 261/81 [1982] ECR 3961.

extra costs. The Court checked the matter in the light of the damage done to the internal market and found no justification for the rule. Any risk of consumer confusion about the nature of the product on offer could be addressed by less restrictive means than stipulating a particular shape, such as mandatory labelling of content. The point is that the disapplication of the offending law opens up the Belgian market to cross-border trade and competition which had previously been suppressed by the rule to the detriment of Belgian consumers. In fact the Court went so far as expressly to note that the price of margarine in Belgium was higher in neighbouring territories and that there was little imported margarine on sale in Belgium. The Court's orthodox approach to free movement law is to insist that it is triggered by an actual or potential effect on cross-border trade, and so this excludes the need for elaborate empirical evidence. But in this case it was clear and irresistible, and so the Court noted the 'protective effect' of the rules in favour of local producers.[53] The case had in fact reached Luxembourg in the context of a breach of contract action. An action for breach of a contract of sale had been initiated before a *Landgericht* in Hamburg in Germany. Walter Rau, a German company, had agreed to sell a quantity of margarine packed in containers having the shape of a truncated cone to de Smedt, a Belgian company. De Smedt, having extracted from the Belgian authorities confirmation that the goods could not be marketed in Belgium, informed Rau that it would not accept the goods. Rau's action against de Smedt was based on the claim that they should have accepted the goods because the Belgian rule was in breach of (what is now) Article 34 TFEU. There was a strong suspicion that the parties had concocted the litigation in order to induce the Court to rule on the compatibility with EU law of the Belgian rule in circumstances where both parties were fully in agreement about what they wanted the outcome to be. The Belgian Government pressed on the Court that it should decline jurisdiction on the basis that there was no genuine dispute. There are a small number of cases in which the Court has taken this view[54] but it did not take it here. It curtly stated that 'there is nothing in the file on the case which provides grounds for doubting that the dispute is genuine'.[55] And indeed there was a dispute about the compatibility of the Belgian rule with EU law which was germane to the litigation, even if the parties themselves were not in dispute about what the answer ought to be. So in this way an action at national level for breach of contract was used to crack open a restriction on cross-border contracting imposed by a regulating State. The result: a more competitive market for margarine in Belgium within the wider EU internal market.

The same pattern applicable to the internal market in services is visible in *Commission v France*, the so-called 'Tourist Guides' case.[56] Just as imported

53 Para. 14.
54 Especially Case 244/80, *Foglia v Novello* [1981] ECR 3045.
55 Para. 9.
56 Case C-154/89, *Commission v France* [1991] ECR I-659.

margarine could be sold in Belgium subject to the condition that its packaging conformed to Belgian law, so too tourist guides from outside France could work in France subject to the condition that they held a French qualification. This impeded both the commercial opportunities of tourist guides and the choice of consumers. The rule prevented tourists choosing 'a guide who is familiar with their language, their interests and their specific expectations'.[57] The Court saw no need for such rules. Competitive pressure within the market, stimulated by the exercise of contractual autonomy, would 'compel companies to be selective in employing tourist guides and exercise some control over the quality of their services'.[58]

The capacity of the consumer to enjoy the benefits of choice is used as a rationale for the replacement of State-level regulation with a deregulated internal market. A huge number of rulings follow this model.[59] National technical standards which do not discriminate on the basis of the origin of goods and services fall for review in the light of free movement law where the fact of inter-State difference in choice of regulatory model causes hindrance to cross-border trade. Such rules survive only if shown to be justified. Most are not. There is no call here to provide further illustrations: this is national 'regulatory contract law' subjected to control in the name of the internal market. One final group of cases is, however, worth brief mention. These are cases where the Court has accepted that national regulation of advertising may impede trade integration and so falls to be checked against the demands of free movement law. Advertising may not be physically associated with a product or service but it forms part of the overall commercial package and to restrict its use in circumstances where use would be allowed in the State of origin is capable of counting as an obstacle to trade caused by divergent national practices on the same model as that identified by the Court in *Cassis de Dijon*. Moreover the Court is astute to the actual context in which advertising is regulated at national level. In *Konsumentombudsmannen v Gourmet International Products* it was faced by a total ban on the advertising of products (alcoholic drinks in Sweden) which applied equally to all products 'on paper'.[60] But this equal application did not mean the ban was immune from review as a barrier to inter-State trade. The Court was receptive to the argument that such a ban might be shown to harm imports more severely than home produced goods where the latter already benefit from the level of consumer familiarity which only an advertising campaign could generate for the former. As the Court has observed 'the possibility cannot be ruled out that to compel a producer to discontinue an advertising scheme which he considers

---

[57] Para. 19.

[58] Para. 20.

[59] For comprehensive treatment see P. Oliver (ed.), *Oliver on Free Movement of Goods in the European Union*, 5th ed., Hart Publishing, Oxford 2010.

[60] Case C-405/98 [2001] ECR I-1795.

to be particularly effective may constitute an obstacle to imports',[61] and it will fall within the scope of the Treaty rules on free movement where it exerts a considerable influence on the behaviour of consumers in such a way as to affect the access of that product to the market of the regulating State.[62] So a ban or even a restriction on advertising is capable of entrenching existing market structures to the advantage of existing incumbents: it may be equal in its legal application, but not in its factual application. It would stand only if justified: public health protection would be the obvious basis for such a claim.

This is national regulatory contract law under the control of the law of the EU's internal market. Where national measures frame the circumstances in which contracts may be concluded, then, provided an adequate effect on inter-State trade is demonstrated, free movement law serves as a basis for review, and where no justification for the national measure of market regulation is shown, the result is deregulation of the national market. So the free movement rules are in fact a *release* of contractual autonomy: they *enable* cross-border contracting.[63] Even if the Charter does not add anything to the legal analysis,[64] it is correct to regard the Treaty rules on free movement as carrying constitutional force.[65] They attack national rules that obstruct cross-border trading freedom and thereby create more generous space for the opportunity to conclude contracts between traders and consumers, employers and workers, and so on.

2.6. THE *UNILEVER* NICHE

Unilever Italia SpA v Central Food SpA was a preliminary ruling triggered by a breach of contract action pursued before the Italian courts.[66] The factual background was pleasingly simple. The parties had agreed by contract that Unilever would supply Central Food with a quantity of olive oil. Unilever delivered the goods. Central Food refused to accept them because they were not labelled in accordance with a relevant Italian law. Consequently, as the ruling makes clear, 'it refused to pay the amount due and called on Unilever to remove

[61] Case C-239/02, *Douwe Egberts* [2004] ECR I-7007, para. 52.

[62] Cf. Case C-142/05, *Åklagaren v Mickelsson, Roos* [2009] ECR I-4273.

[63] See e.g. P. Müller-Graff, 'Basic Freedoms – Extending Party Autonomy across Borders' in S. Grundmann, W. Kerber and S. Weatherill (eds.), *Party Autonomy and the Role of Information in the Internal Market*, De Gruyter, Berlin 2001, Ch. 6, pp. 133–150; G. Davies, 'Freedom of Contract and the Horizontal Effect of Free Movement Law' in D. Leczykiewicz and S. Weatherill (eds.), *The Involvement of EU Law in Private Law Relationships*, Hart Publishing, Oxford 2013, Ch. 4, pp. 53–70.

[64] Case C-390/12, *Pfleger* judgment of 30 April 2014.

[65] See e.g. T. Kingreen, 'Fundamental Freedoms' in A. Von Bogdandy and J. Bast (eds.), *Principles of European Constitutional Law*, 2nd ed., Hart/CH Beck, Oxford/Munich 2010, Ch. 14, pp. 513–549 (the literature in German addressing the 'economic constitution' is much richer than that in English).

[66] Case C-443/98, *Unilever Italia SpA v Central Food SpA* [2000] ECR I-7535.

the goods from its warehouse'.[67] Unilever refused to do so and so 'Unilever commenced proceedings before the Pretore di Milano for an order requiring Central Food to pay a sum corresponding to the price of the consignment'.[68]

The reason why EU law came into play in this contractual dispute was that the Italian law in question, a technical specification governing the marketing of a product, had been brought into force in violation of the obligations imposed on the Italian authorities by the so-called Notification Directive, at the time Directive 83/189, today Directive 2015/1535.[69] This is a measure which requires Member States to notify the Commission of technical rules they plan to introduce and to delay their adoption for a defined period of time after notification. It is designed to give the Commission early warning of potential obstacles to inter-State trade, so that it can intervene to dissuade the application of the national measure where it considers that it is incompatible with EU law as an obstruction to inter-State trade. In short, it allows prevention of potential barriers to trade in preference to their cure achieved through litigation pursued after the measure has been adopted and has already caused harm to the internal market. The Italian labelling rule should have been notified to the Commission in advance of its entry into force and should have been brought into effect only once the envisaged procedures had been followed. But Italy had not complied with its procedural obligations. It was in breach of the Directive.

The question in the case was whether Italy's misconduct had any effect on the action for breach of contract between the supplier, Unilever, and the buyer, Central Food. The Court held that it did, even though the Directive was completely silent on the matter.

The question referred to the Court of Justice asked whether a national court is required, in civil proceedings between individuals concerning contractual rights and obligations, to refuse to apply a national technical regulation which was adopted in breach of the requirements prescribed by the Directive. The Court focused on the point that application of such a technical regulation had the effect of hindering the use or marketing of a product which does not conform to the regulations. In short, application of the Italian rules hindered Unilever from marketing the extra virgin olive oil which it offered for sale. The Court reasoned that the 'effectiveness' of the preventive control envisaged by the Directive would enhanced by an interpretation that thrust it directly into legal proceedings between two contracting parties, with the consequence that the Italian rule was to be treated as unenforceable.[70] The obvious constitutional problem is that it is long established that an EU Directive cannot impose obligations on an individual and cannot therefore be relied on as such against an individual:

67 Para. 19.
68 Para. 21.
69 [2015] OJ L241/1.
70 Para. 44.

this is the denial of the 'horizontal direct effect' of a Directive to which the Court is firmly wedded.[71] The Court confirmed that restraining element in its case law. But this was not a case of this type. Instead the case at hand involved reliance on a Directive to render a technical regulation inapplicable. The absence of 'horizontal direct effect' prevents a Directive imposing an obligation on an individual in proceedings before a national court, but it does not prevent a Directive operating to exclude a rule of national law in such circumstances. And that exclusionary effect was what the Court sanctioned in *Unilever.*

So the national court could not take account of the labelling law. And Central Food therefore had to accept the goods.

In *Unilever* the Court was correct to declare that the Notification Directive created 'neither rights nor obligations for individuals'.[72] The *contract* created rights and obligations. But the invocation of the Directive in the national proceedings completely changed the outcome of the case. Central Food lost as a result. So the allocation of risk under the contract changed radically because of the intervention of EU law. This phenomenon is admittedly different from the mainstream of this chapter, because it was a Directive, not primary law, that caused the adjustment in the position of the contracting parties. But the underlying value is that of protection of the internal market, specifically 'to protect freedom of movement for goods by means of preventive control',[73] so this admittedly niche area is best addressed in the context of this chapter, rather than as a discrete element in EU's effect on contractual autonomy.

Unilever, then, is a useful weapon for a contracting party prejudiced by a technical rule adopted under national law. If that rule has been introduced in defiance of the obligations laid down by (what is now) Directive 2015/1535, then it is unenforceable in proceedings before a national court. But it should be noted that *Unilever* is a troubling decision, and it should not be assumed it will endure indefinitely.

The notion, visible in *Unilever*, that breach of EU law by a public authority may have an incidental prejudicial effect on a private party as a result of legal proceedings at national level is well known in EU law. It has cropped up in a variety of different contexts. For example in *Arcor AG* the German regulatory authorities had approved a funding and connection scheme in favour of Deutsche Telekom, a private company.[74] This had been done in violation of an EU Directive. If the approval were set aside by a German court in proceedings brought by other aggrieved telecommunications firms against the German public authorities, then there would follow obvious prejudice to the position of Deutsche Telekom. However, the Court of Justice held in a preliminary ruling

71 Case C-91/92, *Dori v Recreb* [1994] ECR I-3325.

72 Para. 51.

73 Para. 44.

74 Joined Cases C-152/07 to C-154/07, *Arcor AG* [2008] ECR I-5959.

that this was precisely what should nevertheless follow, provided the relevant provision of the Directive was sufficiently unconditional (which it was). Deutsche Telekom was the victim of 'incidental direct effect' or, in order to capture the idea that it was the third party harmed by litigation between two other parties (one public, one private), one might choose to label this a 'triangular situation'.

Wells v Secretary of State for Transport is another ruling of this type.[75] Delena Wells was a private individual who brought legal proceedings against a public authority which had granted an authorisation to a private mining company to develop a quarry near her home in Somerset. The problem was that the grant was in contravention of applicable EU environmental protection Directives. The Court of Justice held that the national court should require the withdrawal of the authorisation, and was not deterred by the prejudice that would be suffered by the private mining company, which was not party to the litigation. This would not be a case of horizontal direct effect, which the Court in *Wells* explained is ruled out because of the principle of legal certainty, because the Directive did not impose an obligation on the mining company. It would involve an 'incidental' prejudicial effect felt by the mining company as a result of the Directive's insertion into the proceedings brought by Wells against the public authority. So the Directive was apt to require the *exclusion* of the granting decision made by the public authority, in a manner similar to *Unilever* where the Directive caused the exclusion of the Italian technical rule.

The ruling that is closest to *Unilever* and which is its direct inspiration is *CIA Security International SA v Signalson SA and Securitel Sprl.*[76] Like *Unilever*, it involved the Notification Directive. A trader was seeking to extract an order from a court in Belgium to prevent another trader dealing in products (burglar alarms) that were not conformity with a Belgian technical regulation. Policing of the regulated market by a private party in this way was envisaged by Belgian law. But the technical regulation had not been notified to the Commission by the Belgian public authorities. The Court chose an interpretative approach which was founded on enhancing the 'effectiveness' of the notification regime created by the Directive:[77] this is precisely the understanding subsequently adopted by the Court in *Unilever.*[78] This led it to decide that this breach of the procedural obligation to notify meant that the technical regulation should be treated as unenforceable in proceedings before national courts. The order should therefore not be granted.

Once again, there is no question of horizontal direct effect. No obligation was imposed on a private party: the application of the national rule was *excluded*.

---

[75] Case C-201/02, *Wells v Secretary of State for Transport* [2004] ECR I-723.

[76] Case C-194/94 [1996] ECR I-2201.

[77] Para. 48.

[78] Case C-443/98, *Unilever Italia SpA v Central Food SpA* [2000] ECR I-7535: para. 44 cites *CIA Security*.

This, then, is the pedigree from which *Unilever* emerges. But even if the phenomenon of incidental or exclusionary effect acts as a thematic link binding together all these rulings, *Unilever* is in truth something extra. In *Unilever* the impact of the unenforceability of the State measure was felt directly in a contractual dispute between private parties. This was new. There was no contract between private parties in *CIA Security*, nor in *Arcor*, nor in *Wells*. Moreover, in all those three cases the power at stake in the litigation – to suppress non-complying burglar alarms, to remove an authorisation to operate in the telecommunications sector, to remove a grant of permission to operate a quarry – was of a regulatory nature. In *Unilever* the matter was simply enforcement of a private contract.

Unilever, then, takes the phenomenon of incidental or exclusionary effect further than previous case law, and drives it into the heart of an action for breach of contract involving private parties. This is damaging to legal certainty. The anxiety not to disturb the legal certainty of private parties is one reason the Court has given for refusing to extend horizontal direct effect to Directives,[79] yet that anxiety vanishes where the Court is asked to extend the incidental or exclusionary effect of Directives. In *Unilever* Advocate General Jacobs had explained in minute detail the harm that would be done to the legal certainty of private parties relying on national law by permitting the invocation of the Notification Directive in an action for breach of contract, and had strongly advised the Court against such a step. But he was ignored. The Court's eagerness to promote the effectiveness of the notification regime and, through it, the deeper value of the internal market has led it to disturb values embedded in contract law. It has been shrewdly noted that '[w]hat should not be allowed ... is for a private party who cannot possibly be said to derive any right from a provision of EC law to assert that provision against another private party who cannot possibly be said to have any responsibility for the implementation of that provision', yet that is precisely what the Court did in *Unilever*.[80]

The arguments against the Court's ruling in *Unilever*, most of all that founded on the damage done by the ruling for the legal certainty of contracting parties, remain strong. They may yet induce the Court to change its mind. The Court maintained the position it had adopted in *Unilever* in the subsequent ruling in *Sapod Audic*.[81] However, in that decision it embroidered its reasoning. It decided that 'the severity of the sanction under the applicable national law, such as nullity or unenforceability of the contract ... is a question governed by

---

79 Especially in Case C-201/02, *Wells v Secretary of State for Transport* [2004] ECR I-723, para. 56.

80 H. Schepel, 'The Enforcement of EC Law in Contractual Relations: Case Studies in How Not to "Constitutionalize" Private Law' (2004) 5 *European Review of Private Law* 661, 666; see also S. Weatherill, 'Breach of directives and breach of contract' (2001) 26 *European Law Review* 177.

81 Case C-159/00, *Sapod Audic* [2002] ECR I-5031.

national law, in particular as regards the rules and principles of contract law which limit or adjust that sanction in order to render its severity proportionate to the particular defect found.'[82] This is a rather opaque formula, and it plainly opens up the possibility, even likelihood, of different approaches in different Member States to the same violation of the Notification Directive. More subtly, however, it suggests a sensitivity to the implications of invocation of the Directive for the position of contracting parties which is missing from *Unilever.* It cannot be excluded that the Court might one day return to the matter and treat *Unilever* as a step too far and one from which it should backtrack. However, unless and until any such re-consideration takes place, the phenomenon of the incidental or exclusionary effect of Directives remains a niche, but potent, area in which EU law may destabilise the allocation of risk under a contract. Odd enough to ignored in leading textbooks on contract law,[83] *Unilever* nevertheless lurks as a prize for imaginative litigants.[84] It is one of the more vivid instances of how the demands of the internal market upset the assumptions of contract law, but unfortunately, given the Court's insouciant disregard for legal certainty, it is one of the harder to justify too.

2.7. COMPETITION LAW

The Treaty rules on competition share with those on free movement a functional orientation. They are not explicitly aimed at contracts or contract law, or indeed at any other particular practices or sector. They are targeted on the construction and maintenance of an internal market for the EU. Practices, including contracts, fall within their scope where they obstruct in some way the achievement of the internal market.

The Treaty competition rules applicable to private parties are built on two main pillars. Article 101 TFEU prohibits the enforcement of anti-competitive arrangements. Article 102 TFEU prohibits the abuse of a dominant position. Article 101 is concerned with bilateral or multilateral practices, whereas Article 102 is concerned largely with the unilateral practices of dominant firms, and applies only where the necessary threshold of market power is crossed. But as the Court put it in *Continental Can v Commission,* what are now Articles 101 and 102 'seek to achieve the same aim on different levels, viz. the maintenance of effective competition within the common [now internal] market'.[85]

---

[82] Para. 52.

[83] *Unilever* goes unmentioned in e.g. E. Peel, *Treitel on the Law of Contract,* 14th ed., Sweet and Maxwell, London 2015; M. Furmston, *Cheshire, Fifoot and Furmston's Law of Contract,* 16th ed., OUP, Oxford 2012; M. Chen-Wishart, *Contract Law,* 5th ed., OUP, Oxford 2015.

[84] For imagination but probable disappointment see Case C-613/14, *James Elliott Construction Limited v Irish Asphalt Limited* pending before the Court.

[85] Case 6/72 [1973] ECR 215, para. 25.

Both Articles are capable of application to contracts and indeed both explicitly refer to contracts, which is not the case with the Treaty provisions on free movement.

Article 101(1) directs that all agreements between undertakings, decisions by associations of undertakings and concerted practices which may affect trade between Member States and which have as their object or effect the prevention, restriction or distortion of competition within the internal market shall be prohibited. 'Agreements' obviously covers contracts, though it is not limited to contracts. Article 101(1) provides an illustrative list of prohibited practices, covering *inter alia* fixing purchase or selling prices, sharing markets or sources of supply, applying dissimilar conditions to equivalent transactions with other trading parties, thereby placing them at a competitive disadvantage, and making the conclusion of contracts subject to acceptance by the other parties of supplementary obligations which, by their nature or according to commercial usage, have no connection with the subject of such contracts. This plainly affects (*inter alia*) contracts and contractual autonomy. On rare occasions the Court finds a way to immunise contracts from review pursuant to Article 101(1) TFEU. In *Albany International* it decided that an agreement reached collectively between management and labour concerning mandatory affiliation to a sectoral pension fund was not an 'agreement' between undertakings within the meaning of what is now Article 101 TFEU.[86] The Court found that although certain restrictions of competition are inherent in such collective agreements, the social policy objectives which they pursued, which themselves are recognised by the Treaty, would be seriously undermined by the intervention of Article 101. So the nature and purpose of such agreements took them outside its scope. *Wouters* concerned rules of the Dutch bar prohibiting multi-disciplinary partnerships between advocates and accountants.[87] Such rules were plainly restrictive of competition, but the Court was prepared to find no violation of Article 101(1) provided the effects restrictive of competition were inherent in the pursuit of those objectives and were proportionate to them. An assessment of the overall context in which an agreement is struck or produces its effects is required.[88] But these are abnormal instances. The norm is for any contractual arrangements which affect inter-State trade to fall for review in the light of Article 101(1).

The only explicit escape route for practices that fall within the scope of this prohibition is provided by Article 101(3), which permits the application of practices which contribute to improving the production or distribution of goods or to promoting technical or economic progress, while allowing consumers a fair share of the resulting benefit, and which do not impose on the undertakings

86 Case C-67/96, *Albany International* [1997] ECR I-5751.

87 Case C-309/99, *J.C.J. Wouters, J.W. Savelbergh, Price Waterhouse Belastingadviseurs BV v Algemene Raad van de Nederlandse Orde van Advocaten* [2002] ECR I-1577.

88 See also Case C-519/04P, *Meca-Medina and Majcen v Commission* [2006] ECR I-6991 (anti-doping rules in sport).

concerned restrictions which are not indispensable to the attainment of these objectives nor afford such undertakings the possibility of eliminating competition in respect of a substantial part of the products in question. In practice, a great deal of the load involved in determining what is and what is not allowed is taken by Block Exemption Regulations which set out in intricate detail what types of contractual terms are permitted and what are not.

Pursuit of anti-competitive practices is likely to attract the attention of the Commission, which has important powers of investigation and decision-making, including the power to impose fines on defaulting undertakings.[89] But there is also a direct consequence before national courts of pursuit of a practice which is forbidden by Article 101(1). Article 101's bite on contractual enforceability is supplied by the teeth in its second paragraph. Article 101(2) stipulates that '[a]ny agreements or decisions prohibited pursuant to this Article shall be automatically void'. So this is a direct restriction on the enforceability of contracts. Moreover the Court long ago made clear that what is today Article 101 produces direct effects in relations between individuals, thereby creating rights which shall be safeguarded by national courts.[90] The demands of the internal market preclude granting autonomy to contracting parties. This provision, which has always been part of EU law since the Treaty of Rome created the (then) EEC with effect from 1958, is the single most visible and high-profile point of intersection between EU law and national contract law.

Article 102 TFEU prohibits an abuse by one or more undertakings of a dominant position within the internal market or in a substantial part of it. This is stated to be incompatible with the internal market in so far as it may affect trade between Member States. A non-exhaustive list of abusive practices is provided, which covers several practices of a type also addressed by Article 101, *inter alia* directly or indirectly imposing unfair purchase or selling prices or other unfair trading conditions, limiting production, markets or technical development to the prejudice of consumers, applying dissimilar conditions to equivalent transactions with other trading parties, thereby placing them at a competitive disadvantage, and making the conclusion of contracts subject to acceptance by the other parties of supplementary obligations which, by their nature or according to commercial usage, have no connection with the subject of such contracts. Here too there is a direct control over contractual autonomy. And here too the Court considers that what is today Article 102 creates rights which must be safeguarded by national courts.[91] Abuse within the meaning of Article 102 may involve condemnation of a dominant firm as a result of the conclusion of a contract in so far as this is treated as abusive (for example, because pricing is abusively high or predatorily low). It may even require that a

89 Regulation 1/2003 [2003] OJ L1/1.

90 Case 127/73, *BRT v SABAM* [1974] ECR 51.

91 Case 127/73, *BRT v SABAM* [1974] ECR 51.

dominant party enter into a contract with another party, on pain of refusal being found abusive. This is remarkably sensitive: it challenges assumptions about the autonomy of parties to choose with whom to contract, if at all, and, moreover, it risks dampening incentives for firms to invest in search of innovation that will put them ahead of the pack. The Court has gone some way to address such anxieties by making it clear that it is only exceptionally that a refusal to deal will be condemned as abusive: the dominant firm is not routinely required to share its resources or facilities with other firms.[92] But it is possible. It has been openly stated that freedom of contract remains the rule and so it is not open to the Commission to order a party to enter into a contract in order to bring an end to an infringement of Article 101 TFEU,[93] but Article 102 TFEU is different. It is over forty years ago that the Court first made clear that where a refusal to supply is incompatible with (what is now) Article 102, the Commission is entitled to order the supply of quantities of the relevant product.[94] This power has been at the heart of recent inquiries into the conduct of Microsoft.[95] In this way Article 102 TFEU confines the scope of contractual autonomy enjoyed by economically dominant firms. Remedying its violation may entail an obligation to contract. This is not the norm: it is the presence of dominant economic power that explains and justifies intolerance of contractual autonomy.

The State aid rules are a discrete element of EU competition law, but they too may affect the enforceability of contracts. The rules are contained in Articles 107–109 and, unlike Articles 101 and 102, their main concern is with the practices of public authorities. Public authorities are free to invest in the market in the same way as any private party, but once their activities lead to the conferral of an economic advantage on an undertaking which it would not have obtained under normal market conditions, then supervision pursuant to Articles 107–109 TFEU is required for fear that the grant will distort competition within the internal market.[96] This does not automatically mean that such aid will be condemned. Article 107(2) lists types of aid which are compatible with the internal market; Article 107(3) lists types of aid that may be judged compatible with the internal market. The Commission, on which relevant powers are conferred by Article 108, has exclusive competence to determine whether aid which falls within the types listed in Article 107(3) is in the particular circumstances compatible with the

92 e.g. Case C-7/97, *Oscar Bronner* [1998] ECR I-7791; Case C-418/01, *IMS Health* [2004] ECR I-5039.

93 Case T-24/90, *Automec v Commission* [1992] ECR II-2223; the CFI left open that national law may prescribe such a solution, para. 50 of the judgment, and see also Joined Cases C-377/05 and C-376/05, *A. Brünsteiner GmbH, Autohaus Hilgert GmbH v Bayerische Motorenwerke AG (BMW)* [2006] ECR I-11383, paras. 46–51.

94 Joined Cases 6/73 and 7/73, *Commercial Solvents v Commission* [1974] ECR 223.

95 e.g. Case T-201/04, *Microsoft v Commission* [2007] ECR II-3601; Case T-167/08, *Microsoft v Commission* judgment of 27 June 2012.

96 e.g. Case C-39/94, *SFEI and Others v La Poste* [1996] ECR I-3547; Case C-39/14, *BVVG* judgment of 16 July 2015.

internal market. A finding that aid is not so compatible generates an obligation on the Member State to recover it. The concern to protect the effectiveness of the rules clearly means that a recipient may not resist recovery by a claim that it is contractually entitled to retain the aid. The Court considers there can be no legitimate expectation that aid has been granted properly: an economic operator is expected to check that the procedures mandated by EU law have been followed.[97]

The quest to prevent the thwarting of the aim of the system has prompted the Court to intervene surprisingly deeply in matters of national civil procedure. EU law's principle of effective judicial protection serves to lever open established national practice. In *Lucchini* an Italian steel company had been ordered by the Italian public authorities to repay State aid, pursuant to a Commission Decision that the aid was not compatible with EU law.[98] Lucchini argued that as a matter of Italian law its right to the aid, recorded by a final judgment of the Corte d'appello di Roma, could not be challenged: it was, under Italian procedural law contained in the Civil Code, *res judicata*. This, the Court noted, 'would be to frustrate the application of Community law in so far as it would make it impossible to recover State aid that was granted in breach of Community law'.[99] Drawing on the landmark *Simmenthal* ruling, the Court stated that a national court is under a duty to give full effect to provisions of EU law, 'if necessary refusing of its own motion to apply any conflicting provision of national legislation'.[100] Since the assessment of the compatibility of the aid with EU law belongs to the exclusive competence of the Commission, it followed that national rules governing *res judicata* had to be disapplied in so far as their application prevented the recovery of State aid found by the Commission to be incompatible with EU law.

Res judicata plays an important role in promoting legal certainty by securing the finality of litigation and in *Fallimento Olimpiclub* the referring court, noting *Lucchini*, described 'a trend in the case-law of the Court towards considering the principle of *res judicata* to be relative and requiring it to be disapplied in order to uphold the primacy of provisions of Community law and to prevent conflict with those provisions'.[101] The Court was not receptive. *Lucchini* concerned 'a highly specific situation, in which the matters at issue were principles governing the division of powers between the Member States and the Community in the area of State aid'.[102] Such sensitivities will not commonly arise: where they do

---

97 e.g. Case C-5/89, *Commission v Germany* [1990] ECR I-3437, para. 14; Case C-24/95, *Alcan Deutschland* [1997] ECR I-1591, para. 25; Joined Cases C-183/02P and C-187/02P, *Daewoo Electronics Manufacturing España SA (Demesa), Territorio Histórico de Álava – Diputación Foral de Álava v Commission* [2004] ECR I-10609, para. 44.

98 Case C-119/05, *Lucchini* [2007] ECR I-6199.

99 Para. 59.

100 Para. 61 of *Lucchini*: Case 106/77, *Simmenthal* [1978] ECR 629.

101 Case C-2/08, *Fallimento Olimpiclub* [2009] ECR I-7501, para. 16.

102 Para. 25.

not, the worth of *res judicata* will be recognised. That the finality achieved by *res judicata* was displaced in *Lucchini* is powerful evidence of the Court's eagerness to protect the objectives of State aid law when they are imperilled by national practice.

Article 108(3) TFEU creates an obligation on the Member States to notify the Commission of plans to grant or alter aid. If this is not respected, an obligation is placed on a national court not to treat any such procedurally improper aid as enforceable. It is 'unlawful'. This was first developed by the Court[103] and is now carried over in the governing State aid procedural Regulation, Regulation 2015/1589.[104] Its Article 16(3) directs that 'recovery shall be effected without delay and in accordance with the procedures under the national law of the Member State concerned, provided that they allow the immediate and effective execution of the Commission's decision'. The purpose of the State aid rules is to protect the competitive structure of the market, and the Court has noted that situations may arise in which the cancellation of a contract by a national court may be the best way to facilitate the restoration of the competitive situation which existed before the aid was granted.[105] So here too a party may find its contractual expectation is defeated by the obligation imposed on the national court to ensure repayment of the unlawful aid.

Moreover the Court of Justice has specified that the consequences of a violation of the competition rules by a contracting party may generate a liability to compensate parties suffering loss caused by the breach. This stretches far beyond the explicit terms of the Treaty. The principle of *State* liability for loss caused by a violation of EU law was the starting point for the Court. The landmark ruling in *Francovich* rests on the need to secure the full effectiveness of EU rules and the Court insisted that the principle of State liability is 'inherent in the system of the Treaty'.[106] The Court subsequently decided that the principle of liability is capable of application also in the private sphere, in circumstances arising out of infringement of the Treaty competition rules. The ruling in *Courage Ltd v Bernard Crehan* provided the Court with its opportunity.[107] Once again the Court relied on the need to sustain the full effectiveness of EU law, and it reasoned that this aim would be weakened were it not open to any individual to claim damages for loss caused by practices liable to restrict or distort competition in breach of the Treaty. This, then, concerns protecting the victim but also discouraging breach of the rules in the first place. According to the Court, violation must be sufficiently serious to attract such a responsibility to pay

103 See especially Case C-354/90, *Federation Nationale* [1991] ECR I-5505; also Case C-199/06, *CELF, SIDE* [2008] ECR I-469.

104 [2015] OJ L248/99.

105 Case C-275/10, *Residex Capital IV CV v Gemeente Rotterdam* [2011] ECR I-13043 (in which the aid took the form of a guarantee).

106 Cases C-6/90 and C-9/90 [1991] ECR I-5357, para. 35.

107 Case C-453/99 [2001] ECR I-6297.

compensation: a genuinely inadvertent and excusable violation would probably not cross this threshold.[108] The applicant in *Courage v Crehan* was a party to the contract. Subsequently in *Manfredi* the Court relied on *Courage v Crehan* to hold that an individual can claim compensation for the harm suffered where there is a causal relationship between that harm and a practice prohibited by EU competition law in circumstances involving a possible claim by a consumer.[109] This brings the consumer within the circle of those able to seek compensation in proceedings initiated before a national court from parties engaged in unlawful anti-competitive practices and thereby harming the market, although the practical difficulties of pursuing such a claim are doubtless formidable.

In *Kone* the Court added that an individual who suffers loss as a result of high prices charged by an undertaking which is not itself party to a cartel ('umbrella pricing') may claim compensation from members of the cartel even where no contractual link exists between the victim and members of the cartel.[110]

In 2014 an EU Directive was adopted on certain rules governing actions for damages under national law for infringements of the competition rules.[111] It is based on Articles 103 and 114 TFEU. The Directive is, however, not at all radical in its intent or effect. The Court has acted as the pioneer in this area, and in fact the Directive's Preamble declares not only that it 'reaffirms the acquis communautaire ... as stated in the case-law of the Court' but also that it 'does not pre-empt any further development thereof'.[112]

In sum, national contract law, including not only questions of enforceability but also remedies, must embrace the demands of EU competition law.

2.8. EU ANTI-DISCRIMINATION LAW

EU anti-discrimination law has a role to play in confining contractual autonomy. Here too the law is a patchwork, incrementally developed over time, and it is built on primary law (including latterly the Charter), by general principles developed by the Court (some now absorbed by the Charter), and by secondary legislation. It is not based purely on the logic of an internal market. There is a wider vision of equality at stake. But the thematic link for the purposes of understanding the EU's role in matters of contracts and contract law is that rights to non-discriminatory treatment may override the agreed contractual status governing the position of affected parties. Anti-discrimination law is part of a general trend

---

[108] e.g. Case C-352/98P, *Bergaderm v Commission* [2000] ECR I-5291; Joined Cases C-46/93 and C-48/93, *Brasserie du Pêcheur v Germany and R v Secretary of State for Transport, ex parte Factortame* [1996] ECR I-1029.

[109] Joined Cases C-295/04, *Manfredi* [2006] ECR I-6619.

[110] C-557/12 judgment of 18 July 2014.

[111] Dir. 2014/104 [2014] OJ L349/1.

[112] Recital 12.

in EU law to protect the weaker party in particular, *inter alia* in the process of contracting.

2.9. EU ANTI-DISCRIMINATION LAW: EQUAL PAY

The Treaty rules on equal pay have long been the most prominent feature of EU anti-discrimination law.

In the original Treaty of Rome, which entered into force in 1958, what was then Article 119 EEC provided that '[e]ach Member State shall during the first stage ensure and subsequently maintain the application of the principle that men and women should receive equal pay for equal work'. Today this direction is contained in Article 157 TFEU. Reference to 'the first stage', which ended in 1962, has been removed, but the provision's substance remains unaltered. Article 157 TFEU today provides that '[e]ach Member State shall ensure that the principle of equal pay for male and female workers for equal work or work of equal value is applied'. The predominant motivation which prompted the shaping of this rule in the negotiation conducted in 1950s was rooted in anxiety that a Member State with relatively strong legal regulation designed to secure gender equality would suffer in so far as its regime was undercut by Member States with less interventionist (or even no) regimes. In more concrete terms, it was France which objected to Germany's preference to avoid public regulation of pay in the service of gender equality.[113] But even if the main *aim* of the EU's commitment to gender equality in matters of pay was to secure equality in regulatory costs within the internal market, its effect was *also* to establish certain mandatory standards of social protection in favour of the disadvantaged group, which is typically underpaid women. That twofold or dual commitment was strengthened by the Court's landmark ruling in 1976 in *Defrenne v SABENA*.[114] Defrenne was a female air hostess; SABENA was at the time the national airline of Belgium, though it subsequently went into bankruptcy in 2001. Her claim was simple: she wanted compensation for having been paid less than men who were doing the same work.[115] Her contract did not help her, but did EU law? The Court found that the Treaty provision, then Article 119 EEC, now Article 157 TFEU, was directly effective, and so it required no legislative amplification before it could be relied on before national courts. True, that Treaty provision declared, as it declares today, that '[e]ach Member State' shall secure the application of the principle of equal pay for equal work. Did this textual focus on the State push

113 The historical background is explored in J. Kenner, *EU Employment Law: From Rome to Amsterdam and Beyond*, Hart Publishing, Oxford 2003, Ch. 1; and C. Barnard, *EU Employment Law*, 4th ed., OUP, Oxford 2012, Ch. 1.

114 Case 43/75 [1976] ECR 455.

115 The background story is told in Chapter 4 of C. Hoskyns, *Integrating Gender: Women, Law and Politics in the European Union*, Verso, London 1996.

towards restraint in the invocability of the equal pay rule by a *private* party? It did not. The Court could have found the provision capable of application to SABENA on the basis that it was State-controlled, but it preferred a much broader formulation which was apt to lend immense vigour to this Treaty provision. The fact that the Treaty provision was (and is) addressed to '[e]ach Member State' did 'not prevent rights from being conferred at the same time on any individual who has an interest in the performance of the duties thus laid down'.[116] Moreover, the equal pay rule applied 'not only to the action of public authorities, but also extends to all agreements which are intended to regulate paid labour collectively, as well as to contracts between individuals'.[117] The Court tersely dismissed the objection that the application by national courts of the principle of equal pay 'would amount to modifying independent agreements concluded privately or in the sphere of industrial relations such as individual contracts and collective labour agreements' by observing that this followed from the mandatory nature of the prohibition against such discrimination.[118] There is a constitutional hierarchy and, within it, private autonomy is subordinate to the Treaty norm of anti-discrimination in the particular matter of equal pay.

The Court in *Defrenne* confirmed the understanding of the equal pay rule as rooted in *both* economic *and* social motivations. It serves to ensure that undertakings which are established in States which have implemented the principle of equal pay do not suffer a competitive disadvantage when compared with undertakings established in States which have chosen not to legislate; but it also promotes the social objectives of the EU, which embrace social progress and the constant improvement of the living and working conditions of their peoples.[119] So the EU pursues 'a double aim, which is at once economic and social'.[120]

Plenty of forceful rhetoric in the Treaty and the Charter today supports this dual vision. For example since the entry into force of the Lisbon Treaty in 2009 the EU is committed to work for a 'highly competitive social market economy.'[121] But in *Defrenne* in 1976 the Court had already articulated a vision of public regulation of the labour market superimposed on the exercise of contractual autonomy which was driven by *both* the perception that a common set of rules applicable across the whole territory of the EU would correct the competitive distortion caused otherwise by diverse legislative choices among the Member States *and* the embrace of a social purpose embedded within the role of the EU in setting common rules of market regulation. The Court has even gone so far on occasion as to describe the economic aim of the Treaty's equal pay rule as

116 Para. 31.
117 Para. 39.
118 Paras. 38, 39.
119 Paras. 8–10.
120 Para. 12.
121 Art. 3(3) TEU.

'secondary to the social aim pursued'.[122] In sum the Court's finding of a directly effective and horizontally applicable right in *Defrenne* meant that policing the equal pay rule became the province of individual litigants and national courts before which they pursued their cases. Achieving equal pay was no longer bound to the intricacies of the national political process or the gift of the EU's legislative process. Nor was it dependent on socially progressive contracting practices between employers and employees.

However, the glitter spreads only so far. The concrete and clear equal pay rule embedded in (what is today) Article 157 TFEU is atypical. The deal struck in the Treaty negotiations of the 1950s left most matters concerning social policy unaffected by unconditional and precise rules set by primary EU law. The assumption was that most of the field of labour market regulation and social protection more generally rested with the Member States as matters allowing scope for expression of national autonomy, which might over time be subjected to an EU influence through the adoption of secondary legislation at EU level. This, then, did not amount to a wide terrain of individual rights enforceable at a constitutionally superior level to contractual negotiation. The deepening of the EU's aspirations in the field depended on legislative amplification. Such progress as could be made depended on the constitutional scope of the relevant authorisations to legislate supplied by the Treaty, on the institutional readiness of the Commission to exploit them by proposing legislative measures and on the political thirst of the Member States acting in Council and of the Parliament to agree to such measures. The key provision dealing explicitly with social policy is today Article 153 TEU. Article 151 TFEU directs that the Union and the Member States 'shall have as their objectives the promotion of employment, improved living and working conditions, so as to make possible their harmonisation while the improvement is being maintained, proper social protection, dialogue between management and labour, the development of human resources with a view to lasting high employment and the combating of exclusion', and Article 153 TFEU provides a concrete legal base to legislate in (eleven) defined areas. The track record of legislative activity adopted under this legal base and under others of more peripheral significance such as Articles 148 and 149 TFEU on employment and Article 166 on vocational training is incremental and hotly contested. The detail can be found elsewhere:[123] a brief overview of the legislative *acquis*, which comprises mainly Directives, is provided in Chapter 4. This heated contestation is even more plain in the case of measures adopted as legislative harmonisation in the name of the good functioning of the internal market, considered in Chapters 3 and 4; and measures adopted pursuant to

122 Cases C-270/97 and 271/97, *Deutsche Post AG v Sievers, Schrage* [2000] ECR I-929, para. 57; Case C-50/96, *Deutsche Telekom AG v Schröder* [2000] ECR I-743, para. 57.

123 e.g. C. Barnard, *EU Employment Law*, 4th ed., OUP, Oxford 2012; A.C.L. Davies, *EU Labour Law*, Edward Elgar, Cheltenham 2012.

Article 19 TFEU, which, as shown in Chapter 3, provides for a competence to take appropriate action to combat discrimination based on sex, racial or ethnic origin, religion or belief, disability, age or sexual orientation, the predecessor of which is the legal base for Directive 2000/43 on equal treatment between persons irrespective of racial or ethnic origin[124] and Directive 2000/78 establishing a general framework for equal treatment in employment and occupation.[125] Once implemented at national level, these measures plainly exert a significant influence on contractual autonomy, and they are not confined to the workplace or to the internal market more broadly. The intricacy of the policy debate, like the detail of the rules, lies beyond the scope of this book. Its core can, however, be summarised. There are two radically different views. One is, in short, that which animates the Court's understanding of the function of equal pay rule in its ruling in *Defrenne*. This view treats legislative diversity among the Member States as damaging to the competitive structure of the internal market. Costs fluctuate according to local regulatory patterns. On this model, diversity is understood as a distortion of choices made by undertakings and it induces States to cut levels of social protection in order to attract corporate re-location. This is the feared 'race to the bottom', which, it is claimed, robs Europe of the economic and social virtues consequent on a long-term approach to regulation aimed at promoting education, training and job security. The opposite view treats diversity not as a distortion of competition, but quite simply as *competition*! States choose different regulatory patterns according to local preference: some might mandate high protective standards; others might prefer less or no intervention in the market. In so far as those choices lead to competition between jurisdictions as rule-makers, then corporate entities choose the host jurisdiction that best suits their interests, and then that 'market for rules' will reveal which is the best solution. On this view the EU should cherish legislative diversity. It should promote it, not suppress it by adopting common rules. On its most eagerly pressed model this would be to argue for the facilitation of corporate mobility unrestrained by limitations consequent on diverse patterns of market regulation, which in concrete terms would mean a highly sceptical attitude to attempts by national regulators to justify practices that impede cross-border free movement.

The paucity of concrete rules of primary EU law beyond the equal pay rule now found in Article 157 TFEU means that the success of one vision over the other was left to be determined by the political process, which, unsurprisingly, has delivered different degrees of impetus at different times. This will be reviewed in Chapter 4.10. For the purposes of this book, it is plain that preservation of contractual autonomy is – for good or ill – more effectively ensured by a model which is faithful to protecting competition between regulators in the EU than one which insists on the desirability of EU common rules.

---

124 [2000] OJ L180/22.

125 [2000] OJ L303/16.

2.10. EQUALITY LAW MORE BROADLY: GENERAL PRINCIPLES AND THE CHARTER

The subjection of the actions of public authorities to control in the name of fundamental rights has been one of the most significant evolving features of the legal landscape in Europe since the end of the Second World War in 1945. The entry into force of the European Convention on Human Rights in 1953, to which 47 European States are now party, was plainly a moment of immense significance, but each State has its own distinctive narrative concerning choice of form and method whereby to entrench particular political, social and cultural rights beyond the thrust of quotidian majoritarian politics.

In some circumstances it is accepted that control should also reach into the private sphere. In particular rules forbidding discrimination on defined grounds are well-recognised features of modern societies which confine the autonomy of private parties. But how far should the law go in insisting that the standards that apply to public authorities also apply in whole or in part to private contracting parties? How strong is the competing argument in favour of the autonomy of the individual to act without direction from the State? Should, for example, sellers of goods and providers of services be under a legal obligation to treat all customers without regard to their race, age, sexual orientation, nationality and potentially a host of other prohibited grounds? This is to inquire into the *constitutionalistion* of contract law, in the sense that this involves a contestable claim that certain values are of sufficient importance to rank above the value of private autonomy.

All legal systems in Europe grapple with these conundrums. It is a fascinating area of inquiry.[126] The concern of this book is EU law. Nothing in EU law offers a clear articulation of how far the protection of fundamental rights should reach into contract law. Indeed, EU law lacks any clear distinction between public and private law. One of its features is its pursuit of functional objectives, most of all the completion of the internal market, and this may cause it to be blind to such demarcations made under national law and in consequence to destabilise them.

As so often, tracing the impact of EU law in this area therefore involves piecing together a patchwork. There exists no blueprint which sets out the impact of fundamental rights protection under EU law on contractual autonomy and contract law. A great deal depends on the choices made from time to time by the Court. There is a sense of uncertainty and unpredictability

---

126 See e.g. C Mak, *Fundamental Rights in European Contract Law. A comparison of the impact of fundamental rights on contractual relationships in Germany, the Netherlands, Italy and England*, Kluwer Law International, Alphen aan den Rijn 2008; D. Oliver and J. Fedtke, *Human Rights and the Private Sphere: A Comparative Study*, Routledge, London 2007; C. Busch and H. Schulte-Nölke (eds.), *Fundamental Rights and Private Law*, Sellier, Munich 2010.

here, combined too with the sense of the importance of the values at stake. The best way to approach the matter is to inspect the landmarks, and then to try and draw a map.

The ruling which focused attention on the matter in the development of EU law is *Mangold v Helm*.[127] Werner Mangold was a 56-year-old man who worked for Rüdiger Helm, a lawyer. The contract of employment was of limited duration, and the reason for this lay in a statutory provision under German law which was intended to make it easier to conclude fixed-term contracts with older workers (as defined). The key question was simple: was this discrimination on the grounds of age lawful under EU law? It was at least arguable that the *substance* of a relevant Framework Agreement and Directive 2000/78 establishing a general framework for equal treatment in employment and occupation were apt to exclude a national rule of this type which sanctioned diminished protection of older persons in work when compared with other workers. But a *constitutional* problem seemed to defeat this claim. EU law does not permit invocation of a Directive before national courts in order to impose an obligation on a private party: Directives cannot exert horizontal direct effect.[128] This was Mangold's problem: Helm was a private employer.

But the Court found a way to rescue Mangold. He could not rely on Directive 2000/78, but, the Court unexpectedly observed, that Directive 'does not itself lay down the principle of equal treatment in the field of employment and occupation'.[129] Instead the source of the principle lies 'in various international instruments and in the constitutional traditions common to the Member States',[130] and these go to make a general principle of EU law which forbids discrimination on grounds of age. A general principle of this type ranks on a par with the Treaty itself and the Court added that such a general principle enjoys application not only in cases involving public authorities but also, as here, in cases involving private parties. So the Court, by locating the legal protection of Mangold, a party to a contract of employment, at the level of primary law apt to operate 'horizontally', had skipped free of the shackles imposed by the constitutional limits of the application of the Directive as a legal instrument in national proceedings.

Mangold created as much surprise and dismay as any ruling the Court has ever delivered. Tracing the reaction exhaustively is not within this book's ambit: the principal point of criticism was that the Court's identification of a general principle of EU law prohibiting discrimination on the basis of age applicable even in the context of a contract between two private parties stretched beyond what comparative survey of practice in national and transnational legal systems

---

127 Case C-144/04, *Mangold v Helm* [2005] ECR I-9981.
128 Case C-91/92, *Dori v Recreb* [1994] ECR I-3325.
129 Para. 74.
130 Para. 74.

could bear.[131] However, the deed was done and the Court had opened the door to a constitutionalised protection of certain values which is superimposed on contractual autonomy. The question was: which values? And when?

The Charter of Fundamental Rights offers a basis for wider reflection on the matter. It acquired binding force only in 2009 and so was left unmentioned in *Mangold*. But since its Article 21 lists age as one of several prohibited grounds of discrimination within the scope of EU law, it offers a possible basis for a more credible rooting of the claim that EU law forbids discrimination on the basis of age than that concocted by the Court in *Mangold*. And the Grand Chamber ruling in *Seda Kücükdeveci v Swedex GmbH & Co. KG* duly connected *Mangold* to the Charter.[132] This was another employment dispute involving private parties. Under German law periods of employment completed before the age of 25 were not to be taken into account in calculating the applicable notice period. This was treated by the Court as discrimination on grounds of age forbidden by EU law. The Court cited *Mangold* and confirmed that non-discrimination on grounds of age must be regarded as a general principle of EU law, to which Directive 2000/78 gives specific expression. Because the Charter had in the interim been granted binding effect by the reforms made to the Treaty system by the Lisbon Treaty, the Court was able to add that that since its Article 21 prohibits discrimination based on age, the full effectiveness of EU law requires a national court to disapply any provision of national legislation contrary to the principle of non-discrimination. And this is operative also in the context of a contractual dispute.

It seems that we are at an early stage in the story. The Court's landmark 1964 ruling in *Van Gend en Loos* in favour of the direct effect of EU law initiated a series of opportunities for it to clarify just how many provisions of the Treaty were apt for immediate application by national courts and, moreover, which should enjoy horizontal application.[133] The same pattern will now take shape in relation to the Charter. So, for example, in *Association de médiation sociale* the Court ruled that Article 27 of the Charter on workers' rights to information and consultation was not sufficiently precise to provide a basis for mandatory disapplication of national rules that offended against it.[134] Article 27 did not help the applicant – its elaboration must await legislative amplification at EU level. Plenty more cases of this type may be expected to reach Luxembourg as preliminary references in the years to come. So, for example, one might wonder

---

131 For a balanced assessment of the issues and the literature see M. Dougan, 'In Defence of Mangold?' in A. Arnull, C. Barnard, M. Dougan and E. Spaventa (eds.), *A Constitutional Order of States? Essays in EU Law in Honour of Alan Dashwood*, Hart Publishing, Oxford 2011), p. 219. In Case C-427/06, *Birgit Bartsch v BSH* [2008] ECR I-7245 AG Sharpston reflected on academic and judicial reaction to *Mangold*, paras. 31–41 of her Opinion.

132 Case C-555/07, *Kücükdeveci* [2010] ECR I-365.

133 Case 26/62 [1963] ECR 1.

134 Case C-176/12, *Association de médiation sociale* judgment of 15 January 2014.

whether Article 7's respect for private and family life and for the 'home' could be relied on by a consumer to defeat proceedings for foreclosure of a mortgage. Article 7 might not be interpreted to create a right which is enforceable in this manner, and, even if it is, the lender who has not been paid would doubtless seek in turn to rely on its freedom to conduct a business guaranteed by Article 16 of the Charter.[135] The matter is open. The point here is only to remark on the potential for injecting fundamental rights into the resolution of contractual disputes between private parties.

Such cases which elucidate the impact of the Charter in proceedings before national courts, *inter alia* in a horizontal context, will be of importance but it cannot be excluded that the Court will once again be tempted to perform the conjuring trick it unveiled in *Mangold* and to find unexpected general principles of EU law which exist *beyond* the Charter and which bind *inter alia* private parties. However, this is probably not likely. The Charter of Fundamental Rights, endowed with full legitimacy as a result of its location within the process of ratification of the Lisbon Treaty, seems to be the Court's principle source of inspiration today, rather than the more abstract divination of general principles visible in *Mangold*. The Charter, as the constitutional centrepiece of the EU's commitment to protection of fundamental rights, has a good claim to act as ring-fence of any constitutionalising wider ambition on the part of the Court. And, given the troubling unpredictability and harm to legal certainty that a decision such as *Mangold* causes, there is a powerful normative case for treating the Charter as apt to curtail such judicial temptation to play fast and loose with the foundational requirement in Article 5 TEU that the EU shall not act beyond its Treaty mandate and the proviso in Article 13(2) TEU that the EU's institutions shall 'act within the limits of the powers conferred' by the Treaties. After all, there are immensely complex economic and political choices at stake in such circumstances, and a court which is not tethered to a clear legislative mandate is likely to be a relatively poor or at least imperfectly informed decision-maker.

---

135 This example is drawn from O. Cherednychenko and N. Reich, 'The Constitutionalization of European Private Law: Gateways, Constraints, and Challenges' (2015) 23 *European Review of Private Law* 797, 825–26. For further helpful speculation see N. Lazzerini, 'Annotation of Case C-176/12' (2014) 51 *Common Market Law Review* 907; P. Cabral and R. Neves, 'General Principles of EU Law and Horizontal Direct Effect' (2011) 17 *European Public Law* 437; M. De Mol, 'Horizontal Direct Effect of Union Prohibitions of Discrimination' in A. Hartkamp et al. (eds.), *The Influence of EU Law on National Private Law*, Kluwer, Deventer 2014, pp. 219–250; and (more sceptically minded) M. Safjan and P. Miklaszewicz, 'Horizontal Effect of the General Principles of EU law in the Sphere of Private Law' (2010) 18 *European Review of Private Law* 475; M. Fornasier, 'The Impact of EU Fundamental Rights on Private Relationships: Direct or Indirect Effect?' (2015) 23 *European Review of Private Law* 29; M. Dougan, 'The Impact of the General Principles of Union Law upon Private Relationships' in D. Leczykiewicz and S. Weatherill (eds.), *The Involvement of EU Law in Private Law Relationships*, Hart Publishing, Oxford 2013, Ch. 5.

There are hints of such restraint. In *Audiolux* the Court was not willing to extract a general principle attached to the protection of minority shareholders from the existing pattern of rights and obligations created by Directives on company law. What was missing was 'the general, comprehensive character which is otherwise naturally inherent in general principles of law'.[136] This was fully in line with a skilfully written Opinion in the case prepared by Advocate General Trstenjak. She warned that the Court 'may not assume the role of the Community legislature if a gap in the law can be filled by the Community legislature',[137] in the light of the superior democratic legitimation and expertise which the political institutions claim in matters that demand a choice between different political and social interests. She added too that judicial self-restraint should also be dictated by 'grounds of protection of legitimate expectations and legal certainty'.[138] In *Sonia Chacon Navas* the Court refused to accept that non-discrimination on grounds of sickness counts as a general principle of EU law.[139] In *Kaltoft* the Court agreed that discrimination in the workplace on the ground of obesity might in defined circumstances associated with hindering full participation in professional life fall within the scope of discriminatory conduct on the basis of disability forbidden by Directive 2000/78 establishing a general framework for equal treatment in employment and occupation,[140] but it rejected the broader contention that the Charter precludes discrimination on the basis of obesity or that EU law contains any general principle forbidding such discrimination.[141]

The general principles of EU law, now probably contained within and by the Charter of Fundamental Rights, provide a degree of constitutionalised circumscription of the autonomy of contracting parties. They do not offer a wide-ranging or systematic programme whereby private autonomy is subordinated to values in the public interest. And much remains open and undecided. It is probably relatively easy to accept that the full weight of constitutional protection which the individual enjoys against State authorities should not be transplanted to relations between private parties. That would convert every private law dispute into a conflict between constitutional values. It would obliterate the divide between public law and private law, and would be frighteningly intolerant of the value of private autonomy. On the other hand embrace of some degree of legal protection in circumstances of severe economic imbalance even where the consequence is to confine contractual autonomy is a common feature of most

---

136 Case C-101/08, *Audiolux* [2009] ECR I-9823, para. 42. See also C. Herresthal, 'Grundrechtecharta und Privatrecht' [2014] *Zeitschrift für Europäisches Privatrercht* 238.

137 Para. 107, citing 'Louis, J.-V., L'ordre juridique communautaire, 6th edition, Brussels/ Luxembourg 1993, p. 119, 120'.

138 Para. 111.

139 Case C-13/05, *Sonia Chacon Navas* [2006] ECR I-6467.

140 [2000] OJ L303/16.

141 Case C-354/13 judgment of 18 December 2014.

European legal systems, and is especially visible in consumer law, employment law and laws governing tenancy of property. Broader notions of anti-discrimination law also fit this pattern. In part this is based on an understanding that where power is imbalanced 'freedom' of contract is unreal and one-sided. Since freedom for the pike is death for the minnow, the minnow must be granted legal protection: this is to *promote* autonomy (of the minnow) by addressing its unequal relationship with the pike.[142] In part it reflects a sense that there are certain social values that must rank higher than contractual autonomy. So the central quest is to decide not *whether*, but rather *how far*, values inspired by public law and fundamental rights should infiltrate contract law, and in addition to assess how far they should be adapted to take account of the distinct context of private, rather than public, power.[143] In short, what should be the 'key elements' of a constitutionalised EU private law?[144] In the EU the Charter provides a map of sorts, but it is an incomplete and often calculatedly ambiguous document and so a great deal of power is delegated to the Court. How restrained the Court chooses to be will be of critical importance. It should be emphasised that the case *against* an intensively constitutionalised contract law, whether pursued in the name of the Charter or *a fortiori* in developing new general principles, rests not simply on concern to preserve a zone of private autonomy but also on anxiety that judges, rather than legislatures, are poorly equipped to make the necessary politically charged balancing assessments.

2.11. CONCLUSION

An unrestricted version of contractual autonomy is not tolerated where it is shown to impede the cross-border movement of goods and services, but there are relatively few occasions on which purely private arrangements will fall within the scope of the free movement rules, both because of the need to show a restriction to inter-State trade and because of the limited, if uneven, personal scope of the Treaty rules on free movement. Even where such practices are exposed to review, it is open to the regulator to justify such restrictions. The wider phenomenon of regulatory contract law is more readily exposed to the

142 For a good overview in a European context see A. Colombi Ciacchi, 'Freedom of contract as freedom from unconscionable contracts' in M. Kenny, J. Devenney and L. Fox O'Mahony, *Unconscionability in European Private Financial Transactions: Protecting the Vulnerable*, CUP, Cambridge 2010, Ch. 1, pp. 7–25. More generally a highly influential account is M. Trebilcock, *The Limits of Freedom of Contract*, Harvard University Press, Cambridge 1993.

143 See e.g. H. Collins, 'On the (In)compatibility of Human Rights Discourse and Private Law' in H. Micklitz (ed.), *Constitutionalization of European Private Law*, OUP, Oxford 2014, Ch. 2, pp. 26–60.

144 See H. Micklitz, 'Introduction' in H. Micklitz (ed.), *Constitutionalization of European Private Law*, OUP, Oxford 2014, Ch. 1, pp 23–25; and more broadly N. Reich, *General Principles of EU Civil Law*, Intersentia, Cambridge 2013.

supervision of the free movement rules, whether in proceedings instituted by the Commission or more commonly by private parties proceeding initially before national courts, although a key insight is that the controlling influence exerted by EU law is intended to release and promote opportunities for the exercise of cross-border contractual autonomy. The protection of the internal market lies at the heart of these instances where EU law comes into contact with contracts and contract law.

Competition law refuses to sanction a pure model of contractual autonomy because of the harm this may inflict on the functioning of the internal market. A contract which is anti-competitive within the meaning of Article 101 is rendered unenforceable unless it is able to escape the prohibition through the narrowly defined routes covered in section 2.7. Article 102 may cause exploitative or exclusionary activity conducted through use of contracts to be condemned as abusive, and the especially pernicious potential of the economically dominant firm goes so far as to require that in certain circumstances an unwilling firm may be required to enter into a contract in order to put an end to the allegation of abusive conduct.

Anti-discrimination law, in its market-based version best exemplified by *Defrenne*[145] but also pitched at a wider level by the Directives adopted pursuant to Article 19,[146] reveals another zone in which intolerance attaches to a pure model of contractual autonomy and it too may in certain circumstances forbid a party from exercising a choice whether or not to contract where the grounds on which that choice is based are treated as illegitimate as a matter of law. It remains uncertain quite how far this type of wider control over private autonomy reaches, and the evolution of the Charter in the hands of the Court will be crucially illuminating, but the guiding theme is that certain values of social and political significance are constitutionally ranked above that of preserving contractual autonomy. This is the character of primary EU law. However, most of the detailed impact of EU law on contracts and contract law has been elaborated through the adoption of secondary legislation, most of all Directives. It is to this pattern that the rest of the book is devoted. The Treaty authorisations for the adoption of such rules are examined in the next chapter, then Chapter 4 ranges across the landscape of the legislative *acquis* in order to extract the governing themes.

---

145 Case 43/75 [1976] ECR 455.

146 Above nn. 124 and 125.

CHAPTER 3
THE EU AS A SOURCE OF CONTRACT LAW

3.1. SECONDARY LEGISLATION

The previous chapter examined primary EU law as a means to confine the exercise of contractual autonomy. Where it is anti-competitive, where it impedes free movement (of persons and services) or where it involves discrimination on prohibited grounds, EU law prevails. Chapter 2 also considered how national contract law may be subjected to the demands of the internal market. Where it restricts inter-State trade, it is subject to review: where it is not shown to be justified, it must be set aside in so far as it impedes imports.

This chapter moves from primary to secondary law. It concerns regulation of the exercise of contractual autonomy and it largely concerns the scope of EU legislative competence in the field of contract law. Its primary concern is the sturdy raft of Directives that have been adopted as measures of harmonisation with the aim of improving the functioning of the internal market. In this sense it operates at a lower constitutional register than the material considered in the previous chapter. Directives are constitutionally weaker than primary law, in at least two important senses. First, they may be altered 'from within', through the EU's internal legislative process, whereas the Treaty and the Charter can be changed only 'from the outside', with the unanimous support of the Member States acting through processes for revision foreseen by the Treaty superstructure.[1] Second, Directives are denied horizontal direct effect in proceedings before national courts,[2] whereas this attribute readily attaches to many, though not to all, of the relevant provisions of the Treaty and the Charter. In short, primary law paints a bigger, bolder picture of the EU's commitment to regulating contracts and contract law than does secondary law.

Nevertheless, there are quite simply a lot of relevant Directives, to the point that no appreciation of the shape of contract law in Europe can possibly

---

1 Art. 50 TEU.

2 Case C-91/92, *Dori v Recreb* [1994] ECR I-3325; Case C-192/94, *El Corte Inglés v Cristina Blasquez Rivero* [1996] ECR I-1281; Case C-80/06, *Carp Snc v Ecorad* [2007] ECR I-4473; Case C-555/07, *Kücükdeveci* [2010] ECR I-365; Case C-508/14, *Česky telekomunikačni* judgment of 6 October 2015.

disregard the layer of material added by the EU secondary legislation, even if a degree of grumpiness about the *ad hoc* nature of that intervention is commonly visible.[3] Moreover, the fragility of the Directive, as a measure that can be altered through the political process with far less laboriousness than applies to primary law, is strictly *relative*: it is far from easy to achieve change to the EU's legislative *acquis* and it is plain that most of the change that has been adopted within the EU's legislative *acquis* affecting contract law (directly and indirectly) has been to extend, update and widen its reach, not to curtail it. It is also true that the constitutional limits on the application of Directives in proceedings at national level, though real and sometimes vivid in practice,[4] are of no relevance provided Member States implement the Directive properly so that its protection becomes integrated into the national legal order. And even where that is missing the notion of indirect effect, which casts an obligation on a national judge to interpret national law so far as is possible in order to conform with the intent of any relevant Directive, goes a distance towards closing the gap in legal protection of private parties caused by the denial of horizontal direct effect.[5]

In short, this chapter addresses EU secondary legislation, whereas Chapter 2 deals with primary law. The constitutional hierarchy is clear. But both dimensions demand to be understood in an integrated manner in order to make sense of the scope and depth of the contract law of the internal market. The main focus of this Chapter is to show the bases provided in the Treaty on the Functioning of the European Union (TFEU) for legislative activity at EU level, and the next chapter will look more closely at the pattern of legislation that has in fact been adopted in the field of contract law.

3.2. THE PRINCIPLE OF CONFERRAL

The EU's mandate is no wider than its Treaties permit: its competence is that conferred on it by its Member States. This is true of contract law – it is true of any area in which the EU purports to exercise legislative authority. This, the principle of conferral which was mentioned already in Chapter 1, is the starting point in any account of the EU's legislative competence.

Article 5(1) TEU directs that the 'limits of Union competences are governed by the principle of conferral'. Article 5(2) TEU declares that 'the Union shall act only within the limits of the competences conferred upon it by the Member States in the Treaties to attain the objectives set out therein'. It logically follows,

3 See Chapters 4.11 and 7.

4 The fact pattern of Case C-91/92, *Dori v Recreb* [1994] ECR I-3325 is helpfully illustrative: a consumer wished to rely on a Directive to defeat a breach of contract action before a national court but was not able to do so because of the rule against horizontal direct effect.

5 See especially Joined Cases C-397/01 to C-403/01, *Pfeiffer and Others v Deutsches Rotes Kreuz* [2004] ECR I-8835.

as confirmed by Article 5(2) TEU, that competences 'not conferred upon the Union in the Treaties remain with the Member States'. The point, then, is that the EU acquires its competences and powers and, deeper still, its legitimacy from the consensual processes of Treaty ratification performed from time to time at national level through approved domestic constitutional processes. This is its leash. The EU cannot 'self-authorise' an increase in its own competences and powers. It may act only in the areas in which the Member States have given it a mandate. Extension of the grant is made, if at all, by the Member States acting at times of periodic Treaty revision.

Violation of the principle of conferral should mean that an offending act is held invalid as a matter of law. This, according to the Court of Justice, is not only its function, it is also, in order to preserve the uniformity of application of EU law, its *exclusive* function and therefore not one that may be carried out by a national court.[6] But the matter should not be treated as exclusively legal in significance. An attempt to free the EU of the bounds of legitimate but limited authority conferred on it by its Member States according to their particular constitutional arrangements is to threaten the system's foundational roots in consensus among States and democratic approval expressed at national level. Failure to comply with the principle of conferral corrodes the claim of the EU to operate in a legitimate manner. This goes to the very heart of the design of the EU system as a means to manage the interdependence of States while not itself aspiring to become a State.[7]

But that design is deceptive. The EU's competence is in principle limited. But the limits are broad and sometimes they are ambiguous. They are driven most of all by the functional objective of creating an internal market, itself a broad and to some extent ambiguous concept.[8] And contract law, like many other areas of national law and practice, is swept along by this dynamic process of market-making in a way that challenges *in practice* the vitality *in principle* of the notion that the EU has only a limited remit. Unwarranted, or at least inadequately explained, patterns of centralisation tend to generate resistance in any federal or quasi-federal system.[9] The EU is at heart no different.

The previous chapter has already given a clue as to the key issue. The provisions of the Treaties and Charter that concern free movement, competition and non-discrimination make negligible reference to contracts and contract law,

---

6 Case C-314/85, *Foto-Frost v HZA Lübeck-Ost* [1987] ECR I-4199.

7 S. Weatherill, *Law and Values in the European Union*, OUP, Oxford 2016.

8 S. Weatherill, 'The Internal Market as a Legal Concept' in L. Azoulai and M. Cremona (eds.), *Collected Courses of the Academy of European Law*, Vol. XXV, OUP, Oxford forthcoming.

9 For comparative inquiry see e.g. K. Nicolaidis and R. Howse (eds.), *The Federal Vision: Legitimacy and Levels of Governance in the United States and the European Union*, OUP, Oxford 2001; D. McKay, *Designing Europe: Comparative Lessons from the Federal Experience*, OUP, Oxford 2001; E. Fahey and D. Curtin (eds.), *A Transatlantic Community of Law*, CUP, Cambridge 2014.

yet they exert a demonstrably powerful influence as a result of their functionally broad reach. So the EU has a wider role than may be anticipated from a purely textual reading of the Treaties, most of all because of its functionally wide mandate to act in furtherance of market integration. This chapter and the next tell this story in connection with the legislative competence of the EU. The picture is thematically similar. Contracts and contract law are not much mentioned but they are much affected. The evolution has been incremental. The outcome is a 'patchwork' of EU contract law, but, as will be elucidated, there are also visible thematic patterns.

3.3. THE CONFERRED COMPETENCES AFFECTING CONTRACT LAW

There is no competence to be found in the Treaty which confers any general authorisation on the EU to operate in the field of contract law. In fact, references are few and far between. Consequently, given the paucity of references to contract law in the texts of the founding Treaties, one might readily assume that the EU's influence in the field of contract law is negligible. And this would be a large error. Contract lawyers, like any other kind of lawyer, need to be aware that when they encounter the EU they are dealing with a legal order that is able to deliver no more than its founding Treaties permit, but contract lawyers, like any other kind of lawyer, need to appreciate that the text of the Treaties may conceal more than they reveal. And, a consistent theme of this book, it is the internal market which is the magician.

The few explicit references to contracts that are made in the Treaties are fleeting and tangential. But they are worth gathering together.

The competition law provisions of the TFEU, which were examined in the previous chapter, provide two instances. Article 101(1)(e) TFEU includes in the non-exhaustive list of restrictive practices 'the conclusion of contracts subject to acceptance by the other parties of supplementary obligations which, by their nature or according to commercial usage, have no connection with the subject of such contracts'. Article 102 TFEU includes in the non-exhaustive list of prohibited abusive practices 'making the conclusion of contracts subject to acceptance by the other parties of supplementary obligations which, by their nature or according to commercial usage, have no connection with the subject of such contracts'.

Article 151 TFEU on social policy directs that 'the Union and the Member States shall implement measures which take account of the diverse forms of national practices, in particular in the field of contractual relations, and the need to maintain the competitiveness of the Union's economy', and Article 155 TFEU adds that '[s]hould management and labour so desire, the dialogue between them at Union level may lead to contractual relations, including agreements'. Article 153(1)(d) lists as one of the areas where the Union shall support Member State action the 'protection of workers where their employment contract is terminated'.

Article 179(2) TFEU on research and development refers to the opening up of national public contracts; Article 272 provides that the Court of Justice 'shall have jurisdiction to give judgment pursuant to any arbitration clause contained in a contract concluded by or on behalf of the Union'; and Article 340 adds that '[t]he contractual liability of the Union shall be governed by the law applicable to the contract in question'.

And that is the full haul! The *word* 'contract' appears nowhere else in the Treaties. This would lead to an assumption that the EU's relevance to contract lawyers is thin. But it is exactly here that the endemic gap between principle and practice in the matter of the EU's conferred competence yawns. The previous chapter demonstrated this trend in connection with primary law, whereas this chapter addresses the matter with regard to the legislative competence conferred on the EU.

In fact most of the Treaty provisions mentioned immediately above which refer explicitly to 'contract' will be ignored in the remainder of this book. They are devoid of practical and intellectual interest in understanding the EU's influence on contracts and contract law. The main point which animates the exploration conducted in this book is that the road to the EU's influence on contract law runs through the internal market. According to Article 3(3) TEU the EU is committed to the creation of an internal market which 'shall comprise an area without internal frontiers in which the free movement of goods, persons, services and capital is ensured'.[10] As explored in the previous chapter, the Treaty's free movement and competition rules (most of all) and (to a less well-developed extent) its anti-discrimination rules exercise a restraint on contractual enforceability not because the Treaty sets out any developed framework but rather because the exercise of autonomy by contracting parties and contract lawmaking by national authorities may come into conflict with the project to complete the internal market to which the Treaty is wedded. So practices may be blocked in so far as they cannot be shown to meet the standards set by EU internal market law. The concern of this chapter is the EU's own capacity to set rules of contract law and once again the predominant trigger is provided by the empowering force of the internal market. This is noted briefly in connection with Article 81 TFEU, before examination moves to Article 115 and then, by far the most important provision of the Treaty equipping the EU with relevant legislative competence, Article 114. The chapter concludes with a brief glimpse of rule-making that affects contracts and contract law for reasons that reach beyond the internal market. This covers Articles 19 TFEU and 352 TFEU.

10 Article 26(2) TFEU.

3.4. ARTICLE 81 TFEU

Article 81 TFEU provides for the adoption of measures for the approximation of the laws and regulations of the Member States in order to develop judicial cooperation in civil matters 'particularly when necessary for the proper functioning of the internal market'. So Article 81 is not tied exclusively to the pursuit of the internal market law, but it is in part animated by it. Article 81 has a pedigree which goes back only as far as the Treaty of Amsterdam, so the key date for its entry into force here is 1999. The EU's ordinary legislative procedure, mapped out in Article 294 TFEU and involving a proposal by the Commission followed by adoption by the Council (acting by qualified majority vote) and the Parliament, applies, excepting only measures concerning family law with cross-border implications, where unanimity in Council is preserved. The legislative output since the entry into force of what is today Article 81 TFEU has exerted some impact on contract law. Article 81 TFEU or its predecessors have been used as the basis for measures, typically Regulations, addressing matters of private international law and cross-border civil procedure. Regulation 593/2008 on the law applicable to contracts and Regulation 864/2007 on the law applicable to non-contractual obligations are the so-called Rome I and Rome II Regulations.[11] Regulation 1215/2012 on jurisdiction and the recognition and enforcement of judgments in civil and commercial matters is the so-called Brussels Regulation.[12] These instruments are the dominant landmarks in the field, but they are supported by a bloc of more specific material governing enforcement of decisions and civil procedure. Specialist works provide detailed analysis.[13] The concern here is only to locate this source of rule-making as partly, though not exclusively, connected to the project to complete the internal market.[14]

A further point, made here but without pursuit of further elaboration, is that there is a lack of homogeneity in geographical application of the legislative *acquis* that has accumulated in this area. Article 81 is housed within Title V of Part III of the TFEU, which is entitled *Area of Freedom, Security and Justice.* Protocols which are attached to the Treaties set out in painfully contorted terms arrangements which keep the United Kingdom, Ireland and Denmark separate from the mainstream of law- and policymaking governing the area of freedom, security and justice. The United Kingdom and Ireland are not bound by, but have an opportunity to opt in to, rules adopted by the majority of the Member States. Denmark's position is still more opaque: as part of the deal to induce the people of Denmark to vote 'yes' in a 1992 referendum on whether the country should

---

11 [2008] OJ L177/6, [2007] OJ L199/40.

12 Reg. 1215/2012 [2012] OJ L351/1, replacing Reg. 44/2001 [2001] OJ L12/1.

13 See e.g. P. Stone, *EU Private International Law*, 2nd ed., Edward Elgar, Cheltenham 2012; G. Van Calster, *European Private International Law*, Hart Publishing, Oxford 2013.

14 On the trajectory of constitutional reform see K. Gutman, *The Constitutional Foundations of European Contract Law: A Comparative Analysis*, OUP, Oxford 2014, Ch. 10.

ratify the Maastricht Treaty, matters agreed by the other Member States in this particular area may bind Denmark as a matter of international rather than EU law. This is an *uneven* 'area of freedom, security and justice'.[15]

3.5. HARMONISATION

The most conspicuously influential source of EU contract lawmaking is no newcomer to the Treaty. It is harmonisation of laws, which has always been a competence conferred on the EU. The relevant provisions today are Article 114 TFEU and (much less important, for reasons that will be explained) Article 115 TFEU. Articles 114 and 115, unlike Article 81, *require* a contribution to the internal market as a necessary precondition to their invocation. What are today Articles 114 and 115 TFEU have generated a legislative *acquis* relevant to contract law, as the programme of harmonisation of laws in the service of market-making to which those Treaty provisions are dedicated has 'spilled over', even though Articles 114 and 115 do not explicitly recognise a capacity to affect contract law. The programme of legislative harmonisation designed to promote the good functioning of the EU's internal market forms the heartland of what is normally meant by 'EU contract law'.

The original Treaty of Rome included a provision which provided for the 'approximation' of national laws that directly affected the establishment or functioning of the common market. This was Article 100 EEC. It became Article 94 EC in consequence on the Amsterdam Treaty's re-numbering of the EC Treaty effective from 1999. Today it is found in amended form since the entry into force of the Lisbon Treaty in 2009 in Article 115 TFEU. One amendment was to replace its reference to the 'common market' with reference to the 'internal market'. However, Article 115 is of minimal significance today. It has long been overshadowed in importance and impact by a provision introduced by the Single European Act (SEA) with effect from 1987. This was Article 100a, becoming (after amendment) Article 95 EC and today found in Article 114 TFEU. This is the heartland of harmonisation.

Article 114 TFEU provides for the adoption of measures 'for the approximation of the provisions laid down by law, regulation or administrative action in member states which have as their object the establishing and functioning of the internal market.' 'Approximation' – for which the more common term 'harmonisation' is correctly treated as a synonym – may therefore be pursued not for its own sake, but rather in order to achieve the objective of creating an internal market within the EU.

Article 114 has superseded Article 115 as the primary instrument of EU legislative harmonisation chiefly because legislation adopted pursuant to

15 See generally S. Peers, *EU Justice and Home Affairs Law*, 3rd ed., OUP, Oxford 2011.

Article 114 is adopted according to the ordinary legislative procedure, which entails a Commission proposal and subsequent adoption by the Council and by the Parliament. Crucially the Council acts by qualified majority and so no State veto applies. Article 115 is and has always been subject to the stifling requirement of unanimity in the Council. Article 114 is also broader than Article 115 for it permits the adoption of 'measures' of harmonisation, which could conceivably extend beyond Directives to include *inter alia* Regulations, whereas Article 115 is limited to Directives. Article 114 is therefore a great deal more flexible than Article 115, and for that reason Article 115 has largely fallen into disuse. True, Article 114(2) excludes the possibility to harmonise national fiscal provisions, those relating to free movement of persons, and those relating to the rights and interests of employed persons pursuant to Article 114, and so any attempt to harmonise such practices would need to be routed through Article 115. But in practice that would probably be pointless, because there is little likelihood of securing unanimity in Council to act in such sensitive realms. It is in fact their very sensitivity that prompted their exclusion from Article 114 at the time of its negotiation. The obsolescence of Article 115 is the reason that the amendments made with effect from 2009 by the Lisbon Treaty re-located it after, instead of before, Article 114 in the Treaty on the Functioning of the European Union, though a bolder and cleaner reform would have been to delete it entirely. The focus hereafter is on Article 114 as the key Treaty base for legislative harmonisation affecting contract law. It is the fruit of Article 114 TFEU that will be the main focus of this book.

3.6. HARMONISATION AND THE EMPOWERING FORCE OF THE INTERNAL MARKET

Article 114 ties legislative harmonisation to the making of the internal market. Accordingly what is at stake is *not* a conferred competence to replace diverse national laws with a single harmonised EU law. That would be to go too far. Article 114 grants the EU a conferred competence to replace diverse national laws with a single harmonised EU law *only* where that contributes to promoting the establishment and functioning of the EU's internal market. It is specified in Article 114(1)'s first sentence that harmonisation is tied to the achievement of the objectives set out in Article 26 TFEU – which means the establishment of an internal market within the EU, defined in Article 26 as 'an area without internal frontiers in which the free movement of goods, persons, services and capital is ensured in accordance with the provisions of the Treaties.' It is therefore constitutionally stipulated that it is *market-making* harmonisation that is at stake, not harmonisation *per se*. In this vein Article 114 TFEU is supplemented by Articles 53 and 62 TFEU which permit the adoption of measures designed to liberalise the free circulation of persons and services. Variation between national laws has typically been presented as an impediment to market integration, which has prompted a need to pursue harmonisation at EU level. In so far as the national laws subjected to the discipline of harmonisation are national contract laws, then the consequence is the creation of a set of contract law rules at EU level. As will be shown in this book, the process has delivered an increasingly dense set of EU secondary legislation affecting contracts and contract law. In this sense there is a 'dual function' to harmonisation performed by the EU: setting common rules but also choosing the content of those rules. Harmonisation involves a transfer of regulatory responsibility (in whole or in part: Chapter 6) from national level to EU level. It exerts a centralising dynamic.

The constitutionally mandated connection between legislative harmonisation and the good functioning of the internal market is the *limiting* feature of the competence conferred by the Treaty. That harmonisation of laws shall contribute to the establishment and functioning of the internal market, and that it shall not be deployed for broader regulatory objectives, is how the constitutionally fundamental principle of conferral located in Article 5 TEU finds practical expression in the interpretation and application of Article 114 TFEU. So the project to complete the internal market is the platform for the EU's competence to intervene in national contract law by putting in place a harmonised set of EU contract law rules that are apt to promote market integration.

The principal tension is between principle and practice. The internal market, to which Article 114 is tied, is in principle limiting. But the internal market as a legal concept, though not unlimited, is remarkably broad. Moreover, it lacks sharply defined outer margins. So in practice reliance on the internal market tends to empower the EU through the grant of legislative competence to harmonise national rules. It is remarkably easy to cross the threshold and to show that the preconditions for action pursuant to Article 114 TFEU are met. There are several elements to this, which now fall to be considered.

3.7. ARTICLE 114 IS FUNCTIONALLY DRIVEN

The vigour and breadth of Article 114 TFEU is most sharply appreciated by contrasting it with the structure of the large majority of the other provisions in the TFEU which authorise the EU to adopt legislation. Most of the legislative competences which are conferred by the TFEU are sector-specific and they are written with evidently careful attention to their limits. The EU may legislate in the field of environmental protection, but Articles 191–193 TFEU set out in intricate detail precisely where, how and with what effects the EU may act. Articles 151–161 TFEU perform a similar function in the field of social policy. If anything, they are even more cautiously designed, and they are studded with painstakingly crafted boundaries to the EU's mandate. So, for example, the legislative base conferred by Article 153 includes a special proviso in its fifth paragraph which declares expressly that it is not applicable to 'pay, the right of association, the right to strike or the right to impose lock-outs'. Article 168 TFEU provides for Union action relating to public health. Union action 'shall complement national policies' but there is an explicit exclusion of power to harmonise national laws in Article 168(5). Article 169(2)(b) equips the EU with a competence to promote the interests of the consumer, but this is confined to 'measures which support, supplement and monitor the policy pursued by the Member States.' There are many other examples found across the TFEU, and in each instance the key to understanding their design lies in the tough bargaining that accompanies every revision of the Treaties when EU legislative competence is modified or extended. There may be a concern to equip the EU with new competences to address newly emerging problems – environmental protection was for example adopted as an explicit EU competence only with effect from 1987 as a result of the entry into force of the Single European Act and consumer protection joined the party only in 1993 – but the Member States and the EU institutions engage in depth and in detail with the decision about exactly what form and subject to what limits the EU's role should be.

Article 114 is radically different. Article 114 envisages action by the EU where diverse national regulatory choices obstruct the creation of an internal market. Article 114 is *functionally driven* – that means it is driven by the functional task to create an internal market for the EU. It is not sector-specific. *Any* national measure may be subjected to the discipline of harmonisation, whatever its shape, form, colour or intent under national law, provided only that harmonisation improves market integration. The sole exception lies in Article 114(2), which places fiscal provisions, provisions relating to the free movement of persons or to the rights and interests of employed persons beyond the scope of the competence to harmonise provided by Article 114. Those areas of particular sensitivity may be harmonised only pursuant to Article 115 TFEU, but, as mentioned (section 3.5), its requirement of unanimous support in Council tends to bar its use in practice. Aside from the areas listed in Article 114(2), harmonisation pursuant to Article 114 is completely open-ended, subject only to the proviso that the harmonisation adopted at EU level shall contribute to an improvement in the functioning of the internal market.

So if diversity between national contract laws damages the internal market, the EU may harmonise those contract laws. This has the consequence that the EU becomes a contract lawmaker, albeit not for its own sake but rather through the medium of building an internal market for the EU. In short, harmonisation reaches contract law by taking the road that is signposted as the route to the completion of the internal market.

3.8. THE COURT'S INTERPRETATION OF THE SCOPE OF ARTICLE 114

The internal market serves as a means to limit but also to empower the EU as a lawmaker equipped with a competence to harmonise national laws. Its precise meaning depends on the source of authoritative interpretation of EU law, the Court of Justice. In particular the Court here performs an important task of constitutional review: legislative harmonisation that goes beyond the mandate granted by the Treaty should be ruled invalid. This is at bottom the application of the principle of conferral contained in Article 5 TEU. As explained above (section 3.2), fidelity to the principle of conferral is the bedrock of the EU's legitimacy.

The Court's case law discloses three distinct limbs to the competence to harmonise national laws in order to improve the conditions for the establishment and functioning of the internal market. Article 114 TFEU may be validly relied on:

- where there are differences between national rules which are such as to obstruct the fundamental freedoms and thus have a direct effect on the functioning of the internal market; or
- where such differences cause significant distortions of competition; or
- embracing a form of preventive rather than reactive harmonisation so the EU does not have to wait until obstacles are in place and require cure, where it is likely that such obstacles will emerge in the future, because the Member States are about to take divergent measures with respect to a product or a class of products.

A body of case law has built up over the last twenty years in which the Court has consistently set out these formulae as the starting point in any inquiry it is asked to make into whether a challenged piece of legislative harmonisation meets the criteria and is therefore valid as a matter of EU law.[16]

The most striking issue is that that although each of these routes to constitutionally valid legislative harmonisation is based on the existence

---

16 Case C-376/98, *Germany v Parliament and Council* [2000] ECR I-8419; Case C-377/98, *Netherlands v Parliament and Council* [2001] ECR I-7079; Case C-491/01, *British American Tobacco (Investments) and Imperial Tobacco* [2002] ECR I-11453; Case C-210/03, *Swedish Match* [2004] ECR I-11893; Joined Cases C-154/04 and C-155/04, *Alliance for Natural Health and Others* [2005] ECR I-6451; Case C-217/04, *United Kingdom v Parliament and Council* [2006] ECR I-3771; Case C-380/03, *Germany v Parliament and Council* [2006] ECR I-11573; Case C-301/06, *Ireland v Parliament and Council* [2009] ECR I-593; Case C-58/08, *Vodafone Ltd and Others v Secretary of State for Business, Enterprise and Regulatory Reform* [2010] ECR I-4999; Case C-270/12, *United Kingdom v Council and Parliament* judgment of 22 January 2014; Case C-398/13P, *Inuit* judgment of 3 September 2015.

of *limiting* features which correspond to the constitutionally necessary underpinning of the principle of conferral contained in Article 5 TEU, those features are loose-edged and imprecise. Most of all, it is very hard to assemble evidence that is sufficiently concrete to contradict claimed reliance on Article 114 by the EU's legislative institutions.

The Court's case law, summarised above, reveals that differences between national rules must have a *direct* effect on the functioning of the internal market, otherwise what is at stake is simple divergence which is not sufficient to justify harmonisation. Or differences shall cause *significant* – the Court sometimes prefers the adjective *appreciable* – distortions of competition, otherwise what is at stake is simple divergence which is not sufficient to justify harmonisation. Or, finally, preventive harmonisation is permitted subject to the emergence of such obstacles being *likely*. Absent that necessary likelihood, there is no competence (yet) to harmonise in the relevant area.

Each of the italicised words in the previous paragraph carries crucial constitutional weight. They serve to demarcate EU legislative competence from a zone of national autonomy. Where their demands are satisfied, the EU as a regulator is competent to replace diversity with homogeneity; where the threshold is not crossed, legislative diversity between the Member States is left untouched. Yet whether the crucial governing criteria are fulfilled is hard to measure and therefore difficult to deny. When do differences between national rules have a *direct* rather than indirect effect on the functioning of the internal market; when is a distortion of competition *significant* or *appreciable*; when is it *likely* that obstacles will emerge? It is hard to be precise, and so if the EU legislative process is conducted on the basis that the tests are satisfied, it is difficult to show that they are *not*. This third (preventive) criterion is probably the most slippery of all. It follows logically that as public anxiety about a particular matter that is left unregulated at national level increases and public authorities in the Member States come under pressure to consider intervention, then the EU will acquire a legislative competence to harmonise in the area at the exact moment that it becomes 'likely' to be subject to regulation by Member States. So a competence to intervene in the name of market-making may be triggered where it did not exist before, not because the regulatory landscape in the Member States has changed or shows divergence, but because it is likely that it will.

In practice the tests are easily met. The overall impression is that it will be difficult to demonstrate that competence to legislate is missing. The Court's case law demonstrates this. Very rarely are the required tests found to be failed. A small group of examples must suffice, but they are chosen because they are typical of the wide reach allowed to legislative harmonisation pursuant to Article 114 TFEU.

Alliance for Natural Health and Others is a helpfully illustrative decision of the Grand Chamber of the Court of Justice.[17] The litigation arose before

[17] Joined Cases C-154/04 and C-155/04, *Alliance for Natural Health and Others* [2005] ECR I-6451.

English courts as a challenge by economic operators to the United Kingdom's implementation of a harmonisation Directive, 2002/46.[18] Directive 2002/46 harmonises the laws of the Member States relating to food supplements. It was adopted pursuant to Article 95 EC, the predecessor to Article 114 TFEU, and it provides a classic example of regulatory contract law transplanted by harmonisation from national to EU level. Its Preamble explains that products marketed as foods containing concentrated sources of nutrients are regulated in Member States by differing national rules 'that may impede their free movement, create unequal conditions of competition, and thus have a direct impact on the functioning of the internal market'.[19] The adoption of harmonised EU rules eliminates these differences and, since all such products will as a result of the EU's intervention meet the same governing stipulations, it opens up the internal market to products irrespective of their Member State of origin. The consequence is enhanced opportunity for cross-border contracting, to the benefit of suppliers and consumers of such products.

The economic operators, who dealt in food supplements, objected to the restrictive nature of the legislative system instituted by the Directive. They proceeded to attack the validity of the Directive before the English courts and, in accordance with the orthodox rules of EU law, the English court, which is not permitted to find an EU measure invalid,[20] made a preliminary reference to the Court of Justice. But it found the Directive to be valid.

The applicants argued before the Court that the Directive did not contribute to improving the conditions for the establishment and functioning of the internal market. In particular they impressed on the Court that the prohibition on use of certain supplements was motivated by public health considerations, and that Article 152(4)(c) EC denies the EU competence to harmonise national legislation on human health. Article 168(5) EU does this blocking job today.

This, then, was a political and commercial objection to the intensity of EU regulation of the market converted into a constitutional objection to the EU's competence to make this choice of regime.

The Court set out what had already become and would be subsequently further confirmed as its orthodox formula.[21] A 'mere finding of disparities between national rules is not sufficient to justify having recourse to Article 95 EC', now Article 114 TFEU, but 'it is, however, otherwise where there are differences between the laws, regulations or administrative provisions of the Member States which are such as to obstruct the fundamental freedoms and thus have a direct effect on the functioning of the internal market' or where 'the aim is to prevent the emergence of future obstacles to trade resulting from

18 [2002] OJ L183/51.
19 Recital 2.
20 Case C-314/85, *Foto-Frost v HZA Lübeck-Ost* [1987] ECR I-4199.
21 Cf. cases above n. 16.

multifarious development of national laws, the emergence of such obstacles must be likely and the measure in question must be designed to prevent them'.[22]

This, it found, was such a case. It was valid harmonisation. The Court noted the Directive's recitals which referred to the pre-existing diversity in regulation of food supplements which was liable to impede their free movement and thus have a direct impact on the functioning of the internal market. It noted too that cases had been brought before the Court which related to situations in which traders had encountered obstacles when marketing in a Member State other than their State of establishment food supplements lawfully marketed in the latter State. And it drew on the Commission's Explanatory Memorandum to the proposal for the Directive, which insisted on receipt by the Commission services of 'a substantial number of complaints from economic operators' resulting from the differences between national rules.[23] This was enough to lead the Court to the conclusion that reliance on Article 95 EC, today Article 114 TFEU, was justified. The Directive was treated as a valid measure of market-making legislative harmonisation.

The Court did not deny that public health was at stake – quite the reverse. It accepted that human health considerations played a part in the formulation of the provisions concerned.[24] It stated, in line with its previous case law, 'that, provided that the conditions for recourse to Article 95 EC as a legal basis are fulfilled, the Community legislature cannot be prevented from relying on that legal basis on the ground that public health protection is a decisive factor in the choices to be made'.[25] This is logical enough. Legislative harmonisation sets aside national diversity in favour of EU-wide uniformity, and as part of that process the techniques, expectations, demands and objectives found scattered in different ways across the regulatory landscapes of the Member States need to be compressed into a single selected EU regime. So the EU makes regulatory choices – or more precisely, since the EU acts in response to pre-existing and varied Member State actions, the EU engages in *re*-regulation. If what is being subjected to the discipline of legislative harmonisation is national rules governing public health, then the consequence of harmonisation is EU rules governing public health – albeit public health *in the internal market*. This is the dual function of harmonisation. It is, moreover, a connection explicitly mandated by the Treaty and the Charter. The Court in *Alliance for Natural Health* referred to Articles 152(1) and 95(3), which are today Articles 168(1) and Article 114(3) and are buttressed too by Articles 35 and 38 of the Charter. All these provisions assert a constitutional linkage between the protection of public health and of consumers and the definition and implementation of all other EU

22 Paras. 28–29.
23 Para. 37 of the judgment.
24 Para. 40 et seq.
25 Para. 30.

common policies, which certainly includes a linkage to the project to complete the internal market through legislative harmonisation. These several provisions have the effect of embedding (re-)regulatory values in internal market law.

This, then, explains why what was then Article 152 EC, now Article 168 TFEU, does not operate to curtail EU legislative competence under what was then Article 95 EC, now Article 114 TFEU. The EU's competence to address public health *per se* is carefully limited by the terms of Article 168 TFEU, as mentioned above. This is not true of Article 114. The route to harmonisation of rules affecting public health lies through the internal market. Something similar may be said of Article 169 TFEU entitled *Consumer Protection*. This confines Union action to measures which support, supplement and monitor the policy pursued by the Member States, but this narrowly drawn proviso is of no significance whatsoever to Article 114, which certainly may be used and has been used to harmonise national laws in the field of consumer protection – provided that the necessary contribution to making the internal market exists. In this way the EU becomes a law- and policymaker in (partial or total: Chapter 6) replacement for its Member States in an extravagantly wide range of areas which are not only left unmentioned in Article 114 itself but which are mentioned in deceptively constrained terms in the relevant sector-specific legal bases found elsewhere scattered across the TFEU. And precisely this model explains how much of the contract law *acquis* has come into being. If what is being subjected to the discipline of legislative harmonisation is national rules governing contracts and contract law, then the consequence of harmonisation is EU rules governing contracts and contract law – albeit contracts and contract law *in the internal market*.

It follows too that the EU may harmonise rules in the service of the internal market by *prohibiting* particular goods or practices. The Court has made clear that a harmonised rule may consist in requiring all the Member States to authorise the marketing of the product or products concerned, subjecting such an obligation of authorisation to certain conditions, or even provisionally or definitively prohibiting the marketing of a product or products, which it draws from the (re-)regulatory values expressed in what were Articles 152(1) and 95(3) EC, today Articles 168(1) and Article 114(3), buttressed by Articles 35 and 38 of the Charter.[26] The only proviso is that the generally applicable criteria for reliance on Article 114 must be met. This will commonly involve a prohibition which forms part of a regime applicable to a wider category of products or practices than simply those subjected to the harmonised ban. So the EU cannot rely on Article 114 simply to impose a free-standing ban on a particular product or practice, because that would lack the necessary contribution to the creation of an internal market, but it may rely on Article 114 to ban a particular product

26 e.g. Case C-210/03, *Swedish Match* [2004] ECR I-11893, para. 32; Joined Cases C-154/04 and C-155/04, *Alliance for Natural Health and Others* [2005] ECR I-6451, paras. 33–34.

or practice as part of a scheme to open up the market for a wider sphere of permitted products or practices.

So, applying this to contract law, it is open to the EU to adopt harmonised rules which ban particular relevant practices, provided only that an adequate contribution to the functioning of the internal market is demonstrated. Plenty of examples will be met in the next chapter; one is enough here. Directive 2005/29 prohibits unfair commercial practices in order to open up an integrated internal market for fair commercial practices across the territory of the 28 Member States.[27]

Article 114's association with the project of completing the EU's internal market tends to generate an initial impression that it is dedicated to market freedoms. It is, in the sense that its purpose is to permit legislative intervention by the EU which is designed to convert national rules that impede trade integration, yet which survive judicial scrutiny in the name of free movement because they are justified, into a single harmonised EU regime. This is a deregulatory process: at its simplest, 28 diverse systems become just one. And the EU may not introduce common rules – to promote public health, to promote consumer protection – solely on that basis: the market-making component must be present. But once that threshold is crossed – and it readily is – the *content* of the harmonised rule does not have to be purely permissive. The EU's single system may contain strict and interventionist rules. This follows from the understanding that the EU is directed to take full account of regulatory objectives such as consumer protection, public health and environmental protection. This carries with it a market-(re-)regulatory potential.

Vodafone Ltd and Others v Secretary of State for Business, Enterprise and Regulatory Reform tells a similar story to *Alliance for Natural Health*.[28] This is, in fact, a perfect example of how regulatory contract law at national level generates regulatory contract law at EU level, and in both instances it involves a suppression of autonomy to set prices through reliance on contracting. The challenged measure was Regulation 717/2007 on roaming on public mobile telephone networks.[29] It is presented as a classic measure of preventive harmonisation. It adopts a harmonised EU system to regulate the costs of 'roaming' under an assumption that 'there is pressure for Member States to take measures to address the level of international roaming charges'.[30] Regulation 717/2007 states explicitly in its Preamble that contractual freedom is the norm in markets where there is no significant market power on the supply side, but that this is a case where intervention is called for.[31] The market was working

27 Directive 2005/29 [2005] OJ L149/22. See Chapter 4.5.2.
28 Case C-58/08, *Vodafone Ltd and Others v Secretary of State for Business, Enterprise and Regulatory Reform* [2010] ECR I-4999.
29 [2007] OJ L171/32.
30 Recital 9.
31 Recital 12.

imperfectly as a result of market power on the supply side and, on the demand side, intransparency precluded consumers from provoking effective competition. The result was pricing strategies that discriminated against consumers using their mobile phones outside the Member State in which they lived. The Court accepted the claims made in the measure's recital and its supporting explanatory impact assessment that it was likely that national measures would be directed at the malfunctioning market, and so this triggered a basis for the EU to act. Its choice was to restrain the autonomy to set price by contract. The Regulation caps the wholesale and retail charges terrestrial mobile operators may charge for the provision of roaming services on public mobile networks for voice calls between Member States.[32]

The Court added in *Vodafone* that provided that the conditions for recourse to what was then Article 95 EC, now Article 114 TFEU, as a legal basis are fulfilled, the legislature 'cannot be prevented from relying on that legal basis on the ground that consumer protection is a decisive factor in the choices to be made'.[33] So there could be no constitutional objection to intrusive intervention into contractual autonomy – provided only that the harmonisation contributed to the functioning of the internal market. This was fully in line with existing case law, most of which deals with public health protection, and the Court in *Vodafone* was readily able to cite *inter alia* its own ruling in *Alliance for Natural Health*.[34]

The judgment in *Vodafone* is relatively brief and strikingly permissive. It simply cites the relevant recital in the Preamble and repeats the legislature's conclusion that 'there was pressure for Member States to take measures to address the problem of the high level of retail charges for Community-wide roaming services';[35] and then states blandly that the legislature was 'actually confronted with a situation in which it appeared likely that national measures would be adopted aiming to address the problem of the high level of retail charges for Community-wide roaming services through rules fixing the rate of retail charges', and that 'such measures would have been likely to lead to a divergent development of national laws'.[36] The Court ignored the rather powerful argument that national measures capping the cost of roaming were *unlikely* to be adopted because they would have the perverse effect of harming the competitive position of companies based on the regulator's territory while protecting only out-of-State consumers.[37] In fact the Court's own Advocate

---

32 The regime has been subsequently amended: see Reg. 531/2012 [2012] OJ L172/10, for which the legal base is Art. 114 TFEU.

33 Para. 36.

34 Para. 36.

35 Para. 44.

36 Para. 45.

37 Cf. M. Brenncke, 'Annotation' (2010) 47 *Common Market Law Review* 1793, especially at 1804–1806.

General, Mr Maduro, had in his Opinion concluded that the orthodox criteria for preventive harmonisation were not satisfied in the case (although he found another route to uphold the validity of the Regulation). No such anxiety appears on the face of the Court's judgment. The Court took at face value the claims made by the EU legislature. So too the Court accepted in a wholly uncritical manner the explanatory memorandum to the proposal and the impact assessment, which supported the view that there was a likelihood of divergent development of national laws. The Regulation's Preamble recital stated there was pressure for Member States to take measures to address the problem of the high level of retail charges for such roaming services, and the Court added that this had been confirmed by the Commission at the hearing.[38] But of course it would be! The Commission was, after all, responsible for proposing the measure in the first place. It is not a disinterested observer. The Court is in principle responsible for conducting an objective review of the validity of the measure, but in practice the claims made by the EU's political institutions carry considerable weight. *Vodafone* is based on a high degree of mutual reinforcement between the EU's legislative and judicial institutions. Placing a *formal* limit on the EU's conferred competences is central to the constitutional character of the whole project, but the problem lies in the supervision *in practice* of respect for those limits.

Harmonisation involves a vertical transfer of regulatory responsibility from national to EU level and where the transfer concerns contract law the natural consequence is that EU becomes a contract lawmaker. This pattern is central to the claim that a sharp divide between the EU's interest in market integration and the role of the Member States in matters of market regulation cannot be feasibly sustained. The one spills over into the other. The 'competence trigger' is divergence between national laws which affects the internal market, but that trigger is easily pulled.

3.9. HARMONISATION AND THE LIMITING FORCE OF THE INTERNAL MARKET

The question which emerges with force from the survey conducted so far in this chapter is whether there are really limits to Article 114 TFEU at all. Is the truth of the matter that Article 114 subverts the principle of conferral contained in Article 5 TEU? The answer to this question is that it does not, but it does demonstrate that the Treaty is structured in principle to set limits on the scope of EU legislative competence, but that in practice those limits are set remarkably broadly. And Article 114 is the most vivid evidence of this structural trend. In particular provided the legislative process pays careful attention to the need to

38 Para. 44.

demonstrate or at least to assert compliance with the dictates of the principle of conferral mediated through the demands of Article 114, it is highly unlikely that the Court will intervene.

The risk is what has been labelled 'competence creep'.[39] It is to nudge towards an expansion in the EU's competence achieved not by Treaty revision, but by stealth practised from within the EU's legislative process. This is in principle entirely impermissible, for it subverts the constitutional constraint set by the principle of conferral, now found in Article 5 TEU. But, as already suggested, the problem is converting principle into practice.

Tests before the Court were a long time coming. The EU's harmonisation Directives adopted until 1987 were all adopted at a time when unanimous support in Council was necessary for the adoption of harmonisation legislation, under what is now Article 115 TFEU (section 3.5). Unanimity is not easy to assemble – though it was easier then than now, given that there were far fewer Member States thirty years ago – but if it is assembled, there tended to be little anxiety to address sensitive questions about competence. In short, if the Member States wanted to legislate, they legislated. They did not strain to show just why harmonisation measures contributed to the development of the internal market and in truth, especially after the so-called Paris Summit of 1972 committed the EU to acquire a more 'human' face by acting through harmonisation to achieve policies for which the Treaty offered little if any explicit mandate, sometimes they did not. There was little objection, and none with any practical bite.[40]

For the purposes of harmonisation the voting rule in Council was altered from unanimity to the qualified majority vote (QMV) in 1987 on the entry into force of the Single European Act. This was explained above (section 3.5). Thereafter a Member State opposed to a proposed measure of harmonisation could not simply veto it. It could vote against it but, if in a sufficiently small minority in Council, it could find itself outvoted and bound by legislation adopted pursuant to (what is now) Article 114 to which it was opposed. The rise of QMV raised the possibility of a disgruntled Member State taking the matter beyond the political domain on to a specifically constitutional plane. It took time for such litigation to emerge, in part because it remains the case that most measures are supported by unanimity in Council even where this is not formally required. But in 2000 the Court was provided with the opportunity to sharpen

---

39 e.g. M. Pollack, 'Creeping Competence: The Expanding Agenda of the European Community' (1994) 14 *Journal of Public Policy* 95; S. Weatherill, 'Competence creep and competence control' (2004) 23 *Yearbook of European Law* 1.

40 A rare note of constitutional scepticism is found in G. Close, 'The Legal Basis for the Consumer Protection Programme of the EEC and Priorities for Action' (1983) 8 *European Law Review* 221, and see also G. Close 'The Legal Basis for the Consumer Protection Programme of the EEC and Priorities for Action' in G. Woodroffe (ed.), *Consumer Law in the EEC*, Sweet and Maxwell/CCLR, London 1984, Ch. 1, pp. 1–24, but it appears little attention was paid in practice to such principled anxiety.

its view of the scope of legislative harmonisation granted by the Treaty. This is the famous first *Tobacco Advertising* judgment, *Germany v Parliament and Council*.[41]

In this case the Court for the first time annulled a harmonisation Directive on the basis that it failed to make an adequate contribution to the establishment and functioning of the internal market. In it, then, the constitutional limits attached to the EU as a vehicle for harmonisation were laid bare. This emerged in a case which was not about contract law narrowly understood, but it was about what has been described in Chapter 2 and in section 8 of this chapter as 'regulatory contract law'. Its illumination of the limits of Article 114 is of direct relevance to the scope of the harmonisation programme as it affects contract law.

The measure that was challenged was Directive 98/43 on the advertising of tobacco products.[42] It had been adopted pursuant to Articles 57(2), 66 and 100a EC, which are now Articles 53(2), 62 and 114 TFEU, and so it was presented as a measure targeted at the improvement of the functioning of the market for goods and services. National rules which restricted the advertising of tobacco products varied and it was argued that the Directive, by adopting a harmonised regime, improved the functioning of the internal market for tobacco products by promoting cross-border trade, ultimately enhancing the scope for contracting by consumers. Germany had voted against the adoption of the measure in Council, but it had been unable to prevent its adoption because it was supported by a qualified majority of Member States in the Council and by the Parliament.

The principal objection advanced before by the Court by Germany concerned the scope of the Directive. Its Article 3(1) prohibited all forms of advertising and sponsorship of tobacco products and Article 3(4) prohibited any free distribution having the purpose or the effect of promoting such products. Germany's application for annulment of the Directive claimed that this was to go too far: it went beyond the scope permitted by the Treaty provisions governing harmonisation on which the Directive was based. The Court agreed.

The Court pitched its ruling in an explicitly constitutional register. It observed that:

> 'the measures referred to in Article 100a(1) [now Art 114 (1) TFEU] of the Treaty are intended to improve the conditions for the establishment and functioning of the internal market. To construe that article as meaning that it vests in the Community [now Union] legislature a general power to regulate the internal market would … be incompatible with the principle embodied in Article 3b of the EC Treaty [now Article 5 TEU] that the powers of the Community [now Union] are limited to those specifically conferred on it'.[43]

41 Case C-376/98 [2000] ECR I-8419.
42 [1998] OJ L213/9.
43 Para. 83; see also paras. 106–107.

The Treaty confers no competence to harmonise *per se*. The competence is more limited than that and it is, in short, tied to the process of market-building.

In one sense that is trivially obvious. It is the principle of conferral in action, in the particular context of legislative harmonisation. The importance of the ruling in the first *Tobacco Advertising* case is the conversion of that constitutionally fundamental restraint into a test that is apt to police claimed infraction of the principle of conferral by the EU legislative process.

The threshold that must be crossed which emerges from the Court's approach is that a measure of harmonisation must actually contribute to eliminating obstacles to the free movement of goods or to the freedom to provide services or to removing distortions of competition which are appreciable or significant. From this perspective, Directive 98/34 made an inadequate contribution to building the internal market and therefore it was annulled. The implication of the Court's ruling is that this was in truth a measure of public health policy rather than a measure of market-making harmonisation and, as mentioned above (section 3.7), the conferred competence in the field of public health, today Article 168 TFEU, permits only Union action to 'complement national policies' and it contains an explicit exclusion of its use to harmonise national laws.

The Directive had been adopted not as a measure of public health policy because the relevant Treaty provision was simply not sturdy enough to support it, but the Court found that Article 114 could not bear the load either.

The Court did not disagree that diversity between national laws governing the advertising of tobacco products could constitute an obstacle to the functioning of the internal market. It disagreed only with the scope of the problem. It agreed that prohibiting the advertising of tobacco products in periodicals, magazines and newspapers could be pursued by legislative harmonisation as a means to ensure the free movement of press products.[44] It drew an analogy with existing harmonised regulation, according to which television advertising of tobacco products was prohibited in order to promote the free broadcasting of television programmes.[45] There were, the Court conceded, no current obstacles to importation of press products into Member States which prohibited such advertising, but in view of the trend in national legislation towards ever greater restrictions on advertising of tobacco products, the Court treated it as probable that obstacles to the free movement of press products would arise in the future. Preventive harmonisation of this targeted nature would be valid.

But the Court did not accept that this logic could be extended to the full range of the practices subject to the prohibition laid down by the Directive. The prohibition of advertising on posters, parasols, ashtrays and other articles used in hotels, restaurants and cafés, and the prohibition of advertising spots

44 Paras. 97–98.

45 Directive 89/552 is mentioned in para. 98: today the relevant measure is Directive 2010/13 on Audiovisual Media Services [2011] OJ L95/1.

in cinemas, were all mandated by the Directive. But such prohibitions 'in no way help to facilitate trade in the products concerned'.[46] Equally, although the Court was prepared to accept that differences between national rules restricting or banning sponsorship by tobacco firms may give rise to appreciable distortions of competition in so far as certain sports events might be relocated in consequence,[47] it did not agree that such distortion could justify an outright prohibition of advertising of the much broader kind imposed by the Directive.[48] A more narrowly focused Directive prohibiting certain forms of advertising and sponsorship of tobacco products could have been validly adopted, but the measure which the Court was asked to review was fatally flawed as a result of the general nature of the prohibition of advertising and sponsorship of tobacco products.[49]

The ruling is no more than the concrete application of Article 5 TEU's principle of conferral to the particular case of Article 114 as a legislative competence conferred on the EU. It is striking not in principle, but rather in practice. It was the first time that the Court had found a measure invalid for failure to respect the limits of the Treaty conferred competence to harmonise. The ruling insists that it is not open to the EU legislative process to subvert the limits written into the Treaties by the Member States – and it shows that the Court will police such mischief. The Court protects the rights of minorities among the States who have lost the political argument. It also asserts its own position as a constitutional court. The case is a staple of any inquiry into the principle of conferral as a foundational element in the EU's legitimacy.

3.10. COMPETENCE SENSITIVITY IN CONTRACT LAWMAKING

For contract law the message of the first *Tobacco Advertising* case holds that harmonisation of contract law which fails to make the required connection to the building of an internal market will not be permitted. It is at least plausible that some of the older measures of harmonisation concerning contract law, especially consumer contract law, fail to comply with the Court's *constitutionally* driven test. It seems improbable that Directive 85/577 on 'doorstep selling', for example, crossed the threshold which is envisaged by the Court in *Tobacco Advertising*.[50] Its explanations of just why diversity between national laws governing 'doorstep selling' obstructed inter-State trade is at best thin and at worst wholly without

[46] Para. 99.
[47] Para. 110.
[48] Para. 111.
[49] Para. 117.
[50] [1985] OJ L372/31. See Chapter 4.3.

foundation. Its Preamble does no more than assert that 'any disparity between such legislation may directly affect the functioning of the common market'. The political reality was that the Member States were unanimously supportive of the measure: it is a clear example of how the competence to harmonise was in effect borrowed to make real the commitments made at the Paris Summit of 1972 to deepen the social dimension of the EU, even without any enhancement of its formal competences. The Directive's Preamble refers explicitly to the consumer protection and information policies shaped in the wake of the Paris Summit. Since the first *Tobacco Advertising* case any such legislative extravagance is perilous.[51] It is consequently no surprise that the shadow of the first *Tobacco Advertising* case, decided in 2000, hung over the Commission's review of contract law, which was initiated in 2001. A mood of 'competence sensitivity' emerged.

The Commission's July 2001 Communication on European Contract Law initiated the inquiry into the proper role of the EU.[52] Questions associated with competence to act were addressed rather tentatively, but their place in the background was not hard to identify. The Communication called explicitly for information on whether diversity between national contract laws 'directly or indirectly obstructs the functioning of the internal market, and if so to what extent', with a view to considering appropriate action by the EU's institutions.[53] The Commission declared that it was actively seeking to uncover areas in which the internal market was malfunctioning because of deficiencies in the existing patchwork pattern of harmonised EU contract law. The 2001 Communication addresses these issues predominantly in the language of subsidiarity rather than the principle of conferral, which is constitutionally a mistake,[54] but the general perception that justification for EU intervention must be found and carefully explained holds good. The mood was markedly different from, and more sober than, the relatively carefree attitude to questions of competence taken in the development of consumer contract law Directives adopted in the 1980s. It is quite simply the shadow of *Tobacco Advertising*.

The EU's competence to address matters associated with contract became much more keenly contested, not simply among those exercised by principled questions of constitutional sensitivity but also by those aware that as a matter of real practical importance legislative choices may be defeated by judicial intervention. The follow-up February 2003 'Action Plan on a more coherent

---

51 Directive 85/577 has now been replaced by Directive 2011/83 on consumer rights [2011] OJ L304/64, but although that measure pays more attention to the question of competence it cannot be guaranteed that it is valid: see sections 3.12, 4.3.1.

52 COM (2001) 398.

53 Paras. 23–33, 72.

54 S. Weatherill, 'The European Commission's Green Paper on European Contract Law: Context, Content and Constitutionality' (2001) 24 *Journal of Consumer Policy* 339. See Chapter 5 on subsidiarity.

European Contract Law' maintained insistence on having unearthed implications for the internal market arising from legal diversity and devoted five pages to the substance of the matter, albeit without explicit citation of *Tobacco Advertising*.[55] The third and last document published in this initial agenda-setting process, October 2004's 'European Contract Law and the revision of the acquis: the way forward', focused on the question whether the existing level of harmonisation is 'sufficient to eliminate internal market barriers and distortions of competition for business and consumers'.[56] It is entirely understandable that the Commission chose not to pitch its inquiry primarily in the language of the principle of conferral, because it wanted to stimulate a more substantive debate about the proper role of the EU in the field of contract law.[57] But the constitutional rhythm hums in the background to these documents, and it did not go unnoticed.[58] The matter deserves to be assessed from the point of view of commercial practice and contract law, but also from a constitutional perspective associated with the fixing the proper limits of EU legislation competence.[59]

The review of the legislative *acquis* which was pursued as a result of this round of consultation led via a Green Paper released in early 2007[60] to the adoption in 2008 of a proposal for a Directive on Consumer Rights.[61] This would have replaced four Directives (85/577, 97/7, 93/13 and 99/44) with a 'horizontal instrument' that would pursue what the Commission described as *targeted full harmonisation*: that is, targeted at the problems that amount to the most serious blockages to the functioning of the internal market.[62] This did

55 COM (2003) 68, pp. 9–14.

56 COM (2004) 651, p. 4.

57 See S. Weatherill, 'Constitutional Issues – How much is best left unsaid?' in S. Vogenauer and S. Weatherill (eds.), *The Harmonisation of European Contract Law: Implications for European Private Laws, Business and Legal Practice*, Hart Publishing, Oxford 2006, Ch. 6.

58 e.g. M. Kenny, 'The 2004 Communication on European Contract law: those magnificent men in their unifying machines' (2005) 30 *European Law Review* 724; B. Heiderhoff and M. Kenny, 'The Commission's 2007 Green Paper on the Consumer Acquis: deliberate deliberation?' (2007) 32 *European Law Review* 740; M. Ludwigs, 'Harmonisierung des Schuldvertragsrechts in Europa – Zur Rechtweite der gemeinschaftsrechtlichen Zuständigkeit für eine Europäisierung des Privatrechts' [2006] *Europarecht* 370; V. Constantinesco, 'La codification communautaire du droit privé à l'épreuve du titre de competence de l'Union européenne' (2008) 44 *Revue Trimstrielle du Droit Européen* 707.

59 For very good analysis with hindsight, also putting the review initiated in 2001 into a perspective including the full range of projects aimed at some form of Europeansiation of contract law, see K. Gutman, *The Constitutional Foundations of European Contract Law: A Comparative Analysis*, OUP, Oxford 2014, Chs. 4–6; and also L. Miller, *The Emergence of EU Contract Law: Exploring Europeanization*, OUP, Oxford 2011, Ch. 4; R. Schulze, 'European Private Law: Political Foundations and Current Challenges' in R. Brownsword, H. Micklitz, L. Niglia and S. Weatherill (eds.), *The Foundations of European Private Law*, Hart Publishing, Oxford 2011, Ch. 16, pp. 293–307.

60 COM (2006) 744.

61 COM (2008) 614.

62 The proposal also pressed for a maximum model of harmonisation: its failure in this respect is explored in Chapter 6.6.

not attract sufficient political support and ultimately a more modest measure, Directive 2011/83 on consumer rights, was adopted.[63] But this too maintained the thematic connection to the building of the internal market, and its legal base is Article 114 TFEU.

The Commission's review had also moved in a less orthodox direction. The July 2010 Green Paper on policy options for progress towards a European Contract Law for consumers and businesses[64] generated a round of consultation which led in October 2011 to a Commission proposal for a Common European Sales Law – the 'CESL'.[65] This was not conventional harmonisation, but rather intended to put in place a contract law regime at EU level which would be optional. It would serve as an alternative to, not a replacement for, national contract laws. The CESL proposal attracted a high level of antipathy and there is no prospect of it being adopted in the ambitious form originally canvassed by the Commission: this is explained in Chapter 5.9. However, it fits within the narrative of contract law as an instrument to serve the project of the internal market. It was, in the presentation advanced by the Commission, designed 'as a contribution to enhancing growth and trade in the internal market on the basis of freedom of contract and a high level of consumer protection, in line with the principles of subsidiarity and proportionality'.[66] The Explanatory Memorandum accompanying the Proposal was candid: 'The overall objective of the proposal is to improve the establishment and the functioning of the internal market.'[67] The proposed legal base was Article 114 TFEU, although as will be explained (section 3.17), this is unconvincing. There is reason to agree that it would promote the functioning of the internal market but, as a stand-alone new instrument, it would not constitute harmonisation.

3.11. BEYOND THE FIRST *TOBACCO ADVERTISING* RULING: THE SECOND *TOBACCO ADVERTISING* RULING

The first *Tobacco Advertising* ruling created a high degree of 'competence sensitivity'. However, with the advantage of hindsight the Court's judgment in the first *Tobacco Advertising* case is less effective as a means to protect the principle of conferral than it might have appeared at the time. It is today clear that should not be read as a major curtailment of the EU's legislative competence to harmonise, *inter alia* in the field of contract law.

63 [2011] OJ L304/64.
64 COM (2010) 348.
65 COM (2011) 635.
66 COM (2011) 636, p. 7.
67 COM (2011) 635, p. 4.

In the first *Tobacco Advertising* case the Court refused to accept that the Directive as adopted had crossed the threshold required for valid reliance on Article 114: it was, in short, bereft of the necessary market-making element. But a great deal of the judgment was in truth concerned to make clear just how low that threshold truly is, which, it has become evident, was of far greater significance for the future than the finding that that particular challenged Directive had failed to cross it. In this sense what the legislative institutions of the EU lost by the invalidation of Directive 98/43 was amply compensated by the gains made by the Court's readiness to map out what they may do in future in the name of market-making harmonisation pursuant to (what is now) Article 114.

The single best insight into the true impact of the first *Tobacco Advertising* case is provided by inspection of the second *Tobacco Advertising* case.

After Directive 98/34 was annulled in the first *Tobacco Advertising* case the EU legislature responded by adopting a more narrowly drawn measure. This, Directive 2003/33, was aimed only at harmonising laws relating to the advertising of tobacco products and their promotion in the press and other printed publications, in radio broadcasting, in information society services and through tobacco-related sponsorship.[68] It did not seek to deal with ashtrays, parasols and the like. Its legal bases were – again – the Treaty provisions governing harmonisation of laws in the goods and services sectors, today Articles 53(2), 62 and 114 TFEU. Its validity too was challenged by Germany, but without success. This is the second *Tobacco Advertising* case.[69] Germany's failure was hardly surprising, because the Directive's drafting had made conscientious use of the formula prepared by the Court as a blueprint in the first *Tobacco Advertising* case. The Court had there gone out of its way to explain what could be validly achieved in the name of market-making harmonisation. It was openly receptive to the harmonisation of rules affecting tobacco advertising in periodicals, magazines and newspapers as a means to promote the free movement of press products, and to harmonisation of rules governing sponsorship.[70] It was the breadth of the original Directive to which the Court objected, but Directive 2003/33 showed that the legislature had learned the lesson taught by the Court. In its ruling in the second case the Court noted that the Commission's written observations told it that advertising and/or sponsorship in respect of tobacco products were partially prohibited in six Member States, totally prohibited in four, and the subject of legislative proposals seeking a total prohibition in the remaining five. It added that imminent enlargement of the Union created an appreciable risk that those disparities would increase. Moreover the market in press products is a market in which trade between Member States is relatively large and it is set to grow further as a result, in particular, of the link between

68 Directive 2003/33 [2003] OJ L152/16.

69 Case C-380/03, *Germany v Parliament and Council* [2006] ECR I-11573.

70 Case C-376/98, *Germany v Parliament and Council* [2000] ECR I-8419, paras. 97–98, 110–111.

the media in question and the internet, which the Court described as 'the cross-border medium *par excellence*'.[71] This, the Court concluded, was a case where barriers to trade and risks of distortions of competition provided a valid basis for intervention by the EU. Banning advertising in periodicals, magazines and newspapers made a contribution to opening up the wider internal market for periodicals, magazines and newspapers. Directive 2003/33 passed the Court's test, where Directive 98/34 had failed it in the first *Tobacco Advertising* case.

What was in fact at stake here was a perfect example of diversity between national regulatory contract law provoking (harmonised) EU regulatory contract law. Because national laws suppressed or were likely to suppress advertising of tobacco products, the EU suppresses advertising of tobacco products. It shuts down a market for contracting to supply advertising services. But it does so in the service of opening up markets across borders within which to conclude contracts to sell periodicals, magazines and newspapers.

The second *Tobacco Advertising* case is fully in line with the ruling in *Alliance for Natural Health* which was examined above (section 3.8). There is no objection to a harmonised *ban* provided only that the ban serves to promote the functioning of the internal market.[72] In *Alliance for Natural Health* the point was in short to ban suspect products in order to improve the market for safe products; in the second *Tobacco Advertising* case the point was to ban a particular form of advertising in order to promote cross-border competition in press products that carry advertising. In the first *Tobacco Advertising* case the objection was not to a prohibition imposed on advertising, but rather to a prohibition imposed on advertising that did not further the interests of the internal market.

In exactly the same vein the second *Tobacco Advertising* case is fully in line with *Alliance for Natural Health* in its embrace of the appropriateness of public health as a 'decisive factor' in shaping the harmonised regulatory environment.[73] This is the 'dual function' of harmonisation. Indeed the first *Tobacco Advertising* case also conforms to this model. Provided that the measure crosses the threshold for invocation of Article 114, which means that it must make a sufficient contribution to the functioning of the internal market, the EU 'legislature cannot be prevented from relying on that legal basis on the ground that public health protection is a decisive factor in the choices to be made'.[74] The objection in the first *Tobacco Advertising* case was that the threshold was *not* crossed, not that that public health considerations motivated the content of the harmonised regime. As explained above, there is nothing surprising or devious about this. Where national laws are harmonised, the EU unavoidably becomes

71 Case C-380/03, *Germany v Parliament and Council* [2006] ECR I-11573, para. 53.

72 Para. 43.

73 Para. 38, which cites *inter alia Alliance for Natural Health and Others*, para. 30.

74 Case C-376/98, *Germany v Parliament and Council* [2000] ECR I-8419, para. 88.

a (re-)regulator in the area that is harmonised. It must make a choice about the content, quality and technique to be used as the harmonised EU standard. The Treaty and more recently the Charter, routinely cited by the Court in these cases, both recognise this constitutional linkage between market-making and market (re-)regulation.

This connects the *Tobacco Advertising* saga to the treatment of the scope of Article 114 above (section 3.8), where the two chosen illustrations in the case law were *Alliance for Natural Health* and *Vodafone*. Both cases are structurally firmly in line with the second *Tobacco Advertising* case, and in fact they are in line with the large majority of the Court's case law in which it is asked to invalidate measures of harmonisation adopted pursuant to Article 114. Such applications normally fail.[75] This exposes the first *Tobacco Advertising* case as the outlier. It is atypical. Most measures of legislative harmonisation, when challenged, satisfy the Court.

3.12. THE PREDOMINANCE OF POLITICAL OVER CONSTITUTIONAL CONTROLS

What does this inspection of the Court's case law on the limits of Article 114 TFEU reveal? It could suggest that the Court has weakened its intensity of review since the first *Tobacco Advertising* case in 2000; or it could suggest that the legislature has become more scrupulous in its adherence to the limits of Article 114 TFEU. The reality is, it is submitted, a subtle mix. The Directive annulled in the first *Tobacco Advertising* case was a mere four pages long and made no serious attempt to engage with the question of just why prohibiting advertising on ashtrays, parasols and so on counted as a contribution to the better functioning of the internal market. By contrast the measures that have typically survived annulment by the Court have included much fuller and more detailed explanation of how they cross the threshold. This will be considered much more fully in the next chapter, but a brief illustrative flavour is worth including at this stage of the examination in this chapter.

Directive 2002/46 on harmonisation of laws relating to food supplements carefully begins its Preamble by explaining that:

> '(1) There is an increasing number of products marketed in the Community as foods containing concentrated sources of nutrients and presented for supplementing the intake of those nutrients from the normal diet.
>
> (2) Those products are regulated in Member States by differing national rules that may impede their free movement, create unequal conditions of competition, and thus have a direct impact on the functioning of the internal market. It is

[75] See cases above n. 16.

> therefore necessary to adopt Community rules on those products marketed as foodstuffs.'[76]

It is perhaps small wonder that the Court, invited in *Alliance for Natural Health* to review the measure's validity, chose to uphold it.[77] It is not so much that since the first *Tobacco Advertising* case the Court's teeth have become less sharp, it is more that the legislature has been able to absorb the Court's vocabulary and readily present its initiatives as consistent with the strikingly wide scope of Article 114. It is common to find measures of harmonisation which contain in their Preamble assiduous repetition of fidelity to the promotion of the functioning of the internal market. Directive 2014/40 on the manufacture, presentation and sale of tobacco products, for example, includes the phrase 'smooth functioning of the internal market' no fewer than eleven times in its Preamble.[78] In similar vein Directive 2011/83, the Directive on consumer rights which was mentioned above as one of the few fruits of the Commission's quest to renovate the legislative *acquis*,[79] reveals a high level of evident scrupulousness to situate harmonisation within the bounds set by the Court to the scope of Article 114. Its Recital 7 states:

> 'Both consumers and traders should be able to rely on a single regulatory framework based on clearly defined legal concepts regulating certain aspects of business-to-consumer contracts across the Union. The effect of such harmonisation should be to eliminate the barriers stemming from the fragmentation of the rules and to complete the internal market in this area. Those barriers can only be eliminated by establishing uniform rules at Union level'.

The question, however, is whether this is truly a demonstration of legislative fidelity to the principle of conferral or instead simply a demonstration of a readiness to cut and paste the Court's formula and to embroider the legislative record with the decoration that the Court expects to see. That is, the question is whether this is really a matter of substance – that the legislature has applied its mind carefully to what truly is required in order to fulfil the project of completing the internal market – or whether instead it is merely form – that the legislature is smart enough to repeat back to the Court its own competence-defining vocabulary.

Whatever one's assessment, the vital insight is that if the legislative institutions draft their reasons for reliance on Article 114 in careful accordance with the Court's test, it is remarkably difficult to falsify the claims made. A challenge to the validity of an adopted measure needs enough beef to

76 [2002] OJ L183/51.
77 Cases C-154/04 and C-155/04 [2005] ECR I-6451.
78 Directive 2014/40 [2014] OJ L127/1.
79 Directive 2011/83 [2011] OJ L304/64, section 3.10.

persuade the Court that a trinity of the Commission, a qualified majority (at the minimum) of the Member States and the Parliament have conspired to violate the principle of conferral. This involves showing that legislative diversity does not harm the internal market. But commonly it is perfectly plausible that actual or likely regulatory diversity between the Member States exerts at least some kind of restrictive or distortive impact on cross-border trade patterns. True, other matters – linguistic variation, cultural preferences, geography and effective access to justice – may matter *more*, but that does not mean that legal diversity does not matter at all, and in fact empirical evidence, though relatively scarce, tends to support the view that legal diversity is one element in explaining the imperfect nature of the internal market, albeit far from the most important.[80] The problem, then, is rooted in the Treaty itself, in Article 114 TFEU and its loose, ill-defined promise to build an internal market through legislative harmonisation. One might wish to argue that such inter-State diversity is vibrant and worthy of preservation, that it promotes competition between regulators and helps a learning process – but these are political arguments which lack bite before the Court. Broadly, one may criticise harmonisation as culturally and economically insensitive to local autonomy and diversity and a means to impose damaging centralisation on the EU.[81] But none of this is easily converted into a *constitutional* objection apt to block the EU. The reason is that Article 114 is very broad in scope. Constitutionally the threshold is low, and the Court's reticent track record since the first *Tobacco Advertising* case reflects that.

In this sense crossing the threshold in order to bring the matter within the valid scope of Article 114 TFEU requires careful legislative drafting in order to demonstrate or at least assert the necessary connection to the internal market,

---

80 See S. Vogenauer and S. Weatherill, 'The European Community's competence for a comprehensive harmonisation of contract law – an empirical analysis' (2005) 30 *European Law Review* 821; K. Thommes, M. Faure and K. Heine, 'The Internal Market and the Consumer: What Consumers Actually Choose' (2014) 21 *Columbia Journal of European Law* 47. See also G. Low, 'The (Ir)relevance of Harmonization and Legal Diversity to European Contract Law: a Perspective from Psychology' (2010) 18 *European Review of Private Law* 285; H. Collins, *The European Civil Code: The Way Forward*, CUP, Cambridge 2008, Ch. 3; E. McKendrick, 'Harmonisation of European Contract Law: The State we are in' in S. Vogenauer and S. Weatherill (eds.), *The Harmonisation of European Contract Law: Implications for European Private Law, Business and Legal Practice*, Hart/IECL, Oxford 2006, Ch. 2, pp. 5–30.

81 e.g. with reference to contract law F. Gomez and J. Ganuza, 'An Economic Analysis of Harmonization Régimes: Full Harmonization, Minimum Harmonization or Optional Instrument?' (2011) 7 *European Review of Contract Law* 275; A. Wulf, 'Institutional competition of optional codes in European contract law' (2014) 38 *European Journal of Law and Economics* 139; W. Kerber and S. Grundmann, 'An optional European contract law code: Advantages and Disadvantages' (2006) 21 *European Journal of Law and Economics* 215; G. Wagner, 'The Economics of Harmonization: The Case of Contract Law' (2002) 39 *Common Market Law Review* 995. See also L. Miller, *The Emergence of EU Contract Law: Exploring Europeanization*, OUP, Oxford 2011, pp. 58–64.

but in practice judicial intervention is likely to be uncommon.[82] Article 114 is more conspicuously an empowerment of rather than a limitation on EU legislative competence.[83] Harmonisation may even extend to national rules where there is no demonstrated cross-border dimension to their application, provided this is necessary to achieve certainty and predictability in the scope of the EU measure's application in the light of the unfeasibility of locating a sharp demarcation between the purely internal matter and the matter with cross-border effects.[84]

The constitutional significance of the first *Tobacco Advertising* case remains immense, but the legislature's error exposed in that ruling was to fail to infuse the Preamble to (annulled) Directive 98/43 with appropriate wording claiming a connection between harmonisation and market-making. In practice the Court has generated a vocabulary on which the legislature has lately eagerly seized in order to place its choices in practice beyond the scope of judicial invalidation.

'Competence sensitivity' should never be ignored, for it is embedded in the constitutional fabric of the EU as an entity with only a *limited* mandate to act, as stipulated by Article 5 TEU. But this has proved to matter less in practice than in principle. The most prominent strand in this narrative is the *generous* attitude to the scope of EU legislative competence taken by the EU's political institutions and, usually, by its Court. The structural problem is that the internal market itself, far from being an effective limiting legal concept, is a broad and ambiguous one. Its breadth and flexibility endows Article 114, its promoter, with exactly those same features. The internal market is an empowering legal concept. The EU in general and Article 114 in particular do not operate on the basis of a carefully written reservation of national autonomy. Accordingly it is difficult to mount a successful *constitutional* challenge to reliance on Article 114 TFEU. The implication is that those opposed to EU action need to make use of their voice in the political process. Contract law is politically contested. And so it should be, in all circumstances but especially where the constitutional constraints are so loose.

---

82 Cf. S. Weatherill, 'The limits of legislative harmonisation ten years after *Tobacco Advertising*: how the Court's case law has become a "drafting guide"' (2011) 12 *German Law Journal* 827.

83 See D. Wyatt, 'Community Competence to Regulate the Internal Market' in M. Dougan and S. Currie (eds.), *Fifty Years of the European Treaties: Looking Back and Thinking Forward*, Hart Publishing, Oxford 2009; and with special reference to contract law. K. Gutman, *The Constitutional Foundations of European Contract Law: A Comparative Analysis*, OUP, Oxford 2014, Ch. 8.

84 Joined Cases C-465/00, C-138/01 and C-139/01, *Rechnungshof v Österreichischer Rundfunk* [2003] ECR I-4989; Case C-380/03, *Germany v Parliament and Council* [2006] ECR I-11573, para. 80. This expansionist trend is controversial: e.g. C. Twigg-Flesner argues that EU intervention *should* be limited to cross-border cases: *A Cross-Border-Only Regulation for Consumer Transactions in the EU: A Fresh Approach to EU Consumer Law*, Springer, Berlin 2012.

3.13. REVIEW OF THE EXERCISE OF LEGISLATIVE COMPETENCE

The limited scope for successfully challenging the *existence* of a competence to adopt a measure of legislative harmonisation pushes attention to the possibility of claiming that the *exercise* of an admittedly existing competence is legally flawed and therefore invalid. The legal principles that are most intimately associated with the exercise of EU legislative competence are those of subsidiarity and proportionality. Both principles, contained and defined in Article 5 TEU, are conditions of legality attached to EU legislative activity, but they also bleed seamlessly in the wider political debate about the proper scope and intensity of EU regulation. They therefore deserve to be the subject of treatment in a separate chapter. That is Chapter 5.

The concern here is with checks on legality founded on general principles of EU law and the Charter. At stake is judicial review of the quality of the (re-)regulated environment of the internal market. The interesting question asks how far the Court will go in its inquiry into the legality of legislative assessment.

3.14. THE CONSTITUTIONAL OBLIGATION TO REACH HIGH STANDARDS

It has been explained that harmonisation is in principle *not only* a technical matter of fixing common rules *but also* a matter of choosing the quality of the harmonised regime that will prevail across the EU. It has a 'dual function'. The combined force of provisions such as Articles 12, 114(3), 168 and 169 TFEU and Articles 35 and 38 of the Charter ensure that the EU's commitments to public health and consumer protection are constitutionally rooted. This may affect *inter alia* choices about the content of EU initiatives which harmonise regulatory contract law.

However, these provisions are deficient in both legal precision and institutional specificity. Their flavour is more political aspiration than independently enforceable legal norm. It is improbable that the Court could ever be persuaded to rule an EU measure invalid for failure to secure a sufficiently high level of protection, even if in principle such a possibility cannot be excluded given that the norms are contained in primary EU law.

The Court has made clear that the direction to pursue a high level of consumer protection does not mean that the finally agreed harmonised standards must comply with the highest standard found among the Member States. In the *Deposit Guarantee* case the Court decided that the mere fact that a measure of harmonisation may cause a reduction in national standards in some Member

States is not a sufficient basis on which to annul the measure.[85] A degree of political compromise is inevitable within the EU legislative process, and this is precisely the point which the Court is making, albeit by implication: it is to the political process through which the EU measure is adopted that those wishing to secure high standards should turn. It is plausible that a manifest neglect on the part of the legislature to take any account of the protective quality of the harmonised rule or a manifest error of appraisal regarding the applicable conditions would induce the Court to intervene and to rule the adopted act to be invalid.[86] But where the EU legislature is cannily conscientious in drafting a measure to ensure inclusion of the relevant Treaty and Charter provisions on public health and/or consumer protection in the Preamble to adopted legislation it seems improbable that the Court would treat any such measure as legally deficient.

So it is constitutionally possible for EU measures of harmonisation to cause *some* depreciation in existing standards of consumer protection in *some* Member States. The main arena for arguing whether this in fact should occur is the process of political negotiation.

3.15. THE PROTECTION OF FUNDAMENTAL RIGHTS

The competence to harmonise must, like any other legislative competence conferred on the EU, be exercised in conformity with the Charter of Fundamental Rights. In *Fransson* the Court captured this vividly: 'The applicability of EU law entails applicability of the fundamental rights guaranteed by the Charter'.[87] This is a concrete application of the Court's long-standing creative approach which insists that the EU is bound to respect general principles of law, some of which were not and still are not explicitly written into the Treaty.[88]

Legislative fidelity to this requirement is sometimes perfunctory. So, for example, the Preamble to Directive 2011/83 on consumer rights simply asserts that '[t]his Directive respects the fundamental rights and observes the principles recognised in particular by the Charter of Fundamental Rights of the European Union'.[89] There is no elucidation of this claim. The practice will be considered more widely in the next chapter, but the concern of this chapter is with the basic point that any EU measure which fails to adhere to the protection of fundamental rights should be held invalid by the Court. In this sense legislative discretion is confined by the constitutionally superior demands of fundamental rights.

85 Case C-233/94, *Germany v Parliament and Council* (deposit guarantees) [1997] ECR I-2405.

86 Cf. Case C-284/95, *Safety Hi-Tech v S & T* [1998] ECR I-4301, para. 37.

87 Case C-617/10, *Fransson* judgment of 26 January 2013.

88 See T. Tridimas, *The General Principles of EU Law*, 2nd ed., OUP, Oxford 2006.

89 [2011] OJ L304/64, Recital 66.

Legislative harmonisation both promotes commercial freedom, by replacing trade-restrictive regulatory diversity at national level with common rules at EU level, and confines that freedom according to whatever (re-)regulatory scheme is introduced at EU level. This is the familiar 'dual function' of harmonisation. The cases which have reached the Court have tended to involve complaints by commercial operators that the regulatory burdens imposed by the EU go too far and should be treated as invalid. In this vein Articles 16 and 17 of the Charter serve as the most obvious sources of such challenge. Article 16 states that '[t]he freedom to conduct a business in accordance with Union law and national laws and practices is recognised' and Article 17, the *Right to property*, declares in its first sentence that '[e]veryone has the right to own, use, dispose of and bequeath his or her lawfully acquired possessions'. So it is open to commercial operators to complain that (re-)regulatory harmonisation is in violation of these Charter protections. This suggests a *constitutionalised* protection of private economic interests from public regulation. But the Charter is not one-sided. Articles 16 and 17 co-exist with other Charter rights and principles that are favourably inclined to the virtues of intervention in the market the public interest. Article 35 (public health), Article 37 (environmental protection) and Article 38 (consumer protection) all stand for the virtue of confining market freedom in order to achieve broader goals in the collective or public interest. Moreover, Article 17 itself concedes that '[t]he use of property may be regulated by law in so far as is necessary for the general interest', while, more broadly, Article 52(1) admits of limitation on the exercise of the rights and freedoms recognised by this Charter as 'provided for by law', on condition that such limitation shall respect the essence of those rights and freedoms and shall be made only where necessary.

This approach, it should be noted, is not an innovation introduced with effect from 2009, when the Charter acquired binding force as a result of the entry into force of the Treaty of Lisbon. The Charter's impact is to write in a more sophisticated way an approach which the Court has long embraced. The Court recognises the right to property as a general principle of EU law, but has treated it not as an absolute right which defeats intervention in the market in the public interest, but rather as one that must be viewed in relation to its social function. The Court has no objection to legislative restriction on its exercise 'provided that those restrictions in fact correspond to objectives of general interest ... and do not constitute a disproportionate and intolerable interference, impairing the very substance of the rights guaranteed'.[90]

Legislative practice is, as suggested above, vulnerable to criticism as perfunctory, but recitation, if not profound assessment, of the competing

[90] e.g. Case C-491/01, *R v Secretary of State ex parte BAT and Imperial Tobacco* [2002] ECR I-11543; Case C-200/96, *Metronome Musik GmbH* [1998] ECR I-1953. On Article 16 and its pre-history see P. Oliver, 'What Purpose Does Article 16 of the Charter Serve?' in U. Bernitz, X. Groussot and F. Schulyok (eds.), *General Principles of EU Law and European Private Law*, Wolters Kluwer, Alphen aan den Rijn 2013, Ch. 12, pp. 281–300.

provisions of the Charter embroiders recent additions to the *acquis*. For example, Directive 2015/2302 on package travel declares in its Preamble that it 'respects the freedom to conduct a business laid down in Article 16 of the Charter, while ensuring a high level of consumer protection within the Union, in accordance with Article 38 of the Charter'.[91]

The legislative task, then, is in short to balance competing interests. And then the Court's job is to decide how intensively it will review legislative compromise in individual cases where legislative choices about market (re-)regulation are attacked as incompatible with the Charter and, before the Charter's rise to prominence, with the general principles of EU law. In general, the Court embraces respect for a broad legislative discretion where political, economic and social choices are at stake and where complex assessment is demanded. The Court typically brings a measure's validity into doubt only where its impact is manifestly inappropriate in relation to the objective which it seeks to achieve. This relatively light standard of review reflects the Court's anxiety to keep separate judicial and legislative functions.

Sky Österreich GmbH provides a good illustration.[92] The measure in question was Directive 2010/13 on Audiovisual Media Services, which is based on Articles 53(1) and 62 TFEU, the harmonisation provisions in the Treaty which govern the right of establishment and services.[93] Its Preamble supplies the orthodox case in favour of the adoption of harmonised rules to govern the sector 'in order to avoid distortions of competition, improve legal certainty, help complete the internal market and facilitate the emergence of a single information area'.[94] Then – the 'dual function' – the EU is compelled to select the (common) pattern of regulation which will prevail in the sector. In the case the applicant's objection was directed to the Directive's Article 15, which requires Member States to ensure that for the purpose of short news reports, any broadcaster established in the Union has access on a fair, reasonable and non-discriminatory basis to events of high interest to the public even where these are those which are transmitted on an exclusive basis by a broadcaster under their jurisdiction. This entails that public access to reports of this type is widened, but that comes at a cost which is shouldered by the holder of exclusive broadcasting rights, which is denied the right to choose with which broadcasters (if any) it will contract in order to license the making of short news reports. *Exclusivity* is prized in broadcasting markets, because it allows the owner of the rights to charge high prices to viewers eager for access to the relevant material: the Directive robs the right-holder of that lucrative exclusivity. But the Court did not find that any unlawful maltreatment of property rights had occurred. It stated that 'the freedom to conduct a business

---

91 [2015] OJ L326/1, Recital 52. See more fully on this Directive Chapter 4.3.

92 Case C-283/11, *Sky Österreich GmbH* judgment of 22 January 2013.

93 [2006] OJ L95/1.

94 Recital 11.

is not absolute, but must be viewed in relation to its social function'; and it added that 'the freedom to conduct a business may be subject to a broad range of interventions on the part of public authorities which may limit the exercise of economic activity in the public interest'.[95] It then took the view that what was at stake was a 'balance' between on the one hand the importance of safeguarding the fundamental freedom to receive information and the freedom and pluralism of the media guaranteed by Article 11 of the Charter and, on the other, the protection of the freedom to conduct a business guaranteed by Article 16 of the Charter. The Directive involved a valid choice to limit the latter in favour of the former: this was part of 'the necessary balancing of the rights and interests at issue'.[96] In this way the Court refused to disturb the balancing of public and private interests which had been struck through the political process. The implication is that a disgruntled rights-holder, deprived of contractual freedom in an absolute sense by this intervention, must seek to influence the political process if it is to extract a more favourable regime. EU law, in particular the Charter, will not help. In this ruling the Court was staying true to a long-standing unwillingness to use the right to property as an aggressive basis for subversion of regulatory intervention in the market, stretching back long before the Charter acquired binding effect and became the focal point of such inquiry in 2009.[97]

Deutsches Weintor v Land Rheinland-Pfalz has much in common with *Sky Österreich GmbH* both in structure and in outcome.[98] At stake was an orthodox measure of legislative harmonisation, Regulation 1924/2006 on nutrition and health claims.[99] Its Preamble explains that differences between national provisions relating to such claims 'may impede the free movement of foods and create unequal conditions of competition'.[100] So the EU regulates nutrition and health claims in order to promote trade in the sector across the full territory of the internal market. The litigation emerged as a result of German action taken pursuant to the Regulation to suppress the claim that particular wines were 'easily digestible'. Here too, as in *Sky Österreich GmbH*, the applicant could readily rely on Articles 15 and 16 of the Charter to attack such curtailment of its commercial freedom, whereas the Regulation was defended with reference to Article 35 of the Charter, which requires that a high level of human health protection be ensured in the definition and implementation of EU policies and activities. The Court noted that the claim made highlighted *only* the easy digestion of wine, and it risked encouraging consumption leading to increased risks for consumers' health. Consequently 'the prohibition of such claims is warranted in the light of the requirement to ensure a high level of health

95 Paras. 45, 46.

96 Para. 67.

97 Cf. T. Tridimas, *The General Principles of EU Law*, 2nd ed., OUP, Oxford 2006, pp. 313–319.

98 Case C-544/10, *Deutsches Weintor v Land Rheinland-Pfalz* judgment of 6 September 2012.

99 [2006] OJ L404/9.

100 Recital 2.

protection for consumers'.[101] The Regulation was based on a reconciliation of the several fundamental rights at stake, including the right to property and the concern to secure public health, and it struck a 'fair balance' between them.[102] Something very similar happened in *Neptune Distribution*, in which the Court, citing *Deutsches Weintor* and the need for a fair balance and respect for a broad legislative discretion, decided that reliance on Article 16 of the Charter did not upset the suppression pursuant to Regulation 1924/2006 of claims about the sodium content of mineral water, given the weight in favour of such regulatory intervention provided by Articles 35 and 38 of the Charter combined with Articles 9, 12, 114(3), 168(1) and 169(1) TFEU.[103]

It does not follow that use of Article 114 is immune in practice from judicial control in the name of the Charter. In *Digital Rights Ireland* Directive 2006/24 on data retention was found invalid.[104] Its legal base was Article 95 EC, today Article 114 TFEU, because it was adopted as a response to variation between national rules on the retention of data by service providers for the prevention, investigation, detection, and prosecution of criminal offences which, it was asserted in the measure's Preamble, present obstacles to the internal market for electronic communications.[105] The Court, however, found that the Directive amounted to a wide-ranging and particularly serious interference with Charter rights to privacy and personal data which was not accompanied by adequate safeguards. It ruled the Directive to be invalid. But the focus of the regime was on the adoption of common rules which were claimed to be required in order to combat organised crime and terrorism (in response to diverse national measures with similar claimed motivation). It was regulatory contract law in the broadest sense, in that the rules affected commercial activity in the particular services involved, but it was much different from the measures of general market regulation of the type addressed in *Sky Österreich GmbH*, *Deutsches Weintor* and *Neptune Distribution*. Such measures are unlikely to be found invalid for violation of the Charter. The Court is relatively protective of legislative choices conducted pursuant to the practical application of the principle that legislative harmonisation carries a dual function.

3.16. EU RULES AND NON-DISCRIMINATION

Article 19 TFEU provides for a competence exercised according to a special legislative procedure involving unanimity in Council to take appropriate action

---

101 Para. 52.

102 Para. 59.

103 Case C-157/14 judgment of 17 December 2015.

104 Joined Cases C-293/12 and C-594/12, *Digital Rights Ireland* judgment of 8 April 2014. See similarly Case C-362/14, *Maximillian Schrems* judgment of 6 October 2015.

105 [2006] OJ L105/54, Recitals 5 and 6.

to combat discrimination based on sex, racial or ethnic origin, religion or belief, disability, age or sexual orientation. This is not tied to the internal market. It stands for an – inchoate, underdeveloped and not universally applicable– understanding of EU law as a guarantor of equality and dignity.[106] For the purposes of this book, Article 19's significance lies in its role as a base for EU legislation that forbids certain types of discrimination to the detriment of contractual autonomy.

Article 19 TFEU is of itself not capable of being relied on by an individual. It is not a provision that is directly effective and it stands in contrast with the free movement provisions, the competition rules and Article 157 TFEU on equal pay for equal work, all of which were considered in Chapter 2. It requires amplification by secondary legislation. There has been important legislative amplification of this type. Article 19 TFEU succeeded Article 13 EC on the entry into force of the Treaty of Lisbon in 2009, and that immediate predecessor is the legal base for Directive 2000/43 on equal treatment between persons irrespective of racial or ethnic origin[107] and Directive 2000/78 establishing a general framework for equal treatment in employment and occupation.[108] It is also the legal base for Directive 2004/113 implementing the Principle of Equal Treatment between Men and Women in the Access to and Supply of Goods and Services.[109] The Directives are of admittedly limited scope. So, for example, Directive 2004/113 preserves the freedom of the individual who supplies goods or services to make his or her own subjective choice as to contractual partner provided only that that choice is not based on sex.[110] However, once implemented at national level, these measures plainly exert a significant impact on contractual autonomy, and they are not confined to the workplace. It was mentioned in Chapter 2 that the contention that labour market regulation and social policy should be about rights is opposed by those who prefer to emphasise the economic aim of making the market more competitive: by contrast, discrimination and equality law is much more squarely and unarguably part of 'rights discourse'. The power of the grip which these Directives exert on contractual autonomy is best grasped by contrasting them with the assumptions that pervade EU competition law. Articles 101 and 102 TFEU assume that the unilateral practices of an undertaking which is not a position of dominant economic power are immune from review. It can contract (or not) with whomsoever it likes. The same is true of the free movement rules governing goods, persons and services – albeit that there is an unconfirmed and hesitant hint in the case law that unilateral practices restricting

---

106 See e.g. M. Bell, 'The Principle of Equal Treatment: Widening and Deepening' in P. Craig and G. De Burca, *The Evolution of EU Law*, 2nd ed., OUP, Oxford 2011, Ch. 20, pp. 611–639.

107 [2000] OJ L180/22.

108 [2000] OJ L303/16.

109 [2004] OJ L373/37.

110 Art. 3(2), Recital 14.

the free movement of persons may be caught.[111] Such limits simply do not come into play where the matter falls within the scope of the anti-discrimination Directives. So when the director of a firm that supplied doors declared that the company could not employ 'immigrants' as fitters because its customers were reluctant to give them access to their home while the work was done, a violation of Directive 2000/43 was established: this was direct discrimination in respect of recruitment, for such a statement would deter certain candidates from applying for a job and so hinder their access to the labour market.[112] There was no question of preserving the autonomy of the employer. The case had been brought by a Belgian body charged with promoting equal treatment, but there was no proof that an individual applicant had been rejected by the company. The Court took explicit note of the aim of the Directive 'to foster conditions for a socially inclusive labour market' as a reason to refuse to limit its scope to cases in which an unsuccessful candidate for a post had initiated legal proceedings against the employer.[113] In a similar vein a violation of Directive 2000/78 was established in *Coleman v Attridge Law* where a woman brought her contract of employment to an end as a result of discriminatory treatment against her by her employer as a result of her responsibilities as the primary carer of a disabled child.[114] She was not disabled, but her son was, and control of this 'associative discrimination' was found to fall within the purpose of the Directive. The 'need to take appropriate action for the social and economic integration of disabled people' justified a broad interpretation of the Directive.[115] It is a gently provocative exaggeration to describe this as 'the vanishing freedom to choose a contractual partner'[116] but the phrase deftly captures the trend. Where a matter falls within the scope of discrimination prohibited by EU law, the principle of equal treatment ranks above contractual autonomy. Article 19 TFEU and the secondary legislation adopted under it is important in showing that although much of the EU law relevant to contract law is driven by the internal market as a legal concept, it is not exclusively the internal market that provides the animating platform.

The EU's legislative commitments to promoting equality must themselves comply with the commitments made to equality in the Treaty and Charter. As a matter of constitutional hierarchy it is plain that EU legislature may not derogate from the promises made at a superior level by the Treaty and Charter. This might seem an arcane matter without practical bite, but this is not so. In

111 Case C-281/98, *Angonese* [2000] ECR I-4139; Case C-94/07, *Andrea Raccanelli* [2008] ECR I-5939; Case C-379/09, *Maurits Casteels v British Airways* judgment of 10 March 2011. See Chapter 2.3.

112 Case C-54/07, *Firma Feryn NV* [2008] ECR I-5187.

113 Paras. 23–24, citing Recital 8.

114 Case C-303/06 [2008] ECR I-5603.

115 Para. 43.

116 H. Collins, 'The Vanishing Freedom to Choose a Contractual Partner' (2013) 76 *Law and Contemporary Problems* 71.

2011 in *Association belge des Consommateurs Test-Achats* the Court relied on the Charter in finding a provision of the above-mentioned Directive 2004/113 implementing the principle of equal treatment between men and women in the access to and supply of goods and services to be invalid.[117] The flaw lay in the Directive's Article 5(2). This allowed Member States to permit differences relating to sex in the calculation of insurance premiums and benefits. The Court held this to be invalid for violation of Articles 21 and 23 of the Charter which forbid discrimination based on sex and which require that equality between men and women be ensured in all areas. Directive 2004/113 pre-dated the grant of binding force to the Charter, but its Preamble claimed fidelity to Articles 21 and 23 of the Charter which was at the time formally non-binding. The Court therefore took this as a legislative promise that the Directive met the requirements of the Charter.[118] But it did not. In truth Article 5(2) amounted to a blatant contradiction of the principle of equal treatment which the Directive purported to promote.[119] As a matter of constitutional principle, the Court's ruling acts as a strong statement of hierarchy: the exercise of EU legislative competence is conditional on respect for the hierarchically superior Charter. *Test-Achats* brings home vividly that the Member States, by amending the Treaties to grant the Charter 'the same legal value as the Treaties',[120] have limited the scope of legislative discretion that may be practised *within* the EU system.

Sky Österreich GmbH and *Deutsches Weintor* are protective of public regulation that restrains contractual autonomy in the public interest. *Test-Achats* sets aside public regulation which is too weak in its subjection of contractual autonomy to the constitutionalised values of EU law.

3.17. ARTICLE 352 TFEU

Article 352 TFEU provides for legislation to attain one of the objectives of the Union where the Treaty has failed to lay down the necessary powers. It is a type of safety-net competence, allowing action where required to achieve the EU's aims even in the absence of a sector-specific competence. It has always been part of the system since the 1950s, albeit that it has been lightly amended at times of periodic Treaty revision. It requires, as it has always required, unanimous voting in Council. The Court has consistently held that Article 352 can only be

117 Case C-236/09 judgment of 1 March 2011.

118 Para. 17.

119 See e.g. C. Van Schoubroeck, 'Protection of Consumers against Discrimination: the Test-Achats Ruling' in E. Terryn, G. Straetmnans and V. Colaert (eds.), *Landmark Cases of EU Consumer Law: In Honour of Jules Stuyck*, Intersentia, Cambridge 2013, Ch. 2.VII, pp. 239–258.

120 Art. 6(1) TEU.

relied upon where no other Treaty Article provides the necessary powers.[121] It is in principle therefore of limited scope – and that scope has been narrowed each time the Treaty has been revised to add new sector-specific powers. So, for example, the EU's programme of environmental protection was initially developed pursuant to what is now Article 352, often also coupled to what is now Article 115, but this was altered with effect from 1987 by the creation pursuant to the Single European Act of a competence devoted explicitly to environmental protection. This is found today in Articles 191–193 TFEU. In similar and more recent vein the creation of explicit competences in Articles 118 and 194 TFEU in the fields of intellectual property and energy respectively with effect from 2009 as a result of the entry into force of the Lisbon Treaty in principle rules out action in these fields pursuant to Article 352.

It is, however, principally the rule of unanimity in Council which has stripped Article 352 of its vitality. In the past unanimity was an empowering rule, in the sense that if consensus could be assembled among the Member States there was a tendency to legislate with scant concern for the constitutional propriety of the matter. Article 352 (or, more precisely, its predecessors) was conducive to competence creep: it verged on a (quite improper) procedure for revising the scope of the Treaty 'from within'.[122] It is no longer of that type. The expansion of the EU to 28 Member States means that assembly of such uncritical consensus is far less likely. Article 352's poison has been drawn.[123] States are on their mettle.

Before the Lisbon Treaty, Article 352 was confined to legislative action associated with the 'common market': that restriction has been deleted, but was anyway of little practical restraining influence. There is however a particular role that may potentially be played by Article 352 in the creation of an internal market, and this arises where the EU wishes to legislate to promote the functioning of the internal market, but by creating a new regime, rather than by harmonising existing national regimes. Article 114 may be used only where national rules are replaced by common EU rules. It may not be used to create a wholly new and separate EU regime. That is not harmonisation. That is where Article 352 might be required – subject of course to assembling unanimity in Council.

This is clear from *Parliament v Council*, which deals with the validity of Regulation 1435/2003 creating a European Cooperative Society.[124] The chosen

---

121 e.g. Case 45/86, *Commission v Council* [1987] ECR 1493.

122 On past practice, see R. Schütze, 'Organized Change towards an Ever Closer Union: Article 308 EC and the Limits to the Community's Legislative Competence' (2003) 22 *Yearbook of European Law* 79.

123 T. Konstadinides, 'Drawing the Line between Circumvention and Gap-Filling: An Exploration of the Conceptual Limits of the Treaty's Flexibility Clause' (2012) 31 *Yearbook of European Law* 227.

124 Case C-436/03, *Parliament v Council* [2006] ECR I-3733.

legal base was Article 308 EC, which is now in amended form Article 352 TFEU. The Parliament objected. It argued that the measure should have been adopted instead under Article 95 EC (now Article 114 TFEU), and the reason for this objection was that Article 114 allocates to the Parliament a much more influential role in the lawmaking process than does Article 352. But the Court did not sustain the Parliament's objection. It found that was being created was a new EU-level form of cooperative society, existing in addition to national forms which were left unchanged. This might perfectly well have been a measure that advanced the functioning of the internal market, but it simply was *not* harmonisation: Article 114 was not available.

It seems to be a matter of degree. The Regulation did 'not lay down exhaustively all of the rules applicable to European cooperative societies'; 'for certain matters, it refers to the law of the Member State in the territory of which the European cooperative society has its registered office'. But this did not preclude the finding that it should be based on what is now Article 352 as a new EU instrument, since 'that referral is of a subsidiary nature'.[125]

The distinct roles of Articles 114 and 352 are brought into focus in the particular context of contract law by the proposed Common European Sales Law (CESL) considered above. As mentioned (section 3.10), this proposal has run into insuperable political opposition. Therefore extended dissection of its constitutional pedigree is an unnecessary extravagance. Brief mention of the matter is, however, helpful to reinforce the thematic point about the potential practical significance of 'competence sensitivity'. The proposed CESL Regulation was advanced by the Commission as a means to offer an extra contract law regime within the EU, which parties could choose to use in preference to national contract laws. The Commission convincingly argued that this could encourage cross-border trade and that therefore it served the interests of the internal market. However, much less compellingly it claimed that Article 114 would serve as its legal basis. This seems highly improbable in the light of the Court's ruling on the *European Cooperative Society*. The CESL, like the Society, would have been a new free-standing entity in the EU: it did not envisage harmonisation of national law. The correct legal base was Article 352, which, as the Commission was strategically aware, would for sure have condemned its proposal to death for want of unanimity in Council.

Some writers strained with great skill to find a way to justify reliance on Article 114, rather than Article 352. So, it was argued, the CESL could, by revealing particular choices about contract law which proved popular among contracting parties, induce national systems to adapt and adjust towards the EU model. This would be a form of inductive harmonisation.[126]

125 Para. 45.

126 For an optimistic views of the valid use of Art. 114 see G. Low, 'Unitas via Diversitas: Can the Common European Sales Law harmonise through Diversity?' (2012) 19 *Maastricht Journal*

The problem with this argument is, first, that it seems inconsistent with the limits on the use of Article 114 envisaged by the Court in *European Cooperative Society* and, second and more broadly, that it leaves any notion that Article 114 has limits in tatters. If one embraces a logic that treats the creation of a free-standing EU measure as a measure of harmonisation because of the reactions it might provoke, then the role of Article 114 is amplified at the expense of Article 352, and the Court's limiting ruling in the *European Cooperative Society* is in effect neutralised. But, entirely in line with the theme of this chapter, it cannot be discounted that exactly that might be the result of any such litigation before the Court. As with the first *Tobacco Advertising* case's finding that there was no adequate contribution to the making of an internal market, so too with the insistence that EU measures do not amount to 'harmonisation': this is in principle a restraint on the EU's competence to rely on Article 114 to promote market regulation, but in practice the restraint is soft-edged. *United Kingdom v Council and Parliament* was a challenge to the validity of Article 28 of Regulation 236/2012 on 'short selling'.[127] The background was the variety of measures adopted by Member States to restrict or ban short selling in securities for fear that such practices could create systemic risks: the Regulation harmonises such rules in order to promote the proper functioning of the internal market, and its legal base is uncontroversially Article 114 TFEU. But its Article 28 grants powers to the European Securities and Markets Authority to intervene directly in the market in defined and exceptional circumstances. The United Kingdom challenged this provision and found a willing ally in Advocate General Jääskinen, who believed that Article 28 did not amount to harmonisation but instead the replacement of national decision making by EU level decision making. So he thought resort to Article 352 TFEU was necessary. Not so the Court. The Court, in an astonishingly brief analysis which ignores the nuanced Opinion of its Advocate General, asserted that the preconditions for reliance on Article 114 were met, and dismissed the United Kingdom's objections. The lesson is that the Court's ruling in *European Cooperative Society* requires that there be 'harmonisation' before Article 114 may provide a valid basis for an EU measure (as well as a contribution to the functioning of the internal market), and that a proposal such as that for the CESL is suspect, but that this limit to Article 114 is only as sturdy as the Court chooses to make it.

132; also N. Reich, 'EU Strategies in Finding the Optimal Consumer Law Instrument' (2012) 8 *European Review of Contract Law* 1. For comment before the 2011 proposal was released see P. Kuipers, 'The Legal Basis for a European Optional Instrument' (2011) 19 *European Review of Private Law* 545; J. Rutgers, 'European Competence and a European Civil Code, a Common Frame of Reference or an Optional Instrument' in A. Hartkamp et al. (eds.), *Towards a European Civil Code*, 4th ed., Wolters Kluwer, Alphen aan den Rijn 2011, Ch. 13, pp. 311–332. See also K. Gutman, *The Constitutional Foundations of European Contract Law: A Comparative Analysis*, OUP, Oxford 2014, pp. 360–376.

127 Case C-270/12, *United Kingdom v Council and Parliament* judgment of 22 January 2014.

3.18. CONCLUSION

Only a short conclusion is required. Article 114 TFEU is by far the most significant basis for EU legislative action that affects contracts and contract law even though it is not explicitly addressed to contract and contract law at all. It is functionally driven, focused on the project to complete the internal market. In practice, if not in principle, Article 114 strains the limits of EU competence which are promised to exist by Article 5 TEU, which contains the principle of conferral. Contracts and contract law represent one instance of this structural trend in EU law. The internal market as a legal concept is strikingly empowering and it therefore grants to Article 114 exactly this feature. It is difficult to mount a successful *constitutional* challenge to reliance on Article 114 TFEU and moreover, this threshold crossed, the EU enjoys legitimate access to a wide range of factors which properly inform its re-regulatory techniques and choices.

CHAPTER 4

THEMES AND PRINCIPLES IN THE EU'S CONTRACT LAW *ACQUIS*

4.1. INTRODUCTION

The EU's legislative *acquis* affecting contracts and contract law is constructed in line with the constitutionally generous approach mapped in the previous chapter.

Free movement law opens up the internal market by releasing contractual autonomy from the restrictive effect of regulatory barriers to cross-border trading freedom. Then that contractual autonomy is conditioned by controls in the name of competition law. This was covered in Chapter 2. But the limits of free movement law, represented by the available scope to justify barriers to inter-State trade, are also the limits of the internal market as a project built exclusively on deregulation of national markets. Where barriers to inter-State trade survive testing against the standards set by free movement law, progress to the creation of an internal market depends on their (partial or total) replacement by EU-level rules. This is harmonisation. It is the legislative supplement to the judicially driven process of market-making that is founded on the non-absolute requirements of free movement law. Chapter 3 examined this process, and it showed that harmonisation entails deregulation too, in the sense that a multiplicity of diverse national rules are boiled down to a single common rule, set at EU level. But there is a common rule, so the process is deregulatory but simultaneously re-regulatory, in the sense that the EU takes over the responsibility to regulate the market that was previously the preserve of the Member States, performing that task in divergent fashions. In this sense legislative harmonisation has a dual function – both to secure the integration of the markets (by establishing a *common* rule) but also to set the terms according to which conduct shall be (re-)regulated within that integrated market (by establishing a common *rule*). Chapter 3 explained that this dual function is commanded by the Treaty, especially Articles 12, 114(3), 168(1) and 169(1) TFEU, and the Charter of Fundamental Rights, especially Articles 35, 37 and 38, and moreover it has been relied on in a legally significant way by the Court in determining that harmonisation properly possesses this dual function. So the Court in the first *Tobacco Advertising* case did not deny that public health policy and concern for consumer protection may legitimately inform the shaping of the harmonisation programme – quite the reverse. The Court insisted that such concerns form a constituent part of the EU's other policies, including the project to complete the internal market pursued through the adoption of measures of legislative harmonisation.[1] Provided that the measure crosses the threshold for invocation of Article 114, which demands that it shall make a sufficient contribution to improving the functioning of the internal market, the EU legislature cannot be prevented from relying on that legal basis on the ground that protection of public health or consumers is 'a decisive factor in the choices to be made'.[2]

Therefore legislative harmonisation has a promiscuously wide reach. Anything that is or is likely to be the subject of regulation at national level may be subjected to the discipline of harmonisation provided only that that actual or potential intervention in the market at national level may cause harm to the establishment or functioning of the internal market. Harmonisation as a legislative competence is not sector-specific: it is functionally driven by the dictates of the internal market. And once the market-making competence is triggered, the EU has broad scope to make a choice about the preferred content, style and intensity of the harmonised regime.

Contract law is simply one area where the EU's programme of harmonisation bites deep into national regulatory autonomy and causes its re-shaping. But it is the direct concern of this book. This chapter examines harmonisation which affects contract formation, which primarily concerns consumer contracting; content and enforceability, which again focuses on consumer contracting; 'regulatory contract law', which is taken to cover matters such as the regulation of advertising, unfair commercial practices and financial services; passenger law; energy law; public procurement law; and worker protection, labour market regulation and social policy more broadly. None of these categories is clear-edged. But this is of itself illuminating. Harmonisation does not proceed according to treatment of clearly defined and isolated chunks of national law. Article 114 is neither written nor structured nor applied in this way. The empowering concept is the internal market, so *any* national measure, irrespective of its form or category, may be subjected to the discipline of harmonisation where diverse national practices in the field harm the pursuit of the internal market.

The aim of this chapter is not to provide a detailed nuts-and-bolts account of the content of the legislative *acquis*. That is the subject of ample sector-specific literature, which is the subject of citation where appropriate throughout this

1 Case C-376/98, *Germany v Parliament and Council* [2000] ECR I-8419, paras. 78, 88; see also Case C-380/03, *Germany v Parliament and Council* [2006] ECR I-11573, paras. 39, 40.

2 Case C-376/98, *Germany v Parliament and Council* [2000] ECR I-8419, para. 88; Case C-380/03, *Germany v Parliament and Council* [2006] ECR I-11573, para. 38. See Chapter 3.8.

chapter as a means to guide the way to further exploration of the density of the *acquis*. This chapter is ostentatiously selective. Its aim is to emphasise the breadth and depth of the EU's legislative *acquis* that affects contract law directly or indirectly and to show how this flows, sometimes not entirely persuasively, from the constitutional commitment to the concept of the internal market as a foundation stone. The chapter has four themes and each is used in turn to explain the shaping of the categories that are used for descriptive purposes. The chapter's conclusion draws together these four themes.

4.2. FOUR THEMES

The first two themes around which this chapter is structured follow clearly and immediately from the examination provided in the previous chapter. The first theme is competence. The issue is how the quest to improve the functioning of the internal market, defined in Article 26 TFEU and to which the EU is constitutionally committed by Article 3(3) TEU, both limits and empowers the EU to adopt measures of legislative harmonisation. But, as already articulated in Chapter 3, it is the empowering rather than the limiting dimension that shines more brightly in the *acquis*. The second theme is content and re-regulatory choices. As Chapter 3 shows, once the threshold requiring an adequate contribution to the EU's internal market is crossed, the EU enjoys a broad scope in its choice of the content of the common regime. Indeed the Treaty and the Charter both mandate recognition of and respect for certain regulatory values, such as a high level of consumer protection. The *acquis* vividly demonstrates this. These first two themes focus on, in short, the 'dual function' of harmonisation: its deregulatory and (re-)regulatory credentials.

This chapter takes as its third theme one which was only hinted at in the previous chapter. That is the role of the Court. The previous chapter insisted on the importance of the Court's judgments in setting the terms of the scope of legislative harmonisation in the light of the sparsely written and incrementally developed provisions of the Treaty and also in determining questions of validity in the light of the principles of law set by the Treaty and the Charter. This chapter adds in treatment of the interpretative role played by the Court. The Court regularly receives preliminary references from national courts pursuant to the Article 267 TFEU procedure in which it is asked to interpret provisions of the legislative *acquis*. In performing its interpretative role the Court draws on Articles of the Treaty and the Charter, including those directing pursuit of a high level of consumer protection, just as it has done in cases relating to questions of validity which were addressed in Chapter 3, where it accepts that a decisive factor in a measure of harmonisation may legitimately be suppression of particular practices in the name of consumer or health protection, provided only that the measure overall makes a contribution to the functioning of the internal market.[3] A simple example is provided by the Court's view that it is a general principle that derogations from EU rules for the protection of consumers must be interpreted strictly.[4]

In part the involvement of the Court reflects the inevitability of the dual function of harmonisation. Once the legislature has adopted rules, it falls to the Court to interpret their proper scope and meaning. So where national contract law has been subjected to the discipline of legislative harmonisation, with the consequence that the EU has assumed the responsibility to shape contract law, the Court of Justice, asked to do its job by providing interpretation of phrases and concepts contained in these measures, is accordingly transformed into a court with a role to play in developing contract law.

Within the material scope of a measure there is a normal expectation that in the absence of contrary provision it is not national law but rather EU law that shall provide the source of interpretation. Because of the need for a uniform application of Union law there shall be an autonomous and uniform interpretation throughout the Union, having regard to the context of the provision and the objective pursued by the legislation in question.[5] This represents an important claim to be able to discern a distinctively 'Europeanised' method of interpretation. It means that there is a sort of 'EU legal language', distinct from Member States' own specific legal languages.[6] The Commission embedded this basic approach into the inquiry into the EU's role in contract law which it launched in its first Communication on European Contract Law, released in July 2001.[7]

The Court's job is sometimes straightforward and sometimes it is not very interesting. So, for example, its conclusion that inter-State educational exchanges, during which the student stays with a host family free of charge for several months, do not fall within the scope of the Package Travel Directive is doubtless of value to travel agents specialising in educational exchanges, but is scarcely an enticing glimpse of an emergent European contract law methodology.[8] But the case law, examined in this chapter in a selective manner which is nevertheless designed to capture the typical trends, sometimes makes sterner demands of the Court, and sometimes the case law is not only very

---

3 e.g. Case C-380/03, *Germany v Parliament and Council* [2006] ECR I-11573. See Chapter 3.8.

4 e.g. Case C-481/99, *Heininger* [2001] ECR I-9945, para. 31; Case C-203/99, *Henning Veedfald* [2001] ECR I-3569, para. 15.

5 e.g. Case 327/82, *Ekro* [1984] ECR 107, para. 11; Case C-287/98, *Linster* [2000] ECR I-6917, para. 43; Case C-170/03, *Feron* [2005] ECR I-2299, para. 26; Case C-343/13, *Modelo Continente Hipermercados SA* judgment of 5 March 2015, para. 27. The approach may be traced back to Case 75/63, *Hoekstra* [1964] ECR 347.

6 J. Baaij, *Legal Integration and Language Diversity: the Case for Source-Oriented EU Translation*, PhD thesis, Amsterdam 2015.

7 COM (2001) 398, para. 34. See Chapter 3.10.

8 Case C-237/97, *AFS Intercultural Programs Finland* [1999] ECR I-825.

interesting indeed, it is also surprisingly bold in its assertion of the true reach of adopted legislation. The most prominent element in the Court's interpretative approach is an assumption favourable to the protection of the weaker party. For example, in *Oceano Grupo Editorial SA v Rocio Murciano Quintero* the Court concluded that Directive 93/13 on unfair terms 'is based on the idea that the consumer is in a weak position vis-à-vis the seller or supplier, as regards both his bargaining power and his level of knowledge'.[9] As a measure adopted under Article 95 EC – now Article 114 TFEU – the Directive is targeted at improving the functioning of the internal market but it also asserts at EU level a (harmonised) plan of consumer protection. This, as will be shown, has tempted the Court to use its interpretative role amplify the scope of measures of harmonisation beyond that which might be anticipated from a textual inspection. The Court does not always limit itself to the explicit terms of a Directive when it is provided with the opportunity to deliver the autonomous and uniform interpretation of Union provisions to which it is wedded. Moreover, the insight that Directives adopted under what is today Article 114 TFEU are concerned with not only integration of markets but also regulation of markets and of contractual autonomy is highlighted still more brightly by the Court's finding that there are rights to seek compensation in the event that a Member State fails to put in place the envisaged protective regime in the event that a consumer or worker suffers as a result of the conduct of his or her contracting partner.[10] This approach is amply supported today by Article 12 TFEU and by Article 38 Charter, both of which commit the EU to a high level of consumer protection, and, in the matter of protection of the worker, by Article 151 TFEU and Title IV of the Charter.

The fourth and final theme running through this chapter concerns themes, principles and policy. It inquires into the validity of the accusation that the EU's legislative *acquis* deserves to be condemned as a patchwork, intervening opportunistically and without plan into national regimes which are in consequence battered out of their historically and carefully constructed shape. The allegation: the internal market as a legal concept to which the EU's intervention is constitutionally wedded damages the integrity of national contract law. There will be no attempt to deny that this critique deserves to be taken seriously. It will however be demonstrated that there are key themes which animate the legislative *acquis* and which ensure that the rules considered in this chapter make a forceful claim to be understood as a system of sorts and moreover one which, despite its constitutional roots in the project to construct an internal market, is concerned with more than simple market liberalisation. Section 4.11 below tries to tie together the threads of this inquiry and Chapter 7,

9 Cases C-240/98 to C-244/98 [2000] ECR I-4941.

10 e.g. Cases C-178/94 et al., *Dillenkofer* [1996] ECR I-4845 (consumer); Cases C-6/90 and C-9/90, *Francovich and Others* [1991] ECR I-5357 (worker).

the book's Conclusion, operates on a broader plane as it seeks to assess the true nature, purpose and effect of the contract law of the internal market.

4.3. CONSUMERS – CONTRACT FORMATION

4.3.1. COMPETENCE

A mixed bag of Directives regulate the formation of contracts between traders and consumers. They are not identical in their detail and, in aggregate, they fall far short of a systematic programme. But they are all measures of harmonisation and so they derive their constitutional legitimacy from the functional objective of improving the functioning of the internal market.

A breathless paragraph is enough to capture the coverage of these measures. The first was Directive 85/577 on protecting the consumer in respect of contracts negotiated away from business premises, the so-called 'Doorstep Selling' Directive.[11] It survived in force for almost thirty years, until it was repealed and replaced by Directive 2011/83 on consumer rights.[12] Directive 90/314 harmonises rules on package travel, package holidays and package tours.[13] This has been replaced by an updated and extended version, Directive 2015/2302, although the deadline for its implementation by the Member States expires only in 2018.[14] The protection of purchasers in respect of certain aspects of contracts relating to the utilisation of immovable property on a timeshare basis was initially the subject of harmonised regulation in accordance with Directive 94/47,[15] which was subsequently replaced by Directive 2008/122 which widened the scope of the regime to protect consumers in respect of certain aspects of timeshare, long-term holiday product, resale and exchange contracts.[16] The market for consumer credit has been the subject of harmonised rules since 1987.[17] They are today contained in Directive 2008/48 on credit agreements for consumers[18] and they are supplemented by rules governing the particular case of mortgage credit.[19] Directive 97/5 on cross-border credit transfers[20] was replaced by Directive 2007/64 on payment services in the internal market.[21] Several

11 [1985] OJ L372/31.
12 [2011] OJ L304/64.
13 [1990] OJ L158/59.
14 [2015] OJ L326/1.
15 [1994] OJ L280/83.
16 [2009] OJ L33/10.
17 Dir. 87/102 [1987] OJ L42/48 amended by Dir. 90/88 [1990] OJ L61/14 and Dir. 98/7 [1998] OJ L101/7.
18 [2008] OJ L133/66, amended by Dir. 2014/17 [2014] OJ L60/34.
19 Dir. 2014/17 [2014] OJ L60/34.
20 [1997] OJ L43/25.
21 [2007] OJ L319/1.

Directives establish harmonised rules which govern the formation of contracts 'at a distance': that is, typically, where electronic means of communication are employed. Directive 97/7 on distance contracts was among the first such measure responding to technological change.[22] It was repealed and replaced with effect from 2014 by Directive 2011/83.[23] Directive 2000/31 addresses electronic commerce[24] and Directive 2002/65 deals with distance marketing of consumer financial services.[25]

These measures exist on a spectrum of constitutional sincerity. Some – a majority – make a perfectly respectable claim to contribute to the functioning of the internal market by replacing national regulatory diversity with a common rule adopted at EU level. Others – a minority – strain the principle of conferral and hint at a commitment to regulation of the market in the interest of the consumer *per se*.

Timeshare, for example, is a market with a heavy bias towards cross-border purchasing: north European consumers of such property rights in Spain and Portugal, in particular, are common, and it is at least a plausible starting point that diversity of legal regulation operates as an obstacle to the development of the market. The original measure in the field, Directive 94/47, takes as its legal base what is today Article 114 TFEU and its Preamble is based on exactly this case.

> 'Whereas the disparities between national legislations on contracts relating to the purchase of the right to use one or more immovable properties on a timeshare basis are likely to create barriers to the proper operation of the internal market and distortions of competition and lead to the compartmentalization of national markets'.

This is not unconvincing, yet it is illuminating that it is perfunctory and deficient in empirical evidence. There is no evidence of painstaking concern to substantiate the claim to constitutional legitimacy.

Directive 2008/122, which has superseded Directive 94/47 and updated and extended the harmonised regime, is only a little fuller in its explanation. Its Recital 2 states that 'the existing regulatory gaps create appreciable distortions of competition and cause serious problems for consumers, thus hindering the smooth functioning of the internal market'. It asserts the need for a renovated Directive, and, referring to the increasingly important role in the economies of the Member States played by tourism, it adds that 'greater growth and productivity in the timeshare and long-term holiday product industries should be encouraged by adopting certain common rules'.

---

22 [1997] OJ L144/19.
23 [2011] OJ L304/64.
24 [2000] OJ L178/1.
25 [2002] OJ L271/16, amended by Dir 2007/64 [2007] OJ L319/1.

Credit is a market where a cross-border dimension is much less obvious or likely, at least on anything other than a small scale. The original Directive, Directive 87/102, noted in its Preamble that 'wide differences exist in the laws of the Member States in the field of consumer credit', and that 'these differences of law can lead to distortions of competition between grantors of credit in the common market' and 'have an influence on the free movement of goods and services obtainable by consumers on credit and thus directly affect the functioning of the common market'. It then added in aspirational vein that 'the establishment of a common market in consumer credit would benefit alike consumers, grantors of credit, manufacturers, wholesalers and retailers of goods and providers of services'. Studies of this market continued to show that it remains stubbornly resistant to integration: it is largely national.[26] The current and updated measure, Directive 2008/48, contains a thematically similar insistence in its Preamble on the diversity of legislative treatment at national level and adds in its Recital 4 that:

> 'the de facto and de jure situation resulting from those national differences in some cases leads to distortions of competition among creditors in the Community and creates obstacles to the internal market where Member States have adopted different mandatory provisions more stringent than those provided for in Directive 87/102/EEC. It restricts consumers' ability to make direct use of the gradually increasing availability of cross-border credit. Those distortions and restrictions may in turn have consequences in terms of the demand for goods and services.'

It asserts a need to 'facilitate the emergence of a well-functioning internal market in consumer credit'.[27] It is perfectly plausible to dispute the persisting claim that harmonised legal rules are an effective means to secure the integration of the market for consumer credit by pointing out that almost thirty years of EU legislative intervention appears to have done little to promote cross-border patterns of trade. One might think the market is largely national for good reasons associated with language, culture and preference among consumers for readily accessible local access to justice. Crucially, however, this objection has weak constitutional weight. The threshold for harmonisation is very low, as was demonstrated in Chapter 3. A distortion of competition consequent on regulatory diversity among the Member States must be significant or appreciable, according to the Court,[28] but this is hard to measure and it is plainly hard to

---

26 See generally e.g. J. Devenney and M. Kenny (eds.), *Consumer Credit, Debt and Investment in Europe*, CUP, Cambridge 2012.

27 Recital 7.

28 e.g. Case C-376/98, *Germany v Parliament and Council* [2000] ECR I-8419; Joined Cases C-154/04 and C-155/04, *Alliance for Natural Health and Others* [2005] ECR I-6451; Case C-380/03, *Germany v Parliament and Council* [2006] ECR I-11573; Case C-58/08, *Vodafone Ltd and Others v Secretary of State for Business, Enterprise and Regulatory Reform* [2010] ECR I-4999. See Chapter 3.8.

persuade the Court to disagree with the legislative outcome. The Directives on credit do not seem to make much contribution to the development of an internal market in the sector and therefore they strain the principle of conferral. But whether they in fact break it has never been tested before the Court.

However, occasional measures disclose a legislative claim in support of linkage between harmonisation and the functioning of the internal market which is thoroughly implausible. This is where a hint of constitutional insincerity taints the *acquis*.

Directive 85/577 on 'doorstep selling' was mentioned in the previous chapter as an obvious candidate for constitutionally sceptical assessment in the light of the first *Tobacco Advertising* ruling, which of course post-dates the adoption of the Directive by fully fifteen years.[29] The Directive was based on Article 100 EC (which is now Article 115 TFEU). The Preamble to the Directive states that the practice of doorstep selling is the subject of different rules in different Member States. This is perfectly true. The Preamble proceeds to declare that 'any disparity between such legislation may directly affect the functioning of the common market'. This, by stark contrast, is far from obviously true. The claim is not supported by any evidence nor even any explanation.

The Preamble, which looks very short and thin to eyes accustomed to more recent legislative abundance, proceeds to add reference to the commitments to pursue consumer protection, *inter alia* in respect of doorstep selling, found in the EEC's first two programmes for a consumer protection and information policy, adopted in 1975 and 1981.[30] These had been adopted as part of the consumer-specific development of the more general prevailing political consensus, initiated at the famous Paris Summit of 1972, in favour of developing a more 'human face' for (what was then) the EEC. The Member States had expressed a unanimous political commitment to developing a richer texture to EU policymaking, beyond mere trade integration in the narrow sense. But they had not made any constitutional change: they had not revised the Treaty to reflect and support their ambition. Consumer protection as a legislative competence in its own right would not be added to the Treaties until as late as 1993: it is today Article 169 TFEU, mentioned in Chapter 3.7. In the absence at the time of any formal Treaty revision giving effect to these wider aspirations by extending the list of available legislative competences, harmonisation was used as the chosen route. So unanimity in Council was translated into an empowerment of the EU in the guise of harmonisation. The Doorstep Selling Directive is a clear example of how a constitutionally pure 'market-driven' pedigree which seems to be demanded by the relevant provisions in the Treaty may be muddied by political expediency.[31]

---

29 Case C-376/98, *Germany v Parliament and Council* [2000] ECR I-8419. See Chapter 3.9.

30 [1975] OJ C92/2, [1981] OJ C133/1.

31 S. Weatherill, *EU Consumer Law and Policy*, 2nd ed., Edward Elgar, Cheltenham 2013, Ch. 3.

The principle of conferral contained in Article 5 TEU is thereby subverted. But the Court was never granted the opportunity to review the matter in the context of this measure.

Directive 85/577 has now, as mentioned, been replaced by Directive 2011/83 on consumer rights. Directive 2011/83 similarly asserts its market-making credentials. Its Preamble heralds the virtue of creating 'a single regulatory framework based on clearly defined legal concepts' in order 'to eliminate the barriers stemming from the fragmentation of the rules and to complete the internal market in this area'.[32] Its Recital 5 claims that:

> 'The cross-border potential of contracts negotiated away from business premises (direct selling) is constrained by a number of factors including the different national consumer protection rules imposed upon the industry. Compared with the growth of domestic direct selling over the last few years, in particular in the services sector, for instance utilities, the number of consumers using this channel for cross-border purchases has remained flat. Responding to increased business opportunities in many Member States, small and medium-sized enterprises (including individual traders) or agents of direct selling companies should be more inclined to seek business opportunities in other Member States, in particular in border regions. Therefore the full harmonisation of consumer information and the right of withdrawal in distance and off-premises contracts will contribute to a high level of consumer protection and a better functioning of the business-to-consumer internal market'.

This is less perfunctory than the limp reasoning which supported Directive 85/577. But it cannot set aside real doubt whether diversity between national rules governing doorstep selling truly affects the internal market, Directive 2011/83 makes a better fist of the matter than Directive 85/577, but it still lies on the margins of plausibility. The first *Tobacco Advertising* case could yet claim another victim, were a challenge ever to be launched to the validity of this part of Directive 2011/83's claim to promote the good functioning of the internal market.

In conclusion, the structural fear is that an assertion of competence to harmonise in the service of the internal market which is backed up by sufficient political support in the Commission, Council and Parliament is extremely difficult to resist constitutionally. In the case of contract law this leads to the anxiety that the EU exercises an illegitimate reach, subverting the principle of conferral and, taken to a more general level, tending to erode national preference and diversity in favour of unwished and illegitimate homogeneity. Most of the *acquis* in this area associated with contract formation is not vulnerable to such criticism. But some is.

---

32 Recital 7.

4.3.2. CONTENT AND RE-REGULATORY CHOICES

The legislative output reflects the notion that harmonisation concerns the establishment of common rules designed to promote market integration which also are based on appreciation of the need to determine what shall be the quality of the regulated environment – that, in particular, it shall pursue a high level of consumer protection. For example, the first Recital of Directive 2002/65 on distance marketing of consumer financial services provides that:

> 'It is important, in the context of achieving the aims of the single market, to adopt measures designed to consolidate progressively this market and those measures must contribute to attaining a high level of consumer protection, in accordance with Articles 95 and 153 of the Treaty'.[33]

The cited provisions directing pursuit of a high level of protection are today Articles 114 and 168 TFEU, buttressed by Article 38 of the Charter, and a formula of this type is found in forms that are no more than cosmetically different across the harmonised legislative *acquis* dealing with the formation of contracts with consumers.

The measures put in place common rules which are designed to promote the achievement of an internal market in the areas covered by the EU's measures of harmonisation but they also address the quality of those common rules. The question is whether there are any common features which lend a thematic shape to the EU's choice of re-regulatory techniques, or whether this is truly a patchwork of *ad hoc* political opportunism.[34] In fact, for all the admitted eccentricity of a list that flits from doorstep selling to package travel to credit, these are not just isolated dots of legislative intervention. Thematic connections binding together the *acquis* may be excavated. The marketing practice subject to regulation is typically not prohibited by these measures. Instead the chosen technique typically involves mandatory pre-contractual disclosure of information to consumers plus a chance to think again after the deal is agreed and to withdraw within a defined period of time (the so-called 'cooling-off period').

Timeshare is a typical example. Recital 2 of Directive 94/47 declared that it is sufficient for the harmonised rules 'to cover contractual transactions only with regard to those aspects that relate to information on the constituent parts of contracts, the arrangements for communicating such information and the procedures and arrangements for cancellation and withdrawal'. And the body of the Directive contained detailed rules on precisely what is involved. This

---

33 [2002] OJ L271/16.

34 Research into the patterns of supply and demand of harmonised EU consumer contract law is remarkably under-developed: for useful preliminary work see E. O'Connor, 'The limits of contract law harmonisation' (2012) 33 *European Journal of Law and Economics* 505.

is now addressed in Directive 2008/122. Its Article 4 covers pre-contractual information. It provides that '[i]n good time before the consumer is bound by any contract or offer, the trader shall provide the consumer, in a clear and comprehensible manner, with accurate and sufficient information', the content of which is then carefully set out by the Directive. The stipulated information is to be provided free of charge by the trader on paper or on another durable medium which is easily accessible to the consumer. Moreover, Member States shall ensure that the information 'is drawn up in the language or one of the languages of the Member State in which the consumer is resident or a national, at the choice of the consumer, provided it is an official language of the [Union]'.

Article 5 deals with the contract itself. Member States shall ensure that the contract is in writing, on paper or on another durable medium, and drawn up in the language or one of the languages of the Member State in which the consumer is resident or a national, at the choice of the consumer, provided it is an official language of the Union.

Then the Directive proceeds to stipulate a right of withdrawal in defined circumstances and within a defined window of time.

The focus is heavily on transparency, under an assumption that the consumer will be able to make a more informed choice thanks to the disclosure of information, while also ensuring back-stop protection guaranteed by the right of withdrawal for the consumer who has not thought carefully enough in advance and wants to change his or her mind. The Directive does not address the content of the contract. That is left to the market. In this sense the exercise of private autonomy is placed within regulatory boundaries by the EU requirements of information disclosure and withdrawal rights, but its substantive contractual core is left unaffected. This technique is typical across the several measures of harmonisation addressing the formation of consumer contracts. True, the precise detail varies measure by measure, sometimes for plausibly good reasons that are sensitive to the particular sectoral context, but in other circumstances simply because of legislative inattention.[35] This is a matter to which the Commission has paid attention in an attempt to clean up and streamline the *acquis*. The constitutional context of its review, which was initiated in 2001,[36] was considered in Chapter 3.10. Its February 2003 'Action Plan on a more coherent European Contract Law' identified a string of inconsistencies and inadequacies within the *acquis*, including divergent rules governing the right of withdrawal, overlaps between measures, missing or divergent definitions, as well as concern for uneven implementation at national level.[37] Overall the review has so far not been very successful. The tortured process that led to the adoption of Directive

35 See e.g. P. Rekaiti and R. Van den Bergh, 'Cooling-off Periods in the Consumer Laws of the EC Member States: a Comparative Law and Economics Approach' (2001) 23 *Journal of Consumer Policy* 371.

36 COM (2001) 398.

37 COM (2003) 68, paras. 14–51 and Annex.

2011/83, which despite the Commission's best efforts achieves only a modest renovation of the *acquis*, was mentioned at Chapter 3.10 and is explored more fully in Chapter 6.6. It reveals much about the entrenched political blockages to reform.[38]

It would mislead to suggest that none of these Directives touches the content of the contract. Directive 2011/83, for example, is predominantly concerned with the right to information and the right of withdrawal applicable to contracts that fall within its material scope, but it also contains a short Chapter IV, containing six articles and gnomically entitled 'Other Consumer Rights', which include in Article 18 rules governing the time within which delivery should occur, albeit that it is stipulated that the parties may agree otherwise, and in Article 20 rules on the passing of risk. Directive 2015/2302 focuses on the provision of information to consumers of package travel, but also addresses alteration of price and other terms under the contract as well as responsibility for non-performance.[39] However, such direct intervention is relatively uncommon and, where it occurs, it is typically carefully confined: information disclosure remains the dominant regulatory technique. The fact that the content of contracts is affected only occasionally and usually tangentially accentuates the *ad hoc* patchwork nature of the EU's role.

4.3.3. THE COURT OF JUSTICE

Sometimes inspection of the Court's case law is not interesting, and it will not detain the intellectually curious contract lawyer. One example was given above. The Court was asked in a preliminary reference whether inter-State educational exchanges during which the student stays with a host family free of charge for several months fall within the scope of the Package Travel Directive. It ruled that they do not.[40] In similar vein the Court ruled that under the 'e-commerce' Directive (2000/31) a supplier must provide a means for the recipient to make contact rapidly other than by e-mail – but that this does not have to be by telephone.[41] Such rulings are of course important at the level of detail and they help to resolve particular disputes which have arisen before national courts. They are especially important where an EU harmonised measure is of a 'maximum' rather than 'minimum' nature and therefore, since national variation within

---

38 On what needs (still!) to be done, see H. Eidenmüller et al., 'Towards a revision of the consumer acquis' (2011) 48 *Common Market Law Review* 1077; E. Van Schagen, 'The Hidden Potential of Regulatory Impact Assessments (RIAs) in the Private Law Acquis' (2014) 22 *European Review of Private Law* 69.

39 Arts. 10, 11 and 13 Dir. 2015/2302 [2015] OJ L326/1.

40 Case C-237/97, *AFS Intercultural Programs Finland* [1999] ECR I-825.

41 Case C-298/07, *Bundesverband der Verbraucherzentralen v deutsche internet versicherung AG* [2008] ECR I-7841.

its material scope is impermissible, the EU rules, properly interpreted, are the exclusive basis on which to decide the outcome of the dispute.[42]

However, the Court's case law is in some respects more dynamic than this rather static description of a technical process of interpretation suggests. Some of the Directives contain remarkably open-textured notions, the elaboration of which has in effect been the subject of a delegation by the EU legislature to the Court of Justice. This sometimes makes the Court's job thoroughly awkward, but it also provides it with flexibility and power. Particularly good examples are provided by 'unfairness' under Directives 93/13 and 2005/29, which are considered below (sections 4.4 and 4.5). In some instances (but by no means all), the Court itself has taken an aggressively broad view of the scope of concepts and rules that fall within the scope of the harmonised regime and the autonomous interpretation of which therefore belong to it.[43] *Simone Leitner* stands as an atypical but powerful example.[44]

The litigation in *Simone Leitner* concerned Directive 90/314, which harmonises rules governing package travel. According to its Preamble, national laws in the field 'show many disparities' which 'gives rise to obstacles to the freedom to provide services in respect of packages and distortions of competition amongst operators established in different Member States'. It follows the classic 'dual function' model of harmonisation, and introduces at EU level a common rule which protects the consumer by stipulating that he or she shall receive compensation in defined circumstances. In *Simone Leitner* the Court was asked questions about the type of damage for which the consumer is entitled to receive compensation. The Directive's Preamble declares that the organiser and/or retailer 'should be liable for the damage resulting for the consumer from failure to perform or improper performance of the contract unless the defects in the performance of the contract are attributable neither to any fault of theirs nor to that of another supplier of services'. But the body of the Directive does not spell out the type of damage for which the consumer is entitled to claim compensation. In particular, it fails to address the question whether both personal injury and non-material loss, such as a thwarted expectation of an enjoyable holiday, are covered by the Directive. Article 5 is the only provision of the Directive that comes even close. It states that '[i]n the matter of damage other than personal injury resulting from the non-performance or improper performance of the services involved in the package, the Member States may allow compensation to be limited under the contract'. One might assume from this that the Directive requires compensation for personal injury, but that the matter of non-material loss falls to be decided under national law. But this was not the Court's conclusion. In *Simone Leitner* it held that Article 5 is to be interpreted as meaning that the Directive implicitly recognises

42 Chapter 6 examines the maximum/minimum debate.
43 Cf. above n. 5.
44 Case C-168/00 [2002] ECR I-2631.

the existence of a right to compensation for non-material damage. This, of course, extends the impact of EU law, while curtailing the autonomy permitted to national law. It also improves the position of one party to the contract, the consumer, at the expense of the other, the provider.

How did the Court reach its conclusion? It observed that the Directive's purpose of eliminating disparities between national laws in the area of package holidays pushed in favour of bringing rules governing compensation for non-material damage within its scope, for otherwise distortion caused by legal diversity would persist. Moreover the Court pointed out that compensation for non-material damage arising from the loss of enjoyment of a holiday is of particular importance to consumers.

Of course at one level the Court is completely correct. Its interpretation does strengthen the scope of the harmonised regime while also enhancing the protection of contracting consumers. The Court's reasoning is built on the 'dual purpose' of harmonisation – both market integration and regulatory protection – and it treats both ends as advanced by interpreting the Directive to confer on consumers a right to compensation for non-material damage resulting from defective performance. But the objection is that this is to push beyond judicial interpretation and instead to assert a judicial function to embroider a carefully agreed and materially limited legislative text. The Court's reasoning is deficient in respect for the limits of the EU legislative text and for the autonomy of national contract law. This is judicial competence creep: the ruling adjusts the balance between courts and legislatures in favour of the former (at national and at EU levels).[45]

Seen from within the EU system, the Court's approach could be understood as an exercise in gap-filling. It addresses a matter left ambiguous in the legislative text. Seen from within national legal orders there was no gap: what the EU text did not address was dealt with under national law. But now the matter has been wrested away from national law and 'Europeanised'. It is here that the Court is most vulnerable to the accusation that its interpretative ambition undermines the balance between EU and national law.

Furthermore the Court's approach generates a degree of legal uncertainty. Does, for example, the approach to non-material damage revealed in *Simone Leitner* dictate the approach taken beyond the field of package travel? It seems that this does not follow. In *Henning Veenfeld* the Court concluded that under the Product Liability Directive, Directive 85/374, which is a measure of tort

---

45 For a critical account of the Court's sense of adventure see annotation of the case by W.-H. Roth (2003) 40 *Common Market Law Review* 937, and see much more generally L. Niglia, 'Beyond Enchantment – The Possibility of a New European Private Law' (2009) 28 *Yearbook of European Law* 60. The revised Directive, Dir. 2015/2302 [2015] OJ L326/1, retains a provision similar to that at stake in *Leitner* (Art. 14(4)) but does not address the matter of non-material damage in its text – however, its Preamble declares in recital 34 that '[c]ompensation should also cover non-material damage.'

law harmonisation rather than contract law,[46] it is solely for national law to deal with reparation of non-material damage.[47] Article 9 of the Directive defines damage, and is explicitly stated to operate 'without prejudice to national provisions relating to non-material damage'. So an explicit legislative reservation seems to be required to curtail the Court's sense of interpretative ambition.

There is certainly a risk in misrepresenting the trends in the Court's case law. Most of its rulings do not strain the edges of its function in the way that *Simone Leitner* does. The ruling is exceptional. However, it reveals that ambiguity in legislative texts – and in EU law the complex process of negotiation combined with the inevitability of quirks of translation within different language texts of legislation makes ambiguity unavoidable – may tempt the Court to draw on the dual function of harmonisation, rooted in both market integration and market (re-)regulation, to pursue an adventurous approach to interpretation.

4.3.4. THEMES, PRINCIPLES AND POLICY

The emphasis on pre-contractual mandatory disclosure of information combined with the grant to the consumer of a chance to think again after the fact is the *leitmotif* of the Directives considered in this section. Only exceptionally do the Directives concern directly the content of a contract. This regulatory technique reveals a preference for transparency in the market and an associated belief in the virtue of the 'informed consumer'. This is more about choice than rights. The consumer is trusted to react to the supplied information and the right of withdrawal in a way that promotes a more competitive market. Plainly one may readily doubt whether some, even most, consumers are really capable of processing and understanding the information and rights on offer and so too whether it is even rational for them to spend time doing so. This breeds scepticism about a regulatory model which champions access, choice and consumer information.[48] On the other hand, it

---

46 [1985] OJ L210/29.

47 Case C-203/99 [2001] ECR I-3569.

48 See e.g. G. Howells, 'The potential and limits of consumer empowerment by information' (2005) 32 *Journal of Law and Society* 349; F. Rischkowsky and T. Döring, 'Consumer Policy in a Market Economy: Considerations from the Perspective of the Economics of Information, the New Institutional Economics as well as Behavioural Economics' (2008) 31 *Journal of Consumer Policy* 285; C. Willett and M. Morgan-Taylor, 'Recognising the limits of transparency in EU consumer law' in J. Devenney and M. Kenny (eds.), *European Consumer Protection: Theory and Practice*, CUP, Cambridge 2012, Ch. 9. See also more generally S. Grundmann, W. Kerber and S. Weatherill (eds.), *Party Autonomy and the Role of Information in the Internal Market*, De Gruyter, Berlin 2001.

is arguable that rights of withdrawal in particular might induce opportunistic behaviour by consumers.[49] This does not seem very plausible: most consumers are only dimly aware of the rights they enjoy,[50] so few will be smart or sneaky enough to seek to abuse them. But the very fact that such debates are engaged confirms the EU as a thematically driven policymaker. A bolder critique of the EU's preferred approaches would hold that, given consumers' often fragile awareness of information which has been disclosed and to which they are supposed to react, the EU measures are sham corrections to informational and economic asymmetry or, still worse, that they legitimate pernicious commercial practices by falsely suggesting their correction has been achieved. So, for example, the regime governing consumer credit has been criticised for its central concern to open up access to credit in circumstances where this will certainly generate a degree of over-indebtedness among consumers.[51] Even the sketchiest understanding of global trends over the past decade confirms that an inadequately regulated consumer credit market may have deeply damaging social and economic consequences.[52] The less persuaded one is that a model based on information disclosure is adequate to address the risk of harm, the more one tends towards mandatory substantive rules.[53] However, intervention is not cost-free: one must take into account that regulatory intervention to protect a group of identifiably vulnerable consumers may impose costs on other groups of consumers, including the risk of inhibiting supply.[54] The purpose of this book is not to take a stand in this debate: rather the point is, again, is to emphasise that a constitutionally informed inspection of the EU's legislative *acquis* draws one unavoidably into questions of preferred design and political choice. The pattern of harmonised rules reveals an incremental and relatively unsystematic pattern in this area, but there are tangible re-regulatory themes within it.

---

49 M. Hoeppner, 'The unintended consequence of doorstep consumer protection: surprise, reciprocation and consistency' (2014) 38 *European Journal of Law and Economics* 247. See also H. Eidenmüller, 'Why withdrawal rights?' (2011) 7 *European Review of Contract Law* 1.

50 See J. Luzak, 'To Withdraw or Not to Withdraw? Evaluation of the mandatory right of withdrawal in consumer distance selling contracts taking into account its behavioural effects on consumers' (2014) 37 *Journal of Consumer Policy* 91.

51 See I. Ramsay, 'Changing Policy Paradigms of EU Consumer Credit and Debt Regulation' in D. Leczykiewicz and S. Weatherill (eds.), *The Images of the Consumer in EU Law*, Bloomsbury/Hart/IECL, Oxford 2016, Ch. 5, pp. 159–182.

52 See H. Micklitz and I. Domurath (eds.), *Consumer Debt and Social Exclusion in Europe*, Ashgate, Farnham 2015.

53 Cf. e.g. O. Cherednychenko, 'Freedom of Contract in the Post-Crisis Era: Quo Vadis?' (2014) 10 *European Review of Contract Law* 390.

54 e.g. S. Grundmann, 'Targeted Consumer Protection' in D. Leczykiewicz and S. Weatherill (eds.), *The Images of the Consumer in EU Law*, Bloomsbury/Hart/IECL, Oxford 2016, Ch. 9, pp. 223–244.

4.4. CONSUMERS – CONTENT AND ENFORCEABILITY OF CONTRACTS

4.4.1. COMPETENCE

A pair of Directives are more ambitious than those addressed in the previous section. Directive 93/13 prohibits unfair terms in consumer contracts.[55] Directive 99/44 on certain aspects of the sale of consumer goods and associated guarantees imports standards of required quality into consumer contracts.[56] These measures go beyond contract formation and information disclosure. Instead they assert control over the content of the bargain. Most of the Directives concerning contract formation examined in the previous section are probably safely relegated to footnotes in national contract law textbooks, if they are mentioned at all. Not so the two measures addressed in this section.[57]

The constitutionally striking feature of these two Directives is that they emphasise a contribution to the functioning of the internal market from both the supply side and the demand side. Directive 93/13 asserts in its Preamble that 'the laws of Member States relating to the terms of contract between the seller of goods or supplier of services, on the one hand, and the consumer of them, on the other hand, show many disparities'. This is doubtless true. Its Preamble then asserts that in consequence 'distortions of competition may arise amongst the sellers and suppliers, notably when they sell and supply in other Member States' and also that 'consumers do not know the rules of law which, in Member States other than their own, govern contracts for the sale of goods or services' and that 'this lack of awareness may deter them from direct transactions for the purchase of goods or services in another Member State.' Harmonising rules prohibiting unfair terms will, it is claimed, generate intensified cross-competition and an improved internal market, but the driving perception is that both traders and consumers will be encouraged thereby to treat the market as unfragmented by national frontiers.

Directive 99/44 does not simply cut and paste this reasoning, but it follows a similar line. Its Preamble asserts the existence of legislative diversity among the laws of the Member States concerning the sale of consumer goods, and draws from this that 'competition between sellers may be distorted'. But it too stresses the place of 'consumers who are keen to benefit from the large market by purchasing goods in Member States other than their State of residence [who]

---

55 [1993] OJ L95/29.

56 [1999] OJ L171/12.

57 So, e.g., E. Peel, *Treitel on the Law of Contract*, 14th ed., Sweet and Maxwell, London 2015 contains several references to Dirs. 93/13 and 99/44, but of the measures mentioned in section 4.3 it mentions only Dirs. 2000/31, 2002/65 and 2011/83; M. Furmston, *Cheshire, Fifoot and Furmston's Law of Contract*, 16th ed., OUP, Oxford 2012 mentions only Dir. 93/13.

play a fundamental role in the completion of the internal market' and argues that 'the creation of a common set of minimum rules of consumer law, valid no matter where goods are purchased within the Community, will strengthen consumer confidence and enable consumers to make the most of the internal market'. In fact the Preamble inverts the order: consumer protection comes first in the motivation, followed by the pursuit of the internal market.

Reliance on the notion that legislative diversity causes distortion of competition and an absence of confidence is particularly significant where the national practices that are subject to harmonisation would not readily be treated as obstacles to trade within the meaning of Articles 34 or 56 TFEU. This is likely to be the case where national measures on unfair terms and quality guarantees are concerned. Provided they apply without discrimination on the basis of the origin of goods, services, traders and consumers, they probably escape the reach of Articles 34 and 56 TFEU as interpreted by the Court.[58] The claim made in the motivation for these Directives holds that in the absence of harmonised legal regulation the internal market will be deficient: what is required is a confidence-building bloc of EU rules, even where the areas of national practice subject to that harmonisation would not have been direct obstacles to cross-border trade.

This, then, is to grant a wider reach to Article 114 than to Articles 34 and 56. There is ample academic support for this view. It has been noted that if Article 114 could be directed only at barriers to trade within the meaning of Articles 34 or 56 its vigour in promoting the smooth functioning of the internal market would be severely compromised. So Article 114 needs to be interpreted more broadly in order to make good Article 3(3) TEU's commitment to the creation of an internal market in the EU.[59] The obvious objection to treating the competence to legislate pursuant to Article 114 as broader in scope than the control exercised over national measures pursuant to free movement law is that it pushes Article 114 towards a scope that is in practice unlimited: how can one contradict a claim to legislate in order to promote confidence in the market?[60] As explored in Chapter 3, the retort seems to be that this breadth is exactly the design planned by the Treaty. The Court has never explicitly endorsed this broad understanding of the scope of Article 114. It has, however, acknowledged this line of reasoning, In *Simone Leitner*, which concerned compensation for damage under the Package Travel Directive, it noted that the Directive was designed

---

58 Especially Cases C-267/91 and C-268/91, *Keck and Mithouard* [1993] ECR I-6097. See Chapter 2.4.

59 See e.g. A. Von Bogdandy and J. Bast, 'The EU's vertical order of competences: the current law and proposals for its reform' (2002) 39 *Common Market Law Review* 227; G. Davies, 'Can selling arrangements be harmonised?' (2005) 30 *European Law Review* 370; J. Basedow, 'A Common Contract Law for the Common Market' (1996) 33 *Common Market Law Review* 1169.

60 e.g. M. Ludwigs, 'Harmonisierung des Schuldvertragsrechts in Europa – Zur Rechtweite der gemeinschaftsrechtlichen Zuständigkeit für eine Europäisierung des Privatrechts' [2006] *Europarecht* 370.

to eliminate disparities between national laws 'which are liable to give rise to distortions of competition between operators established in different Member States' and that the particular issues at hand, diversity in the scope of obligations to provide compensation for non-material damage, 'would cause significant distortions of competition'.[61] A State placing such an obligation on traders operating on its territory would probably not be obstructing inter-State trade within the meaning of Articles 34 or 56 TFEU, provided the obligation applied equally to all traders irrespective of their origin. But the Court seems prepared to treat the fact of diversity as a significant distortion of competition, and so the competence to harmonise pursuant to Article 114 is triggered.

This, then, is probably the way in which to conclude that Directives 93/13 and 99/44 are constitutionally valid as measures of legislative harmonisation designed to improve the functioning of the EU's internal market.

4.4.2. CONTENT AND RE-REGULATORY CHOICES

Both Directive 93/13 and Directive 99/44 fit comfortably into the model of EU legislative harmonisation which was explained in the previous chapter. They are presented as means to improve the functioning of the internal market by replacing existing legislative diversity among the Member States with a single common EU rule, albeit one that is pitched at a minimum level. But that inevitably requires the EU to engage with questions associated with regulatory design. National regimes are being replaced – but by what, precisely? This is the re-regulatory dynamic which is endemic to legislative harmonisation. It is the 'dual function' of harmonisation.

The point is well captured by Directive 93/13's Preamble. It declares that 'it is the responsibility of the Member States to ensure that contracts concluded with consumers do not contain unfair terms'. Harmonisation re-allocates that responsibility to EU level. So harmonisation is called for in order to improve the functioning of the internal market, but that in turn demands that the EU choose a regulatory model, which is to forbid unfair terms falling within the material scope of the Directive. National consumer law is thereby adjusted by the EU's harmonisation programme and more generally the EU becomes a factor in the pattern of lawmaking provoked by the widely visible scepticism about the virtue of permitting unrestricted contractual freedom in relationships that are economically imbalanced. It is in this sense a matter of consumer protection, and the Preamble to Directive 93/13 cites the Community programmes for a consumer protection and information policy which also appear in the Preamble to Directive 85/577 on Doorstep Selling, as explained above (section 4.3.1). But it is also a matter of building an internal market.

---

61 Case C-168/00 [2002] ECR I-2631, paras. 20, 21.

Article 3 of Directive 93/13 provides that a contractual term which has not been individually negotiated shall be regarded as unfair if, contrary to the requirement of good faith, it causes a significant imbalance in the parties' rights and obligations arising under the contract, to the detriment of the consumer.

Article 6 directs that unfair terms used in a contract concluded with a consumer by a seller or supplier shall not be binding on the consumer and that the contract shall continue to bind the parties upon those terms if it is capable of continuing in existence without the unfair terms. In addition Article 7 envisages public enforcement of the prohibition, but the point of Article 6 is that it makes clear that Member States must equip ordinary courts dealing with the enforcement of contracts with the power to refuse to treat unfair terms as binding on the consumer. It is therefore everyday judicial practice to decide whether a term is unfair, in so far as the dispute in question falls within the scope of Directive 93/13.

The Annex to the Directive contains an indicative and non-exhaustive list of the terms which may be regarded as unfair. The aim is to elucidate just what the test of unfairness embraces. The Annex contains a list of terms, (a)–(q), which might be treated as unfair depending on the circumstances. It is, then, a 'grey list', rather than 'black list': the terms on the list are not inevitably to be treated as unfair. One might in practice feel pessimistic about persuading a judge that a term that appears on the list is in fact fair, but it is at least in principle possible. The grey list is characterised by particular thematic anxieties. The types of term that attract particular suspicion are those that exclude the liability of the supplier,[62] impose disproportionately onerous obligations on the consumer,[63] attribute unilateral decision-making power to the supplier,[64] and more generally are tainted by intransparency.[65] The Court's role is considered more fully below (section 4.4.3), but it is already worth noting here that in *Aziz* it offered a concrete view on how to apply this test. To find an imbalance arising contrary to the requirement of good faith, the national court must assess 'whether the seller or supplier, dealing fairly and equitably with the consumer, could reasonably assume that the consumer would have agreed to such a term in individual contract negotiations'.[66]

Article 3(2) addresses the meaning of individual negotiation. It is only absent such negotiation that review occurs. Roughly put, the concern is to

---

62 e.g. (a) excluding or limiting the legal liability of a seller or supplier in the event of the death of a consumer or personal injury to the latter resulting from an act or omission of that seller or supplier.

63 e.g. (e) requiring any consumer who fails to fulfil his obligation to pay a disproportionately high sum in compensation.

64 e.g. (f) authorising the seller or supplier to dissolve the contract on a discretionary basis where the same facility is not granted to the consumer.

65 e.g. (i) irrevocably binding the consumer to terms with which he had no real opportunity of becoming acquainted before the conclusion of the contract.

66 Case C-415/11, *Aziz* judgment of 14 March 2013, para. 69.

ensure review of the fairness of standard-form terms over which the consumer has no possibility to exert influence. Where there is individual negotiation the assumption appears to be that the consumer can look after him or herself.

Article 4(2) also operates to limit the scope of review. It provides that assessment of the unfair nature of the terms 'shall relate neither to the definition of the main subject matter of the contract nor to the adequacy of the price and remuneration, on the one hand, as against the services or goods supplies in exchange, on the other', although this protection from review is lost in so far as the terms are not in plain intelligible language. Article 4(2) therefore ensures there is a core to the contract which enjoys immunity from review against the standard of unfairness. This is best explained as a reflection of a perceived need to show some respect for contractual autonomy and also a concern to preclude the problem of a judge determining whether or not a price is fair. That, it seems, belongs to the market not the courts. It is, however, awkward to determine exactly where lies the margin between the (in short) unreviewable core and the rest of the agreement. Following general principles of interpretation which favour consumer protection and by adopting an analogy with the above-mentioned *Aziz* approach to unfairness, it is probable that an assessment needs to made from the perspective of the consumer. So if a consumer would not regard a term as defining 'the main subject matter of the contract' it should be open to review.

Whereas Directive 93/13 requires the suppression of terms in a contract with a consumer where they are tainted by unfairness, Directive 99/44 requires the inclusion of terms concerning quality into such a contract. Its Article 2(1) stipulates that '[t]he seller must deliver goods to the consumer which are in conformity with the contract of sale'. The rest of Article 2 amplifies what this entails. Article 3 then addresses the rights of the consumer. The basic position is that the seller shall be liable to the consumer for any lack of conformity which exists at the time the goods were delivered, but it is carefully listed which remedies shall be available to the consumer and how they inter-relate. At stake are repair, replacement, an appropriate reduction made in the price, or rescission of the contract. The consumer may require the seller to repair or replace the goods, in either case free of charge, unless this is impossible or disproportionate.

The seller shall be held liable where the lack of conformity becomes apparent within two years from the date of delivery of the goods. A special rule provides in addition that unless proved otherwise, any lack of conformity which becomes apparent within six months of delivery of the goods shall be presumed to have existed at the time of delivery unless this presumption is incompatible with the nature of the goods or the nature of the lack of conformity.

Article 6 of Directive 99/44 deals with guarantees, which shall be legally binding on the offeror under the conditions laid down in the guarantee statement and the associated advertising. The Directive provides amplifying detail.

4.4.3. THE COURT OF JUSTICE

The Court has taken on the task of explaining more fully what the purpose of both of these Directives is. It is Directive 93/13 which has commanded the lion's share of the preliminary references made to the Court. In fact there have been a large number of such references, with the consequence that the Court's interpretation of Directive 93/13 and, to a lesser extent, of Directive 99/44 has given more concrete shape to the regime than the legislative texts alone deliver.

Article 6(1) of Directive 93/13 requires the Member States to provide that unfair terms shall not bind the consumer. One might understand this as a means to protect the consumer as the typically weaker and less well-informed party to the negotiation or as a means to protect the consumer who simply chooses not to read every last line of a standard-form contract but rather to do something more interesting with his or her time. It is the former model which the Court openly embraces. The Court has developed a commonly used formula, in which it describes Article 6(1) as a mandatory provision which, taking into account the weaker position of one of the parties to the contract, aims to replace the formal balance which the contract establishes between the rights and obligations of the parties with an effective balance which re-establishes equality between them.[67] This, then, is a direct check on the enforceability of contractual terms which is motivated by concern to tackle the imbalance that flows from permitting contractual freedom free rein in the economically asymmetric relationship that normally, albeit not always, prevails between the trader and the consumer. In this sense Directive 93/13 is about promoting the autonomy of weaker parties. It is not about undermining freedom of contract. It is about promoting it.

The Court's chosen description of the purpose of the Directive is not mere flashy rhetoric. The Court, exploiting the interpretative opportunities offered by periodic preliminary references made by national courts, has used it in a concrete manner to require adaptation of national practice. Article 6(1) requires deletion of the offending unfair clause, so it is not open to a national court to revise it to remove its worst effects. This interpretation is necessary to protect the aim of the Directive, for if a national court enjoyed such a power of revision the consequence would be to weaken the dissuasive effect on sellers or suppliers minded to use unfair terms.[68] However, the Court's case law, fed by national litigation generating preliminary references, has been drawn into realms of

67 e.g. Case C-168/05, *Mostaza Claro v Centro Móvil Milenium* [2006] ECR I-10421, para. 36; Case C-137/08, *VB Pénzügyi Lízing* [2010] ECR I-10847, para. 47; Case C-618/10, *Banco Español de Crédito v Joaquín Calderón Camino* judgment of 14 June 2012, paras. 40, 63; Case C-415/11, *Aziz* judgment of 14 March 2013, para. 45; Case C-470/12, *Pohotovost' s.r.o. v Vašuta* judgment of 27 February 2014, paras. 39–41; Case C-169/14, *Sánchez Morcillo* judgment of 17 July 2014, para. 23; Case C-8/14, *BBVA SA* judgment of 29 October 2015, para. 17. See S. Weatherill, *EU Consumer Law and Policy*, 2nd ed., Edward Elgar, Cheltenham 2013, Ch. 5.

68 Case C-488/11, *Asbeek Brusse* judgment of 30 May 2013.

sophisticated nuance. Revision is not excluded in all circumstances. The Court has held that a national court may delete an unfair term and replace it with a supplementary provision of national law to avoid the contract being annulled where that annulment would prejudice the consumer.[69]

Whether a term is in fact fair or not is a judgement to be made by a national court. The Court will interpret the general criteria in the Directive, but assessment of the fairness of a particular term belongs with the national court which is able to consider the circumstances of the particular contractual relationship at stake and the costs and benefits to the consumer of the clause.[70] This includes the taking into account of the applicable rules of national law in the absence of agreement between the parties, an investigation in which the national court's expertise plainly outweighs that of the Court of Justice.[71] It has already been mentioned, but deserves repetition, that the Court has interpreted the governing test contained in Article 3(1) that a term shall be regarded as unfair 'if, contrary to the requirement of good faith, it causes a significant imbalance in the parties' rights and obligations arising under the contract, to the detriment of the consumer' by ruling that a national court 'must assess for those purposes whether the seller or supplier, dealing fairly and equitably with the consumer, could reasonably assume that the consumer would have agreed to such a term in individual contract negotiations'.[72]

Directive 99/44 too has drawn the Court into some relatively detailed exercises in interpretation, although the preliminary references inquiring about the intent of this Directive are far less abundant than those addressing Directive 93/13. In *Quelle AG v Bundesverband* it held that the German law of sale did not comply with the Directive because it permitted the supplier to require the consumer to pay an indemnity to cover use where he or she has a non-conforming product replaced.[73] This interpretation favours the consumer: the ruling is in fact explicitly constructed on this thematically familiar preference.[74] The re-regulatory dimension of harmonisation is thereby accentuated. That same concern for effective protection of the consumer is present too in *Weber, Putz*.[75] At stake was replacement of defective goods. Under German law the seller did not have to bear the cost of removing the defective goods or installing

69 Case C-26/13, *Árpád Kásler* judgment of 30 April 2014; Joined Cases C-482/13, *Unicaja Banco SA* judgment of 21 January 2015; Case C-90/14, *Banco Grupo Cajatres v Pinilla* judgment of 8 July 2015.

70 Case C-237/02, *Freiburger Kommunalbauten v Hofstetter* [2004] ECR I-3403; Case C-137/08, *VB Pénzügyi Lízing* [2010] ECR I-10847; Case C-472/10, *Nemzeti* judgment of 26 April 2012.

71 Case C-226/12, *Constructora Principado SA* judgment of 16 January 2014, para. 21; Case C-415/11, *Aziz* judgment of 14 March 2013, para. 68.

72 Case C-415/11, *Aziz* judgment of 14 March 2013, para. 69.

73 Case C-404/06 [2008] ECR I-2685. See S. Stijns and S. Jansen, 'Consumer Sales – Remedies' in E. Terryn, G. Straetmnans and V. Colaert (eds.), *Landmark Cases of EU Consumer Law: In Honour of Jules Stuyck*, Intersentia, Cambridge 2013, Ch. 5.XI, pp. 701–724.

74 e.g. paras. 30, 35, 36; see similarly AG Trstenjak's Opinion in the case.

75 Joined Cases C-65/09 and C-87/09, *Weber, Putz* judgment of 16 June 2011, esp. paras. 52, 57, 72.

the replacement. The Court interpreted Article 3 of the Directive to mean that the seller must bear the costs – were it otherwise, the 'free of charge' proviso in Article 3 would be thwarted. However, in response to detailed questions asked by the national court, it added that where replacement is the only possible remedy but it involves disproportionate cost because of the need to remove the goods not in conformity, Article 3(3) of the Directive does not preclude the consumer's right to reimbursement from being limited to an amount proportionate to the value the goods would have had if there were no lack of conformity. This would establish 'a fair balance between the interests of the consumer and the seller',[76] but the Court stressed that any such reduction must not cause the consumer's right to reimbursement to be effectively rendered devoid of substance. The Court described the consumer 'as the weak party to the contract', to whom the Directive grants 'complete and effective protection from faulty performance by the seller of his contractual obligations'.[77] The assumption, then, is that the consumer cannot extract such protection through contractual negotiation pure and simple, and therefore requires protection. The detail is important to contract lawyers: the broader lesson is that the Court is sometimes tempted to address in considerable detail matters that are not dealt with at all in the more broadly written text of a Directive.[78] In this way the Court of Justice chooses to become a court with responsibility for shaping contract law.

The most conspicuously bold group of cases decided under (particularly) Directive 93/13 are those in which the Court relies on the need to ensure the achievement of the Directive's aims as a basis for extending its interpretative mandate into matters of civil procedure that lie beyond the explicit text of the Directive and which one might have initially thought belonged exclusively to the autonomy of national law.

The single most striking general manifestation of this tendency lies in the Court's insistence that a national court has a duty to evaluate the fairness of terms of its own motion.[79] It bases its consistently repeated reasoning on the system of protection introduced by the Directive, which the Court interprets as based on the idea that the consumer is in a weak position in his or her dealings with the seller or supplier. So the effective protection of the consumer envisaged by the Directive can be achieved only by requiring the reinforcement which is supplied by casting an obligation on the national judge to intervene. The

---

76 Para. 75.

77 Para. 75.

78 For discussion see S. Grundmann, 'Consumer Sales – the *Weber-Putz* Case Law: From Traditional to Modern Contract Law' in E. Terryn, G. Straetmnans and V. Colaert (eds.), *Landmark Cases of EU Consumer Law: In Honour of Jules Stuyck*, Intersentia, Cambridge 2013, Ch. 5.XII, pp. 725–742.

79 e.g. Case C-168/05, *Mostaza Claro v Centro Móvil Milenium* [2006] ECR I-10421, para. 38; Case C-243/08, *Pannon GSM Zrt* [2009] ECR I-4713, para. 32; Case C-397/11, *Erika Jörös* judgment of 30 May 2013, para. 28.

consequence is to convert national autonomy in this particular corner of civil procedure into a matter of mandatory EU law.[80]

Cases on arbitration provide particularly vivid examples of how the Court uses the need to protect the aims pursued by (particularly) Directive 93/13 to assert a basis for detailed and concrete intervention into matters of civil procedure. In *Elisa María Mostaza Claro v Centro Móvil Milenium SL* (*'Mostaza Claro'*) the Court was asked questions about the Spanish transposition of Directive 93/13.[81] The contract in question was between Móvil, a supplier of mobile telephones, and a consumer, Ms Mostaza Claro. The contract contained a clause under which any disputes arising from the contract were to be referred for arbitration. A dispute did indeed arise, because Ms Mostaza Claro did not comply with the minimum subscription period. Móvil initiated arbitration proceedings which found in its favour. Ms Mostaza Claro then contested that arbitration decision on the basis that the arbitration clause itself was unfair, and that therefore the arbitration agreement was accordingly void.

This was the dispute before the Spanish court which led to the referral of questions to the Court in Luxembourg. The Spanish court had no doubt that the arbitration agreement was indeed tainted by inclusion of an unfair contractual term.[82] But under Spanish procedural law Ms Mostaza Claro had failed to plead that the arbitration agreement was invalid during the arbitration proceedings and therefore it was now too late for her to raise the matter in the subsequent action of annulment. So, under Spanish law, the arbitration award against her had to stand – even though that decision involved neglect of the EU Directive.

Directive 93/13 has nothing at all to say about such procedural questions. And although the Spanish rule clearly obstructed the faithful application of EU law, finality of arbitration is a well-recognised value embedded in procedural law. It promotes the efficient administration of justice by ensuring that all parties know where they stand once the stipulated deadlines are passed. The Court noted that 'it is in the interest of efficient arbitration proceedings that review of arbitration awards should be limited in scope and that annulment of or refusal to recognise an award should be possible only in exceptional circumstances'.[83] It found, however, that the circumstances prevailing in the case *were* exceptional. The Court relied heavily on the Directive as a means to protect the consumer who is in a relatively weak position.[84] It added that the

80 For a brilliant uncovering of the impulses that drove the Court to this remarkable conclusion see F. Nicola and E. Tichadou, 'Oceano Grupo: Missed Opportunities and a Second Life for EU Consumer Law' in F. Nicola and B. Davies (eds.), *EU Law Stories: Contextual, Critical and Comparative Histories of European Jurisprudence*, CUP, Cambridge 2016, Ch. 20.

81 Case C-168/05 [2006] ECR I-10421.

82 Cf. Dir. 93/13 [1993] OJ L95/29, Annex 1(q).

83 Para. 34.

84 Paras. 25, 36. See also e.g. Case C-137/08, *VB Pénzügyi Lízing* [2010] ECR I-10847, para. 47, Case C-618/10, *Banco Español de Crédito v Joaquín Calderón Camino* judgment of 14 June 2012, paras. 40, 63.

Directive's aim to strengthen consumer protection constitutes 'a measure which is essential to the accomplishment of the tasks entrusted to the Community', citing Article 3(1)(t) EC.[85] This is frankly to strain the reach and sturdiness of that Treaty provision, but if the Court was willing to do so then, in 2006, its claim is on much firmer ground today since the entry into force of the amending Lisbon Treaty in 2009, thanks to the support provided by Article 12 TFEU and Articles 38 and 47 of the Charter. It concluded that a court dealing with an action for annulment of an arbitration award must be able to determine whether that award is void because the agreement contains an unfair term even where the consumer failed to plead the invalidity of the arbitration agreement in the course of the arbitration proceedings.

Spanish law had to yield. For otherwise the 'regime of special protection established by the Directive would be definitively undermined'.[86]

An analogous approach breathed life into Directive 99/44's vitality in matters of procedure in *Froujke Faber*.[87] The Court held that a national court must determine whether an individual counts as a 'consumer' even if the buyer has not relied on that status in the proceedings, for otherwise the rights intended to be conferred by the Directive would be jeopardised. The Court explicitly cited case law dealing with Directive 93/13, and stressed the common rationale of using EU measures of harmonisation to address the consumer's relatively weak position while also seeking to advance the internal market.[88] The *quality* of the harmonised landscape is constitutionally significant, and this feeds into the Court's techniques of interpretation.

Adopting this perspective, the Court is not deterred by the absence of any directly relevant legislative material adopted at EU level. It declared in *Mostaza Claro* that the detailed procedural rules designed to ensure the protection of the rights which individuals acquire under EU law fall to be decided by the domestic legal order of each Member State 'under the principle of the procedural autonomy of the Member States'.[89] But this autonomy is not unconditional. It is subject to two EU law controls: that they are not less favourable than those governing similar domestic situations (the principle of equivalence) and that they do not render impossible in practice or excessively difficult the exercise of rights conferred by the EU legal order (the principle of effectiveness). Today Article 19(1) TEU provides that Member States shall provide remedies sufficient to ensure effective legal protection in the fields covered by Union law, and this is supplemented by Article 47 of the Charter, which stipulates that everyone whose rights and freedoms guaranteed by EU law are violated 'has the right to an effective remedy before a tribunal in compliance with the conditions laid

---

85 Para. 37.
86 Para. 31.
87 Case C-497/13 judgment of 4 June 2015.
88 AG Sharpston's Opinion in the case is particularly lucid on this point.
89 Para. 24.

down in this Article'. Both provisions have been a formal part of primary EU law only since 2009, and they are to all intents and purposes mere codification of the Court's long-standing and remarkably rich practice, of which *Mostaza Claro* forms part.

The Court has embarked on an adventure that is not mapped by any concrete EU rules. A clear risk is that national procedural rules will be overthrown as a result of resort to the claim that EU law requires effective protection of the rights it has created and that there will be considerable uncertainty as a result. This anxiety can be appreciated by attempting to pin down just when national rules on procedure which suppress relevant aspects of EU law will be upset. This will not occur in the context of commercial litigation where the consumer is not involved. The background to the litigation in *Van der Weerd* was the Dutch implementation and application of Directive 85/511 introducing measures for the control of foot-and-mouth disease.[90] The applicants were the subject of an order concerning the slaughter of their animals. They challenged the order but the national court rejected their pleas. However, that court noted significant arguments based on EU law which had not been raised by the applicants – and which therefore could not, under Dutch procedural law, be taken into account. Such a court was required to give its ruling solely on the basis of the issues which are put before it. Did this prejudice the effective application of EU law and so require adjustment? The Court recited its familiar deferral to the autonomy of the domestic legal system of each Member State to lay down the detailed procedural rules governing actions for safeguarding rights which individuals derive from EU law, subject to compliance with the principle of equivalence and the principle of effectiveness. In the matter of effectiveness, the Court required an analysis by reference to the role of that provision in the procedure, its progress and its special features, viewed as a whole, before the various national instances. Limiting the power of the national court was based on the assumption that in a civil suit it is for the parties to take the initiative, and that as a result the rights of the defence are safeguarded and the proper conduct of proceedings is ensured, involving, in particular, protecting them from the delays inherent in examination of new pleas.[91] The Court addressed explicitly the argument that this was out of line with (*inter alia*) *Mostaza Claro*, decided a year earlier.[92] However, it denied its relevance. *Mostaza Claro*, and other cases decided in the light of Directive 93/13 where the Court imposed a duty on the national court to raise relevant points of EU law of their own motion, are 'justified by the need to ensure that consumers are given the effective protection' which the Directive seeks to achieve.[93] The applicants in *Van der Weerd* had had their chance to

90 Joined Cases C-222/05 et al., *van der Weerd* [2007] ECR I-4233.
91 Paras. 33, 35–36.
92 Para. 39.
93 Para. 40.

raise a plea based on EU law and had not taken it, and their protection was not important enough to justify subverting national procedural law that prevented relevant points of EU law being raised.

Concern to preserve legal certainty is embedded in EU law, and accordingly a misapplication of EU law at national level may go uncorrected.[94] But the rule is not absolute. As the Court made explicit in *Van der Weerd*[95] the introduction of the consumer into the fact pattern diminishes the Court's willingness to respect national procedural autonomy and its concern for legal certainty.[96] The Court accordingly gives special force to EU consumer law and, via its application by national courts, it accentuates the contours of consumer law as a distinct category within national legal orders. Context matters. However, nuance breeds nuance. It is not the case that all consumer cases attract this level of intervention, while all commercial cases do not. The Court has refused to intervene in some circumstances where even consumers risk being treated in violation of the protective norms mandated by EU law. In *Mostaza Claro* the consumer had raised the matter of unfairness in proceedings contesting an earlier adverse arbitral finding. In contrast in *Asturcom Telecomunicaciones* the consumer was even more dilatory.[97] She had neglected even to challenge the arbitral award within the time limit stipulated by national law. Here the Court of Justice refused to help. It accepted that the importance of *res judicata* and ensuring the sound administration of justice should prevail over the consumer interest in re-opening the matter. So EU law treats the aim of consumer protection made concrete by Directive 93/13 as a motivating force which is strong enough to require adaptation of national rules of civil procedure in some but not all circumstances.

The Court has also been peculiarly unwilling to invest consumer associations with any special protective status. *Asociación de Consumidores Independientes de Castilla y León v Anuntis Segundamano España SL* concerned Spanish rules on territorial jurisdiction in litigation which work to the advantage of the trader rather than the consumer representative organisation seeking to act against unfair terms.[98] The Court was familiar with the phenomenon. In *Océano*

94 See similarly Case C-392/04 and C-422/04, *i-21 Germany and Arcor v Germany* [2006] ECR I-8559; Case C-455/06, *Heemskerk BV* [2008] ECR I-8763.

95 Especially paras. 39–40 of the judgment.

96 The reasoning could be extended beyond the consumer context: see e.g. J. Jans and A. Marseille, 'Annotation' (2008) 45 *Common Market Law Review* 853, which considers *inter alia* environmental and health protection. See also on the reach of EU law G. Bermann, 'Navigating EU law and the Law of International Arbitration' (2012) 28 *Arbitration International* 397; and beyond arbitration S. Whittaker, 'Who Determines What Civil Courts Decide? Private Rights, Public Policy and EU Law' in D. Leczykiewicz and S. Weatherill (eds.), *The Involvement of EU Law in Private Law Relationships*, Hart Publishing, Oxford 2012, Ch. 6, pp. 89–130.

97 Case C-40/08 [2009] ECR I-9579.

98 Case C-413/12, *Asociación de Consumidores Independientes de Castilla y León v Anuntis Segundamano España SL* judgment of 5 December 2013.

Grupo Editorial and Salvat Editores it had made plain its view that such a clause which conferred jurisdiction in respect of all disputes arising under the contract on the court in the seller's territorial jurisdiction worked solely to the benefit of the seller and, conferring no conceivable compensating advantage on the individual consumer, was therefore unfair.[99] But in *Asociación de Consumidores Independientes de Castilla y León v Anuntis Segundamano España SL* the Court explained its case law was based on the perception that an individual consumer is in an inferior position, but that this does not apply to a consumer association. This judgment seems to be based on an assumption that consumer associations acting collectively are powerful enough to counteract the economic power of suppliers even where suppliers are privileged by domestic procedural rules. The Court took a similarly cautious approach in *Pohotvost' s.r.o. v Vašuta* when it refused to find a breach of the requirements of effective protection in a case involving a Slovak law which prevented a consumer protection association from intervening in support of a consumer in procedures for enforcement of an arbitration award against the consumer.[100] Such a ruling preserves national autonomy. However, it may be convenient to draw a bright line in this way between consumer associations and individual consumers, but in reality some consumer associations are doubtless sufficiently well resourced to able to enter into combat with traders on an equal footing, while others are doubtless not. It would have been more in the spirit of the Court's earlier case law, and more in tune with Article 12 TFEU and Articles 38 and 47 of the Charter, had the Court left national courts to make a case- and context-specific inquiry into whether such rules obstructed the effective protection of consumers.

The case law is vast: it is time to call a halt for fear of being overwhelmed by its torrid detail. How to judge the Court's output? A benevolent view treats it as nuanced and, though more ambitious than the explicit terms of the relevant legislative texts, nonetheless justified by the concern to achieve the objectives of those texts, against a constitutional background driven by the commitments to a high level of consumer protection and effective redress mandated by Article 19(1) TEU, Article 12 TFEU and Articles 38 and 47 of the Charter of Fundamental Rights. It is socially progressive consumer contract law. A more sternly critical view condemns it as *ad hoc* and opportunistic, and endemically biased in favour of subverting balanced solutions carefully constructed over time at national level in favour of an insensitive homogenised EU influence. It is judicial competence creep. There is no simple answer to the question whether the Court has been too aggressive.[101] The case law discussed in this section is best understood as revealing that both analytical strains have a degree of truth within them.

---

99 Joined Cases C-240/98 to C-244/98, *Océano Grupo Editorial and Salvat Editores* [2000] ECR I-4941.

100 Case C-470/12, *Pohotvost' s.r.o. v Vašuta* judgment of 27 February 2014.

101 See e.g. A. Ward 'Do unto others as you would have them do unto you' (2008) 33 *European Law Review* 739; M. Dougan, 'The Vicissitudes of Life at the Coalface: Remedies and

To conclude, two examples from the case law reveal how the tension between intervention to protect the values promoted by EU law and the preservation of national autonomy is a live and sensitive issue within the Court itself. *Banco Español de Crédito v Joaquín Calderón Camino* is another of the many cases arising out of Directive 93/13.[102] A Spanish rule precluded a court before which an application for repayment of a loan had been made against a consumer from assessing whether a term concerning interest on late payments was unfair where the consumer has not lodged an objection. Such a rule plainly prejudices consumers and tends to undermine the effective protection intended by Directive 93/13. But this matter of procedure is not explicitly addressed by the Directive and such a rule helps to achieve speedy and efficient administration of civil justice, as the Court's judgment itself admits.[103] So which prevails? The Court cited both *Mostaza Claro* (a ruling motivated by effectiveness) and *Asturcom Telecomunicaciones* (a ruling which is respectful of national autonomy) and concluded that the Spanish rule did not meet the requirements of effectiveness under EU law. The delicately difficult nature of the choice is exposed by appreciation that in her Opinion in the case Advocate General Trstenjak had proposed the Court find no breach of EU law: her Opinion stresses a preference for the virtue of national autonomy. There is an echo here of the same Advocate General's Opinion in *Audiolux*, mentioned in Chapter 2.11, which expressed scepticism about finding a general principle of EU law asserting protection of minority shareholders.[104] In that case her anxiety was directed at the Court trespassing on the prerogatives of the EU's political institutions rather than those of the Member States and moreover in *Audiolux*, in contrast to *Banco Español de Crédito v Joaquín Calderón Camino*, the Court agreed with her call for judicial restraint. But the thematic concern to decide just how aggressively interventionist shall be EU law in general, and the Court in particular, runs in common. Precisely the same tension and difference of opinion is visible in *Sánchez Morcillo*.[105] Spanish rules governing the enforcement of mortgages were successfully attacked before the Court on the basis they failed to provide effective protection of the consumer as required by Directive 93/13 on unfair terms. The ruling draws on the long-standing thematic and principled concern to adopt an interpretation that is apt to protect the consumer as the weaker party.[106] But the Opinion in the case delivered by Advocate General Wahl had advised the Court to leave the matter to national autonomy, and expressed anxiety about the

Procedures for enforcing Union Law before the National Courts' in P. Craig and G. De Burca (eds.), *The Evolution of EU Law*, 2nd ed., OUP, Oxford 2011, Ch. 14, pp. 407–438.

102 Case C-618/10, *Banco Español de Crédito v Joaquín Calderón Camino* judgment of 14 June 2012.

103 Para. 52.

104 Case C-101/08, *Audiolux* [2009] ECR I-9823.

105 Case C-169/14, *Sánchez Morcillo* judgment of 17 July 2014.

106 Especially paras. 22–23.

legitimacy of intervention in such a matter of procedure under the guise of the slippery notion of effectiveness.

These are truly fine lines. The enduring message is that a rule of national law which obstructs the enjoyment of rights conferred by EU law is vulnerable to attack. Especially where consumer protection is at stake, one may have a sound expectation of success in using EU law to lever open the blockage to effective application of EU law. National procedural autonomy is a myth.[107]

4.4.4. THEMES, PRINCIPLES AND POLICY

Article 169 TFEU is the consumer-specific legal base in the Treaty. It was inserted with effect from 1993 as a result of the amendments made by the Maastricht Treaty. It is narrowly drawn and has been rarely used as a basis for legislation and so no one would dream of claiming it as evidence that the EU possesses a programme of consumer policy. Article 169(2)(b) limits Union action to promote the interests of consumers and to ensure a high level of consumer protection to 'measures which support, supplement and monitor the policy pursued by the Member States'. Article 114 by contrast, to which Article 169(2)(a) makes bland cross-reference, provides the basis for a rather dense network of legislative harmonisation which affects consumer protection generally and consumer contract law in particular. This material, examined in this section but also the one that precedes it and the one that follows, does form the basis for a credible description of 'EU consumer law and policy'.[108] The EU is not at all the exclusive source of consumer protection law across the 28 Member States, but no examination of the pattern of consumer protection law in the EU can feasibly be confined to national law alone. Harmonisation spills over, and the *acquis* has become relatively dense. One can therefore construct a sector-specific consumer EU policy out of material adopted not under the sector-specific legal bases, but rather pursuant to the functionally broad Article 114. The road is that which leads to the internal market, but the result of market-making harmonisation is a

---

107 M. Bobek, 'Why There is no Principle of Procedural Autonomy of the Member States' in B. de Witte and H. Micklitz (eds.), *The European Court of Justice and Autonomy of the Member States*, Intersentia, Cambridge 2011.

108 For example – and by no means adopting the same descriptive or normative perspective – G. Howells and T. Wilhelmsson, 'EC Consumer Law: has it come of age?' (2003) 28 *European Law Review* 370; J. Basedow, 'Freedom of Contract in the European Union' (2008) 16 *European Review of Private Law* 901; J. Davies, 'Entrenchment of New Governance in Consumer Policy Formulation: a platform for European Consumer Citizenship Practice?' (2009) 32 *Journal of Consumer Policy* 245; M. Dani, 'Assembling the Fractured European Consumer' (2011) 36 *European Law Review* 362; I. Ramsay, 'Regulation and the Contribution of the EU Single Market: the Contribution of Consumer Law' (2010) 50 *Canadian Business Law Journal* 322; H.-W. Micklitz, 'The expulsion of the concept of protection from the consumer law and the return of social elements in the civil law: a bittersweet polemic' (2012) 35 *Journal of Consumer Policy* 283.

distinct pattern of consumer protection generally and consumer contract law in particular.

It is admittedly not a systematic programme. There are images of the consumer, rather than a single image.[109] But there are linking themes. Transparency was identified as a *leitmotif* in the previous section. It is visible in this section too. Article 4(2) of Directive 93/13 opens up review of the fairness of even the main subject matter of a contract and the adequacy of the price where the terms are not in plain intelligible language. This gives the prize of immunity from review to the contracting party who uses plain intelligible language. Article 5 directs that terms offered in writing must be drafted in plain intelligible language, and in the event of doubt about a term's meaning, the interpretation most favourable to the consumer shall prevail. The Annex to the Directive has a list of terms that are capable of being regarded as unfair, depending on the context, and want of transparency is plainly a corrupting factor.[110]

The Court has enhanced this thematic regulatory preference for the promotion of transparency through its interpretation of the sanction of unfairness. For example, *Árpád Kásler* concerned the interpretation of Directive 93/13 in the context of a challenge to a term dealing with the exchange rate applicable to repayment of a loan denominated in a foreign currency.[111] Article 4(2) of the Directive, as mentioned, directs that assessment of the unfair nature of terms shall relate neither to the definition of the main subject matter of the contract nor to the adequacy of the price 'in so far as these terms are in plain intelligible language'. This, the Court reasoned, imposes a 'requirement of transparency' which, given the consumer's 'position of weakness', must be interpreted broadly.[112] Therefore the requirement that a contractual term must be drafted in plain intelligible language covers not only formal grammatical intelligibility but also a transparent explanation of how the term shall operate, as a means to ensure the consumer is in a position to evaluate on the basis of clear criteria the economic consequences.[113] So, in the particular circumstances, the contract should set out transparently exactly how the mechanism of conversion for the foreign currency shall operate. If it does not, the relevant term does not escape review by a court pursuant to Article 4(2) of the Directive.

More generally Directive 93/13 and Directive 99/44 are both based on the perception that the consumer is normally the weaker party to a transaction and that therefore a legal guarantee – of insulation from unfair terms and of

---

109 D. Leczykiewicz and S. Weatherill (eds.), *The Images of the Consumer in EU Law*, Bloomsbury/Hart/IECL, Oxford 2016.

110 e.g. (i) irrevocably binding the consumer to terms with which he had no real opportunity of becoming acquainted before the conclusion of the contract.

111 Case C-26/13 judgment of 30 April 2014.

112 Paras. 71–72. See also Case C-96/14, *Van Hove v CNP Assurances SA* judgment of 23 April 2015, esp. paras. 40–49.

113 Para. 75.

guaranteed conformity with expected quality standards – must be introduced which is independent of contractual negotiation. On this platform is built the detailed rules in the Directives, which in turn prompt the Court to adopt a generously pro-consumer interpretative preference. These measures are readily understood not as restrictions on autonomy but as quite the reverse: they are devices for promoting freedom of choice by consumers and immunity from coercion by more powerful actors. If unregulated 'freedom of contract' consolidates or even promotes existing inequality, then intervening to structure and channel its exercise is not to diminish freedom, it is to give it genuine content.

A concluding remark is that it is extraordinary just how many preliminary references the Court has received in this area. These are consumer cases – by definition they are often relatively small scale, often involving relatively small amounts of money and typically needing quick resolution. Yet preliminary references, which take well over a year on average to provoke a ruling from the Court, abound. It seems clear that litigants are able to extract greater protection from EU law than national law provides, and it is clear too that national judges are ready to exploit the EU dimension as a means to escape from restrictive rules to which they would be tied in a purely national context.[114] Cases on repossession in Spain in the wave of mortgage debt and house repossessions in consequence on the economic crisis are especially fruitful examples of reliance on EU law to force change – both *in casu* and through legislative reform – which will upgrade protection enjoyed by the consumer facing loss of accommodation. It is far from uncommon that an individual preliminary reference conceals a host of similar wrangles tormenting a national legal order.[115] The Court is frequently eager

114 Cf. e.g. F. Nicola and E. Tichadou, 'Oceano Grupo: Missed Opportunities and a Second Life for EU Consumer Law' in F. Nicola and B. Davies (eds.), *EU Law Stories: Contextual, Critical and Comparative Histories of European Jurisprudence*, CUP, Cambridge 2016; H. Micklitz, 'Judicial activism and the development of a European social model in anti-discrimination and consumer law' in U. Neergard, R. Nielsen and L. Roseberry (eds.), *The Role of Courts in Developing a European Social Model – Theoretical and Methodological Perspectives*, Djøf Publishing, Copenhagen 2010, pp. 25–63.

115 Case C-415/11, *Aziz* judgment of 14 March 2013, concerning mortgage repossessions, is explained in this vein by R. Iglesias Sánchez, 'Annotation' (2014) 51 *Common Market Law Review* 955. See also subsequent to post-*Aziz* reforms, Case C-8/14, *BBVA SA* judgment of 29 October 2015; Case C-539/14, *Sánchez Morcillo* judgment of 16 July 2015. The problem is not exclusive to Spain: Case C-34/13, *Monika Kušionová* judgment of 10 September 2014 (Slovakia); Case C-32/14, *ERSTE Bank* judgment of 1 October 2015 (Hungary). A narrative of unfair price rises for the supply of energy in Germany underpins Case C-92/11, *RWE Vertrieb AG* judgment of 21 March 2013: see N. Reich, 'I want my money back: Problems, Successes and Failures in the Price Regulation of the gas supply market by civil law remedies in Germany', Florence, EUI LAW 2015/05, http://cadmus.eui.eu/handle/1814/34862. An early wave of cases in this vein concerned the German *Schrottimmobilien*, e.g. Case C-481/99, *Heininger* [2001] ECR I-9945, on which see H. Micklitz, 'Judicial activism and the development of a European social model in anti-discrimination and consumer law' in U. Neergard, R. Nielsen and L. Roseberry (eds.), *The Role of Courts in Developing a*

to adopt an ambitious approach to the scope of protection in cases that reach it: its case law addressing the scope and meaning of 'unfairness' and its wider role in causing adaptation of national law of procedure and remedies has itself become an important part of the process of shaping this protective regime.[116] This doubtless makes involving it in litigation ever more appealing to the disadvantaged consumer and to the active national judge, thus adding further fuel to the engine of preliminary references and the dynamic process of multi-level judicial interaction.

4.5. REGULATORY CONTRACT LAW

4.5.1. COMPETENCE

A huge range of legal rules regulate economic activity in particular sectors. They channel the way in which parties may operate: they set boundaries to the way in which contractual autonomy is exercised. As has already been introduced in Chapter 2.5, this is conveniently labelled 'regulatory contract law'. Its density at national level has generated an EU response. In the first place this occurs in the context of the application of the free movement rules, where obstacles to cross-border trade in goods and services caused by such regulatory contract law fall for review in the light of EU law and must be set aside in so far as there is an impediment to the importation of goods and services on to the regulated territory, unless they are shown to be justified. Where justification is successfully demonstrated, the internal market can be advanced only by a supplementary legislative contribution at EU level. Obstacles to inter-State trade caused by such measures of market regulation are addressed by the adoption of common EU rules which promote market integration while also absorbing at EU level the motivations which underpinned (diverse, justified) national laws. This, then, fully conforms to the re-regulatory momentum – this is the thematically familiar dual function of harmonisation.

The concern of this section is the EU's brand of regulatory contract law, adopted as harmonised standards to replace diverse national standards. The regulation of advertising provides an absolutely typical and long-established example of the EU's ready assertion of a competence to put in place harmonised

European Social Model – Theoretical and Methodological Perspectives, Djøf Publishing, Copenhagen 2010; N. Reich, 'Balancing in Private Law and the Imperatives of the Public Interest' in R. Brownsword, H. Micklitz, L. Niglia and S. Weatherill (eds.), *The Foundations of European Private Law*, Hart Publishing, Oxford 2011, Ch. 12, pp. 221–248.

116 Surveying the case law, H. Micklitz and N. Reich, 'The Court and Sleeping Beauty: The Revival of the Unfair Contract Terms Directive' (2014) 51 *Common Market Law Review* 771; O. Gerstenberg, 'Constitutional Reasoning in Private Law: The Role of the CJEU in Adjudicating Unfair Terms in Consumer Contracts' (2015) 21 *European Law Journal* 599.

EU rules to replace diverse but justified national restrictions on the freedom to advertise and thereby to induce consumers to enter into contracts to buy the advertised goods and services. Recourse to the lubricating effect of advertising is especially important when an attempt is made to penetrate a new market in which a product or service is unfamiliar to consumers, and this suggests it is likely to be particularly helpful in attempts to gain traction in a market in another Member State.

The EU's first intervention in the field was Directive 84/450 harmonising national measures concerning misleading advertising.[117] Directive 84/450 was amended by Directive 97/55[118] to include coverage of comparative advertising and was further amended by Directive 2005/29 on unfair commercial practices.[119] The incremental growth of this regime damaged its intelligibility and accordingly the decision was taken to codify the regime. This was achieved by Directive 2006/114 concerning misleading and comparative advertising, which is now the governing measure in this area.[120]

At each stage, from 1984 to 2006, the logic was clear and open: national rules in the field diverge and cause impediments to the functioning of the internal market. They must accordingly be replaced by common rules adopted at EU level. Such rules open up a cross-border market in advertising, because the fragmentation caused by regulatory divergence among the Member States has been eliminated. That market is subject to the rules adopted to (re-)regulate it at EU level, which here means rules to suppress misleading advertising and to permit on carefully defined terms comparative advertising. The Preamble to codifying Directive 2006/114 reveals scrupulous attention to the limits of Article 95 EC, which is now Article 114 TFEU. It is there stated that 'the laws against misleading advertising in force in the Member States differ widely' and that this 'has a direct effect on the smooth functioning of the internal market'.[121] Moreover, 'the differences between the laws of the Member States on advertising which misleads business hinder the execution of advertising campaigns beyond national boundaries and thus affect the free circulation of goods and provision of services'.[122] Harmonisation will therefore liberalise cross-border trade and stimulate competition in the internal market.

Directive 89/552 introduced an EU regime for the regulation of television broadcasting.[123] It too has been subsequently amended, in the course of which the regime was re-labelled with effect from 2007 Audiovisual Media Services (AVMS) in recognition of technological adaptation in the sector, which has

117 [1984] OJ L250/17.
118 [1997] OJ L290/18, corrig. [1998] OJ L194/54.
119 [2005] OJ L149/22.
120 [2006] OJ L376/21.
121 Recital 2.
122 Recital 5.
123 [1989] OJ L298/23.

stretched broadcasting media far beyond conventional television. The regime is now codified in Directive 2010/13, the AVMS Directive.[124] The Directive is a measure of harmonisation based on Articles 53(1) and 62 TFEU, which locates it as a contribution to integrating markets for legal and natural persons wishing to establish themselves in another Member State and for the provision of services across borders. It fits comfortably and illuminatingly into the pattern which has become familiar in this chapter. National level regulation of the sector varies, causing obstacles to the creation of an EU broadcasting market. This provides the case for market-making harmonisation. However, the sector has been the subject of a wide range of socially and culturally motivated interventions over the century or so since television broadcasting was first developed and these are necessarily absorbed by and reflected in the EU's choice of (re-)regulated regime. So the dual function of harmonisation is readily visible. In this vein Recital 11 to Directive 2010/13 asserts that it 'is necessary, in order to avoid distortions of competition, improve legal certainty, help complete the internal market and facilitate the emergence of a single information area, that at least a basic tier of coordinated rules apply to all audiovisual media services', and Recital 5 adds that audiovisual media services 'are as much cultural services as they are economic services' and that their 'growing importance for societies, democracy – in particular by ensuring freedom of information, diversity of opinion and media pluralism – education and culture justifies the application of specific rules to these services'. That this is more than a merely transient political preference is underlined by Recital 6, which cites Article 167(4) TFEU as a source of the requirement that the Union shall take cultural aspects into account in law- and policymaking, in particular in order to respect and to promote the diversity of its culture.

These claims seem compelling. There is here no hint of the borderline constitutional insincerity that plagues some of the measures associated with contract formation, where the suspicion, aired above (section 4.3.1), is that the internal market has been on occasion borrowed as a means to promote a policy of consumer protection with negligible market-making credentials. Nor is there here any risk of awkward questions about whether a distortive effect, absent any direct impediment to cross-border trade, is at stake, of the type observed in connection with Directive 93/13 (section 4.4.1). The landscape of regulatory contract law is different. Such rules at national level are commonly and convincingly found to act as barriers to inter-State trade in goods and services and this in turn generates a competence to adopt harmonised standards in replacement for national measures.

In the judgment in the first *Tobacco Advertising* case the Court chose to go out of its way to confirm the validity of harmonisation of this type.[125] In

[124] [2010] OJ L95/1.

[125] Case C-376/98, *Germany v Parliament and Council* [2000] ECR I-8419. See Chapter 3.9.

suggesting the scope of a Directive prohibiting the advertising of tobacco products in periodicals, magazines and newspapers it drew an analogy with (what was then) Article 13 of Directive 89/552's prohibition on television advertising of tobacco products as a means to promote the free broadcasting of television programmes.[126] There is a genuine market-making thrust to this regime. It is not constitutionally fragile.

An advertising campaign is an important element in the successful marketing of a great many goods and services today. Advertising, however, is just one strategy in the range of commercial practices that may be deployed by suppliers of goods and services to attract consumers to contract with them. Already at the time the first Directive in the field was adopted in 1984[127] the Commission was acutely aware there was a wider landscape of 'regulatory contract law' that needed to be addressed.[128] Progress was relatively slow. In 2001 the Commission published a Green Paper on Consumer Protection which gathered information on the layers of diverse national laws that were relevant to the regulation of marketing practices in a broad sense.[129] The Green Paper described the number of legal obligations that arise in the several Member States as 'off-putting' to 'nearly all businesses but those who can afford to establish in all Member States', and, in addition, it explained that they acted as a brake on the confidence of consumers to treat the market as integrated. This analysis was plainly intended to establish competence to set harmonised rules in the field, while also presenting a substantive case in favour of EU intervention in the regulation of marketing practices. In the language of the previous chapter, the Green Paper revealed 'competence sensitivity' (Chapter 3.10). The Commission published a follow-up document in 2002 which reported that consultation had revealed strong support for the adoption of an EU measure.[130] This paved the way to a proposal adopted by the Commission which successfully negotiated the legislative process and was ultimately adopted as Directive 2005/29 on unfair business-to-consumer commercial practices.[131]

Directive 2005/29's legal base was Article 95 EC, which is today Article 114 TFEU. The motivation presented in the Directive's Preamble has much in common with the above-mentioned measures concerning advertising. It situates harmonisation of national laws on unfair commercial practices which

126 Case C-376/98, *Germany v Parliament and Council* [2000] ECR I-8419, paras. 97–98.

127 Dir. 84/450 [1984] OJ L250/17.

128 See L. Kraemer, 'Marketing Practices' in G. Woodroffe (ed.), *Consumer Law in the EEC*, Sweet and Maxwell/CCLR, London 1984, Ch. V, pp. 69–75.

129 COM (2001) 531, 2 October 2001. See M. Radeideh, *Fair Trading in EC Law*, Europa Publishing, Groningen 2005.

130 COM (2002) 289.

131 [2005] OJ L149/22. See B. Keirsbilck, *The new European law of unfair commercial practices and competition law*, Hart Publishing, Oxford 2011; S. Weatherill and U. Bernitz (eds.), *The Regulation of Unfair Commercial Practices under EC Directive 2005/29: New Rules and New Techniques*, Hart Publishing, Oxford 2007.

prejudice consumers' economic interests in the economic context of the project to improve the functioning of the internal market. According to the Preamble, '[t]he development of fair commercial practices within the area without internal frontiers is vital for the promotion of the development of cross-border activities';[132] and moreover disparities between national laws in the area 'cause uncertainty as to which national rules apply to unfair commercial practices harming consumers' economic interests and create many barriers affecting business and consumers'.[133]

Article 1 identifies the 'purpose' of the Directive as twofold: to contribute to the proper functioning of the internal market and to achieve a high level of consumer protection. This is immediately visible as the thematically familiar 'dual function' of harmonisation. The first Recital in the Directive's Preamble cites what were then Articles 153(1) and 153(3)(a) EC, now Articles 12 and 169 TFEU, in asserting that the EU 'is to contribute to the attainment of a high level of consumer protection' by the measures it adopts pursuant to the competence to introduce market-making legislative harmonisation. Here, then, the protection of the consumer literally comes first.

Examples of regulatory contract law adopted at EU level abound, but since the model according to which a competence is shown to exist is more or less consistent exhaustive coverage is not called for. One further example shall suffice. Directive 2001/83 on the code relating to medicinal products for human use contains sector-specific rules on the advertising of medicinal products.[134] Recital 43 in its Preamble claims that all Member States have adopted further specific measures concerning the advertising of medicinal products, that there are disparities between these measures, and that these disparities are likely to have an impact on the functioning of the internal market, 'since advertising disseminated in one Member State is likely to have effects in other Member States'. This is orthodox and convincing. The EU's competence to act is securely based on Article 114 TFEU.

4.5.2. CONTENT AND RE-REGULATORY CHOICES

These measures are good examples of the point that where the EU is competent to harmonise, it is free to adopt a re-regulatory standard that restricts or even forbids particular forms of trading practice throughout the territory of the EU. This was explored in Chapter 3.8. The Court's point is that the threshold of a required sufficient contribution to the improvement of the conditions for the establishment and functioning of the internal market must be crossed before

132 Recital 2.
133 Recital 4.
134 [2001] OJ L311/67.

the competence to harmonise exists, but then the values of *inter alia* a high level of consumer protection may (and must) play their part in shaping the content of the harmonised regime. In the first *Tobacco Advertising* case the problem was that the Directive banned advertising on products such as ashtrays, billboards and parasols for use in street cafés without opening up the market for any other kind of product.[135] The problem was not the ban *per se*: a ban that is part of a wider market-making regime is lawful.[136] Many of the Directives addressing 'regulatory contract law', such as those dealing with advertising and commercial practices more widely, are of this type. As explained in the previous subsection, it is clear that harmonisation, which eliminates regulatory diversity in national practice, contributes to an improvement in the functioning of the internal market. This takes the measures over the threshold of constitutional validity, whereupon commitments to regulatory protection, achieved *inter alia* by prohibition of particular practices, may validly supply the 'decisive factor' in the shaping of the EU regime, to use the Court's standard vocabulary on the matter.[137] So a harmonised ban on misleading advertising opens up the market for advertising more widely; a harmonised ban on unfair commercial practices opens up the market for commercial practices which are not unfair.

Directive 2010/13 on Audiovisual Media Services (AVMS) supplies a good detailed example of how harmonisation is concerned not only with integrating the EU market through the adoption of common rules but also with the choice of (re-)regulatory model.[138] Article 9 of the Directive provides that Member States shall ensure that audiovisual commercial communications for alcoholic beverages shall not be aimed specifically at minors. This is supplemented by Article 12, which directs that Member States shall take appropriate measures to restrict on-demand audiovisual media services which might seriously impair the physical, mental or moral development of minors. Through this Directive, the EU becomes engaged in making choices about how to regulate the market to protect minors. So too the Directive touches those with disabilities. Its Article 7 directs that Member States 'shall encourage media service providers under their jurisdiction to ensure that their services are gradually made accessible to people with a visual or hearing disability'. Article 9(1)(c)(ii) provides that audiovisual commercial communications shall not include or promote any discrimination based on (*inter alia*) disability. The EU, pursuing its programme of legislative harmonisation, is not competent to introduce such protective measures for their

135 Case C-376/98, *Germany v Parliament and Council* [2000] ECR I-8419.

136 e.g. Case C-380/03, *Germany v Parliament and Council* [2006] ECR I-11573, and more fully Chapter 3.8.

137 e.g. Case C-376/98, *Germany v Parliament and Council* [2000] ECR I-8419, para. 88; Case C-380/03, *Germany v Parliament and Council* [2006] ECR I-11573, para. 38. The case law is considered more fully in Chapter 3.8.

138 Dir. 2010/13 [2010] OJ L95/1.

own sake, but it is competent to do so once its competence to act in the service of the internal market is established. As elaborated in Chapter 3.8, there is no shady subterfuge at stake here. If the Member States regulate the market to protect minors and the disabled and choose different ways to achieve this protective aim, then it is inevitable that the EU, setting harmonised standards that replace national diversity, will have to absorb and reflect those protective aims in its own reactive rule-making. So the objectives of the Directive are 'the creation of an area without internal frontiers for audiovisual media services whilst ensuring at the same time a high level of protection of objectives of general interest, in particular the protection of minors and human dignity as well as promoting the rights of persons with disabilities'.[139]

Directive 2005/29's core requirement is contained in Article 5(1). It could not be more textually simple: 'Unfair commercial practices shall be prohibited'. This means that matters previously assessed in the light of Articles 34 or 56 TFEU now fall for assessment in the light of the Directive in so far as they fall within its material scope. And since Directive 2005/29 applies a regime of maximum harmonisation, there is no scope for variation at national level.[140] Unfair practices must be suppressed. Practices that are not unfair which fall within the material scope of the Directive must be permitted.

A key question in the practical application of the regime is how one can achieve a harmonised understanding of 'unfairness'. This is vital to the practical success of its twin aims, to promote an integrated market while also protecting consumers from unfair practices. The EU's re-regulatory scheme needs to be rather sophisticated if it is to deliver its promised benefits. In particular, the appeal of open-textured norms such as 'unfairness' is that they permit context-specific application, but at the same time they are resistant to a predictably uniform understanding across the entire EU. In pursuit of the required clarity of definition Article 5(2) amplifies the notion of unfairness. A commercial practice shall be treated as unfair if (a) it is contrary to the requirements of professional diligence[141] and (b) it materially distorts or is likely to materially distort the economic behaviour[142] with regard to the product of the average consumer whom it reaches or to whom it is addressed or of the average member of the group when a commercial practice is directed to a particular group of consumers.

---

139 Recital 104.

140 Chapter 6 examines the nature of maximum harmonisation.

141 Defined in Art. 2(h) to mean 'the standard of special skill and care which a trader may reasonably be expected to exercise towards consumers, commensurate with honest market practice and/or the general principle of good faith in the trader's field of activity'.

142 Defined in Art. 2(e): 'to materially distort the economic behaviour of consumers' means using a commercial practice to appreciably impair the consumer's ability to make an informed decision, thereby causing the consumer to take a transactional decision that he would not have taken otherwise.

These two cumulatively applicable elements of 'unfairness' are the subject of further elucidation in Article 5(4) of the Directive. This provides that in particular, commercial practices shall be unfair where they are misleading as set out in Articles 6 and 7 or aggressive as set out in Articles 8 and 9. These provisions set out a degree of detail apt to make more concrete the test: the Directive's structure is therefore to apply a general test of unfairness supplemented by the control of two particular types of unfair practice, the misleading and the aggressive. The harmonised norm is granted still more concrete shape by the 'black list' contained in Annex I, which contains a list of 31 practices that are 'in all circumstances considered unfair'. 23 are 'misleading', eight are 'aggressive'. The Directive therefore strives to create a harmonised concept of unfairness on paper, but the size of the challenge in creating a workably uniform scheme is emphasised by appreciation that understanding how consumers actually behave demands a distinct scientific inquiry from simply supposing in the abstract how they should behave.[143] The aim is best understood as the initiation of a process of convergent understanding of the harmonised standard of 'unfairness' rather than any top-down imposition of an impeccably uniform rule.[144]

The generally applicable benchmark is that of the average consumer. Not all consumers are the same, nor are all of them average. The Directive also shows a degree of sensitivity to special types of consumers in its Article 5(3). This states that commercial practices which are likely to materially distort the economic behaviour 'only of a clearly identifiable group of consumers who are particularly vulnerable to the practice or the underlying product because of their mental or physical infirmity, age or credulity in a way which the trader could reasonably be expected to foresee' shall be assessed from the perspective of the average member of that group. The purpose of this proviso is to leave space for the suppression of practices that would not harm the average consumer but would have a particular impact within a clearly identifiable group of consumers. There is a glimpse of protection of the weaker party and, in particular, the vulnerable consumer. This is a flavour of the rich nuance to be found in the EU's re-regulatory harmonised *acquis*.

The coverage contained in this section is necessarily selective. There is in truth an increasing number of domains of sector-specific regulatory contract law in the EU, all designed to promote a functioning internal market in the sector in questions while also demonstrating a thematic commitment to its (re-)regulation, both in the adoption of rules and increasingly through the

---

143 Cf. e.g., insisting on the relevance of behavioural economics, A.L. Sibony, 'Can EU Consumer Law Benefit from Behavioural Insights? An Analysis of the Unfair Practices Directive' (2014) 22 *European Review of Private Law* 901; J. Trzaskowski, 'Lawful Distortion of Consumers' Economic Behaviour – Collateral Damage under the Unfair Commercial Practices Directive' [2016] *European Business Law Review* 25.

144 Cf. A. De Vries, 'The Aim for Complete Uniformity in EU Private Law: An Obstacle to Further Harmonization' (2012) 20 *European Review of Private Law* 913.

establishment of supportive administrative agencies.[145] Telecommunications is an example. The harmonised rules in the sector conform to the orthodox model of 'dual regulation'; they set common rules applicable across the territory of all 28 Member States apt to promote an integrated and competitive market for telecommunications in the EU while also setting a framework within which contractual autonomy in that market may be exercised. This, vividly demonstrated by the discussion of the Court's ruling in *Vodafone* which was examined in Chapter 3.8,[146] does not mean a wholly deregulated sector. Instead the EU responds to anxieties that have prompted intervention at national level – in fact, as *Vodafone* shows, to anxieties that are perceived to be *likely* to prompt intervention – and, by harmonising, loads a method to address such anxieties at EU level. So the measure at stake in *Vodafone*, today Regulation 531/2012, the 'Roaming Regulation',[147] contains rules that require prices to be capped for cross-border provision of services on the basis that intransparency in the market has been shown to prevent genuine price competition that would, through the exercise of the contracting power of consumers, otherwise constrain the conduct of suppliers. This is just one of several EU measures: Directive 2002/22, for example, concerns universal service and users' rights.[148] Looking broadly over the increasingly dense legislative framework in this sector, it has been astutely observed that the EU provides 'regulated autonomy in the information society'.[149] The financial services sector is another example of a sector that is heavily (re-)regulated at EU level in order to promote the internal market.[150] The plan is familiar: the existence of common EU rules promotes cross-border trade and, more specifically, it facilitates cross-border contracting. Intellectual property law, subject only since the entry into force of the Lisbon Treaty with effect from 2009 to an explicit competence granted by the Treaty, Article 118 TFEU, is another field worthy of such investigation.[151] Moreover, beyond concern for regulation designed to protect the economic interests of consumers,

---

145 See e.g. A. Ottow, 'Europeanisation of the Supervision of Competitive Markets' (2012) 18 *European Public Law* 191; also, with rich referencing to the store of literature, H. Micklitz, 'The Transformation of Enforcement in European Private Law: Preliminary Considerations' (2015) 23 *European Review of Private Law* 491.

146 Case C-58/08, *Vodafone Ltd and Others v Secretary of State for Business, Enterprise and Regulatory Reform* [2010] ECR I-4999.

147 [2012] OJ L172/10.

148 [2002] OJ L108/51.

149 e.g. G. Comparato and H. Micklitz, 'Regulated Autonomy between Market Freedoms and Fundamental Rights in the Case Law of the CJEU' in U. Bernitz, X. Groussot and F. Schulyok (eds.), *General Principles of EU Law and European Private Law*, Wolters Kluwer, Alphen aan den Rijn 2013, Ch. 4, pp. 121–154.

150 See N. Moloney, *EU Securities and Financial Services Regulation*, 3rd ed., OUP, Oxford 2014. On the place of constitutional values, discussed in Chapter 2.11, see O. Cherednychenko, 'Fundamental Rights, European Private Law, and Financial Services' in H. Micklitz (ed.), *Constitutionalization of European Private Law*, OUP, Oxford 2014, Ch. 6, pp. 170–209.

151 See J. Pila and P. Torremans, *European Intellectual Property Law*, OUP, Oxford 2016.

the regulation of safety – in connection with medicines, cosmetics, and goods generally – provides yet another field of inquiry into regulatory contract law. EU rules set boundaries to the permitted scope of supply. To attempt to provide a remotely comprehensive account would require the writing of a very long book, and that is not the ambition of this project, which is concerned to trace the constitutional context of the contract law of the internal market.

4.5.3. THE COURT OF JUSTICE

Preliminary references have supplied the Court with ample opportunity to rule on the proper interpretation of several of these Directives. Its orthodox interpretative technique, which is favourable to the protection of the consumer, is readily visible.

So, for example, the Court treats comparative advertising as valuable as a means to promote competition between products and services to the advantage of the consumer. When invited to define its scope and the limits that may permissibly be placed upon it, it has therefore taken an approach whereby 'the conditions required of comparative advertising must be interpreted in the sense most favourable to it'.[152] This has much in common with the thematic concern to promote the provision of information to the consumer in order to secure transparency. The Court has similarly emphasised the consumer benefit from comparative advertising in relation to the use of trademarks. In *L'Oreal* it therefore carefully spelled out what an advertiser may and may not do with a rival's trademark.[153] In another *L'Oreal* case it refined the scope of permissible use of a trademark by a third party selling goods via an online marketplace (*in casu*, ebay).[154]

Directive 2005/29 which harmonises rules governing unfair business-to-consumer commercial practices by prohibiting them is marked by a comparable pro- consumer interpretation, which reveals the Court's understanding of the purpose of the measure. The Court has consistently insisted that pursuit of a high level of consumer protection is a reason to reject a restrictive interpretative approach to the scope of the Directive.[155] So, for example, in *Nemzeti Fogyasztovedelmi Hatosag* the Court, making exactly this connection between the quest for a high level of consumer protection and the proper interpretation

152 Case C-356/04, *Lidl Belgium v Franz Colruyt* [2006] ECR I-8501, para. 22. See also Case C-59/05, *Siemens* [2006] ECR I-2147, paras. 22–24.

153 Case C-487/07 [2009] ECR I-5185. See also Case C-533/06, *O2 Holdings* [2008] ECR I-4231.

154 Case C-324/09, *L'Oreal* judgment of 12 July 2011; Case C-323/09, *Interflora* judgment of 22 September 2011.

155 e.g. Case C-122/10, *Ving Sverige AB* [2011] ECR I-3903; Case C-428/11, *Purely Creative Ltd and Others v OFT* judgment of 18 October 2012; Case C-435/11, *CHS Tour Services* judgment of 19 September 2013.

of the Directive, made clear that this precluded the imposition of restrictions on its material scope which were not explicitly foreseen by the Directive.[156] The consumer, it noted, is 'economically weaker and less experienced in legal matters' than the trader.[157] The message is that the Court is conscientious is interpreting the Directive both to promote an integrated market (in fair practices) and to ensure its protective re-regulatory ambitions are met (by sheltering consumers from unfair practices).

The case law is mostly illustrative and does not deserve exhaustive treatment.[158] It is, however, largely internally consistent. The key message is that the internal market is no neutral legal concept: it involves choices about the quality of the re-regulatory environment which are conducive to protection of weaker parties.

4.5.4. THEMES, PRINCIPLES AND POLICY

A national lawyer might wish to assert a sharp distinction between contract law narrowly understood and the wider pattern of market regulation labelled in this book 'regulatory contract law'. One, in short, is private law; the other public law. But EU law in general and legislative harmonisation in particular is blind to such distinctions. In either instance EU law reaches national choices in so far as they come into contact with and impede the project of market integration. Their status under national law is of no constitutional significance. Consequently EU law tends to erode relatively well recognised and sometimes cherished patterns of classification under national law. The internal market, to which harmonisation pursuant to Article 114 is dedicated, is driven by functional aims, and the categorisations on which this chapter is constructed are for convenience of exposition, and they are not intended to suggest sharp or principled demarcations.

Directive 2005/29 on unfair commercial practices contains a rather neat illustration.[159] Its Article 3(2) states that the Directive 'is without prejudice to contract law, and in particular to the rules on the validity, formation or effect of a contract'. In formal terms this is doubtless correct. However, Directive 2005/29's suppression of unfair practices surely affects the way some rules of national contract law are applied, especially those pertaining to practices occurring before a enforceable contract comes into existence. The Directive's 'black list' of practices that are to be considered unfair in all circumstances includes

---

156 Case C-388/13 judgment of 16 April 2015.

157 Para. 53.

158 On Directive 2005/29 see J. Stuyck, 'The Court of Justice and the Unfair Commercial Practices Directive' (2015) 52 *Common Market Law Review* 721.

159 [2005] OJ L149/22.

several that are connected to the sin of intransparency,[160] which establishes a thematic link with the EU Directives considered in section 4.3 above which have a significant impact on pre-contractual information disclosure. These are formally separate matters, but they share the regulatory assumption of the virtue of transparency.[161]

One could make a similar observation about the relationship between Directive 2005/29 and Directive 93/13 on unfair terms. The Court has relied on Article 3(2) of Directive 2005/29 in pointing out that Directive 2005/29 applies without prejudice to the rules on the validity, formation or effect of a contract and that in consequence a finding that a commercial practice is unfair has no direct effect on the validity of a term.[162] Directive 2005/29 stipulates particular forms of administrative action against the offender and the practice. It is Directive 93/13 which prevents enforcement of any unfair term. They are formally distinct. However, a finding that a commercial practice is unfair counts as one element in the assessment which a competent court is required to make in checking whether a contractual term is unfair within the meaning of Article 4(1) of Directive 93/13.[163] Moreover, use of unfair terms within the meaning of Directive 93/13 may constitute an unfair commercial practice within the meaning of Directive 2005/29.[164]

This patchwork model is remote from the complementarity between public and private enforcement which can be delivered by astute design.[165] It underlines the limits of the EU's competence as well as the political sensitivity associated with its exercise. However, the crossover in substance between the regulatory ambitions of Directive 93/13 and Directive 2005/29 is real, and the insulation promised by Article 3(2) Directive 2005/29 is comprehensible only if one takes a narrow formal view of what 'contract law' comprises.[166] Article 3(2) is probably

---

160 Dir. 2005/29 [2005] OJ L149/22, Annex I, points 5, 6, 7, 8, 11, 19, 31.

161 For a corresponding attempt to elucidate a general duty of pre-contractual information from this material, see M. Durovic, 'The Subtle Europeanization of Contract Law: The Case of Directive 2005/29 on Unfair Commercial Practices' (2015) 23 *European Review of Private Law* 715.

162 Case C-453/10, *Pereničová and Perenič* judgment of 15 March 2012.

163 Case C-453/10, *Pereničová and Perenič* judgment of 15 March 2012.

164 Cf. S. Orlando, 'The Use of Unfair Contractual Terms as an Unfair Commercial Practice' (2011) 7 *European Review of Contract Law* 25.

165 Cf. e.g. the highly influential account by S. Shavell, 'A Model of the Optimal Use of Liability and Safety Regulation' (1984) 15 *Rand Journal of Economics* 271. In the EU context, see O. Cheredychenko, 'Public and Private Enforcement of European Private Law: Perspectives and Challenges' (2015) 23 *European Review of Private Law* 481 (introducing a Special Issue of the journal on the matter); F. Weber, *The Law and Economics of Enforcing European Consumer Law: A Comparative Analysis of Package Travel and Misleading Advertising*, Ashgate, Aldershot 2014.

166 See e.g. S Whittaker, 'The Relationship of the Unfair Commercial Practices Directive to European and National Contract Law' in S. Weatherill and U. Bernitz (eds.), *The Regulation of Unfair Commercial Practices under EC Directive 2005/29: New Rules and New Techniques*, Hart Publishing, Oxford 2007, Ch. 8, pp. 139–158.

best understood as a formal statement designed to placate those alarmed by the EU's apparent invasion of private law through harmonisation of regulatory contract law. But they are right to be attentive, if not necessarily alarmed, because the EU's emphasis on building the internal market through legislative harmonisation may be oddly shaped, but it has bred precisely this transgression of boundaries recognised at national level.

So, in conclusion, 'European regulatory private law can be defined as the rules laid down by the EU legislator that seek to facilitate private law relationships whilst also pursuing specific policy goals, such as consumer protection or the integration of the EU internal market'.[167] It opens up space (in the internal market) for intensified competition and cross-border contracting, while also channelling the way in which commercial activity may be conducted with a view to inducing consumers to agree to enter into contracts to buy goods or services. This is the heartland of the development of a regulatory policy for the EU within the broader project of constructing a contract law of the internal market.[168]

4.6. PASSENGERS

4.6.1. COMPETENCE

Regulation 261/2004 is among the most high profile of all the EU's legislative measures.[169] It establishes common rules on compensation and assistance to passengers in the event of denied boarding and of cancellation or long delay of flights. Its existence is well known and it is frequently newsworthy, even if its detailed provisions are often only imperfectly understood. By providing a basic level of protection for passengers on air transport who suffer from denied boarding, cancellation or long delay of flights it assumes that the matter should not be left to contractual negotiation. Instead public regulation supports the process of contracting. This is a particular niche of regulatory contract law.

The legal base of the Regulation is Article 80 EC, which is today Article 100 TFEU. This appears in the Title of Part III of the TFEU, which is dedicated to Transport. Article 100 TFEU itself permits action taken according to the ordinary legislative procedure to 'lay down appropriate provisions for sea and air transport'. The aim of the Title is to develop a common transport policy, and, as a broad observation, Article 100 is in this sense a sector-specific application of the general idea that common rule-making is required at EU level in order to

167 V. Mak, 'The Consumer in European Regulatory Private Law' in D. Leczykiewicz and S. Weatherill (eds.), *The Images of the Consumer in EU Law*, Bloomsbury/Hart/IECL, Oxford 2016, Ch. 16, pp. 381–400, at p. 381.

168 Cf. the wealth of academic reflection cited above n. 108.

169 [2004] OJ L46/1.

make real the Treaty commitment to an integrated market. Regulation 261/2004 forms part of the package.

Its Preamble makes very clear that its motivation follows a pattern familiar to the student of legislative harmonisation generally. Its very first Recital states that action 'in the field of air transport should aim, among other things, at ensuring a high level of protection for passengers' and that 'full account should be taken of the requirements of consumer protection in general'. This is a clear embrace of the dual function of EU rule-making. This is reinforced in Recital 4: the aim is 'both to strengthen the rights of passengers and to ensure that air carriers operate under harmonised conditions in a liberalised market'.

This is admittedly a niche area of legal regulation and it tends to reinforce the impression of EU intervention as a patchwork. However, passengers using railways,[170] ships,[171] buses and coaches[172] also enjoy a degree of protection in the event of delays and cancellations under measures adopted pursuant to the Title on Transport in the TFEU or its predecessor, and there is an additional significant layer of protection established under international agreements.[173]

4.6.2. CONTENT AND RE-REGULATORY CHOICES

The protection envisaged covers assistance and compensation for disappointed passengers.

The scope of protection in the event of denied boarding, cancellation or delay is spelled out by Regulation 261/2004. Article 4 goes into some detail in specifying how the possibility of denied boarding shall be handled. It is well known that carriers 'overbook', in the expectation that some travellers will not in fact arrive at the airport, and this may mean on occasions when fewer than the norm fail to show that a flight cannot accommodate all intended passengers. Article 4 states that a carrier shall ask for volunteers to surrender their reservations in exchange for benefits to be agreed: hearing such an invitation, usually over a malfunctioning public address system, is a frequent occurrence for the regular air traveller. Where an insufficient number of volunteers come forward to allow the remaining passengers with reservations to board the flight, the operating air carrier may then deny boarding to passengers. This triggers an obligation to compensate them in accordance with Article 7 of the Regulation and also assist them in accordance with Articles 8 and 9.

Article 5 deals with cancellation. The passengers concerned shall be offered assistance by the carrier in accordance with Articles 8 and 9 of the Regulation

170 Reg. 1371/2007 [2007] OJ L315/14.

171 Reg. 1177/2010 [2010] OJ L334/1.

172 Reg. 181/2011 [2011] OJ L55/1.

173 See B. Havel and G. Sanchez, *The Principles and Practice of International Aviation Law*, CUP, Cambridge 2014.

and shall have the right to compensation in accordance with Article 7, unless they are informed of the cancellation in advance within a window of time defined in precise detail in the Regulation. Article 5(3) relieves a carrier of the obligation to pay compensation 'if it can prove that the cancellation is caused by extraordinary circumstances which could not have been avoided even if all reasonable measures had been taken'. One would readily predict this rough-edged exception would trigger litigation and it has duly done so. This is covered below (section 4.6.3).

Article 6 deals with delay. Here too there is carefully written detail about the circumstances, in particular the length of the delay, that trigger an obligation to offer help to the passenger which goes beyond anything that have been agreed in the contract, but the core protection concerns provision of the assistance specified in Articles 8 and 9. Compensation is not mentioned in Article 6 and, therefore and logically, references in Article 7, which provides detail on the calculation of compensation, are only to denial of boarding or cancellation, not delay. Here, however, all is not as it seems and it is explained below that the Court has ruled that delayed passengers are entitled to compensation.

Article 14 covers the obligation to inform passengers of their rights. It fits easily into the theme of transparency. The carrier shall ensure that at check-in 'a clearly legible notice' is displayed in a manner clearly visible to passengers, and goes so far as to stipulate the exact wording:

> 'If you are denied boarding or if your flight is cancelled or delayed for at least two hours, ask at the check-in counter or boarding gate for the text stating your rights, particularly with regard to compensation and assistance'.

Moreover, Article 14(2) requires a carrier to provide each passenger affected with a written notice setting out the rules for compensation and assistance in line with this Regulation. Article 15 adds that obligations owed to passengers pursuant to this Regulation may not be limited or waived by a derogation or restrictive clause in the contract of carriage. These are mandatory rules.

4.6.3. THE COURT OF JUSTICE

The Regulation is the subject of frequent criticism by carriers, especially by low-cost carriers which complain that the costs involved in compliance with the Regulation damage their commercial position both in absolute terms and relative to high-cost carriers for which the costs of compliance represent a much smaller percentage of the cost of the ticket price. This antipathy to public regulation is reflected in patterns of litigation which have reached the Court via preliminary references made to it by national courts.

Carriers have tried to escape or limit their obligations. The basic and thematically familiar approach taken by the Court is to interpret restrictions on the protection of consumers in a narrow manner.[174] Mere illustrations of attempts by carriers to confine the extent of their liabilities are provided here; this is not an exhaustive account.[175] In *Finnair v Lassooy* the Court was asked to determine whether 'denied boarding' under Regulation 261/2004 related exclusively to cases where boarding is denied because of overbooking or whether it also applies to cases where boarding is denied on other grounds, such as operational reasons (*in casu*, a strike at Barcelona airport).[176] The Court adopted the broader interpretation. It noted that placing a limit on the scope of 'denied boarding' so that it attached exclusively to cases of overbooking would reduce the available protection and would therefore run contrary to the Regulation's aim of ensuring a high level of protection for passengers. This interpretative approach plainly conforms to that found in EU consumer protection generally.[177]

Other illustrative case law has been generated by the proviso in Article 5(3) of the Regulation to the effect that compensation is not payable if the carrier can prove that cancellation is 'caused by extraordinary circumstances which could not have been avoided even if all reasonable measures had been taken'. Carriers have naturally striven to interpret this as much in their favour as possible.[178] It falls to the Court to provide an authoritative interpretation. It has decided that Article 5(3)'s reliance on 'extraordinary circumstances' demands a problem which stems from events which, by their nature or origin, are not inherent in the normal exercise of the activity of the air carrier concerned and are beyond its actual control.[179] A technical problem in an aircraft is not covered by the concept of 'extraordinary circumstances' unless these extra ingredients are present.

Carriers have also attacked the very validity of the Regulation, but without success. Airlines specialising in cheap flights have protested bitterly that to impose an obligation to compensate delayed consumers which is unconnected to the price of a ticket discriminates against 'budget' airlines which, as a result, carry a higher liability in percentage terms judged according to price than their more luxurious and more expensive competitor airlines. But the Court of Justice did not find this to be legally objectionable. It rejected the argument that the Regulation was invalid for violation of the principle of equal treatment, and it

---

174 Cf. above n. 3.

175 See M. Bobek and J. Prassl (eds.), *Air Passenger Rights: Ten Years On*, Bloomsbury/Hart, Oxford 2016.

176 Case C-22/11 judgment of 4 October 2012.

177 As is clear from the treatment above in sections 4.3, 4.4 and 4.5.

178 See e.g. Case C-294/10, *Eglitis, Ratnieks* judgment of 12 May 2011; Joined Cases C-402/07 and C-432/07, *Christopher Sturgeon, Gabriel Sturgeon and Alana Sturgeon v Condor Flugdienst GmbH and Stefan Böck and Cornelia Lepuschitz v Air France SA* [2009] ECR I-10923.

179 Case C-549/07, *Wallentin-Hermann* [2008] ECR I-11061; Joined Cases C-402/07 and C-432/07, *Sturgeon* [2009] ECR I-10923.

pointed out that the loss suffered by consumers was the same irrespective of the identity of the carrier with which they happened to be booked.[180]

Lately airlines have grasped for the Charter of Fundamental Rights in the hope of finding a legal means to attack the costs they incur as a result of the EU's regulatory requirements. In *Denise McDonough v Ryanair Ltd* the Court was asked by an Irish court to assess the scope of the obligation to provide care for passengers in the event of cancellation of a flight imposed by Regulation 261/2004.[181] The background to the dispute was the eruption of the Eyjafjallajökull volcano in Iceland during the spring of 2010, which had led to serious disruption of air traffic and so had triggered a wave of claims by affected passengers. The reference made by the Irish court asked the Court to consider the potential application of Articles 16 and 17 of the Charter, dealing with freedom to conduct a business and the right to property respectively. However, as has already been noted in Chapter 3, the Charter is not only concerned with commercial freedom, it is also infused with respect for the values of public regulation. In its ruling in *McDonough* the Court drew on Article 38 of the Charter which commits the EU to a high level of consumer protection. The Court found that the obligation imposed on airlines by Regulation 261/2004 struck 'a fair balance' between the several Charter rights at stake.[182] Therefore, it did not breach Articles 16 and 17 of the Charter. This case stands with others considered in Chapter 3.15 which confirm that the EU is a legitimate regulator of markets.[183]

The Court's interpretation of the Regulation is fuelled by its understanding of the constitutional weight placed on the protection of the consumer in EU law. However, one of its judgments pushes the impetus to protect with especially startling vigour.

In *Sturgeon* the Court interpreted the Regulation to cover compensation not only for passengers on cancelled flights, but also those on delayed flights.[184] This is not expressly foreseen by the Regulation. The Sturgeons had suffered a delay of more than 25 hours on a flight from Toronto to Frankfurt. The carrier, Condor, refused to pay compensation, since the Regulation provides for a right to compensation only in the case of a cancellation of the flight. The applicants claimed first of all that this was in truth not a delay, but, given the duration, a cancellation. This failed to persuade the Court. A flight is delayed for the purposes of Article 6 of Regulation 261/2004 'if it is operated in accordance with the original planning and its actual departure time is later than the scheduled

---

180 Case C-344/04, *ex parte IATA* [2006] ECR I-403, para. 98.

181 Case C-12/11, *Denise McDonagh v Ryanair Ltd* judgment of 31 January 2013.

182 Para. 64.

183 Cf. Case C-544/10, *Deutsches Weintor v Land Rheinland-Pfalz* judgment of 6 September 2012; Case C-283/11, *Sky Österreich GmbH* judgment of 22 January 2013; Case C-101/12, *Herbert Schaible v Land Baden-Württemberg* judgment of 17 October 2013.

184 Joined Cases C-402/07 and C-432/07 [2009] ECR I-10923.

departure time' whereas by contrast a flight in cancelled where a flight that was previously planned does not operate.[185] So 'cancelled flights and delayed flights are two quite distinct categories of flights'.[186] And the Sturgeons had travelled on a delayed flight. This seemed fatal to their chances of securing compensation. But it was not. The Court admitted that the express terms of the Regulation provide a right to compensation in the event of cancellation, but not in the event of delay. But it then insisted on the need to examine not only the measure's wording, 'but also the context in which it occurs and the objectives pursued by the rules of which it is part'.[187] This brought it to a conclusion that a right to compensation applied also in the event of delay. Its reasoning is worryingly tenuous. It is based on three main strands. If first noted that Article 5(3) of the Regulation excludes carriers from an obligation to compensate in the event of cancellation where 'extraordinary circumstances' prevail, but noted too that Recital 15 in the Preamble to the regulation states that that ground may also be relied on where an air traffic management decision in relation to a particular aircraft on a particular day gives rise to 'a long delay [or] an overnight delay'. So, the Court argued, this connection between the notion of long delay and 'extraordinary circumstances' meant also a connection between long delay and the right to compensation. But this is to pursue interpretation of the measure by elevating an odd twist in the Preamble above the absence of any treatment of compensation for delay in the body of the Regulation. Second, the Court insisted on the aim to ensure a high level of protection for air passengers dictated a broad interpretation of the protective rules, and that since cancellation and delay cause similar inconvenience, 'it cannot automatically be presumed that passengers whose flights are delayed do not have a right to compensation and cannot, for the purposes of recognition of such a right, be treated as passengers whose flights are cancelled'.[188] Were this to be a motivating statement provided by a legislature one would not be surprised. But it is remarkable to find a court correcting a piece of legislation in this way. Thirdly, the Court also drew on the principle of equal treatment, which requires that comparable situations must not be treated differently and that different situations must not be treated in the same way unless such treatment is objectively justified. It took the view that passengers whose flights have been cancelled and passengers affected by a flight delay suffer similar damage: they are in comparable situations. The Regulation treats them differently without any objective ground capable of justifying such a difference in treatment. So, interpreting the Regulation in order to comply with the principle of equal treatment, the Court found that passengers whose flights are delayed may rely on the right to compensation laid down in Article 7 where they

---

185 Paras. 32, 33.
186 Para. 33.
187 Para. 41.
188 Para. 46.

suffer a delay of three or more hours. Again, here the Court is readily accused of choosing a preferred policy outcome rather than genuinely interpreting the existing legislative text. It is striking how eagerly the Court relied on the principle of equal treatment to improve the position of passengers, whereas by contrast it has been uninterested in exploiting it in favour of low-cost carriers in the *IATA* case.[189] This is plainly an approach that is in the service of consumer protection but under a very exaggerated reading of the judicial function. It was achieved by an interpretative stretch, based on reference to the context and objectives of the legislative scheme, and open to sceptical review.[190]

Subsequently in *Germanwings* the Court was invited by Landgericht Köln to reconsider its approach, and especially to address the question whether the ruling in *Sturgeon* amounted to a violation of the principle of separation of powers.[191] Unsurprisingly the Court disagreed with the accusation. It simply portrayed *Sturgeon* as a matter of legitimate interpretation of a legislative text.

The Court's approach fits into a model whereby the interest in protecting consumers is treated as of high significance and the regulatory burdens are a natural consequence to which operators may not object as a matter of law. A case such as *McDonough v Ryanair* shows judicial disinclination to upset the balancing of interests struck though the legislative process. The Court is however on the very edge of the legitimate limits of judicial interpretation when, as in *Sturgeon*, it upsets what gave every impression of being a carefully struck legislative compromise on the proper scope of intervention into contractual autonomy.

4.6.4. THEMES, PRINCIPLES AND POLICY

Provided one appreciates that legislative coverage is far from comprehensive, the label EU 'travel law' or 'passenger law' as a means to capture this niche area of regulation is not far-fetched.[192] This regime pushes beyond the model of information disclosure typical of the measures found in section 4.3 which deal with the formation of contracts with consumers. It protects the weaker party by insisting on a basic level of protection and compensation for passengers irrespective of contractual negotiation. However, the thematic concern for transparency surfaces in Article 14 of Regulation 261/2004. Carriers must have

---

189 Case C-344/04 [2006] ECR I-403.

190 For discussion see S. Garben, 'Sky-High Controversy and High-Flying Claims? The Sturgeon Case Law in Light of Judicial Activism, Euroscepticism and Eurolegalism' (2013) 50 *Common Market Law Review* 15; F. Le Bot, 'La protection des passagers aériens dans l'Union européenne' (2013) 49 *Revue Trimestrielle de Droit Européen* 753.

191 Case C-413/11, *Germanwings GmbH v Thomas Amend* judgment of 18 April 2013.

192 Cf. J. Karsten, 'Travel Law' in C. Twigg-Flesner (ed.), *The Cambridge Companion to European Union Private Law*, CUP, Cambridge 2010, Ch. 15, pp. 201–215.

a notice at check-in which invites passengers to ask for a text stating their rights in the event of denied boarding, cancellation or delay for at least two hours, and should such an eventuality occur, the carrier must provide each passenger affected with a written notice setting out the applicable rules.

4.7. ENERGY

4.7.1. COMPETENCE

The amending Lisbon Treaty introduced a new provision on energy into the TFEU. This is Article 194 TFEU and, on the entry into force of the Lisbon Treaty in 2009, it conferred on the EU for the first time a competence specific to energy. It sets out the aims of EU energy policy, and locates it explicitly in 'the context of the establishment and functioning of the internal market' and 'with regard for the need to preserve and improve the environment'. At stake is ensuring the functioning of the energy market and security of energy supply, the promotion of energy efficiency and the development of new and renewable forms of energy, and the promotion of the interconnection of energy networks. The ordinary legislative procedure governs the adoption of measures necessary to achieve these objectives, excepting where those measures 'are primarily of a fiscal nature' which, according to Article 194(3) and thematically in line with practice elsewhere in the EU lawmaking process where fiscal matters are at stake, unanimity in Council is required.[193]

There is however a substantial body of EU secondary legislation which concerns the energy sector and it mostly pre-dates the arrival of Article 194 in the Treaty with effect from 2009. The driving force of this accumulated legislative *acquis* is the completion of the internal market. A body of harmonised rules aim to replace divergent national measures, often revealing a high level of State control in the sector, with common EU rules as a means to create an internal market for energy in the EU. This is firmly in line with the patterns of regulatory contract law examined in section 4.5.

It is not the aim of this book to provide an exhaustive treatment of the legislation in this sector: other sources perform that function admirably.[194] The point here is to demonstrate how the building of an internal market draws the EU legislative institutions into the complex job of shaping the environment within which cross-border contracting in the supply of energy is released.

---

193 Cf. Arts. 113, 114(2) TFEU.

194 For detail see A. Johnston and G. Block, *Energy Law in Europe*, OUP, Oxford 2012; K. Talus, *EU Energy Law and Policy: A Critical Account*, OUP, Oxford 2013; M. Roggenkamp, C. Redgwell, A. Rønne and I. Del Guayo (eds.), *Energy Law in Europe: National, EU and International Regulation*, 3rd ed., OUP, Oxford 2016.

Directive 2009/72 on the internal market for electricity[195] and Directive 2009/73 on the internal market for natural gas[196] are both based on Articles 47(2), 55 and 95 EC, which are today Articles 53(2), 62 and 114 TFEU. This is therefore harmonisation aimed at improving the functioning of the internal market in goods and services. A series of other important measures are based exclusively on Article 95 EC, today Article 114 TFEU: these include Directive 2005/89 on the security of supply of electricity,[197] Regulation 713/2009 on the Agency for the Cooperation of Energy Regulators,[198] Regulation 714/2009 on conditions for access to the network for cross-border exchanges in electricity[199] and Regulation 715/2009 on conditions for access to natural gas transmission networks.[200]

The rise of the energy-specific Treaty competence will change the packaging but not the motivation of secondary legislation in this area. Regulation 994/2010 on the security of supply of natural gas is based on Article 194(2),[201] but the measure it replaces, a 2004 Directive, is an orthodox internal market measure.

4.7.2. CONTENT AND RE-REGULATORY CHOICES

The familiar pattern of the dual function of harmonisation is plainly evident in this legislative *acquis*.

A brief inspection of the names of the key Directives conveys what is at stake: in particular, measures on the internal market for electricity and for natural gas combined with measures on security of supply of electricity and of natural gas reveal the concern both to integrate the market and to (re-)regulate that market by policing security of supply. Although it is thematically important that the consumer's capacity to enjoy the benefits of choice is treated as a rationale for setting aside State-level regulation in favour of a deregulated and more competitive internal market, this is not a ubiquitous model. The case of energy is different from that of consumption of timeshare or air travel. This is not a question of choice; it is a question of necessity. The creation of competitive cross-border markets is therefore a concern that co-exists with the need to prevent shortage of supply.[202] States do not leave such vital markets unregulated and so it follows that neither should the EU, when it acts as a re-regulator. This fully conforms to the consistently visible theme that the EU assumes a degree of regulatory responsibility for the shape of the market that it is creating through

195 [2009] OJ L211/55.
196 [2009] OJ L211/94.
197 [2005] OJ L33/22.
198 [2009] OJ L211/1.
199 [2009] OJ L211/15.
200 [2009] OJ L211/36.
201 [2010] OJ L295/1.
202 For detail see A. Johnston and G. Block, *Energy Law in Europe*, OUP, Oxford 2012, Chs. 9 and 10.

the pursuit of its internal market project. This is not an exclusively deregulatory endeavour.

Protection of 'vulnerable' consumers also appears in the EU's legislative *acquis* governing energy supply. So, for example, Directive 2009/72 establishes common rules for the internal market in electricity, and includes provision for universal service and the protection of vulnerable consumers.[203] The EU regime cannot be considered comprehensive. It deals with some matters more clearly and more fully than others. But the developing pattern of legislative activity at EU level is in the process of creating an increasingly dense network of rules. That the EU legislative *acquis* addresses universal service and consumer vulnerability at all, however imperfectly, is of itself a demonstration of how social protection, not simply choice in the market, has become part of the EU's pattern of (re-)regulation. There is here legislative material that tends towards an obligation imposed on a supplier to enter into a contract, albeit not of a systematic nature.

A much richer set of constitutional norms lies in the background. Article 36 of the Charter declares that the Union 'recognises and respects access to services of general economic interest as provided for in national laws and practices, in accordance with the Treaties, in order to promote the social and territorial cohesion of the Union.' Article 14 TFEU is more intricate, but at its heart it too commits to the virtue of services of general economic interest 'in the shared values of the Union' and directs that both the Union and the Member States shall take care that such services operate on the basis of principles and conditions which enable them to fulfil their missions. It is beyond the scope of this book to provide an in-depth account of the treatment in EU law of services of general economic interest: at stake is debate about the proper role of public intervention in the market[204] and, broader still, a human rights perspective as a means to examine the social and economic tensions at stake.[205] Energy law in the internal market is one window on this debate.

4.7.3. THE COURT OF JUSTICE

Information disclosure as a regulatory technique in the pre-contractual phase was discussed above in section 4.3; the thematic importance of transparency in the application of Directive 93/13 on unfair terms in particular is a *leitmotif* in the

203 For detail see A. Johnston and G. Block, *Energy Law in Europe*, OUP, Oxford 2012, Ch 7.

204 See A. Johnston, 'Seeking the EU "Consumer" in Services of General Economic Interest' in D. Leczykiewicz and S. Weatherill (eds.), *The Images of the Consumer in EU Law*, Bloomsbury/Hart/IECL, Oxford 2016, Ch. 4, pp. 93–138; also e.g. W. Sauter and H. Schepel, *State and Market in the European Union: The Public and Private Spheres of the Internal Market before the EU Courts*, CUP, Cambridge 2009.

205 e.g. I. Benöhr, *EU Consumer Law and Human Rights*, OUP, Oxford 2013.

Court's case law.[206] A comparable approach may be found in the supply of energy to consumers. In *Alexandra Schulz and Josef Egbringhoff* the Court was asked to consider a standard term contract for the supply of gas.[207] The relevant standard terms, established by a German legislative measure, provided for the possibility of unilateral increases in price without indicating the reasons and preconditions for that adjustment or its scope, but ensured that customers were informed of any increase in rates and that they were free to terminate their contract. When Ms Schultz found the price she paid had been increased in this manner four times in the space of two years, she challenged the terms. Mr Egbringhoff was in a similar predicament, though he was a consumer of both electricity and gas. Directive 93/13 did not help. It excludes from its scope contractual terms which reflect mandatory provisions, and the German measures at stake were of this type. But the consumers were nevertheless able to claim protection pursuant to Directives 2003/54 and 2003/55, the Directives on the internal market for electricity and gas that are the immediate predecessors of those mentioned above.[208] The Court 'noted that the aim of those directives is to improve the operation of the internal market in electricity and gas' and immediately added that '[n]on-discriminatory, transparent and fairly priced network access is necessary for competition to function and of paramount importance in completing the internal electricity and gas market'.[209] Furthermore, '[c]onsumer protection concerns underpin the provisions of Directives 2003/54 and 2003/55'.[210] The Court ruled that the Directives require Member States to ensure a high level of consumer protection in relation to the transparency of the contract terms and conditions. In order to permit challenge to adjustments to the price of supply, it is required that *before* the adjustment takes effect the consumer be given adequate notice of the reasons and preconditions for the adjustment, and its scope. German law was in this regard deficient.

This ruling ties together market-making, consumer protection and transparency and extracts concrete conclusions from it. The Court emphasised the force of its ruling by rejecting pleas to limit the temporal effect of its judgment to the future for fear of significant economic damage caused by obligations to repay. It was not persuaded that there would follow consequences on such a scale.

4.7.4. THEMES, PRINCIPLES AND POLICY

Energy law, like passenger law (section 4.6), amounts to a sector-specific area of EU regulatory contract law. It reveals that the EU is concerned with transparency

---

206 e.g. Case C-26/13, *Árpád Kásler* judgment of 30 April 2014, esp. paras. 70–72. See section 4.4.3.

207 Joined Cases C-359/11 and C-400/11 judgment of 23 October 2014. Cf. also Case C-92/11, *RWE Vertrieb AG* judgment of 21 March 2013.

208 Above n. 195, 196.

209 Para. 39.

210 Para. 40.

in the market, but not only with that. It pushes further to protect security of supply, and dips albeit hesitantly into matters of protection for vulnerable consumers. The detail is important, but more generally a politically contested debate is required to fix the appropriate balance between market liberalisation, on the one hand, and regulation of that market more intensively than would be delivered by reliance on competition law alone on the other.[211]

4.8. COMMERCIAL CONTRACT LAW

4.8.1. COMPETENCE

It is not only consumer contract law which makes up the legislative *acquis*, though that provides the bulk of it and it is typically the main focus of academic and practical attention. There is a small amount of harmonised commercial contract law. A Directive deals with rules on self-employed commercial agents[212] and another with combating late payment in commercial transactions.[213] The 'Services Directive' contains significant provisions dealing with pre-contractual information disclosure and the prohibition of discrimination which affect commercial contracts as well as consumer contracts.[214]

Directive 86/653 on commercial agents cites in its Preamble 'differences in national laws concerning commercial representation' which, it is claimed, 'substantially affect the conditions of competition and the carrying-on of that activity within the Community'. So harmonisation is called for 'to the extent required for the proper functioning of the common market'.

Directive 2011/7 on late payment in commercial transactions is based on equally familiar logic. Its Recital 5 states that '[d]istortions of competition would ensue if substantially different rules applied to domestic and transborder operations'. So diverse national responses to the hindrances to liquidity and competitiveness which are caused by late payment generate an EU competence to address the matter at the level of the internal market.

This cupboard is not bare, but it has little in it. There is only a small pocket of harmonised contract law beyond the consumer sphere. This is largely because the impetus to develop a harmonised *acquis* in the field of consumer contract law derives from the transformative political commitments made at the Paris Summit of 1972 which were focused on consumer protection (within the

211 See e.g. A. Johnston, 'The Future Shape of EU Energy Law and Policy' in A. Arnull et al. (eds.), *A Constitutional Order of States? Essays in EU Law in Honour of Alan Dashwood*, Hart Publishing, Oxford 2011.

212 Dir. 86/653 [1986] OJ L382/17.

213 Dir. 2011/7 [2011] OJ L48/1, replacing the original Dir. 2000/35 [2000] OJ L200/35.

214 Dir. 2006/123 [2006] OJ L376/36.

internal market), not the commercial sphere.[215] This bias was also accentuated by an institutional dimension: there has long been a unit within the Commission with specific responsibility for consumer policy, albeit that its precise location and resources have not remained static over the last five decades, whereas by contrast there is no equivalent with direct responsibility for commercial law. In addition, however, there is a coherent constitutional reason why consumer contract law has been subjected to a much more intensive harmonised impact than commercial contract law. At national level intervention to adopt mandatory rules that are designed to protect the consumer, as the weaker party, is a long-established feature of the regulated market, whereas there is in general a much higher level of readiness to permit commercial parties to make their own choices about contracting. Legislative diversity is the trigger to EU harmonisation. As a general observation the fact that consumer contract law is more heavily regulated at national level than commercial contract law is the reason why it is in turn more heavily regulated at EU level. This is the re-regulatory dynamic of harmonisation in the internal market.

4.8.2. CONTENT AND RE-REGULATORY CHOICES

Directive 86/653 addresses the legal status of the relationship between commercial agents (as defined) and their principals. Its Chapter II sets out rights and obligations. So in performing his or her activities a commercial agent must look after his principal's interests and act dutifully and in good faith, while a principal too must act dutifully and in good faith. This is the subject of more elaborate detail in the Directive, but it is important that Article 5 states that the parties may not derogate from these requirements. They therefore prevail over contractual autonomy.

Chapter III addresses remuneration. Article 6 declares that 'a commercial agent shall be entitled to the remuneration that commercial agents appointed for the goods forming the subject of his agency contract are customarily allowed in the place where he carries on his activities'. This is however subject to the proviso that this applies in the absence of any agreement on this matter between the parties. So thematically a preference for contractual autonomy is here visible.

Chapter IV deals with conclusion and termination of the agency contract. Here too there is some limited degree of supplement to contractual autonomy. Article 15, for example, stipulates the notice periods that shall apply where an agency contract is concluded for an indefinite period, but leaves it to the parties to fix notice periods for contracts concluded for a finite period. Article 17 provides for the indemnification or compensation of the agent on termination of the contract, subject to exceptions set out in Article 18. Article 19 precludes the

[215] See sections 3.9, 3.10 and 4.3.1.

parties derogating from Articles 17 and 18 to the detriment of the commercial agent before the agency contract expires.

Directive 2011/7 directs that in commercial transactions between undertakings, the creditor shall be entitled to interest for late payment without the necessity of a reminder, where stipulated conditions are satisfied. This, in short, is a move beyond a pure model of contractual autonomy. The Preamble to the Directive states that it 'should prohibit abuse of freedom of contract to the disadvantage of the creditor'.[216] But the Directive itself reveals the tensions involved. Its Article 3(4) directs that where a procedure of acceptance or verification, by which the conformity of the goods or services with the contract is to be ascertained, is provided for, Member States shall ensure that the maximum duration of that procedure does not exceed thirty calendar days from the date of receipt of the goods or services, but this is not unconditional. It is added that this applies 'unless otherwise expressly agreed in the contract and provided it is not grossly unfair to the creditor within the meaning of Article 7'. Similarly Article 3(5) states that Member States 'shall ensure that the period for payment fixed in the contract does not exceed 60 calendar days, unless otherwise expressly agreed in the contract and provided it is not grossly unfair to the creditor within the meaning of Article 7'.

There are, in addition, special rules applicable where the debtor is a public authority.

Article 8 is entitled 'Transparency and awareness raising'. Member States shall ensure transparency regarding the rights and obligations stemming from this Directive, including by making publicly available the applicable rate of statutory interest for late payment.

4.8.3. THE COURT OF JUSTICE

There is a small amount of case law dealing with these Directives, but much less than is visible in connection with other Directives considered in this chapter, especially Directive 93/13 on unfair terms (section 4.4.3).

The purposes of the Commercial Agents Directive have been explained by the Court as the protection of commercial agents in their relations with their principals, the promotion of the security of commercial transactions, and the facilitation of trade in goods between Member States by means of harmonisation.[217] The Court has been asked to elucidate the meaning of the Directive, which in several respects is lacking in precise detail. So, for example,

[216] Recital 28.

[217] Case C-465/04, *Honyvem Informazioni Commerciali* [2006] ECR I-2879, para. 19; Case C-348/07, *Turgay Semen* [2009] ECR I-2341, para. 14; Case C-338/14, *Quenon K. Sprl* judgment of 3 December 2015, para. 23.

it has been asked in preliminary references to clarify how the indemnity for termination of contract mandated by Article 17 shall be calculated. It has insisted that Article 19 of the Directive means that a derogation from the provisions of Article 17 may be accepted only if, judged ex ante, there is no possibility that at the end of the contract the derogation will prove to be detrimental to the agent.[218] Asked to supply detailed guidance on how to calculate the indemnity for termination of contract which is mandated by Article 17, it has left the matter to the discretion of the Member States, albeit that this must be exercised in the light of the objectives pursued by the Directive.[219]

In *Ingmar v Eaton Leonard Technologies* the Court was asked questions about Article 19's preclusion of the parties' ability to derogate from the protections envisaged by Articles 17 and 18.[220] An agent was seeking payment of commission and compensation for damage suffered as a result of the termination of a contract. The problem was that the contract was stated to be governed by the law of California. It was pressed on the Court that 'the freedom of contracting parties to choose the system of law by which they wish their contractual relations to be governed is a basic tenet of private international law and that that freedom is removed only by rules that are mandatory'.[221] But the Court concluded this was such a mandatory rule. It took an approach which would be immediately familiar to the student of its case law concerning consumer contract law. It identified the Directive's dual function: it is aimed at both the protection of commercial agents and at making the conditions of competition within the EU uniform. So where the commercial agent carries on activity within the EU, the requirements of the Directive may not be evaded by 'the simple expedient of a choice-of-law clause'.[222]

Caffaro Srl arose under the first iteration of the Late Payment Directive (2000/35).[223] The Court noted the limited scope of the measure. It includes rules on interest for late payments, retention of title and procedures for recovery of unchallenged claims. But the Court found that rules governing forced execution did not fall within the harmonised regime. National law therefore governed such matters. This was not an inevitable conclusion. A recital to the Directive stated that it does not regulate 'the various procedures of forced execution' of an enforceable title, but – contrary to the Court's claim in the judgment – the Directive does not make it explicit that national law shall apply to such matters.[224] In some other rulings – most conspicuously in *Simone Leitner*[225] –

218 Case C-465/04, *Honyvem Informazioni Commerciali* [2006] ECR I-2879.

219 Case C-465/04, *Honyvem Informazioni Commerciali* [2006] ECR I-2879; Case C-338/14, *Quenon K. Sprl* judgment of 3 December 2015.

220 Case C-381/98 [2000] ECR I-9305.

221 Para. 15.

222 Para. 25.

223 Case C-265/07 [2008] ECR I-7085.

224 Recital 15 to the Directive; see para. 17 of the judgment.

225 Case C-168/00 [2002] ECR I-2631.

the Court has exploited a lack of legislative decisiveness to shift regulation of a particular issue to EU level, at the expense of national autonomy. In *Caffaro* the Court was more restrained.

It would be a mistake to read too much into this shallow pool of *ad hoc* preliminary rulings, but it is at least plausible that the commercial context, devoid of any element in which the Treaty mandate to pursue a high level of consumer protection might play a role, prompts a degree of judicial interpretative restraint.

4.8.4. THEMES, PRINCIPLES AND POLICY

It would be a stretch to extract substantial themes from such a slim body of legislation dealing with commercial contract law, although transparency is a visible element that deserves attention as a regular theme in the EU's legislative *acquis*. In fact, although both Directives contain some mandatory rules, the caution attached to curtailment of contractual autonomy visible in both the Commercial Agents and the Late Payment Directives combined with, more broadly, the very paucity of initiatives is itself revealing: it is best understood as an indication that the main theme here is to permit autonomy as a general rule in the commercial context.

Part of this story is that commercial parties have the expertise and resources to operate across national borders in the internal market without needing the comfort of harmonisation of laws. This will be more true of some businesses than others, and a clear theme of the Commission's review of contract law, initiated in 2001 and explained in Chapter 3.10, is to promote harmonisation as a means to induce not only consumers but also small and medium-sized enterprises (SMEs) to treat the internal market as a resource. In this vein the Commission argued that for 'consumers and SMEs in particular, not knowing other contract law regimes may be a disincentive against undertaking cross-border transactions' and that 'disparate national law rules may lead to higher transaction costs, especially information and possible litigation costs for enterprises in general and SMEs and consumers in particular'.[226] There is therefore a case that consumer protection should not be treated as an isolated category. The margins may blur – a small business may be every bit as vulnerable as a consumer when dealing with a powerful business, and in fact Article 1 of Directive 2011/7 on late payment declares its aim is to foster 'the competitiveness of undertakings and in particular of SMEs'. However, although there are hints of special concern for SMEs in EU law,[227] in general the EU's policy to protect SMEs is far less elaborate

226 COM (2001) 398, paras. 30, 31.

227 e.g. on justifications for restrictions on free movement, see Case C-464/05, *Maria Geurts* [2007] ECR I-9325; on special treatment in the light of the State aid rules, Regulation

than that which has developed to protect consumers. This is highly conspicuous in relation to contract law.

4.9. PUBLIC PROCUREMENT

4.9.1. COMPETENCE

The law of public procurement constitutes an atypically well-developed area of 'Europeanisation' of national contract law. Directives impose structure and limitations on the process of soliciting bids for public contracts and the method for their award, and moreover there is explicit legislative treatment of remedies to be made available at national level. This is something of a niche area, and tends to be the exclusive preserve of specialists dealing chiefly with its high commercial significance. Sector-specific works examine the law in intricate detail.[228] However, niche though it may be, it royally deserves wider appreciation as an example of how (and why) internal market law may come into close connection with national contract law.

There have been four rounds of secondary legislation designed to promote competitive public procurement in the EU. The first set of Directives, adopted in the 1970s, were subsequently amended and updated to meet the challenge of completing the internal market by the end of 1992 and beyond. Then the package was renovated once again by measures adopted in 2004 before the fourth and current iteration of legislative renewal. With effect from 18 April 2016, the governing Directive is Directive 2014/24 on public procurement, supported by the special sector-specific regime of Directive 2014/25 on procurement by entities operating in the water, energy, transport and postal services sectors.[229] These Directives are supplemented by Directive 2014/23 on concession contracts.[230] The Directives on remedies, of which there are three, have been adopted according to a different rhythm. They are the general remedies Directive 89/665,[231] which was

651/2004 declaring certain categories of aid compatible with the internal market in application of Articles 107 and 108 of the Treaty [2004] OJ L187/1 and Regulation 2015/1588 on the application of Articles 107 and 108 of the Treaty on the Functioning of the European Union to certain categories of horizontal State aid [2015] OJ L248/1. See also M. Loos and I. Samoy (eds.), *The Position of Small and Medium-Sized Enterprises in European Contract Law*, Intersentia, Antwerp 2014; M. Hesselink, 'SMEs in European Contract Law' in K. Boele-Woelki and W. Grosheide (eds.), *The Future of European Contract Law: Essays in Honour of Ewoud Hondius*, Kluwer Law International, Alphen aan der Rijn 2007, pp. 349–371.

228 See S. Arrowsmith, *The Law of Public and Utilities Procurement*, Vols. 1 and 2, 3rd ed., Sweet and Maxwell, London 2014.

229 [2014] OJ L94/65, [2014] OJ L94/243. See F. Lichère, R. Caranta and S. Treumer (eds.), *Modernising Public Procurement: The New Directive*, Djøf Publishing, Copenhagen 2014.

230 [2014] OJ L94/1.

231 [1989] OJ L395/33.

amended by Directive 2007/66,[232] supplemented by Directive 92/13 operative in the water, energy, transport and telecommunications sectors.[233] There is very little legislation in the EU which addresses remedies before national courts, so these are rarities and their existence is of interest for that reason, though, given the bite they add to the consequences of breach of the EU's public procurement rules, certainly not only for that reason.

All these Directives are measures of legislative harmonisation and, stretching back to the 1970s, they have all been firmly based on the Treaty provisions governing harmonisation as means to improve the functioning of the internal market for goods and services. Their basic aim is to promote cross-border trade in the supply of goods and services to public authorities and to make those markets more competitive through integration. Directive 2014/24 is the core measure today.[234] Its legal base is provided by Articles 53(1), 62 and 114 TFEU.

This, then, is heartland internal market law. It is in fact the pressing need to accelerate the integration of markets for public contracts that explains the existence of this relatively elaborate sector-specific pattern of secondary legislation. There is no difficulty in condemning as a violation of EU law contracting practices which assert bias based on the origin of the bidder, typically expressed in favour of local suppliers. A local authority in Ruritania which decides to 'buy Ruritanian' thereby favours goods and services on the basis of their origin rather than quality. This contradicts the basic assumptions of the internal market. This is a straightforward violation of the law of free movement. It is not difficult to find cases of this type on the record.[235] It is moreover clear that free movement law is not merely focused on substance, but rather that it also has a procedural dimension. When a public authority operates a process that will lead to the grant of, for example, a licence to pursue a particular type of supply, it is required that the procedures be open, non-discriminatory and transparent: to operate such a procedure without an adequate level of openness that will permit genuine competition between suppliers is itself in violation of EU law.[236]

These cases are relatively plentiful. But the governing perception is that there are not enough of these types of cases to reveal, prevent and deter endemic discriminatory practices in markets for public procurement.

---

232 [2007] OJ L335/31.

233 [1992] OJ L76/14.

234 [2014] OJ L94/65.

235 e.g. Case 45/87, *Commission v Ireland* [1988] ECR 4929; Case C-3/88, *Commission v Italy* [1989] ECR 4035; Case C-243/89, *Commission v Denmark* [1993] ECR I-3353.

236 e.g. Case C-24/00, *Commission v France* [2004] ECR I-1277; Joined Cases C-25/14 and C-26/14, *UNIS* judgment of 17 December 2015; Case C-375/14, *Rosanna Laezza* judgment of 28 January 2016; Case C-336/14, *Sebat Ince* judgment of 4 February 2016.

The Commission's 1985 White Paper on completing the internal market set the tone. It observed that:

> 'Public procurement covers a sizeable part of GDP and is still marked by the tendency of the authorities concerned to keep their purchases and contracts within their own territory. This continued partitioning of individual national markets is one of the most evident barriers to the achievement of a real internal market'.[237]

Public procurement has been treated as a persisting 'problem area' in the Commission's regular surveys of progress made towards the completion of the internal market. It covers some 15% of GDP in the EU, so the size of the market for public contracts means that there would be significant gains from converting it from a largely national scale into one that is genuinely competitive across borders in the internal market, but it is stubbornly resistant to such alteration. In 2011 the Commission's 'Single Market Act: twelve levers to boost growth and strengthen confidence, working together to create new growth' picked as one of its 'twelve levers' public procurement.[238] The sector's resistance to cross-border integration continues to command attention. The 2011 document concludes that 'the proportion of public contracts which are awarded to suppliers from other Member States is still quite low, in particular in comparison with the level of import penetration in private procurement'.[239] The Commission continues anxiously to monitor the sector. A closely argued and empirically driven survey published in April 2015, 'Economic efficiency and legal effectiveness of review and remedies procedures for public contracts', is rich in detail and information, but concedes that, over forty years since the EU first adopted secondary legislation in the field, suppliers continue not to seek review of contracting malpractice, 'the two most common reasons being lack of confidence in the success of the complaints and a fear of retaliation by the awarding authority'.[240]

It seems relatively easy to conceal discriminatory practices in this sector. It will frequently be hard to prove why a contract has been placed locally. And disappointed bidders have incentives not to take legal action against offending public authorities, but rather to suffer in silence in the hope of better luck next time. The size and economic strength of awarding public authorities is precisely the reason why they are able to thwart the expectations of internal market law. So the Directives put in place much more concrete and detailed rules, under an assumption that the true potential of the internal market cannot be realised without deeper cuts into national autonomy than are envisaged by the rules of primary EU law alone.

---

237 COM (85) 310, para. 81.

238 COM (2011) 206.

239 Page 19.

240 European Commission, Final Study Report MARKT/2013/072C, p. 12.

4.9.2. CONTENT AND RE-REGULATORY CHOICES

Directive 2014/24 is the most important general measure of secondary legislation governing public procurement in the EU.[241] Its core aim is to channel the process of public contracting within defined pathways. The intricacy of its design is readily appreciated by noting its length: it covers 94 Articles, it is padded by 138 Recitals in its Preamble and it is then supported by 15 Annexes which provide further detailed definitional support. It occupies 177 pages of the Official Journal of the EU. The abiding concern is to promote transparency and open competition uncontaminated by bias based on the origin of the supplier of goods and services. The aim is to foster a genuine internal market by confining contractual autonomy, the exercise of which has demonstrably tended to impede the achievement of that genuine internal market. This fits within the general concept of 'regulatory contract law' which is explored in this chapter, albeit that it is here targeted at placing constraints on the contractual autonomy of public authorities, not private suppliers.

Recital 1 of Directive 2014/24 offers a helpful summary of the regime:

> 'The award of public contracts by or on behalf of Member States' authorities has to comply with the principles of the Treaty on the Functioning of the European Union (TFEU), and in particular the free movement of goods, freedom of establishment and the freedom to provide services, as well as the principles deriving therefrom, such as equal treatment, non-discrimination, mutual recognition, proportionality and transparency. However, for public contracts above a certain value, provisions should be drawn up coordinating national procurement procedures so as to ensure that those principles are given practical effect and public procurement is opened up to competition'.

Directive 2014/24's Title I covers 'Scope, Definitions and General Principles' and stretches from Article 1 to Article 24. Article 1(1) states that '[t]his Directive establishes rules on the procedures for procurement by contracting authorities with respect to public contracts as well as design contests, whose value is estimated to be not less than the thresholds laid down in Article 4'. Procurement within the meaning of the Directive 'is the acquisition by means of a public contract of works, supplies or services by one or more contracting authorities from economic operators chosen by those contracting authorities, whether or not the works, supplies or services are intended for a public purpose'.[242] Article 2 defines 'contracting authorities'. They cover 'the State, regional or local authorities, bodies governed by public law or associations formed by one or more such authorities or one or more such bodies governed by public law'. This is plainly designed to be a broad definition, a point which

241 [2014] OJ L94/65.
242 Art. 1(2).

the Court has repeatedly confirmed in its interpretation of this Directive's predecessors.[243]

Article 18, 'Principles of procurement', states that '[c]ontracting authorities shall treat economic operators equally and without discrimination and shall act in a transparent and proportionate manner'. The Directive, then, is broadly concerned to require equal treatment and transparency, but, more significant in practice, it prescribes the use of procedures that will promote the likelihood of compliance with these aspirations. This is where it builds beyond the basic free movement rules of the Treaty. The aim is greater competition and economic efficiency in a sector which has sorely lacked such features over an extended period.

Title II of Directive 2014/24 is entitled 'Rules on Public Contracts'. It comprises Articles 25–73 of the Directive. It sets out the procedures among which contracting authorities may select, and crucially it defines the way they shall be structured and conducted with considerable precision, with particular concern for encouraging participation by bidders and confining the scope for excluding would-be bidders. Transparency is a clear *leitmotif*. The options are open procedure, restricted procedure, competitive procedure with negotiation, competitive dialogue, innovation partnership, and negotiated procedure without prior publication. Electronic means are widely used today and the Directive sets out in detail the governing arrangements. Getting to grips with exactly what these rules entail is the lifeblood of practice in the commercially significant field of public procurement law.[244] At a wider thematic level, the point is to channel contractual autonomy under an assumption that, left unrestrained, it will be exercised in a manner that will not be conducive to the achievement of an internal market for the EU.

Article 67, 'Contract award criteria', provides that 'contracting authorities shall base the award of public contracts on the most economically advantageous tender'. This falls to be identified 'on the basis of the price or cost, using a cost-effectiveness approach, such as life-cycle costing in accordance with Article 68'; it 'may include the best price–quality ratio, which shall be assessed on the basis of criteria, including qualitative, environmental and/or social aspects, linked to the subject-matter of the public contract in question'. Further elucidation of the criteria is supplied, under an instruction that '[a]ward criteria shall not have the effect of conferring an unrestricted freedom of choice on the contracting authority'.[245] Moreover the contracting authority shall specify 'the relative weighting which it gives to each of the criteria chosen to determine the most

---

243 e.g. Case 31/87, *Beentjes v Netherlands* [1988] ECR 4635; Case C-337/06, *Bayerische Rundfunk* [2007] ECR I-11173; Case C-305/08, *CoNISMa* [2009] ECR I-12129.

244 See S. Arrowsmith, *The Law of Public and Utilities Procurement*, Vols. 1 and 2, 3rd ed., Sweet and Maxwell, London 2014. The *Public Procurement Law Review* offers regular useful insight into matters that are awkward in practice.

245 Article 67(4).

economically advantageous tender, except where this is identified on the basis of price alone'.[246] The thematic concern for transparency is plain.

This serves as only a short summary: the Directive overall provides a relatively dense framework within which to pursue public contracting. The additional legislative commitment to remedies is striking and, as mentioned, unusual in EU law.[247] The norm in EU law is to leave it to national systems to determine the nature of the procedures and remedies to be placed at the service of rights granted by EU law. This is subject to the admittedly rather highly evolved EU law principles of equivalence and effectiveness, first nurtured and developed by the Court of Justice in some of its more ground-breaking rulings[248] and now recorded as a Treaty commitment by Article 19 TEU. The Court's readiness to use the principle of effectiveness (in particular) as a springboard from which to dive deep into national patterns of procedure and remedies was tracked earlier in this chapter in connection with most of all Directive 93/13 on unfair terms (section 4.4.3) to the point where one could plausibly conclude that national procedural autonomy is a myth.[249] Remedies law governing public procurement is built on these foundations, but goes further. For public procurement, in contrast to virtually all other areas of EU law and policy, the scope of national remedies has not been left to national law applied in the light of the Court of Justice's broad but vague notion that there shall be effective judicial protection of EU law rights before national courts. Secondary legislation sharpens the requirements imposed by EU law. As with the channelling Directives mentioned above, the concern is to make more concrete the obligations imposed by EU law in the hope that this will improve policing of the rules governing contracts awarded by public authorities and in consequence develop further the construction of a true internal market in this sector.

The original Directive, Directive 89/665,[250] is quite short. It occupies only three pages of the Official Journal of the EU and it contains just three substantive Articles. Article 1 directs the Member States to take the necessary measures to ensure effective review of contract award procedures that infringe EU law. Article 2 stipulates that the measures available shall include

---

246 Art. 67(5).

247 Other examples, all niches, include injunctions in consumer cases (Dir. 2009/22 [2009] OJ L110/30), competition law (Dir. 2014/104 [2014] OJ L349/1), enforcement of intellectual property rights (Dir. 2004/48 [2004] OJ L195/16) and access to environmental justice (Dir. 2003/35 [2003] OJ L156/17).

248 Most spectacularly those dealing with claims for damages: e.g. Cases C-6/90 and C-9/90, *Francovich and Others* [1991] ECR I-5357; Joined Cases C-46/93 and C-48/93, *Brasserie du Pêcheur v Germany and R v Secretary of State for Transport, ex parte Factortame* [1996] ECR I-1029; Case C-453/99, *Courage v Crehan* [2001] ECR I-6297.

249 M. Bobek, 'Why There is no Principle of Procedural Autonomy of the Member States' in B. de Witte and H. Micklitz (eds.), *The European Court of Justice and Autonomy of the Member States*, Intersentia, Cambridge 2011.

250 [1989] OJ L395/33.

interim measures, the setting aside of decisions taken unlawfully and the award of damages to persons harmed by an infringement. Article 3 provides for Commission intervention in a case of clear and manifest infringement, generating a defined path of dialogue between Commission and national authorities.

Article 2 is the most interesting provision of the Directive because of what it reveals about the delicacy of the collision between the pursuit of the internal market and the sanctity of contracts. It begins by directing that Member States shall ensure provision for powers to take interim measures with the aim of correcting the alleged infringement or preventing further damage to the interests concerned, including measures to suspend or to ensure the suspension of the procedure for the award of a public contract or the implementation of any decision taken by the contracting authority; and ensure the setting aside of decisions taken unlawfully, including the removal of discriminatory technical, economic or financial specifications in the invitation to tender, the contract documents or in any other document relating to the contract award procedure; and award damages to persons harmed by an infringement.

The obvious awkward question is whether a violation of the rules of EU law has any impact on a contract that has already been concluded. Article 2(6) is clear and it is deferential. It provides that '[t]he effects of the exercise of the powers referred to in paragraph 1 on a contract concluded subsequent to its award shall be determined by national law'. Moreover, Article 2(6) adds that 'except where a decision must be set aside prior to the award of damages, a Member State may provide that, after the conclusion of a contract following its award, the powers of the body responsible for the review procedures shall be limited to awarding damages to any person harmed by an infringement'. There is, then, a sensitivity to the uncertainty that would flow from requiring the unravelling of contractual obligations that have come into existence. This means that a contract awarded pursuant to improper procedures may be allowed to remain in force, should a Member State so choose, pushing the aggrieved party to pursue a damages claim. This gives a route to evade the intended impact of the EU's rules. There is an incentive for the public authority to ensure a contract is signed quickly, because it cannot later be set aside. It became apparent that the possibility of a damages award recognised by Directive 89/665 was not enough to deter this 'rush to signature'. There are real practical obstacles to pursuing a claim for damages where a contract has been awarded in breach of the requirements of EU law, such as the shrewd preference of a wrongly excluded bidder to hope to win the next contract rather than cause disturbance by litigating over a lost contract and, even where a bidder is defiant enough to litigate, the difficulty of showing a quantifiable loss caused by the public authorities' default, a particular problem where the bidder is wrongfully excluded before it is able to show it has lost anything more concrete than a chance to participate in a competitive process.

Directive 89/665 was therefore amended by Directive 2007/66.[251] In consequence of its amendment of the regime, there is now an Article 1 in Directive 89/665 which is expanded in detail, albeit that it follows the original pattern in that it requires Member States to provide for effective review of contract award procedures that infringe EU law. There is also an expanded Article 3: it too follows the original pattern which is to envisage Commission intervention in cases of misfeasance leading to dialogue with national authorities. However, Article 2, which deals with review and sanction procedures to be made available at national level, is much expanded.

Under an assumption that the possibility of a damages claim is not enough to deter malpractice by contacting authorities, amending Directive 2007/66 is driven by the need to combat the 'rush to signature'. Recital 4 of the Directive provides a brief summary of the existing weaknesses in the scheme. These cover 'in particular the absence of a period allowing an effective review between the decision to award a contract and the conclusion of the contract in question'. The point, it is explained, is that contracting authorities wishing to make irreversible the consequences of the disputed award decision tend to proceed 'very quickly to the signature of the contract'. This plainly harms the interests of those tenderers who have not yet been definitively excluded, and more broadly it undermines the pro-competitive aim of the EU's intervention into this market. The Recital explains that 'it is necessary to provide for a minimum standstill period during which the conclusion of the contract in question is suspended, irrespective of whether conclusion occurs at the time of signature of the contract or not'.[252] So the key idea is to stop the contract being concluded as a means to improve enforcement of the EU rules. This would improve legal protection for disgruntled bidders and help to forestall a faulty and hasty process.

Directive 2007/66 inserted a new Article 2a into Directive 89/665. It establishes a 'standstill period'. This is intended to deter the 'rush to signature' which has undermined legal protection in practice hitherto. So a contract may not be concluded following the decision to award it before the expiry of a period of at least ten calendar days with effect from the day following the date on which the contract award decision is sent to the tenderers and candidates concerned if fax or electronic means are used, or longer, as defined by the Directive, if other means are used. Article 2b provides for derogations from the standstill period. These, one might suppose based on previous experience of poor conduct by awarding authorities, will be important in practice. Article 2d deals with

[251] [2007] OJ L335/31. For a collection of essays, see D. Fairgrieve and F. Lichère (ed.), *Public Procurement Law: Damages as an Effective Remedy*, Hart Publishing, Oxford 2011.

[252] The problems and the motivation for this remedy are explained more fully in COM (2006) 195.

the 'ineffectiveness' of contracts in some circumstances. This is probably the most innovative aspect of the amending Directive. It is provided that 'Member States shall ensure that a contract is considered ineffective by a review body independent of the contracting authority or that its ineffectiveness is the result of a decision of such a review body' in any of three cases: where award has been made without required prior publication of a notice in the Official Journal; where particular defined infringements have deprived the tenderer applying for review of the possibility to pursue pre-contractual remedies or the chances to obtain the contract; and, third, in particular defined circumstances associated with a framework agreement and a dynamic purchasing system.

The first of these is of the widest application. Failure to publicise in the Official Journal, a key component of the overall scheme promoting transparency, shall lead to a decision that the contract is 'ineffective'. But what does this entail? 'Ineffective' is not a term of art in English contract law. The word used in other language versions is similarly lacking in precision.[253] One might assume it should therefore be granted an autonomous meaning under EU law, as considered in section 4.2 above. However, it is not defined by Directive 2007/66. Article 2d(2) directs that '[t]he consequences of a contract being considered ineffective shall be provided for by national law'. Here one is immediately reacquainted with the sensitivity of intervention in concluded contracts. Article 2d(2) adds that '[n]ational law *may* provide for the retroactive cancellation of all contractual obligations or limit the scope of the cancellation to those obligations which still have to be performed' – the emphasis is added to reinforce the point that this is a national choice. Article 2d(3) provides – and here again the emphasis is added for the same purpose – that:

> 'Member States *may* provide that the review body independent of the contracting authority may not consider a contract ineffective, even though it has been awarded illegally on the grounds mentioned in paragraph 1, if the review body finds, after having examined all relevant aspects, that overriding reasons relating to a general interest require that the effects of the contract should be maintained'.

In such a case Member States shall provide for 'alternative penalties within the meaning of Article 2e(2)', which shall be applied instead. These cover the imposition of fines on the contracting authority or the shortening of the duration of the contract. Article 2e(2) makes explicit what is in fact a general principle of EU law, that such alternative penalties must be effective, proportionate and dissuasive. Generally Article 2e is intended to sharpen penalties in the case of disregard of the rules.

So Article 2d(3) leaves it open to Member States to bar the sanction of ineffectiveness, which reveals the abiding sensitivity at stake once a contract has

253 e.g. *dépourvu d'effets, privo di effetti, unwirksam, onverbindend.*

been awarded, even if the award is procedurally flawed as a matter of EU law.[254] The threshold set by the Directive is whether 'overriding reasons relating to a general interest require that the effects of the contract should be maintained'. The key is what this means. Article 2d(3) cautions that '[e]conomic interests in the effectiveness of the contract may only be considered as overriding reasons if in exceptional circumstances ineffectiveness would lead to disproportionate consequences' and that 'economic interests directly linked to the contract concerned shall not constitute overriding reasons relating to a general interest'. Economic interests directly linked to the contract are defined to 'include, inter alia, the costs resulting from the delay in the execution of the contract, the costs resulting from the launching of a new procurement procedure, the costs resulting from the change of the economic operator performing the contract and the costs of legal obligations resulting from the ineffectiveness'.

Article 2f places time limits on pursuit of these newly introduced forms of review, in order to protect legal certainty.

So the principal intrigue and mystery of this regime lies mainly in the content of contractual 'ineffectiveness'. Recital 14 to Directive 2007/66 declares that '[i]neffectiveness is the most effective way to restore competition and to create new business opportunities for those economic operators which have been deprived illegally of their opportunity to compete'. But this begs the question of what 'ineffectiveness' entails. There loom questions of interpretation about the proper mix between EU law and national contract law. The Directive's Article 2d(2) directs that '[t]he consequences of a contract being considered ineffective shall be provided for by national law'. As explained above, this is subject to a certain amount of elaboration by the Directive. But there is room for the Court of Justice to develop an autonomous EU law understanding of when a contract shall be considered 'ineffective' and, in addition, to use EU law's principle of effectiveness to make concrete what shall be the consequences of such a designation. Article 2d(2)'s reservation of that matter to national law should be read with awareness of the Court's predilection elsewhere to treat national law which gives effect to the intent of Directives as itself conditioned by the overall requirements of EU law, including the need for its effective application. The case law under Directive 93/13 on unfair terms, discussed in section 4.4.3, is the most vivid illustration of this trend. The EU lawyer's suspicion is that the Court of Justice will be tempted to be bolder in its interpretation of this remedies regime than might be expected under a rigidly textual approach. In fact one may predict that it is likely to promote an effective interpretation of ineffectiveness.

---

254 Some information on the choices made by Member States under this and other optional provisions of the Directive may be found in European Commission, Final Study Report MARKT/2013/072C, pp. 63–65; see also pp. 91–96 on practice.

4.9.3. THE COURT OF JUSTICE

The Court has been given a great many opportunities to elucidate its general view of the regime. There is a large amount of litigation in this sector, although, as mentioned above (section 4.9.1), the Commission's strong view is that it has not been sufficiently vigorous to promote any significant correction of the national bias that contaminates the public procurement sector in the EU.

The Court has identified the principle of equal treatment of tenderers as going to the essence or the 'very heart' of the Directive.[255] Moreover, it treats exposure to Union law as a promotion of 'competition in accordance with the procedures provided for by the Directive which avoids the risk of the public authorities indulging in favouritism'.[256] The Court insists on the interest of the EU and of the contracting authority 'to ensure the widest possible participation by tenderers in a call for tenders'.[257] Moreover, the Court has always given a wide interpretation to the 'contracting authorities' which are subject to the obligations laid down by the Directive.[258] The Court's aim is to secure achievement of the Directive's pro-competitive objectives.

Its interpretative interventions are not confined to matters of procedure but also touch remedies. Examples must suffice: the case law is extensive and detailed.[259] In *Stadt Graz v Strabag* the Court relied on 'the wording, context and objective of the provisions of Directive 89/665' to rule against a requirement that a damages claim be conditional on a finding that the contracting authority involved was at fault.[260] It is for the national system to lay down the detailed rules of procedure that support a claim based on the EU Directive, but this is subject to the overriding requirement that there be effective protection of EU rights, and this militated against the restrictive rule requiring fault on the part of the public authority.

The Court has also been asked on a number of occasions to judge whether time limits imposed under national law are compatible with EU law. Plainly a time limit, beyond which litigation is precluded, promotes legal certainty, but it may also foreclose the opportunity to correct a misapplication of the law, including EU law, in the original process. The Court does not adopt a stance which is in principle intolerant of time limits, but the shorter and

---

255 See e.g. Case C-19/00, *SIAC v Mayo County Council* [2001] ECR I-7725; Joined Cases C-226/04 and C-228/04, *La Cascina, Zilch* [2006] ECR I-1347; Case C-213/07, *Michaniki AE* [2008] ECR I-9999.

256 e.g. Case C-399/98, *Ordine degli Architecti delle Province di Milano e Lodi and Others* [2001] ECR I-5409, para. 75; Case C-213/07, *Michaniki AE* [2008] ECR I-9999, para. 53.

257 e.g. Case C-538/07, *Assitur* [2009] ECR I-4219, para. 26; Case C-305/08, *CoNISMa* [2009] ECR I-12129, para. 37; Case C-376/08, *Serrantoni* [2009] ECR I-12169, para. 40.

258 e.g. Case 31/87, *Beentjes v Netherlands* [1988] ECR 4635.

259 S. Arrowsmith, *The Law of Public and Utilities Procurement*, Vol. 2, 3rd ed., Sweet and Maxwell, London 2014.

260 Case C-314/09 [2010] ECR I-8769.

the more uncertain the limit, the less likely the Court is to find it compatible with EU law.[261] The requirement to adopt a context-specific inquiry, visible in section 4.4.3 in connection with the challenges to the finality of arbitration, is thematically visible here too. So, for example, in *Lämmerzahl GmbH v Bremen* the Court confirmed that a time limit under national law may be in principle compatible with EU law but not where its application to a particular bidder defeats the requirements of effectiveness: in the case the contracting authority had been evasive in supplying the details of the contract.[262] In *MedEval* the Court addressed an absolute time limit.[263] Austrian law required that a party wishing to bringing an action for damages in respect of the violation of a rule of public procurement law had to secure a prior declaration that the procedure was unlawful; and that action for a declaration was subject to a six-month limitation period beginning on the day after the date of the award of the contract. No account was taken of whether the aggrieved party knew or could know of the malpractice. This, the Court ruled, runs contrary to the principle of effectiveness.

The Court has not yet had much opportunity to address the notion of contractual 'ineffectiveness' introduced into the regime by Directive 2007/66. In *Fastweb* the Court ruled that if the conditions in Article 2d(4), which carve out an exception from the sanction of ineffectiveness, are met, the effects of the contract must be maintained.[264] Since legal certainty is a consideration that militates against finding contracts ineffective, exceptions to the rules concerning ineffectiveness are to be interpreted narrowly but are not to be deprived of their effect. It added that Article 2d(4) does not violate Article 47 of the Charter, which asserts a right to an effective remedy. Instead that Article 'seeks to accommodate divergent interests'.[265] In *MedEval* the Court noted that rendering a contract ineffective 'puts an end to the existence and possibly the performance of that contract', which can cause considerable upset and financial loss to tenderer, awarding authority and to the public, and so the concern to preserve legal certainty is more compelling in actions for a declaration that a contract is ineffective than in actions for damages.[266] As suggested above (section 4.9.2), the Court is likely to be offered richer fare in future preliminary references asking it to elucidate the meaning and consequences of contractual 'ineffectiveness'.

---

261 e.g. Case C-470/99, *Universale Bau* [2002] ECR I-11617; Case C-327/00, *Santex SpA* [2003] ECR I-1877; Case C-406/08, *Uniplex* [2010] ECR I-817.

262 Case C-241/06, *Lämmerzahl GmbH v Bremen* [2007] ECR I-8415.

263 Case C-166/14 judgment of 26 November 2015.

264 Case C-19/13, *Fastweb* judgment of 11 September 2014.

265 Para. 63.

266 Case C-166/14 judgment of 26 November 2015, para. 40.

4.9.4. THEMES, PRINCIPLES AND POLICY

The channelling effect of EU law is prominent in this sector. Contractual autonomy must be exercised in particular carefully defined ways in order to promote competition and the building of an internal market. Transparency is a strong impulse in the design of the rules. The rules on remedies reveal a relatively rare instance of willingness in EU secondary legislation to address directly questions associated with the validity of contracts, but their detailed content reveals too the real sensitivity attached to such intervention. The rules, especially those concerning the 'ineffectiveness' of contracts, are both cautious and ambiguous.

Perhaps the most intriguing question is one that goes beyond the scope of this book. The public procurement sector is one of the most densely regulated in the whole EU legal order. It also remains one of the most dismally fragmented along national lines. The question, then, is whether this exposes that the EU, which operates by adopting 'top down' rules but has minimal legal competence or material resources to do anything further, is simply inadequately equipped to tackle entrenched obstacles to the functioning of the internal market caused by local culture, preferences, and tradition. Top-down lawmaking is not transformative enough.

4.10. WORKER PROTECTION AND LABOUR MARKET REGULATION

4.10.1. COMPETENCE

Chapter 2 explained how primary EU law grants a right to non-discriminatory treatment on grounds of gender in the matter of pay. The relevant provision on equal pay for equal work is today Article 157 TFEU, having originally been Article 119 EEC, and its significance was greatly enhanced by the Court's ruling in *Defrenne v SABENA*[267] which explained the Treaty provision as a commitment both to social protection and to eliminating the distortive effect of variation between national regimes governing such matters of employment law and practice, while also insisting on its capacity for direct effect without any further legislative amplification even in 'horizontal' situations, that is in cases involving private employers and employees with no connection to the public sector. This set a course for the regulation of the employment relationship pursuant to EU law which was prepared to suppress contractual autonomy in favour of harmonised standards motivated both by social progress across the territory

[267] Case 43/75 [1976] ECR 455. See Chapter 2.9.

of the EU and also by the suppression of the distortive effect of local regulatory diversity. So, as the Court expressed the matter in *Defrenne*, the EU pursues 'a double aim, which is at once economic and social'.[268] The analogy to legislative harmonisation's 'dual function', a theme of this chapter, is immediately resonant.

However, the deal struck in the 1950s left most matters concerning labour market regulation and social policy more generally untouched by concrete rules set by primary EU law. The provision on which Ms Defrenne could rely, today Article 157 TFEU, was atypical: the Treaty went little further in the grant of immediately enforceable individual rights. Further concrete elaboration depended on political will to make use of the Treaty to adopt amplifying secondary legislation. This depends on the assembly of a constellation of supporting political motivations and in particular it requires a political willingness to follow the Court's understanding of the role of the EU in this field. Much of the shaping of EU labour market regulation has been characterised by political disagreement among, on the one hand, those willing to endorse and promote the Court's vision of the dual function of common rule-making at EU level, frequently concerned too to regulate at EU level to combat the risk of the deregulatory spiral to which the label 'social dumping' is commonly attached, and, on the other, those who, by stark contrast, prefer a quite distinct approach which would characterise inter-State regulatory diversity not as a distortion of competition but instead quite simply as competition – that is, competition between jurisdictions. This perspective, most closely but not exclusively associated with Conservative-led governments in the UK, would oppose regulation at EU level that sets aside contractual autonomy and local regulatory preference, and would leave choices to be made within the Member States.

This struggle has been conducted against the background of the available competence to adopt measures of EU secondary legislation addressing labour market regulation. The political debate about whether to act has salience only if the EU is competent to act.

The original Treaty of Rome offered little explicit scope for legislation aimed explicitly at labour market regulation or at social policy, However, it was noted in relation to consumer policy at section 4.3.1 above that a commitment to put a more 'human face' on the process, which was cemented at the politically transformative 'Paris Summit' of 1972, led to an intensification of legislative activity. The same impulse generated momentum in the field of labour market regulation. And the same constitutional pattern, whereby legal bases in the Treaty lacking express connection to the topic were exploited to covert political consensus into binding legal rules, was visible. The chosen bases were Articles 235 and 100 EEC, today, in amended form, Articles 352 and 115 TFEU.[269] By asserting that social policy counts among the EU's objectives and is

---

268 Para. 12.

269 Chapter 3.17, 3.5.

part of the process of creating an internal market the EU began to give legislative shape to political aspiration.

Directive 76/207 on equal treatment for men and women as regards access to employment, vocational training and promotion, and working conditions was based on Article 235 EEC.[270] Directive 77/187 on safeguarding of employees' rights in the event of transfers of undertakings was adopted pursuant to Article 100 EEC.[271] It has now been replaced by Directive 2001/23, which takes the same – albeit today amended – legal base, Article 94 EC, now Article 115 TFEU.[272] Directive 75/129 and its successor Directive 98/59 on collective redundancies were both based on Article 100 EEC.[273] Directive 80/987 on the protection of employees in the event of the insolvency of their employer was based on Article 100 EEC.[274]

Some of these measures were accompanied by no more than a curt explanation of why Article 100 EEC was used. Here too, as in the case of consumer policy (section 4.3.1), a political commitment made by all the Member States was converted into concrete legislative activity by claiming an attachment to the project to build an internal market for the EU. Market-making acted as a constitutionally convenient load-bearer. The presence of unanimity among the Member States suppressed any political need or practical desire to explore lurking intricacies of constitutional legitimacy. The political message, however, was in tune with the double aim announced by the Court in *Defrenne*: it asserts a link between market-making and social protection. So, for example, Directive 77/187 explained in its Preamble that differences between Member States' protection of employees can have a direct effect on the functioning of the common market, and that accordingly harmonisation is required while maintaining the improvement in working conditions then described in Article 117 EEC, now set out in Article 151(1) TFEU.

Some of these measures have been supplemented and in some instances superseded by reliance on the more explicit social policy provisions which have been added to the Treaty incrementally over time, so that EU social policy has acquired a more coherent shape than that promised by what were Articles 100 and 235 EEC. Directive 76/207 has been replaced by the broader Directive 2006/54 on the implementation of the principle of equal opportunities and equal treatment of men and women in matters of employment and occupation, which takes as its basis the more specific Article 141(3) EC, now Article 157(3) TFEU.[275] Directive 80/987 on the protection of employees in the event of the insolvency of their employer was replaced by Directive 2008/94, which takes Article 137(2)

270 [1976] OJ L39/40.
271 [1977] OJ L61/26.
272 [2001] OJ L82/16.
273 [1975] OJ L48/29, [1998] OJ L225/16.
274 [1980] OJ L283/23.
275 [2006] OJ L204/23.

EC, now Article 153 TFEU, as its base, and its Preamble makes greater play than its predecessor of the protective element rather than simply the need to address regulatory divergence among the Member States.[276]

In an EU of 28 Member States the unanimity requirement built into Articles 100 and 235 EEC, today Articles 115 and 352 TFEU, is restricting rather than empowering. Its blocking effect has pushed those provisions into disuse. Nor may Article 114 TFEU be used, for Article 114(2) directs that it may not be used to harmonise measures that affect the rights and interests of employed persons.[277] Social policy *per se*, rather than harmonisation, is now the label used. The ordinary legislative procedure which rests on the assembly of a qualified majority vote (QMV) in Council has become the norm in legislative activity which addresses social policy, and the key provisions are today contained in Title X of Part Three of the TFEU, which is entitled 'Social Policy'. They stretch from Article 151 to Article 161 TFEU. This story, politically contested, of how the Treaty has been revised over time to enhance the EU's legislative competence in labour market regulation in particular and social policy in general cannot be explained in full here – it needs a lengthy diversion to follow all the wrangles that have led to the uneven inflation of an explicit social policy competences over time.[278] Article 151 TFEU directs that the Union and the Member States 'shall have as their objectives the promotion of employment, improved living and working conditions, so as to make possible their harmonisation while the improvement is being maintained, proper social protection, dialogue between management and labour, the development of human resources with a view to lasting high employment and the combating of exclusion'. Article 153(1) provides a list of areas in which the Union shall support and complement the activities of the Member States with a view to achieving the objectives of Article 151. Article 157 TFEU's commitment to equal pay, the modern successor to the provision that provided the platform for *Defrenne*,[279] is locked into the Treaty, but most of the relevant protective rules that apply in common across the territory of the EU are found in secondary legislation, mostly Directives. States that are politically opposed to the shaping of an EU social policy must seek to win that argument in the legislative process. Since the relevant provisions today almost all involve QMV in Council, a dissenting State normally needs allies to halt an initiative.

The measures that have been adopted under Article 153 TFEU, or its immediate predecessor Article 137 EC, are not confined to measures that are a renovation of earlier initiatives based on Article 100 and/or 235 EEC. The Working Time Directive, which in its current form is Directive 2003/88 based

276 [2008] OJ L283/36.
277 See Chapter 3.5.
278 See C. Barnard, *EU Employment Law*, 4th ed., OUP, Oxford 2012, Chs. 1–3.
279 Case 43/75 [1976] ECR 455.

on Article 137 EC,[280] was first adopted in 1994 as a measure to protect workers' health and safety.[281] The legal base that permitted legislation of this type was introduced into the Treaty with effect from 1987 as a result of the amendments made by the Single European Act (SEA). Other measures adopted under Article 137(2) EC include Directive 2002/14 establishing a general framework for informing and consulting employees.[282] It is, however, true that legislative activity has grown sluggish more recently. Even the conferral of an expanded competence and the enhanced scope to act by qualified majority in Council has not set aside the real political blockages to deepened EU legislative activity in this field. Quite a lot of activity has been displaced from orthodox EU lawmaking to softer methods of action, such as the Open Method of Co-ordination (OMC).[283] However, the thematic thread is a readiness to regulate the labour market (in some way) and not simply to rely on the contractual autonomy of employers and employees.

4.10.2. CONTENT AND RE-REGULATORY CHOICES

The Court's statement in *Defrenne* that the EU pursues 'a double aim, which is at once economic and social' provides a ready connection between the material contained within this section and that covered elsewhere in this chapter.[284] There is a politically contested debate about how far the EU should go in establishing common rules governing the employment relationship and social policy more broadly, but where the political commitment to act exists the aim and the consequence of such rule-making is to put in place common rules and at the same time to commit to a particular form of regulation of the market at EU level.

The legislative *acquis* is neither complete nor systematic, partly for reasons of want of comprehensive legal competence, partly because of the fluctuatingly contested political context. Nevertheless in this area the thematic regulatory concern to protect the weaker party is conspicuous.

Inspection of the legislative *acquis* must necessarily be selective: specialist works examine the field in detail and in more broadly reflective fashion.[285]

---

280 [2003] OJ L299/9.

281 Dir. 93/104 [1993] OJ L307/18.

282 [2000] OJ L80/29.

283 In the employment context see C. Barnard, *EU Employment Law*, 4th ed., OUP, Oxford 2012, Ch. 3; A.C.L. Davies, *EU Labour Law*, Edward Elgar, Cheltenham 2012, pp. 53–64; and also D. Ashiagbor, 'Evaluating the Reflexive Turn in Labour Law' in A. Bogg, C. Costello, A. Davies, and J. Prassl, *The Autonomy of Labour Law*, Hart Publishing, Oxford 2015, pp. 123–148. For broader discussion of shifting patterns of governance see K. Armstrong, 'The Character of EU Law and Governance: From Community Method to New Modes of Governance' (2011) 64 *Current Legal Problems* 179.

284 Case 43/75 [1976] ECR 455, para. 12.

285 See e.g. C. Barnard, *EU Employment Law*, 4th ed., OUP, Oxford 2012; A.C.L. Davies, *EU Labour Law*, Edward Elgar, Cheltenham 2012.

Two Directives deserve attention to allow an illustrative glimpse of the EU's re-regulatory strategy.

As mentioned above, the EU has applied common rules to safeguard employees' rights in the event of a transfer of an undertaking since 1977. The governing measure today is Directive 2001/23.[286] The legal base has always been what is today Article 115, so the measure is constitutionally tied to the project of creating an internal market for the EU. Its content, however, is inspired by the perception that employees require protection when the business for which they work is bought. The matter shall not, in short, rest exclusively with the contractual status of employer and employee. In its Preamble, the Directive's social motivation comes first. It is first declared that it is 'necessary to provide for the protection of employees in the event of a change of employer, in particular, to ensure that their rights are safeguarded', and only thereafter that there are differences between the Member States in the extent of the protection of employees and that 'these differences should be reduced'.[287]

The heart of the envisaged protection holds that when a business is transferred, the rights and obligations arising from a contract of employment or from an employment relationship existing on the date of a transfer are transferred too. This includes an obligation to observe the terms and conditions set out in a collective agreement. So too it is stipulated that the transfer shall not in itself constitute grounds for dismissal by either the transferor or the transferee, although a special proviso adds that this does not stand in the way of dismissals that may take place for economic, technical or organisational reasons entailing changes in the workforce.[288] Naturally the Directive is festooned with definitional detail, in particular to determine precisely when a 'transfer' occurs. This is required reading for those engaged in advising on the sale or purchase of a business in the EU. However, the overall scheme is plainly intended to place a layer of protection above that which is negotiated as a matter of contract between the owner of a business and its employees. The Directive is also stated by its Article 8 not to affect the right of Member States to apply rules, including collective agreements, which are more favourable to employees. The EU standards are mandatory, but are set at a minimum level.[289]

The EU's regulation of working time dates from 1993. Directive 93/104 on working time was based on Article 118a EC, a provision which, as mentioned above, was introduced by the SEA in order to confer a competence on the EU to legislate to address health and safety, particularly in respect of the working environment.[290] In an unsuccessful application for the Working Time Directive's

286 [2001] OJ L82/16.

287 Recitals 3 and 4.

288 Articles 3 and 4.

289 Chapter 6.4 explains the Court's – mistaken – attempt in Case C-426/11, *Alemo-Herron* judgment of 18 July 2013 to cut across this legislative choice.

290 [1993] OJ L307/18.

annulment brought by the United Kingdom on the basis that the measure had been improperly classified as a measure of health and safety, the Court ruled that the measure's principal aim was the protection of the health and safety of workers, and so the Directive was valid.[291] But it did not deny that the measure had ancillary effects on the establishment and functioning of the internal market. In short it had a dual function. The Directive was subsequently adapted and re-made as Directive 2003/88,[292] adopted under Article 137(2) EC, which is today in amended form Article 153(2) TFEU. The Directive tends to be one of the EU's measures that is most quickly cited by those opposed to perceived over-intrusive regulation of the workplace in general or its regulation by the EU in particular. It has become an ideological battleground. At a more detailed level, there is no denying that it is a measure which is complicated, in part because it represents a necessarily arduous attempt to accommodate divergent traditions among the Member States on how working time is to be regulated, if at all. States vary too in whether they prefer to emphasise public regulation or private bargaining. The result is a politically hard-won Directive that is marked by imprecision, compromise and derogations. The detail is beyond the scope of this book.[293] It fits, however, into the broad shape of this chapter because it asserts a concern to protect the weaker party by placing certain matters beyond and above the terms of the contract of employment. The Preamble states that 'improvement of workers' safety, hygiene and health at work is an objective which should not be subordinated to purely economic considerations'.[294] Nor, one may readily add, is it left exclusively to contractual negotiation. So the Directive regulates matters such as periods of daily rest, weekly rest and annual leave, aspects of night work and shift work and patterns of work. Its Article 15 provides that Member States remain free to apply provisions more favourable to the worker.

4.10.3. THE COURT OF JUSTICE

The Court has transposed the reasoning used in its pioneering ruling in *Defrenne*,[295] which concerned primary law, to its interpretation of the body of secondary legislation which addresses protection of workers.

Directive 77/187, the first measure concerning the transfer of undertakings, was at stake in *Commission v United Kingdom*.[296] The Court's explanation of

---

291 Case C-84/94, *United Kingdom v Council* [1996] ECR I-5755.

292 [2003] OJ L299/9.

293 In detail, see C. Barnard, *EU Employment Law*, 4th ed., OUP, Oxford 2012, Ch. 11; A.C.L. Davies, *EU Labour Law*, Edward Elgar, Cheltenham 2012, Ch. 7.

294 Recital 4.

295 Case 43/75 [1976] ECR 455.

296 Case C-382/92 [1994] ECR I-2435.

how measures of this kind may be based on what was Article 100 EEC (and is now Article 115 TFEU) offered a plain echo of *Defrenne*. It stated that:

> 'By harmonising the rules applicable to the safeguarding of employees' rights in the event of transfers of undertakings, the Community legislature intended both to ensure comparable protection for employees' rights in the different Member States and to harmonise the costs which those protective rules entail for Community undertakings'.[297]

The 'dual function', both social and economic, is clearly visible. The EU is motivated both to develop a common regulatory strategy at EU level apt to protect employees and to put in place common rules apt to promote the good functioning of the internal market. The protective or social rationale in combination with the economic rationale for harmonisation is easy to trace through the EU's legislative *acquis* and the associated interpretative rulings of the Court which now stretch over several decades.[298]

As explained above (section 4.10.1), the EU enjoys an explicit social policy competence conferred by Title X of Part Three of the TFEU, comprising Articles 151–161 TFEU. This is the base for important measures of secondary legislation. But reliance on Article 100 EC, today Article 115 TFEU, is to make a constitutional claim that harmonisation of labour market regulation is also embedded within the project to complete the internal market.

The Working Time Directive, as mentioned above (section 4.10.2), is a measure concerned with health and safety rather than directly with the internal market.[299] It is, however, thematically important that the Court's interpretative approach to the Directive openly embraces an understanding of the employee as 'the weaker party to the employment contract' and in that vein the Court has identified the need 'to prevent the employer being in a position to disregard the intentions of the other party to the contract or to impose on that party a restriction of his rights.'[300] Trends in EU labour law veer towards practical alignment with those already met in this chapter in connection with EU consumer contract law in particular, but also passenger law and energy law.

In *Union syndicale Solidaires Isère* the Court found that exclusion of a particular group of casual and seasonal members of staff at holiday and leisure centres from entitlement to a sufficiently long daily rest period was a violation of

---

297 Para. 15.

298 e.g. on transfer of undertakings Case C-164/00, *Katia Beckmann* [2002] ECR I-4893, para. 29; Case C-561/07, *Commission v Italy* [2009] ECR I-4959, para. 30; on collective redundancies, regulated by Directive 98/59, also adopted under Article 100 EEC, Case C-55/02, *Commission v Portugal* [2004] ECR I-9387, para. 48; Case C-385/05, *CGT* [2007] ECR I-611, para. 43.

299 Dir. 2003/88 [2003] OJ L299/9.

300 Joined Cases C-397/01 to C-403/01, *Pfeiffer and Others v Deutsches Rotes Kreuz* [2004] ECR I-8835, para. 82; Case C-429/09, *Günter Fuß v Stadt Halle* [2010] ECR I-12167, para. 80.

the Directive.[301] It reached that conclusion by insisting on the need to interpret Directive 2003/88 broadly, which is mandated both by its wording and its purpose, which is to encourage improvements in the health and safety of workers at work. These are 'rules of European Union social law of particular importance from which every worker must benefit as a minimum requirement necessary to ensure the protection of his health and safety'.[302] In *Jaeger* the Court decided that time spent by doctors 'on call' constituted working time. Harmonisation is intended to guarantee improved protection of the safety and health of workers by ensuring that they are entitled to minimum rest periods. It did not matter that an 'on call' employee was permitted to sleep at times when he or she was not required to work, since what mattered in the calculation of working time was the existence of an obligation to be at the workplace.[303]

The Court's sense of interpretative adventure is also visible in the area of discrimination in the workplace. In *Belinda Coote v Granada Hospitality* it crafted a ruling which has implications for understanding of the reach of contractual liability.[304] Ms Coote complained that her former private sector employer, Granada, had refused to provide a reference on her behalf as she applied for new jobs because Granada wished to punish her for having pursued a sex discrimination claim while she was in its employ. The question was whether this could be addressed under Directive 76/207 on equal treatment for men and women in access to employment, given that she was no longer an employee of Granada. The Directive did not address this issue at all.

Article 6 of the Directive directs Member States to introduce into their national legal systems such measures as are necessary to enable all persons who consider themselves victims of unlawful discrimination to pursue their claims by judicial process. This, the Court observed, requires that the Member States must take measures which are sufficiently effective to achieve the aim of the Directive. Moreover, that recourse be available to the courts was nothing less than a 'general principle of law which underlies the constitutional traditions common to the Member States' as well as being found in the European Convention on Human Rights.[305] Today Article 47 of the Charter could be included in this armoury of legal protection. Armed with this 'principle of effective judicial control'[306] the Court insisted that the Directive would be deprived of an essential part of its effectiveness if the envisaged protection did not cover the circumstances raised in the case. Without such protection, employees would be deterred from seeking

---

301 In Case C-428/09, *Union syndicale Solidaires Isère* [2010] ECR I-9961.

302 Para. 36. See also e.g. Case C-266/14, *Federación de Servicios Privados del sindicato Comisiones obreras v Tyco* judgment of 10 September 2015, para. 24.

303 Case C-151/02 [2003] ECR I-8389.

304 Case C-185/97 [1998] ECR I-5199.

305 Para. 21.

306 Para. 24.

redress when victims of discrimination. So the Directive covers action taken after the employment relationship has ended.

Article 7 of the Directive provides that Member States shall take the necessary measures to protect employees against dismissal by the employer as a reaction to a complaint or legal proceedings, but makes no reference to any other sort of sanction, such as that encountered by Ms Coote. The Court refused to treat the explicit coverage of the measure as determinative of its limits. Relying on the objective of the Directive in achieving 'real equality of opportunity for men and women'[307] it asserted that only a clear legislative indication would be effective to confine protection to instances of dismissal as a form of retaliation. *Coote* has much in common with many of the cases covered in this chapter, perhaps most of all those which look beyond the text of Directive 93/13 on unfair terms to ensure that national law governing procedure and remedies is applied in a way that ensures effective protection of the aim of the Directive.[308]

The approach taken in these Directives and, in their interpretation, by the Court is readily matched with that taken in other contexts to the Charter of Fundamental Rights. One might see such intervention as hostile to the right to property and analogous enterprise rights asserted by commercial operators which are found in Articles 15, 16 and 17 of the Charter. But those rights are not absolute and they need to be balanced against the rights and principles expressed elsewhere in the Charter, especially in its Chapter IV which is entitled 'Solidarity'. It is here that the EU's commitments to health care, environmental protection and consumer protection are located.[309] As cases such as *Sky Österreich,*[310] *Deutsches Weintor*[311] and *McDonough,*[312] mentioned in section 4.6.3 and considered more fully in Chapter 3.15, demonstrate, the legislative institutions are required to balance the competing interests and the Court is required to ensure there is no violation of EU law. Commercial freedom is by no means an overriding value. This is a model that opens up scope for permissible regulation of the market in the public interest, even where costs may be imposed on commercial parties. Chapter IV of the Charter also includes material relevant to the worker. Article 27 concerns information and consultation; Article 28 refers to a right of collective bargaining; and Article 31 provides that every worker 'has the right to working conditions which respect his or her health, safety and dignity' and 'the right to limitation of maximum working hours, to daily and weekly rest periods and to an annual period of paid leave'. It would be easy to regard the several Directives adopted before the

307 Para. 27.
308 e.g. Case C-168/05, *Mostaza Claro v Centro Móvil Milenium* [2006] ECR I-10421. See section 4.4.3.
309 Arts. 35, 37 and 38 Charter respectively.
310 Case C-283/11, *Sky Österreich GmbH* judgment of 22 January 2013.
311 Case C-544/10, *Deutsches Weintor v Land Rheinland-Pfalz* judgment of 6 September 2012.
312 Case C-12/11, *Denise McDonagh v Ryanair Ltd* judgment of 31 January 2013.

arrival of the Charter which are considered in this section as reflections of the aspirations to regulate the EU labour market which are now mapped by this part of the Charter. So one would anticipate that any attempt to rely on Articles 15, 16 and 17 of the Charter to attack the validity of regulation of matters such as working time or transfer of undertakings would find little favour before the Court. The worker, as the weaker party to the contract of employment, is a proper subject of protection.

One ruling of the Court, however, causes a dent in the confidence of this claim. This is *Mark Alemo-Herron and Others v Parkwood Leisure Ltd*, hereafter simply '*Alemo-Herron*'.[313]

Alemo-Herron concerned the transfer of undertakings. As mentioned above, this has been the subject of regulation by the EU since 1977, and the governing measure today, which was also that at stake in *Alemo-Herron*, is Directive 2001/23.[314] The Supreme Court of the United Kingdom made a preliminary reference to the Court of Justice asking whether a particular judicial approach to the interpretation of the Directive was correct. The choice lay between a so-called 'dynamic' view of the place of collective bargains in determining the rights of employees of transferred undertakings and a 'static' view. The basic issue which fuelled the litigation concerned linkage between a contract of employment and a collective agreement covering the sector. The employment contract between a public authority in London and its workers provided that the latter would enjoy the benefit of the terms and conditions negotiated by the local government collective bargaining body. The collective agreements were not themselves binding as a matter of law but they were contractually enforceable as a result of their incorporation into relevant contracts of employment. So, in effect, the content of the contract of employment was determined from outside, by the collective agreements negotiated from time to time. The business was transferred from the public authority to a private operator, Parkwood. Parkwood was not represented on the collective bargaining body and, in fact, given its status as a private sector undertaking, it was not entitled to be. The key question was whether Parkwood was bound by changes made to the collective agreement after the transfer had occurred.

The 'static' approach said no – the collectively agreed rules become part of the employment contract at the moment of transfer but then remain fixed. The 'dynamic' approach said 'yes' – the collectively agreed rules become part of the employment contract but may then be updated after the transfer, for as long as the agreement remains in place.

The dynamic view was plainly the more generous to the employee (and it was the one favoured by the English judiciary). The Court of Justice, however, decided that the 'static' approach was the correct one.

---

313 Case C-426/11 judgment of 18 July 2013.

314 [2001] OJ L82/16.

This could be treated as a rather technical interpretative ruling of marginal importance beyond the particular dispute in which it arose. The problem, however, was the Court's reasoning. It did not reach its conclusion in favour of the 'static' approach through a narrow textual examination of the Directive. It took a much broader approach. Most of all it drew on the protection of fundamental rights guaranteed by the Charter. The Court of Justice approached the matter on the basis that the Directive required the striking of a 'fair balance' between the transferee employer and the employee,[315] and it considered that only the static approach would deliver this. It emphasised the importance of securing the managerial flexibility of the company to which the transfer is made, and it relied on Article 16 of the Charter, which it declared covers 'freedom of contract', although in fact it does not do so explicitly: its focus is freedom to conduct a business.[316] The judgment claims that were the English courts' interpretation to prevail, then the private firm, to which the business has been transferred, would find its contractual freedom seriously reduced to the point that there may be damage to the very essence of its freedom to conduct a business. So, in short, the more generous 'dynamic' interpretation of the protective effect of the Directive was ruled out in favour of the 'static' and less protective interpretation.

There is no objection in general to the quest for a 'fair balance' between competing interests. The objection lies in the Court's vigorous concern to highlight the costs incurred by the employer and largely to neglect the benefits to the worker. This is a 'balance' which seems highly one-sided and, in particular, the Court's ruling wholly neglects the animating concern in the legislative *acquis* in this area to protect the weaker party. Most of all, the Court stands accused of an improperly inflated reliance on Article 16 of the Charter. Its claim in *Alemo-Herron* that the 'dynamic' interpretation would so seriously reduce the contractual freedom of the transferee that that there may be damage to the very essence of its freedom to conduct a business is a wholly implausible exaggeration. If Article 16 of the Charter is treated as engaged and violated so very easily, a great deal of the regulatory *acquis* examined in this chapter, not only that concerning workers, is as a constitutional matter horribly fragile. It is frankly shocking that *Alemo-Herron*, drawing on Article 16 of the Charter to maximise managerial and commercial flexibility, claims a direct connection with the rulings in *Sky Österreich* and *Deutsches Weintor*. Those rulings, mentioned above (in this section and in section 4.6.3) and dissected in Chapter 3.15, authorised legislative *restrictions* on contractual and commercial freedom.

Alemo-Herron has been flayed mercilessly in the academic commentary.[317] It is a ruling of a five-judge Chamber and has not been relied on more widely in

---

315 Para. 29.

316 Para. 32.

317 See S. Weatherill, 'Use and Abuse of the EU's Charter of Fundamental Rights: on the improper veneration of freedom of contract' (2014) 10 *European Review of Contract Law* 157; J. Prassl, 'Freedom of Contract as a General Principle of EU law' (2013) 42 *Industrial*

the Court's practice. It should be treated as an aberration. Its chosen approach would, if extended, threaten a whole host of the measures considered in this chapter which protect weaker parties from market failure, and would grotesquely destabilise the long-established balance in EU secondary legislation between integration of markets and their regulation. *Alemo-Herron* is incompatible with the scepticism about the reality of freedom of contract in economically imbalanced relationships which animates much of the EU's consumer and employee protection legislation and the Court's interpretation of it: in fact, the ruling seems unaware of this past history. It cannot be wished out of existence and it will doubtless be exploited by litigious commercial operators seeking to weaken regulation of the EU market. If the Court allows this door to be kicked open, it would deliver a very different kind of internal market. But it should close the door. *Alemo-Herron* is, in fact, not compatible with the commitments made the Treaty and the Charter to the quality of the regulatory environment in the internal market which were examined in Chapter 3.8.

4.10.4. THEMES, PRINCIPLES AND POLICY

The purpose(s) of EU labour market regulation and social policy more generally remain illuminatingly contested. At the political level the battle between those who would champion a common floor of protection applicable across the EU and those who by contrast promote room for inter-jurisdictional competition between State regulators is, as articulated above,[318] an enduring feature. There is a range of explanations – which sometimes compete with each other and which sometimes fluctuate over time – for the EU's incursion into labour market regulation and social policy more generally.[319] Constitutionally, however, the EU has proven able to deliver common rules, should the political process lend adequate support to that vision, most of all through action taken pursuant to what are today Articles 115 and 153 TFEU.

The thematic thread is shared with the discussion elsewhere in this chapter: the EU's intervention possesses a 'dual function'. It promotes the functioning of the internal market by removing the (perceived) distortive effect of diversity between national rules of labour market regulation and it achieves social objectives by embedding at EU level particular protective values and techniques. The concern for the worker as the weaker party, unable to take realistic

Law Journal 434; D. Gudmundsdottir, 'A renewed emphasis on the Charter's distinction between rights and principles: is a doctrine of judicial restraint more appropriate?' (2015) 52 *Common Market Law Review* 685, 716–718.

318 See section 4.10.1, also Chapter 2.9.

319 See e.g. C. Barnard, *EU Employment Law*, 4th ed., OUP, Oxford 2012; A.C.L. Davies, *EU Labour Law*, Edward Elgar, Cheltenham 2012; P. Syrpis, *EU Intervention in Domestic Labour Law*, OUP, Oxford 2007.

advantage of the notion of contractual autonomy, is prominent. This paradigm is shared with the EU's *acquis* affecting consumer contract law (section 4.4), although there are thematic policy differences as well as similarities between EU labour law and consumer law: in particular the animating concern in labour market regulation to address 'social dumping' is not part of the discourse about consumer law.[320] The Court's ruling in *Defrenne* conforms to the 'dual function' vision as a landmark interpretation of primary EU law and this has been absorbed and integrated into the development and interpretation of EU secondary legislation. True, there is nothing systematic or comprehensive about EU policy in this area. It is rather fragmented; it is largely, though not exclusively, related to employment; it is *ad hoc*, often a product of moments of political opportunity. This too is a pattern shared with other areas considered in this chapter. The 'informed consumer' is a paradigm that is both descriptively and normatively contested, as is explained in section 4.3.4: the 'European Social Model' takes descriptive and normative contestation on to a much higher plane and its very vitality as an aspiration has been called into serious question by economic recession and enforced labour market 'reforms' in some Member States of the Eurozone.[321]

4.11. CONCLUSION

4.11.1. COMPETENCE

The EU has developed a significant role in contract law. This covers judging the justifiability of national laws which impede cross-border trade, the subject matter of Chapter 2, as well as review of contracts themselves in some circumstances where they hinder cross-border or distort competition or, the least sharply defined area of all, where they violate certain anti-discrimination norms, also addressed in Chapter 2. It also emerges through the need to elaborate the substantive content of legislative harmonisation. The constitutional contours were drawn in Chapter 3: the current chapter provides a necessarily selective examination of how the competences conferred on the EU have been relied on to build a significant body of legislative material that directly or indirectly regulates contractual autonomy.

---

320 H. Collins, 'Social Dumping, Multi-level Governance and Private Law in Employment Relationships' in D. Leczykiewicz and S. Weatherill (eds.), *The Involvement of EU Law in Private Law Relationships*, Hart Publishing, Oxford 2012, Ch. 10, pp. 223–252.

321 Cf. e.g. C. Barnard, 'EU Employment Law and the European Social Model: The Past, the Present and the Future' (2014) 67 *Current Legal Problems* 199; N. Countouris and M. Freedland (eds.), *Resocialising Europe in a Time of Crisis*, CUP, Cambridge 2013; D. Schiek, 'The EU Constitution of Social Governance in an Economic Crisis: In Defence of a Transnational Dimension to Social Europe' (2013) 20 *Maastricht Journal* 185.

The narrative in this chapter reveals how and why there is no room to understand the internal market to be based on a neat separation between the EU as a promoter of market integration and the Member States as the source of regulatory protection. The impact of the EU has broadened and deepened, blurring the viability of this demarcation of functions. Contract law is one example of this evolution, though it is a feature of the development of the internal market generally. The general lesson therefore extends far beyond contract law. It holds that a programme which is presented as an exercise in securing market freedom inevitably involves a sustained commitment to rule-making.[322] Markets need framing rules, and this is especially pertinent in the case of the European Union's internal market which is constructed against the background of centuries of regulatory fragmentation along national and local lines.

In a sense the very character of EU contract law is instrumental. The EU reaches contract law because it is engaged with making the internal market. Diverse national contract laws get in the way, by obstructing inter-State trade or by distorting competition. But having reached contract law via the internal market, the EU has a wide scope within which to choose what shall be its model of (usually regulatory) contract law. This means that EU contract law is neither systematic nor comprehensive, and it means too that it may damage the supposed integrity of legal classifications under national law, most of all those that separate public from private law. Moreover the internal market, rather than any broader concerns for, say, distribution of resources within society and social justice, is its starting point. But market-making is not the finishing point of the EU's endeavours.

So, for consumer law, features such as mandatory information disclosure, concern for the weaker party and protection of legitimate expectations help to provide a thematic and principled account of EU consumer policy which aspires to transcend mere detailed examination of individual Directives. The sub-discipline of 'EU consumer policy' has grown: it is founded on, but it is not limited by, the internal market.[323] EU labour law reveals comparable patterns,[324] and so too do smaller niches such as passenger law (section 4.6), energy law (section 4.7) and the law of public procurement (section 4.9). The point, rooted in the Court's reading of the constitutional pattern of harmonisation, is that there is a low threshold to invocation of Article 114 TFEU as a basis for the adoption of measures of legislative harmonisation which are designed to improve the

---

322 Cf. e.g. M. Egan, *Constructing a European Market*, OUP, Oxford 2001; and from a more specifically legal perspective, S. De Vries, *Tensions within the Internal Market: The Functioning of the Internal Market and the Development of Horizontal and Flanking Policies*, Europa Law Publishing, Groningen 2006.

323 Cf. the multiple sources cited above n. 108. H.-W. Micklitz, 'The expulsion of the concept of protection from the consumer law and the return of social elements in the civil law: a bittersweet polemic' (2012) 35 *Journal of Consumer Policy* 283 provides perhaps the most plangent account of the risks involved in using the internal market as the chief framing device.

324 See especially sources above n. 285.

functioning of the internal market, but once that threshold is crossed, there is no objection to the pursuit of regulatory protection, which may potentially encompass suppression of unsafe or pernicious practices, serving as a 'decisive factor' in shaping the harmonised regulatory environment.[325] This is the 'dual function' of harmonisation. It is underpinned by Articles 35, 37 and 38 of the Charter combined with Articles 9, 12, 114(3), 168(1) and 169(1) TFEU.

4.11.2. CONTENT AND RE-REGULATORY CHOICES

There is no call here to repeat the rather dense treatment provided throughout this chapter: the re-regulatory dynamic of legislative harmonisation has propelled the EU to make important choices about the content of its common rules. Transparency and the protection of the weaker party probably stand as the most prominent features which provide a thematic binding for the *acquis*. There are also niches within which to find concern for minors and the disabled (section 4.5.2), the vulnerable consumer (sections 4.5.2 and 4.7.2) and the recipient of universal service (section 4.7). It is entirely plausible to understand the *acquis* as a means, albeit admittedly far from systematic, to promote private autonomy by tackling substantive inequalities. The EU has adopted important rules of mandatory law to protect weaker parties such as consumers, passengers and workers, albeit that it also commonly, but not exclusively, operates according to a model of information disclosure which makes certain implausible assumptions about the capacity and willingness of addressees to digest such information. The more the anxiety about imbalance recedes, the higher the respect accorded to contractual autonomy. The Directives on late payment and commercial agents have a whiff of protection of the weaker party but also reveal hesitation about introducing mandatory rules that detract from party autonomy (section 4.8). The rules on public procurement demonstrate exquisite sensitivity about the uncertainty that flows from setting aside concluded contracts even where a violation of EU law has contaminated the process of award: the notion of the 'ineffectiveness' of contracts is in this vein instructively evasive (section 4.9.2).

At bottom, however, the Court's declaration that once an adequate contribution to the functioning of the internal market is shown, it is proper that the pursuit of protection of matters such as public health, consumer protection or protection of the worker serves as the 'decisive factor' in the legislative choice has been eagerly exploited by the EU legislature. There is a relatively dense pattern of 'regulatory contract law' adopted at EU level, and it is constitutionally justified as a contribution to the functioning of the internal market which requires also

325 e.g. Case C-376/98, *Germany v Parliament and Council* [2000] ECR I-8419, para. 88; Case C-380/03, *Germany v Parliament and Council* [2006] ECR I-11573, para. 38. The case law is considered more fully in Chapter 3.8.

that a choice be made at EU level about its content, technique and intensity. This, as has been neatly captured by Comparato and Micklitz, is 'regulated autonomy' in the EU's internal market.[326] Moreover, it tends to erode the coherence of categories kept separate under national law. The divide between public law and private law is well recognised in Europe, albeit that there exists no single version. It carries implications at the abstract level associated with the legitimacy of the exercise of State power, on the one hand, and the value attached to private autonomy on the other, as well as more practical consequences associated with applicable procedures and competent courts. Even EU law has its own glimpses of it: the rejection of the horizontal direct effect of Directives,[327] the refusal to allow the horizontal application of some but not all of the Treaty provisions on free movement[328] and the 'State' element to the State aid rules[329] are all moments when EU law makes a separation which is loosely of this type. But EU law's emphasis on the functional imperative of creating an internal market means its sight is not aimed at the character of a rule but rather at its effect. So it may be indifferent to formal patterns of classification which are cherished within national legal orders. The discussion of the rough-edged relationship between the EU's regulation of unfair terms and unfair commercial practices provided in section 4.5.4 offers a particularly helpful insight. The former is in formal terms a matter concerning the validity of terms in an individual contract whereas the latter is a matter of administrative regulation of market practices. But the crossover between the two regimes is real, even if left unstitched at the level of detail, and in consequence the very viability of sustaining a sharp divide between private and public law at national level is damaged by the EU's commitment to (re-)regulating the internal market. On occasion the point is made explicitly by the Court – it has openly treated the public or private character of a supplier as irrelevant to the scope of both Directive 93/13 and Directive 2005/29[330] – but in general it is embedded, though commonly unspoken, in the functionally driven assumptions of EU internal market law.[331]

---

326 G. Comparato and H. Micklitz, 'Regulated Autonomy between Market Freedoms and Fundamental Rights in the Case Law of the CJEU' in U. Bernitz, X. Groussot and F. Schulyok (eds.), *General Principles of EU Law and European Private Law*, Wolters Kluwer, Alphen aan den Rijn 2013, Ch. 4, pp. 121–154.

327 Case C-91/92, *Dori v Recreb* [1994] ECR I-3325; Case C-192/94, *El Corte Inglés v Cristina Blasquez Rivero* [1996] ECR I-1281; Case C-80/06, *Carp Snc v Ecorad* [2007] ECR I-4473; Case C-555/07, *Kücükdeveci* [2010] ECR I-365; Case C-508/14, *Česky telekomunikační* judgment of 6 October 2015.

328 See Chapter 2.3.

329 See Chapter 2.7.

330 Case C-537/13, *Birute Šiba* judgment of 15 January 2015, para. 28 (Dir. 93/13); Case C-59/12, *BKK Mobil Oil* judgment of 3 October 2013, para. 37 (Dir. 2005/29).

331 See also C. Semmelmann, 'The General Principles of European Union Law in the Light of the Public-Private Distinction' in S. Besson and P. Pichonnaz (eds.), *Principles in European Law*, Schulthess, Zürich 2011; H. Micklitz, 'Rethinking the public/private divide' in

4.11.3. THE COURT OF JUSTICE

The Court occupied a profoundly important and powerful place in the development of the contract law of the internal market. This follows naturally from its role as the authoritative source of interpretation of EU law and also from its function in checking the validity of EU secondary legislation. However, it deals frequently with ambiguous material, the product of compromise struck within through the political process, and it is required too to apply the Treaty and Charter directions in favour of particular regulatory values.

On occasion the Court's choices are adapted by the legislature. In *Heininger* the Court decided that where a supplier has failed to inform the consumer of the right to withdraw mandated under Directive 85/577 the right endures and cannot be subject to a cut-off set by national law (one year under German law, *in casu*).[332] The legislature returned to this matter when Directive 85/577 was replaced by Directive 2011/83 on consumer rights.[333] Its Article 10 provides for a twelve-month cut-off where the trader fails to inform the consumer of the right to withdraw. The EU legislature therefore concluded that the Court's adventurous interpretation amounted to excessively generous protection of the consumer to the detriment of legal certainty.[334]

Sometimes the Court provokes the legislative process. The Misleading Advertising Directive, adopted in 1984, excluded regulation of comparative advertising in the face of political disagreement among the Member States, but the harmonised regime was amended in 1997 to include qualified liberalisation of comparative advertising. Crucially, those who had wished to restrain EU legislative intervention grasped that their resistance was already undermined by the Court's interpretation of free movement law which curtailed national autonomy to restrain comparative advertising.[335] Mapping the relationship between the Court and the legislative process is intriguing, though rarely explored in a systematic way.[336] However, much of the time the Court enjoys a high level of autonomous power which has been delegated to it by the Member States and by the EU's legislative institutions.

M. Maduro, K. Tuori and S. Sankari (eds.), *Transnational Law: Rethinking European Law and Legal Thinking*, CUP, Cambridge 2014, Ch. 10, pp. 271–306.

332 Case C-481/99 [2001] ECR I-9945.

333 [2011] OJ L304/64.

334 See especially Recital 43. *Heininger* itself would not be revisited at all today, since Art. 3(3)(d) of Dir. 2011/83 excludes contracts for financial services from its scope.

335 e.g. Case C-362/88 *GB-INNO v CCL* [1990] ECR I-667. See S. Weatherill, *EU Consumer Law and Policy*, 2nd ed., Edward Elgar, Cheltenham 2013, Ch. 2; L. Ballon, 'Comparative Advertising: Price Comparisons' in E. Terryn, G. Straetmnans and V. Colaert (eds.), *Landmark Cases of EU Consumer Law: In Honour of Jules Stuyck*, Intersentia, Cambridge 2013, Ch. 4.III, pp. 359–372.

336 For groundwork see P. Syrpis, 'The Relationship between Primary and Secondary Law in the EU' (2015) 52 *Common Market Law Review* 461.

The case law does not reveal merely neutral or passive choices. Rather, as has been made plain time and again in the course of this chapter, the Court's interpretative approach is heavily influenced by a particular view of the quality of the harmonised rules.[337] They are designed not only to establish common rules apt to nurture an internal market but also they are designed to protect particular interests, frequently those of weaker parties for whom contractual autonomy is not freedom at all but, left unregulated, risks serving as a route to subordination to the preferences of more powerful parties.

The Court is certainly not wholly consistent: its interpretative boldness 'oscillates wildly'.[338] On occasion the Court exploits its autonomy too eagerly, at the expense of institutional restraint. *Mangold v Helm* was met with coolness in Chapter 2.10[339] In this chapter enough attention has been devoted to its exorbitant rulings in *Simone Leitner* and *Sturgeon*, examined in sections 4.3.3 and 4.6.3 respectively.[340] Pursuit of the effective protection of the consumer as the weaker party to the contract has acted as a springboard to the interpretation of rules of civil procedure relevant to the vindication of consumer rights (section 4.4.3): this too is adventurous and differences between the Court and its Advocates General on the proper reach of EU law into national autonomy betray the sensitivities involved.[341] The Court's brief flirtation with embrace of 'general principles of civil law' as a means to interpret the *acquis* suggested a troublingly exaggerated claim to impose a system on the pattern of EU contract law.[342] True, in all three decisions concerning contract law in which the Court floated this approach the result of reliance on these general principles was in fact to *limit*, not to extend, the intrusive effect of EU consumer protection law.[343] But, if pursued more widely, the methodology would not inevitably lead in this direction in all cases. For some this is a desirable means to achieve a higher degree of 'systematisation', while others are conspicuously more cautious about the legitimacy of such judicial engagement.[344] The matter now seems dormant,

---

337 Cf. K. Gutman, *The Constitutional Foundations of European Contract Law: A Comparative Analysis*, OUP, Oxford 2014, Ch. 2.

338 H. Collins, *The European Civil Code: The Way Forward*, CUP, Cambridge 2008, p. 60.

339 Case C-144/04, *Mangold v Helm* [2005] ECR I-9981.

340 Case C-168/00 [2002] ECR I-2631; Joined Cases C-402/07 and C-432/07 [2009] ECR I-10923.

341 See especially Case C-618/10, *Banco Español de Crédito v Joaquín Calderón Camino* judgment of 14 June 2012 and Case C-169/14, *Sánchez Morcillo* judgment of 17 July 2014.

342 Case C-412/06, *Annelore Hamilton v Volksbank Filder* [2008] ECR I-2383; Case C-489/07, *Pia Messner v Firma Stefan Krüger* [2009] ECR I-7315; Case C-215/08, *E. Friz* [2010] ECR I-2947. The starting point was Case C-277/05, *Société thermale d'Eugénie-les-Bains v Ministère de l'Économie, des Finances et de l'Industrie* [2007] ECR I-6415, which refers to 'the general principles of civil law' at para. 24, but that case concerned liability to tax, not contract law.

343 See M. Hesselink, 'The general principles of civil law: their nature, roles and legitimacy' in D. Leczykiewicz and S. Weatherill (eds.), *The Involvement of EU Law in Private Law Relationships*, Hart Publishing, Oxford 2012, Ch. 7, pp. 131–180, esp. pp. 159–160.

344 Contrast (sceptical) S. Weatherill, 'The "principles of civil law" as a basis for interpreting the legislative acquis' (2010) 6 *European Review of Contract Law* 74 with (positive) A. Hartkamp, 'The General Principles of EU law and Private Law' (2011) 75 *RabelsZ* 241.

since the Court has stopped relying on such 'general principles of civil law', but the general point is that the more one emphasises 'system' at EU level, the more forceful becomes the perceived case for projecting legal interpretation beyond the detail of the *acquis*, but the less space is allowed for national autonomy and variation. The constitutional concern is that the Court risks treading beyond the role of interpretation of Treaty texts and secondary legislation and becoming instead, in short, a lawmaker. This may lead it to invade territory reserved to the EU legislative process and/or to national autonomy.

However, one should not exaggerate the peril. Sometimes there are hints that the Court might develop a generalised and systematised approach to interpretation across the sweep of the *acquis*, but more often it is narrower in its approach.[345] In the main it is properly inclined to a protective interpretative bias, and in matters of validity it is attentive to the regulatory ambitions of the EU to which the Treaty and Charter express multiple commitments even where it is pressed to prefer commercial freedom. It is a vitally important actor in the overall pattern, and its readiness to operate as a source of interpretation which helps to develop a 'European civil society'[346] shapes the development of the system, usually in a direction which is fully consistent with that authorised by the Treaty and the Charter. Its case law has repeatedly improved the level of protection beyond that 'afforded to consumers by often recalcitrant and reluctant national legal systems'.[347]

This chapter has referred on several occasions to the frequent emphasis on the protection of the weaker party: it has been convincingly argued that through legislative act and judicial interpretation this has become a principle of EU law.[348] Concern for vulnerable consumers is visible in the *acquis*, in particular in the regulation of the energy sector (section 4.7) but also in Article 5(3) of Directive 2005/29 on unfair commercial practices (section 4.5.2). The coverage

---

See also K. Purnhagen, 'Principles of European Private or Civil Law?' (2012) 18 *European Law Journal* 844; O. Lando, 'Is Good Faith an over-arching General Clause in the Principles of European Contract Law?' (2007) 15 *European Review of Private Law* 841; H. Rösler, 'Auslegungsgrundsätze des Europäischen Verbraucherprivatsrechts in Theorie und Praxis' (2007) 71 *RabelsZ* 495. M. Hesselink, 'The general principles of civil law: their nature, roles and legitimacy' in D. Leczykiewicz and S. Weatherill (eds.), *The Involvement of EU Law in Private Law Relationships*, Hart Publishing, Oxford 2012, provides an excellent survey of possibilities and limitations.

345 This point is made in connection with *Simone Leitner* in the Commission's 'Action Plan on a more coherent European Contract Law', COM (2003) 68, para. 21.

346 H. Micklitz and N. Reich, 'The Court and Sleeping Beauty: The Revival of the Unfair Contract Terms Directive' (2014) 51 *Common Market Law Review* 771, 806.

347 O. Gerstenberg, 'Constitutional Reasoning in Private Law: The Role of the CJEU in Adjudicating Unfair Terms in Consumer Contracts' (2015) 21 *European Law Journal* 599, 620.

348 See especially N. Reich, *General Principles of EU Civil Law*, Cambridge, Intersentia 2014, Ch. 2; also H. Rösler, 'Protection of the Weaker Party in European Contract Law: Standardized and Individual Inferiority in multi-level Private Law' (2010) 18 *European Review of Private Law* 729.

is admittedly not systematic: this remains primarily a matter for national law.[349] But the re-regulatory *acquis* shows that although the EU's Treaty mandate grants it no general distributive aspiration, nor is it confined to a narrow, exclusively functional preoccupation with market liberalisation. And perhaps the most striking feature is the sheer quantity of preliminary references made to the Court, which has fuelled its ability to promote its understanding of the nature and purpose of the contract law of the internal market.[350]

The general message holds that the programme of legislative harmonisation is broad in its scope, yet its impact may be broadened yet further by judicial interpretation.

4.11.4. THEMES, PRINCIPLES AND POLICY

This chapter does not purport to address every single area of law where the EU's legislative activity has touched contract law or contractual autonomy. Nor does it purport to provide exhaustively detailed examination of the several areas of legislative activity which have been chosen for investigation. Nor is the treatment of the Court's case law designed to be comprehensive. Any inquiry that offered a nuts-and-bolts inspection of every twist and turn would be unbearably dense. Specialist works provide such sector-specific inquiry and they have been the subject of cross-reference in the course of this chapter.[351] This chapter, then, is selective in its coverage. It is, however, a targeted selection. The matters subjected to examination reveal the abiding themes of the EU's legislative acquis where the project of making an internal market crosses over with contract law and contractual autonomy. Transparency and the protection of the weaker party probably stand as the most prominent features which provide a thematic binding for the *acquis*. But most important of all is the claim that although this is a contract law of the internal market there is a great deal more to it than market liberalisation. Contractual autonomy is regulated in the internal market.

---

349 See M. Friant-Perrot, 'Le consommateur vulnerable à la lumière du droit de la consummation de 'Union européenne' (2013) 49 *Revue Trimestrielle de Droit Européen* 483; L. Waddington, 'Vulnerable and Confused: The Protection of "Vulnerable" Consumers under EU Law' (2013) 38 *European Law Review* 757; S. Weatherill, 'Empowerment is not the only Fruit' in D. Leczykiewicz and S. Weatherill (eds.), *The Images of the Consumer in EU Law*, Bloomsbury/Hart/IECL, Oxford 2016, Ch. 8, pp. 203–221. See also European Parliament Resolution on a strategy for strengthening the rights of vulnerable consumers [2013] OJ C264E/11.

350 Cf. above n. 114 on exploitation of EU law by litigants and courts at national level. There is evidence that lower instance courts are more eager to refer than higher courts: H. Rösler, 'Das Rechtsgespräch zwischen dem EuGH und den verschiedenen zivilgerichtlichen Instanzen über das Vertrags- und Deliktsrecht' [2014] *Europäisches Zeitschrift für Wirtschafts-recht* 606.

351 Above nn. 31, 131, 150, 194, 228, 285.

CHAPTER 5
IMPROVING THE REGULATORY ENVIRONMENT

5.1. THE NEED FOR A POLITICAL AS WELL AS A LEGAL APPROACH

The story told in Chapters 3 and 4 is of the practical difficulty in making sharp and effective use of the promise of a *limited* role for the EU which is made by the principle of conferral contained in Article 5 TEU. Several features militate against the prosecution of a compelling constitutional case that the limits of EU legislative competence have been exceeded. Most of all, the internal market, to which legislative harmonisation adopted pursuant to Article 114 TFEU is dedicated, is in principle a limiting concept but in practice an empowering one. The threshold which must be crossed is low: the Court is reluctant to intervene in legislative choices provided the constitutionally necessary incantation of a contribution to the functioning of the internal market adorns the legislative measure's reasoning. Seen from the opposite standpoint, it is very difficult to make a plausible case against the validity of measures of legislative harmonisation, since it is so easy for a political preference to act to be endowed with the necessary sheen of constitutional respectability. The case law, examined in Chapter 3, duly reveals that most challenged measures survive attack before the Court.[1]

The problem, then, lies in the limited worth of the currently applicable legal rules in giving substance to the corollary of the principle of conferral, which is that competences not conferred on the EU belong with the Member States. This is important enough to be made explicit twice in the common provisions

---

1 Case C-376/98, *Germany v Parliament and Council* [2000] ECR I-8419; Case C-377/98, *Netherlands v Parliament and Council* [2001] ECR I-7079; Case C-491/01, *British American Tobacco (Investments) and Imperial Tobacco* [2002] ECR I-11453; Case C-210/03, *Swedish Match* [2004] ECR I-11893; Joined Cases C-154/04 and C-155/04, *Alliance for Natural Health and Others* [2005] ECR I-6451; Case C-217/04, *United Kingdom v Parliament and Council* [2006] ECR I-3771; Case C-380/03, *Germany v Parliament and Council* [2006] ECR I-11573; Case C-301/06, *Ireland v Parliament and Council* [2009] ECR I-593; Case C-58/08, *Vodafone Ltd and Others v Secretary of State for Business, Enterprise and Regulatory Reform* [2010] ECR I-4999; Case C-270/12, *United Kingdom v Council and Parliament* judgment of 22 January 2014; Case C-398/13P, *Inuit* judgment of 3 September 2015.

at the beginning of the TEU, in Articles 4(1) and 5(2) TEU, but it is not backed up by operationally useful rules. The Treaty does not make explicit provision to exclude particular areas from the influence of the EU. In fact, by stark contrast, it is structured to grant functionally broad competences to the EU. Article 114 TFEU is the most supple of these, and, as explained in principle in Chapter 3 and explored in legislative practice in Chapter 4, it is a poor guardian of the notion of 'States' rights' which seems to be promised by Articles 4(1) and 5(2). In this sense the Court is open to criticism as a weak guardian of the areas of State autonomy protected by the principle of conferral and of the limits of Article 114 TFEU in particular, but a response is that this is largely because the Treaty makes it so. Part of the Court's concern is to avoid asserting an overly intrusive constitutional review of politically balanced judgments, but part too is dictated by the very structure of the Treaties. Any reforming agenda must involve attention to that political context to show greater appreciation of the sensitivities involved in the distribution of competences between the EU and its Member States, which in turn should be informed by the underlying tensions associated with the need to find a way to achieve a better balance between uniformity and centralisation, on the one hand, and diversity and local autonomy, on the other. It cannot all be law: it must also be politics. This chapter is about the constitutional context of incubating a more questioning political culture in the debate about the contract law of the internal market, which is itself but one aspect of a much wider sensitivity about the trajectory of European integration.

5.2. SUBSIDIARITY AND PROPORTIONALITY

Chapter 3 examined the legislative competences relevant to contract law which are conferred on the EU by its Treaties. The existence of a legislative competence conferred on the EU does not entail that it shall be exercised. There are in law conditions that must be met before the exercise of a conferred legislative competence is valid. The two most prominent principles that guide and limit the exercise of EU legislative competences are those of subsidiarity and proportionality. This is clear from Article 5 TEU and it entails that even where a legislative competence *exists* – the domain of conferral – its *exercise* will be invalid if it trespasses beyond the restraint imposed on legislative action by the principles of subsidiarity and proportionality.

It is therefore a condition of validity of a measure of legislative harmonisation that it shall comply with the principles of subsidiarity and proportionality.

Both principles contain eminently sensible instructions about the character of EU rule-making. In distinct though overlapping ways they require that the EU shall act only in such a way as to promote a superior regulatory environment than that which can be delivered by the Member States acting on their own. But even to depict the principles in that rough-and-ready fashion is immediately to raise the two key questions. First, how is it really to be decided what is a superior regulatory environment and, second, who decides. Most of all, subsidiarity and proportionality are legal principles which are intimately attached to contested political calculations. They open a window on the need for a vibrant political debate about the virtue and vice of replacing local autonomy and diversity with centralised and uniform rule-making – one which is explored in this chapter and in the next. In this chapter in particular the inquiry is into how far these legal principles are apt to generate a useful reflective and critical debate about the contours of EU contract law. Legal rules (and their policing) cannot do it all, or even very much, but they can be designed in a way that will give space for and promote the necessary political reflection.

The problem, however, is a familiar one. It is that the restraint imposed is in principle a good deal more impressive than its significance in practice. Chapter 3 explored this theme in relation to the principle of conferral: the current chapter contains a similar rhythm in its examination of the principles that govern the exercise of EU competence. The problem, in short, lies in the remarkably ambiguous character of these principles, which tends to means that if there is adequate political support for legislative action it is improbable that the Court will be persuaded to intervene. So although conferral is a logically distinct (and a *priori*) matter from subsidiarity and proportionality, the rhythms are thematically similar: ambiguity in legal concept tends to shield political choices from being set aside by judges.

Each principle deserves separate examination, first subsidiarity and then proportionality, although, as will be explained, they have a degree of interconnection.

5.3. SUBSIDIARITY

The principle of subsidiarity was first introduced into the Treaties as a general principle with effect from 1993 as a result of the entry into force of the amending Maastricht Treaty. It was a reflection of a political concern to express in legal form the need for some kind of balance between centralising tendencies in the EU, most evident at the time of the Maastricht Treaty in the shaping of economic and monetary union, and the countervailing virtue of local autonomy. This tension has certainly not diminished in the years since 1993. Today Article 5(3) TEU houses the principle of subsidiarity. It provides that:

> 'In areas which do not fall within its exclusive competence, the Union shall act only if and in so far as the objectives of the proposed action cannot be sufficiently achieved by the Member States, either at central level or at regional and local level, but can

rather, by reason of the scale or effects of the proposed action, be better achieved at Union level'.

Areas of exclusive competence are few.[2] The only one of any significance to the subject matter of this book, contracts and contract law, is the establishment of the competition rules necessary for the functioning of the internal market.[3] Competition law is examined in Chapter 2.7. Everything else that is examined in this book is *not* a matter of exclusive EU competence. Subsidiarity is therefore in principle of general application to the subject matter of this book, excepting only competition law. The challenge, however, lies not in determining the scope of the application of the principle of subsidiarity, but rather what this in fact entails for EU activity.

That the Union shall be confined in the exercise of its competences to action which can 'by reason of the scale or effects of the proposed action, be better achieved at Union level' is at one level rather straightforward and uncontroversial. It is a simple direction that the best level for law- and policymaking should be preferred. Who would argue? It should immediately be noted that subsidiarity is not based on preconceptions about centralisation or decentralisation. It does not, contrary to some popular misconception, mandate a preference for State action over EU action, save only in the unlikely case where all things are otherwise equal. Instead it directs in short that the Union acts only where it adds value to action taken by the Member States – but where it does so, subsidiarity militates in favour of action at EU level in preference to State level.

There is a ready association between subsidiarity in EU law and general questions which arise in any system of divided power. Any system which divides power between levels of government – national/local, federal/State – needs to decide who shall do what. This needs rules and it also needs process and institutions. There are very different designs to be found in different systems across the world. In the matter of choosing what shall be decided centrally in common and locally and therefore in divergent manner the patterns of American federalism differ from those in Canada, from those in Germany and from those in Australia, and so on. But it is crucial to grasp too that American federalism now differs from American federalism fifty years ago and even more from two hundred years ago before the Civil War. Canadian and German and Australian federalism have mutated over time too. Sometimes this is the consequence of direct adjustment to the basic constitutional rules. These, however, are typically hard to change, and so frequently more significant, though less overt, are mutations as a result of political decisions and sometimes as a result of key decisions of supreme or constitutional courts. Federal patterns vary and they tend to be cyclical. Subsidiarity is a window on the EU's own particular version

2 They are listed in Art. 3 TFEU.

3 Art. 3(b) TFEU.

of the debate about centralisation and homogenisation versus diversity and local autonomy.[4]

This is a debate of huge legal, economic and cultural sensitivity: there are no right answers, only contested choices. This chapter confines its inquiry to contract law. But contract law is a good case study into the law and practice of subsidiarity. It offers an opportunity to ask not simply how much centralised contract law making is required and how much diversity can be tolerated or indeed encouraged, but also to reflect on how one makes such calculations. The core of the objection to subsidiarity lies in its lack of precision and predictability. The legal discussion has a ready connection to economic questions – the costs and benefits of a centralised model versus one based on interjurisdictional competition – and it has wider cultural resonance too. The quest to convert subsidiarity from catchphrase into a reliable set of principles for guiding the exercise of Treaty competences is formidably and enduringly difficult. This is visible in both legislative practice and the role of the Court.

5.4. SUBSIDIARITY AND LEGISLATIVE ACTIVITY IN THE FIELD OF CONTRACT LAW

References to subsidiarity dot the record of policy elaboration even before its arrival as a general principle of the EU legal order with effect from 1993 on the entry into force of the Maastricht Treaty. Much of the contract law *acquis* emerged from the Commission's preoccupation with consumer policy, as was explained in Chapter 4, and in its consumer policy Action Plan 1990–1992 the Commission declared under the heading 'Subsidiarity Principle' that:

> 'Practical consumer policy must be effectively managed in the member states on an ongoing basis with the management and control of safety, information and redress being adapted in each instance to local needs. It would be unrealistic to undertake such tasks continuously at a Community [now Union] level'.[5]

This suggests a readiness to reflect on the proper allocation of tasks and responsibilities within the EU, but plainly subsidiarity is more a means to frame the debate than to supply concrete prescriptions.

---

4 Cf. e.g. K. Nicolaidis and R. Howse (eds.), *The Federal Vision: Legitimacy and Levels of Governance in the United States and the European Union*, OUP, Oxford 2001; X. Groussot and S. Bogojević, 'Subsidiarity as a Procedural Safeguard of Federalism' in L. Azoulai (ed.), *The Question of Competence in the EU*, OUP, Oxford 2014, Ch. 11, pp. 234–252; J. Gutierrez-Fons, 'Transatlantic adjudication techniques: The Commerce Clause and the EU's internal market harmonisation clause in perspective' in E. Fahey and D. Curtin (eds.), *A Transatlantic Community of Law*, CUP, Cambridge 2014, Ch. 4, pp. 69–100.

5 COM (90) 98.

Legislative practice reveals faithful readiness to assert compliance with the principle of subsidiarity. It is normal to find that the Preamble of a measure of harmonisation includes reference to subsidiarity. So, to take a banal but entirely typical example, Regulation 1924/2006 on nutrition and health claims states that:

> 'Since the objective of this Regulation, namely to ensure the effective functioning of the internal market as regards nutrition and health claims whilst providing a high level of consumer protection, cannot be sufficiently achieved by the Member States and can therefore be better achieved at Community level, the Community may adopt measures, in accordance with the principle of subsidiarity'.[6]

Not a word more is offered about subsidiarity in the text of the measure. This is more assertion than explanation. But it is standard legislative practice.

Directive 2011/83 on consumer rights offers another good example of perfunctory engagement with the assessments that are engaged by the principle of subsidiarity.[7] Its Preamble mentions subsidiarity just twice:

> 'In accordance with Article 26(2) TFEU, the internal market is to comprise an area without internal frontiers in which the free movement of goods and services and freedom of establishment are ensured. The harmonisation of certain aspects of consumer distance and off-premises contracts is necessary for the promotion of a real consumer internal market striking the right balance between a high level of consumer protection and the competitiveness of enterprises, while ensuring respect for the principle of subsidiarity'.[8]

> 'Since the objective of this Directive, namely, through the achievement of a high level of consumer protection, to contribute to the proper functioning of the internal market, cannot be sufficiently achieved by the Member States and can therefore be better achieved at Union level, the Union may adopt measures, in accordance with the principle of subsidiarity as set out in Article 5 of the Treaty on European Union. In accordance with the principle of proportionality, as set out in that Article, this Directive does not go beyond what is necessary in order to achieve that objective'.[9]

Directive 2015/2302 on package travel provides a final but entirely typical example.[10] Its Preamble notes that the objective of the Directive is to contribute to the proper functioning of the internal market and to the achievement of a high and as uniform as possible level of consumer protection and adds that this cannot be sufficiently achieved by the Member States, but rather can be better

---

6 [2006] OJ L404/9, Recital 34.
7 [2011] OJ L304/64.
8 Recital 4.
9 Recital 65.
10 [2015] OJ L326/1, Recital 52. See more fully on this Directive Chapter 4.3.

achieved at Union level. So 'the Union may adopt measures, in accordance with the principle of subsidiarity as set out in Article 5 of the Treaty on European Union'.[11] It's that simple!

The lesson holds that routine legislative recitation of subsidiarity is usually devoid of any substance or depth. Complying with subsidiarity is, in this sense, a question of ticking the box. If there is political will to act, the measure will find itself adorned with the shimmer of claimed compliance with subsidiarity. Only on rare occasions is something more concrete visible. The area of cross-border credit transfers provides an atypical example. The perceived problem in this market was intransparency: consumers did not readily understand the available terms, including pricing, so cross-border competition was sluggish. In 1990 a Recommendation was adopted on the transparency of banking conditions relating to cross-border financial transactions.[12] This is 'soft law': the Recommendation is not a binding EU legal act, according to what is now Article 288 TFEU. This, however, was judged inadequate to solve the problem. The structure of the market was shown to be unaffected by the Recommendation. So the Commission proposed the adoption of binding legislation, and explained this explicitly with regard to the dictates of subsidiarity. This led to the adoption of Directive 97/5, which was subsequently replaced by Directive 2007/64, which today governs the field.[13] So subsidiarity was used to justify the adoption of binding EU rules: it did not operate to insulate national autonomy. This example is, however, atypical. Subsidiarity is rarely used in such concrete directing fashion. Normally subsidiarity plays no demonstrated role in guiding the EU towards the choice between action at EU level or inaction which leaves the matter in the hands of the Member States. Subsidiarity lacks constitutional bite.

Subsidiarity does not have to be mere window-dressing. It is not devoid of potential as a means to invigorate a debate about how to balance the competing merits of, on the one hand, centralised rule-making and uniformity and, on the other, local autonomy, cultural particularity, diversity and permitted scope for national-level experimentation and regulatory learning.[14] But that potentially remains untapped. The nature of the blockages to the constructive invocation of subsidiarity in the EU lawmaking process were helpfully captured in 2002 by Jean-Claude Piris, who was at the time Director General of the Council's Legal Service. In evidence which M. Piris presented to the Subsidiarity Working Group of the Convention on the Future of Europe, he was ready to confess that the Legal Service itself had expressed doubts about the compliance of proposals with the principle of subsidiarity only on rare occasions, but his principal point was

---

11 Recital 51.

12 Rec. 90/109 [1990] OJ L67/39.

13 [1997] OJ L43/25, [2007] OJ L319/1.

14 e.g. E. Carbonara, B. Luppi and F. Parisi, 'Self-Defeating Subsidiarity' (2009) 5 *Review of Law and Economics* 742; G. Gelauff, I. Grilo and A. Lejour (eds.), *Subsidiarity and Economic Reform in Europe*, Springer, Berlin 2008.

to highlight the breadth of the problem.[15] On his account it is typical that once a political consensus is achieved according to which it is decided to introduce rules at EU level, the process of negotiation typically involves Member States striving to secure a result as close as possible to their own pre-existing systems. Their concern is, in short, to reduce the costs of adaptation at national level once the EU standard is set. The outcome is therefore commonly cumulative. The EU process generates a package deal which loads the harmonised standard with the weight of many aspects of the pre-existing varied national standards. The diversity of national regulatory practice which inhibits the completion of the internal market provides incentives to Member States to abandon national rule-making in favour of common EU-level legislative standards, but then the desire to contain the costs of adaptation affects the shape and content of the EU standard. Chapters 3 and 4 insisted that EU (re-)regulation necessarily requires the EU to make choices about the *quality* of the harmonised environment: this is mandated by provisions such as Articles 12, 114(3), 168(1) and 169(1) TFEU and by Articles 35, 37 and 38 of the Charter. Here the point is more political: the EU rule tends to accumulate vestiges of pre-existing varied national rules. The EU does not regulate *de novo* when it harmonises: politically it is structurally inhibited from pursuing light-touch regulation.

It is plainly true that many of the measures of harmonisation discussed in this book which are advanced as beneficial to the consumer also impose costs that will be spread across all consumers in the form of increases in prices of goods and services. The victim of the cancellation of a flight is compensated by all consumers of flights.[16] One might well accept that such distributional outcomes are quite proper, but the point is that there is a cost/benefit analysis that deserves to be conducted, and frequently the costs of EU regulation are less openly weighed than the benefits.[17] This deserves consideration both in respect of the level of protection and the style of the regulatory regime.

In the context of harmonisation, subsidiarity might have some power in support of a case for *less dense* EU-level regulation, but it does not operate to support preservation of national regulatory competence through *no* EU-level regulation. Perhaps it should: but once the decision to act pursuant to Article 114 is taken, subsidiarity comes too late to the political party to change the tune being played.[18] The nature of EU political bargaining tends to generate an intensification of rule-making damaging to expression of local autonomy. As a

---

15 WD-004 WG I 13 July 2002.

16 Reg. 261/2004 [2004] OJ L46/1, examined in Chapter 4.6.

17 See, tracking this in both legislative and judicial practice, D. Leczykiewicz, 'Regulatory Cost, the Consumer and the EU Constitutional Framework' in D. Leczykiewicz and S. Weatherill (eds.), *The Images of the Consumer in EU Law*, Bloomsbury/Hart/IECL, Oxford 2016, Ch. 11, pp. 257–278.

18 e.g. G. Davies, 'Subsidiarity: the wrong idea, in the wrong place, at the wrong time' (2006) 43 *Common Market Law Review* 63.

general observation subsidiarity has become embedded within the debate about EU contract law and EU lawmaking practice in general, but for many critics it fares poorly as an operationally useful means to allay anxieties that the EU has contributed to *over*-centralisation in Europe.

5.5. SUBSIDIARITY AND THE COURT

No legislative act has ever been annulled by the Court of Justice for non-compliance with the principle of subsidiarity.

In fact, it seems improbable that one ever will be. The ruling in *R v Secretary of State ex parte BAT and Imperial Tobacco* set the tone.[19] This case is one of the slew decided after the first *Tobacco Advertising* case in which the Court dismissed attempts to show that measures of harmonisation were not validly based on what is today Article 114 TFEU.[20] The particular Directive that was unsuccessfully challenged in the case harmonised rules on labelling on tobacco products and tar and nicotine yields.[21] The Court found that the Directive made an adequate contribution to the internal market by replacing diversity in legislative treatment at national level with a common EU regime, and so it was validly based on what is today Article 114 TFEU. It complied with the principle of conferral. The Court logically then proceeded to check whether, as an exercise of a conferred competence, it complied with the principle of subsidiarity – an inquiry it had not pursued in the first *Tobacco Advertising* case for the equally logical reason that the Directive successfully attacked in that case had been shown to lack a valid basis for want of adequate contribution to the functioning of the internal market. In *ex parte BAT* the Court found no violation of the principle of subsidiarity. The Court's cunning formula deserves citation in full:

> '[T]he Directive's objective is to eliminate the barriers raised by the differences which still exist between the Member States' laws, regulations and administrative provisions on the manufacture, presentation and sale of tobacco products, while ensuring a high level of health protection, in accordance with Article 95(3) EC [now 114(3) TFEU]. Such an objective cannot be sufficiently achieved by the Member States individually and calls for action at Community level, as demonstrated by the multifarious development of national laws in this case … It follows that, in the case of the Directive, the objective of the proposed action could be better achieved at Community level'.[22]

---

19 Case C-491/01 [2002] ECR I-11543.

20 Case C-376/98, *Germany v Parliament and Council* [2000] ECR I-8419. See above n. 1 and Chapter 3.

21 Directive 2001/37 [2001] OJ L194/26.

22 Paras. 181–183.

The objective, the elimination of the barriers raised by the differences between State laws, cannot be sufficiently achieved by the Member States individually – indeed it is the variety of approaches taken that causes the problem to which harmonisation is the solution! The Court concluded that the matter therefore called for action at EU level. Once the objective is the adoption of common rules, as is clearly the case with Article 114, it seems according to this reasoning that it is unavoidable that the EU will be treated as better able to deliver those common rules than the Member States, and so EU action will satisfy the dictates of the principle of subsidiarity. In fact, this is an approach which makes it difficult to imagine circumstances in which a harmonisation measure, or indeed any EU measure setting common rules, will *ever* be found to violate the demands of subsidiarity. This was no accident: it has become the Court's orthodox formula in cases where a measure is impugned for infringement of the principle of subsidiarity.[23] Its application means that it is hard to imagine that, other than where the procedural obligation to support an act with reasons as required by Article 296 TFEU is not met, an EU measure could ever be held invalid for want of compliance with subsidiarity. This is true of Article 114 as a legal base but it is true of most of EU law – when it legislates, adopting common rules is the norm for the EU. Compliance with the principle of conferral is rarely found wanting, as Chapter 3's examination of the case law since the first *Tobacco Advertising* case revealed, but it will be still more unexpected to find a legislative act invalidated for want of compliance with subsidiarity.

The Court's formula has the effect of sustaining subsidiarity as a legal principle which must be met, but treating it as such in practice met with remarkable ease. The result, dampened judicial review, is to concede much in practice to legislative discretion. This too is no accident. The impression that the Court has adopted a narrow approach to subsidiarity as a legal concept according to an assumption that it is in the political sphere in which subsidarity concerns should be addressed in depth. There are in fact open hints to this effect on the record. In an address delivered in 2002 the President of the Court at the time, Gil Carlos Rodriguez Iglesias, made precisely this distinction. He argued that 'subsidiarity is a principle of an essentially political nature' and he expressed a concern to purge the Court's diet of 'political hot potatoes'.[24] This is a rather good summary of the impact of the Court's formula first devised in

23 See similarly Case C-103/01, *Commission v Germany* [2003] ECR I-5369, para. 47; Cases C-154/04 and C-155/04, *Alliance for Natural Health and Others* [2005] ECR I-6451, paras. 99–108; Case C-58/08, *Vodafone Ltd and Others v Secretary of State for Business, Enterprise and Regulatory Reform* [2010] ECR I-4999, paras. 72–80; Case C-539/09, *Commission v Germany* judgment of 15 November 2011, para. 84.

24 'The Court of Justice, Principles of EC Law, Court Reform and Constitutional Adjudication' (2004) 15 *European Business Law Review* 1115, 1117. Cf. B. Bertrand, 'Un principe politique saisi par le droit. La justiciabilité du principe de subsidiarité en droit de l'Union européenne' (2012) 48 *Revue Trimistrielle de Droit Européen* 329.

the *ex parte BAT* case.[25] There is good reason to be sympathetic to this reticent approach. Subsidiarity is a statement of evident good sense as a general principle of governance, but it lacks the precision characteristic of a justiciable norm. Its aggressive application to upset political compromises would expose the Court to allegations that it is intent on trespassing beyond the proper role of the judiciary. The Court's stance has a clear association with its concern to leave space for political decision-making which, as explored in Chapter 3.15, similarly animates the Court's relatively light-touch review of re-regulatory compromises which are typically struck in legislative harmonisation.[26] Therefore there is much to be said in favour of treating 'subsidiarity' as no magic word, but rather as a label for the debate in the EU about the balance between centralisation and preservation of local autonomy – a debate which, as suggested above, has plain echoes of similar debates that take place frequently in any system of divided political power.[27] There is no 'right answer' to the question 'who does what?': preferences and rhythms alter over time. The Court has not denied that there is a legal requirement for EU measures to comply with the principle of subsidiarity. Nor could it make any such denial given that subsidiarity is written into the Treaty. But it has interpreted the principle in a way that makes legislative compliance with it frankly routine. Given that subsidiarity is not only a legal principle but also a principle with contested political, economic and cultural significance, one can understand the Court's motivation in shunning its aggressive application in cases of judicial review of EU acts.

5.6. PROPORTIONALITY

Proportionality, like subsidiarity, is a principle of EU law which is stipulated by the Treaty and compliance with it is a condition of validity of EU legislative acts. Proportionality, like subsidiarity, is in practice very rarely found to be violated. Therefore proportionality, like subsidiarity, is much more a general statement of good governance than a concrete rule with practical significance of assistance to those opposing the style and form of an EU act.

Article 5(4) TEU provides that that according to the principle of proportionality 'the content and form of Union action shall not exceed what is necessary to achieve the objectives of the Treaty'. In the abstract this makes perfect sense. In fact, the roots of the principle of proportionality lie in the case law of the Court, which took shape long before the principle was admitted

25 Case C-491/01, *British American Tobacco (Investments) and Imperial Tobacco* [2002] ECR I-11453.

26 e.g. Case C-544/10, *Deutsches Weintor v Land Rheinland-Pfalz* judgment of 6 September 2012; Case C-12/11, *Denise McDonagh v Ryanair Ltd* judgment of 31 January 2013.

27 Above n. 4.

explicitly to the Treaty itself, and as a general observation its role has always been aimed at the control of legislative excess.[28]

Legislation must comply with the principle of proportionality, but, in the light of the analysis provided above of the typically eager textual embrace of subsidiarity in the drafting of EU acts, it will be no surprise that Preambles routinely make a similar claim to the required fidelity to the dictates of proportionality. So, to take a perfectly typical example, Directive 2011/83 on consumer rights simply asserts that '[i]n accordance with the principle of proportionality, as set out in that Article, this Directive does not go beyond what is necessary in order to achieve that objective'.[29] No amplification of this claim is provided. Directive 2015/2302 on package travel provides another example.[30] Its Preamble simply notes that '[i]n accordance with the principle of proportionality, as set out in that Article, this Directive does not go beyond what is necessary in order to achieve that objective'.[31]

If such perfunctory claims are to be shown to be legally flawed, then it falls to the Court of Justice to intervene, but, as is true of subsidiarity, the Court shows a high degree of caution when invited to condemn legislative measures as incompatible with the demands of the principle of proportionality. In fact, it is common for challenges to legislative action to be based *inter alia* on both subsidiarity and proportionality, and it is common too for both pleas to be dismissed. In fact, there is a clear overlap between the scope of the two principles, in particular when the contested issue is the intensity of the EU action, and it is common to find the Court using the same type of reasoning to dismiss both the subsidiarity-based and the proportionality-based claims. So, for example, in *ex parte BAT* the Court found that 'the intensity of the action undertaken' was 'in keeping with the requirements of the principle of subsidiarity in that …, as paragraphs 122 to 141 above make clear, it did not go beyond what was necessary to achieve the objective pursued'.[32] The cited paragraphs, the analysis in which was simply recycled, were concerned with proportionality.

The consequence is respect for a broad discretion enjoyed by the EU legislative institutions where political, economic and social choices are at stake and where complex assessment is demanded. This fits the normal pattern of judicial review of legislative harmonisation examined in Chapter 3.

Two rulings examined in Chapter 3.8 in connection with the basic question of the scope of the competence conferred by Article 114 are equally revealing

---

28 See generally T. Tridimas, *The General Principles of EU Law*, 2nd ed., OUP, Oxford 2006, Chs. 3 and 4.

29 Recital 65.

30 [2015] OJ L326/1, Recital 52. See more fully on this Directive Chapter 4.3.

31 Recital 51.

32 Case C-491/01, *British American Tobacco (Investments) and Imperial Tobacco* [2002] ECR I-11453, para. 184.

of the Court's attitude to the policing of the principle of proportionality. Both concern regulatory contract law.

In *Alliance for Natural Health* the Court was asked to consider the validity of Directive 2002/46.[33] This Directive permitted the marketing of nutrients only where they had received a favourable opinion from the competent scientific authorities – a so-called 'positive list' system. It was more intrusive than the obvious alternative, a system that permitted use of nutrients provided they had not been shown to present a risk to human health – a 'negative list'. The Court found that the Directive contributed to the functioning of the internal market by replacing diverse national practice with a common EU system, and so it was validly based on what is today Article 114: this was explored in Chapter 3.8. It then added that the Directive was compatible with the principle of proportionality. It cited the obligation of the EU legislature to ensure a high level of protection of human health and found that the measures were appropriate for achieving that objective and that they did not go beyond what was necessary to attain it.[34] Clearly the system chosen by the EU legislature was more burdensome than that preferred by the applicants, who were traders in products containing nutrients, but this did not make it an unlawfully disproportionate choice. It lay within the scope of legitimate discretion granted to the political process. That this was neither simple nor inevitable is clear from awareness of the approach preferred by Advocate General Geelhoed's Opinion in the case. He was heavily critical of the legislative regime. He thought the 'positive list' system needed to be designed 'with prudence and precision' in order to meet the expectations of traders, but in his disdainful view the stipulated administrative procedure was in fact marked by 'the transparency of a black box'.[35] He believed it was not in conformity with the dictates of the principle of proportionality. The Court, by contrast, was far more generous to the legislative choice that had emerged. It is regrettably common for the Court simply to ignore contrary views expressed by its Advocates General, but it was not so rude in *Alliance for Natural Health*. The Court accepted that it 'would, no doubt, have been desirable' for the Directive to have included provisions governing transparency and time limits, but it was nonetheless content to rely on 'the responsibility of the Commission' to operate the procedure in accordance with standards of sound administration.[36] The measure survived attack.

Vodafone, O2 and Others v Secretary of State is similarly revealing of the Court's unwillingness to adopt an intensive review of legislative choices in the

---

33 Joined Cases C-154/04 and C-155/04, *Alliance for Natural Health and Others* [2005] ECR I-6451.

34 Para. 111.

35 Paras. 66 and 85 of his Opinion.

36 Paras. 81–82 of the judgment.

name of proportionality.[37] As explained in Chapter 3.8 the Court concluded that the measure, the so-called 'Roaming Regulation' applicable to mobile telephone networks, was a valid exercise of the conferred competence to adopt measures of 'preventive harmonisation', although in this instance it chose to ignore the contrary views expressed by its Advocate General, Mr Maduro, who did not believe the orthodox criteria governing preventive harmonisation were satisfied. The applicants then claimed a violation of the principle of proportionality committed as a result of the intensity and scope of the EU's harmonised regime. In particular they complained that the Regulation capped prices not only for wholesale charges but also for retail charges. This was indeed the intent of the regime, but the Court emphasised the legislature's broad discretion. It reviewed the stated reasons for this legislative choice and in its ruling it decided they provided a basis for a legitimate political view that regulation of the wholesale market alone would not have met the objectives pursued by the measure. The Court concluded that the Regulation was not 'manifestly inappropriate having regard to the objective which the competent institution is seeking to pursue'.[38] A test of this nature is plainly heavily protective of legislative discretion. Such a relatively light degree of scrutiny reflects the Court's general anxiety to keep separate judicial and legislative functions. It treats proportionality, like subsidiarity and fundamental rights, as generating demanding and politically charged questions about the proper intensity of regulation which are not familiar or comfortable material to use in judicial review of acts which are, by definition, supported by the Commission, Parliament and a majority of Member States. Those institutions are thereby allowed a generous room for manoeuvre.

5.7. THE POLITICAL TURN

Subsidiarity is commonly invoked in a call for less intrusive EU rules. So, it is sometimes said, the EU should not introduce harmonised standards but instead should leave in place national diversity subjected to an obligation of mutual recognition of products and services that meet the standards required in their Member State of origin. This, it must be appreciated, is not to exclude EU lawmaking. Quite the reverse, it is to require it, since the obligation of mutual recognition needs to be agreed and imposed on Member States though agreement achieved within the EU legislative process. So the debate is about the style and intensity of EU rule-making, not the existence of it. Subsidiarity is in truth an invitation to engage in debate about how to achieve effective governance for the internal market and for the EU more generally. The principle of subsidiarity

37 Case C-58/08, *Vodafone Ltd and Others v Secretary of State for Business, Enterprise and Regulatory Reform* [2010] ECR I-4999.

38 Para. 52.

does not in itself offer concrete answers. The Court's point in the case law examined above (section 5.5) is to push the resolution of critical decisions to the political process. It could not do otherwise without itself taking a position on the proper balance of regulation in the EU, which is not its role and anyway is not the subject of any concrete policy direction provided by the Treaties. And in a similar vein the Court has retreated from any temptation to apply the proportionality principle in an aggressive way that would curtail legislative discretion. But, as explained above, the political process shows relatively little commitment to reflecting on the costs and benefits of centralisation in the EU. At least once measures are adopted, the engagement with the restraining influence of the principles of subsidiarity and proportionality is basically no more than perfunctory. The EU, it is widely though sometimes to an inflated degree alleged, is infected by a bias in favour of common rule-making. If, as suggested in the introduction to this chapter, the fate of all federations and federal-type systems is to reflect introspectively on just how to manage the tension between homogeneity and diversity, it seems that the EU is peculiarly poorly equipped to voice and protect the latter virtue.

The EU has been engaged on a quest to do better for some time. There are two adjustments that deserve attention. The first is the embrace of national parliaments as more critical voices in the process of EU lawmaking (sections 5.8–5.10). The second is the Commission's commitment to Better Regulation (section 5.11). Both processes assume there is a need to think more carefully about the reasons for and against EU action than is ensured under the orthodox processes of lawmaking and judicial review. Both are of general application to the management of the tension between centralising homogeneity and diversity and local autonomy in the EU, but both have particular content and salience in relation to contract law.

5.8. THE RISE OF NATIONAL PARLIAMENTS

Recent Treaty revision has been motivated by a desire to incubate a more critical culture surrounding the assertion of EU legislative competence generally and in relation to the application of the subsidiarity principle in particular. This debate has taken many twists and turns which need not be recounted in full for the purposes of this book.[39] The most significant innovations that have emerged concern the position of national parliaments. As a result of the entry into force

---

39 See e.g. S. Weatherill, 'Competence creep and competence control' (2004) 23 *Yearbook of European Law* 1; V. Constantinesco, 'Les compétences et le principe de subsidiarité' (2005) 41 *Revue Trimistrielle de Droit Européen* 305; W. Swenden, 'Is the EU in need of a Competence Catalogue? Insights from comparative federalism' (2004) 42 *Journal of Common Market Studies* 371.

of the amending Treaty of Lisbon national parliaments enjoy with effect from 2009 a direct right of participation in the EU lawmaking process for the very first time.

The post-2009 renovated 'competence method' of the EU involves both rules and process, as most federal or quasi-federal systems do. As far as rules are concerned, what are now Articles 2–6 TFEU collect together the nature and scope of the EU's competences in a far more transparent and organised way than was previously available. They define the three main types of competences enjoyed by the EU – exclusive, shared and supporting – and they allocate particular types of activity to each category. They are not the last word on the matter and they skate over some intricate detail contained elsewhere in the Treaty,[40] but as an introduction to the nature of the EU's competence they are very helpful. The key aim is to promote a more transparent and informed debate about what the EU does, how it does it, and why. These rules are supplemented by process: this means institutional reform. National parliaments had no explicit place in the EU lawmaking process until 2009. It was assumed that their views would be represented by Ministers in Council. Practice often proves otherwise. The dislocation between domestic parliamentary oversight and the behaviour of ministers as members of the Council is notorious: what happens in 'Brussels' is sometimes concealed or at least hard to grasp, and the result is a tendency for the Council to serve as an exacerbation of the power of executives at State level. Under the reforms instituted by the Treaty of Lisbon, the system for monitoring the existence and exercise of the EU's conferred competences is enhanced and deepened by creating an explicit and direct role for national parliaments in the EU legislative process, in supplement to that which they perform imperfectly through national processes in seeking to hold ministers to account.

Article 12 TEU brings national parliaments explicitly into the EU institutional architecture. They 'contribute actively to the good functioning of the Union'. In the matter of competence monitoring, this is achieved by their being informed by the institutions of the Union and having draft legislative acts of the Union forwarded to them. This occurs in accordance with the Protocol on the role of national parliaments in the European Union which is attached to the Treaties. Moreover national parliaments are charged with the task of seeing to it that the principle of subsidiarity is respected in accordance with the procedures provided for in the Protocol on the application of the principles of subsidiarity and proportionality which is also attached to the Treaties.

The Protocol on the role of national parliaments in the EU deals in detail with the procedures for the distribution of information to national parliaments. It allows for the submission of a reasoned opinion in cases of suspected violation of the subsidiarity principle or (mis)use of Article 352 TFEU. It establishes an eight-week 'standstill' period designed to give national parliaments a real practical

40 See S. Weatherill, *Law and Values in the European Union*, OUP, Oxford 2016, Ch. 2.

opportunity to intervene in cases of troublesome draft legislative acts, applicable in all but urgent cases. The Protocol on subsidiarity and proportionality absorbs and amplifies this procedure. Where reasoned opinions on non-compliance represent at least one third of all the votes allocated to national parliaments, the draft legislation must be reviewed. This, following an analogy with football, has become known as the 'yellow card'. The Commission may then maintain, amend or withdraw the draft, and it must give reasons for its choice. Where reasoned opinions on non-compliance represent a simple majority of votes cast by national parliaments, then the Commission must review the proposal. This has become known as the 'orange card', which has no footballing equivalent, and it is plainly sterner in its braking power. The Commission, if it decides to maintain the proposal, must itself present a reasoned opinion dealing with its view defending the proposal. These opinions are then made available to the Union legislator and shall be considered. Plainly the aim is to maximise the opportunity for dialogue and for the voice of the national parliaments to be heard effectively. But national parliaments are *not* granted a veto over a legislative proposal. To sustain the analogy with sanctions imposed on recalcitrant footballers, there is no 'red card' made available to national parliaments under this procedure.

National parliaments are in this way granted their own distinct institutional identity at EU level. They are, after all, the bodies most obviously and directly prejudiced by over-hasty and over-intrusive legislative activity at EU level and they are therefore the bodies most likely to hold an incentive to interject a critical voice into EU lawmaking. It is worth noting that, compared to some of the other plans advanced during the process of negotiation that ultimately led to the Treaty of Lisbon and in particular those aired at the Convention on the Future of Europe,[41] these devices are relatively modest. Of particular relevance to the internal market, the deletion of (what are now) Articles 114 and/or 352 TFEU had its advocates, but not enough of them. Fears about the damaging loss of flexibility at EU level that would follow from deletion of these two functionally driven legal bases was enough to persuade the majority to reject pressure to abolish either or both legal bases. This is to highlight an abiding background tension in the debate about reform: alleged 'competence creep' opens the EU to criticisms rooted in want of formal legitimacy, and yet the more restrictive the rules and procedures under which it is forced to labour, the more it risks becoming unresponsive and ineffective, to the detriment of its ability to gather legitimacy through effective problem-solving on behalf of its Member States.[42] The refusal to grant national parliaments a red card is exactly in this spirit. The collective intervention of national parliaments, focused on the yellow and orange card procedures applicable to compliance with the subsidiarity principle, is

41 Cf. above n. 39.

42 Cf. S. Weatherill, 'Competence and Legitimacy' in C. Barnard and O. Odudu (eds.), *The Outer Limits of European Union Law*, Hart Publishing, Oxford 2009, Ch. 2, pp. 17–34.

best appreciated as an attempt to promote *dialogue* 'from below' about whether particular EU proposals are valid or well-intentioned. To grant a veto to national parliaments was, it was concluded, to allow them too brutal an intervening power in defence of State autonomy. The basic structure of the EU's lawmaking process is therefore left untouched, but a new and probably more openly critical voice – that of national parliaments – is added to the pattern of negotiation.

It should be emphasised that the involvement of national parliaments in the monitoring of the subsidiarity principle does not at all remove the *legal* requirement that EU acts must comply with the principle of subsidiarity. The role allocated to national parliaments by the reforms instituted with effect from 2009 was and is designed to supplement, not to replace, judicial control. However, as explained above,[43] the Court has in practice placed subsidiarity largely beyond the reach of judicially-based control. And it has been suggested (section 5.5) not only that it probably did so according to a sense that it wished to avoid addressing fiercely contested political questions about the virtues and vices of centralised rule-making *versus* preservation of divergent local preference and autonomy, but also that its sensitive reticence is well judged. The point, then, is not to abandon, but to move beyond, a purely legal understanding of subsidiarity. The reasoned opinion procedure centred on national parliaments represents an attempt to enliven the *political* debate about the risks associated with centralising bias in the EU. In this spirit it is clear from the Commission's Annual Reports that in practice the reasoned opinions submitted by national parliaments stretch far beyond subsidiarity as conventionally understood, engaging proportionality too, from which subsidiarity is sometimes not easily separated,[44] and frequently engage with the political merits of legislative proposals.[45] The Commission has been encouraged to embrace this stretching of the scope of the reasoned opinion procedure by COSAC, the Conference of Parliamentary Committees for Union Affairs of Parliaments of the European Union, which is obviously no impartial source.[46] However, this trend deserves to be welcomed, because it promises a richer debate about the relative virtues and vices of EU intervention that that which would be delivered by subsidiarity understood in a narrowly legal sense. The cautiously minimalist attitude to judicial review on the basis of subsidiarity adopted by the Court should not be the model for the development of the reasoned opinion procedure, or else it will be condemned to uselessness.

The Commission's reviewing of practice has typically endeavoured to maintain an optimistic tone about the reasoned opinion procedure: national

43 Case C-491/01, *British American Tobacco (Investments) and Imperial Tobacco* [2002] ECR I-11453, section 5.5.

44 Case C-491/01, *British American Tobacco (Investments) and Imperial Tobacco* [2002] ECR I-11453.

45 The Commission's Annual Reports on 'Better Lawmaking', which contain relevant detail, are at: http://ec.europa.eu/smart-regulation/better_regulation/reports_en.htm.

46 e.g. Contribution of the LII COSAC [2015] OJ C181/1, section 2.

parliaments have 'further enriched the discussions'.[47] It is no panacea. The lack of time and energy to exercise effective oversight over not only domestic politics but also 'Brussels' is an endemic problem among national parliaments. It is pertinent too that national executives dominate parliaments most of the time in most of the Member States, so the fountain of fresh critical thinking erupting from national parliaments may be more aspiration than reality. National parliaments submitting studious reasoned opinions will not convert the EU into a system that satisfies everyone that the tensions of centralisation *versus* local autonomy have been soothed. However, the aim, which is to raise the profile of national-level political processes and controls and to join them in a more structured and communicative way to the EU lawmaking process, is well intentioned. It has been the subject of critical approval in the main.[48] There has moreover been encouragement to expand it.[49]

There were 64 reasoned opinions submitted by national parliaments in 2011, relating to 28 different proposals.[50] In 2012 there were 70 reasoned opinions, on 23 different proposals. In 2013, there were 88 reasoned opinions, on 36 different proposals. In 2014 the number of reasoned opinions submitted dropped significantly. Only 21 were received by the Commission, on 15 different proposals, though the Commission explains this in its Annual Report with reference to the decrease in the number of legislative proposals it has made: it does not think national parliaments are losing interest.

So far the weight of reasoned opinions submitted has resulted in two yellow cards and no orange card. Neither of the two yellow cards has been in relation to a measure adopted under Article 114 TFEU and neither was remotely close to contract law. One concerned the so-called 'Monti II' legislative proposal of the Commission which was directed at balancing protection of collective labour rights and the free movement of companies.[51] The Commission was duly cowed and it withdrew the proposal, but it did not admit to violation of the subsidiarity principle. Instead it simply cited absence of adequate political

---

47 COM (2011) 344, page 10.

48 e.g. R. Schütze, 'Subsidiarity after Lisbon: Reinforcing the Safeguards of Federalism' (2009) 68 *Cambridge Law Journal* 525; P. Kiiver, 'The Early-Warning System for the Principle of Subsidiarity: the National Parliament as a *Conseil d'Etat* for Europe' (2011) 36 *European Law Journal* 98; A. Cygan, 'The Parliamentarisation of EU Decision-Making? The Impact of the Treaty of Lisbon on National Parliaments' (2011) 36 *European Law Review* 480; C. Bickenbach, 'Das Subsidiaritätsprinzip in Art. 5 EUZ und seine Kontrolle' [2013] *Europarecht* 523; B. Guastaferro, 'Coupling National Identity with Subsidiarity Concerns in National Parliaments' Reasoned Opinions' (2014) 21 *Maastricht Journal* 320.

49 D. Jančić, 'The Game of Cards: National Parliaments in the EU and the Future of the Early Warning Mechanism and the Political Dialogue' (2015) 52 *Common Market Law Review* 939.

50 The Commission's Annual Reports on 'Better Lawmaking', which contain these statistics, are at: http://ec.europa.eu/smart-regulation/better_regulation/reports_en.htm. National parliaments' opinions are available via IPEX, www.ipex.eu/IPEXL-WEB/search.do.

51 COM (2012) 130, prepared as a response to the rulings in Case C-438/05, *Viking Line* [2007] ECR I-10779 and Case C-341/05, *Laval* [2007] ECR I-11767, met in Chapter 2.5.

support.[52] The other yellow card concerned the Proposal for a Council Regulation on the establishment of the European Public Prosecutor's Office. The Commission has decided not to abandon this proposal.[53] But the influence of the reasoned opinion is not confined to instances of the thresholds for cards being crossed. The Commission's report for calendar year 2014 tells that early in 2015 the Commission withdrew a proposal for a Directive amending existing Directives which would have addressed in detail the recycling of municipal waste and packaging waste.[54] Three national parliaments had submitted reasoned opinions expressing the view that the proposal did not comply with the principle of subsidiarity. So this did not cross the threshold required for a 'yellow card'. But still, it seems, national parliaments had played a part in creating an environment that was not conducive to proceeding with EU legislative action. They have influence beyond the formal limits of the reasoned opinion procedure.

5.9. CONTRACT LAW

Contract law was not and is not at the centre of the debate about the rising profile of national parliaments as guardians of the subsidiarity principle in particular and the balance of competences between the EU and its Member States more generally. However, consideration of contract law fits perfectly neatly into the thematic concerns which have animated reform of the EU's system of competence in recent years.

The Consumer Rights Directive, 2011/83, was discussed in Chapter 4 as a measure of harmonisation.[55] It was mentioned in Chapter 3, and will be explored much more fully in Chapter 6, that the Commission's original ambitions in proposing legislation in the field had to scale back dramatically for want of adequate political support for, most of all, its preference for a model of maximum harmonisation. Chapter 6.6 tells a story of preservation of diversity (in control of unfair terms and consumer sales) driven by a distrust of the cost/benefit calculation advanced by the Commission in its zeal to make the internal market more coherent (but national law less coherent, and potentially less protective of the consumer too).

---

52 The story is told by The Adoptive Parents, 'The Life of a Death Foretold: The Proposal for a Monti II Regulation' in M. Freedland and J. Prassl (eds.), *EU Law in the Member States: Viking, Laval and Beyond*, Hart Publishing, Oxford 2014, Ch. 5, pp. 95–112; F. Fabbrini and K. Granat, 'Yellow Card but no Foul: the role of the national parliaments under the subsidiarity protocol and the Commission proposal for an EU regulation on the right to strike' (2013) 50 *Common Market Law Review* 115.

53 COM (2013) 851.

54 COM (2015) 315, pp. 9–10.

55 [2011] OJ L304/64, Chapter 4.3.

The proposal for a Common European Sales Law was met in Chapter 3.[56] There too the Commission's plans had the wind taken out of their sails by political and academic disquiet about the proposed model. The contaminating absence of a healthy and questioning political debate about the virtue and vice of centralisation has been diagnosed as lying at the core of such fractious debates about the shape of EU legislative initiatives in the field of contract law, and it has been persuasively argued that the national parliaments deserve to be promoted as a means to provoke the missing more intense debate about the purposes and consequences of an EU intervention into contract law.[57]

In fact, one of the legislative proposals targeted by national parliaments' reasoned opinions in 2011, receiving four reasoned opinions within the deadline, was that for the Regulation on a Common European Sales Law (CESL), which raised awkward constitutional and substantive questions already introduced in Chapter 3. The CESL would have created a new EU level instrument of contract law, which would co-exist with national forms. It would not have been a classic measure of harmonisation: it would have added one extra diverse regime at EU level to the existing patterns of diversity at the level of the Member States. It would, in the Commission's thinking of 2011, have established a 28th regime of contract law in the EU – which would now, thanks to Croatia's accession, be a 29th regime or in fact (because there are two different systems of contract law in one Member State, the United Kingdom) a 30th regime. The Commission's guiding explanation was *choice*. The regime would be voluntary. Traders and consumers could opt in to the new model provided by the CESL if they so chose. Alternatively they could stick with national law. The CESL's success or failure would be determined by its appeal to users.

The Proposal for a Regulation of the Parliament and the Council on a Common European Sales Law was published by the Commission in October 2011.[58] The first sentence of the Explanatory Memorandum states that '[d]ifferences in contract law between Member States hinder traders and consumers who want to engage in cross-border trade within the internal market'. The proposal was expressly presented as a contribution designed to improve the establishment and the functioning of the internal market. The supporting Communication could not have been clearer about the internal market focus of the proposal: its title was 'A Common European Sales Law to Facilitate Cross-Border Transactions in the Single Market'.[59] The Communication is built on a sustained and thematically familiar insistence that differences between national contract law systems hinder cross-border trade in the EU.

---

56 COM (2011) 635, Chapter 3.10, 3.17.

57 e.g. M. Bartl, 'The Way we do Europe: Subsidiarity and the *Substantive* Democratic Deficit' (2015) 21 *European Law Journal* 23.

58 COM (2011) 635.

59 COM (2011) 636.

The Commission's proposed legal base was Article 114. It explained its proposal from the perspective of subsidiarity as a contribution to the proper functioning of the internal market which could not be sufficiently achieved by the Member States acting within the framework of their uncoordinated national systems. It added that stakeholders had acknowledged that the existence of differences in contract laws had led to legal fragmentation which can affect the functioning of the internal market.

The proposed CESL was poorly received, as was mentioned in Chapter 3.10. The Commission's Work Programme for 2015 includes the CESL in its list of proposals to be withdrawn or modified.[60] It is there declared that the CESL in its original relatively ambitious form will not be pursued and that instead there will be only a replacement modified proposal targeted at promoting e-commerce in the development of a wider Digital Single Market.

The four reasoned opinions issued by national parliaments which objected to the proposed CESL deserve attention.[61] The original CESL proposal may now have been vanquished, but the insight which the reasoned opinions provide into the capacities and preoccupations of the national parliaments are of value into the future. Each opinion is written with economy, but a number of important points about the virtues and vices of EU rule-making emerge.

That submitted by the UK's House of Commons, which covers twelve pages, begins badly by stating that '[t]he principle of subsidiarity is born of the wish to ensure that decisions are taken as closely as possible to the citizens of the EU'. This is at best an incomplete observation, at worst plain wrong: Article 5(3) TEU directs a search for the level of action best able to achieve the objectives of the proposed action. The reasoned opinion prepared by the House of Commons takes as its main objection the lack of detail provided by the Commission on the implications of its proposal for EU law, national law and users of contract law, combined with protest at the short time it has been allowed to address the matter. It also objects that the damage done by diverse contract laws is exaggerated by the Commission, while the complexity and harm to legal certainty is underestimated. The objections are presented expressly as based on subsidiarity, though the opinion plainly ranges more widely and also engages (critically) with the merits of the initiative.

The Austrian Federal Council (Bundesrat) submitted a three-page opinion. It also objects to the level of uncertainty associated with the CESL, noting that it would take years, and rulings of the Court of Justice, to firm up understanding of its provisions, and that in any event the CESL is not exhaustive in its coverage and so would still depend on existing and varied national law. It also protests

60 http://ec.europa.eu/atwork/key-documents/index_en.htm.

61 They are at www.ipex.eu/IPEXL-WEB/dossier/document/COM20110635.do#dossier-COD 20110284.

that the Commission is aiming at the wrong target. Drawing on data collected through Eurobarometer, it argues that:

> 'Consumers are reluctant to engage in cross-border transactions not because of differences in legal regimes, but due to factual and practical problems, such as language barriers, fear of fraud, delays in delivery or problems encountered in the event of deficient products received. Traders themselves indicate that they do not consider differences in legal regimes a substantial obstacle to cross-border activities. General considerations of economic efficiency play a greater role.'

This objection lacks constitutional bite. It was explained in Chapter 3 that even though it is probable that actual or likely regulatory diversity between the Member States exerts less restrictive or distortive impact on cross-border trade patterns than other matters such as the 'factual and practical problems' to which the Austrian opinion draws attention, this still does not rule out the existence of a legislative competence to harmonise. Article 114 has a low threshold: there is empirical evidence that inter-State legislative diversity has *some* detrimental impact on the internal market.[62] However, the Austrian anxieties are certainly the sorts of concern that should animate the political debate about whether the EU *should* exercise its competence, given that there is evident doubt about the advantage to be gained from harmonisation. The principles of subsidiarity and proportionality open a window towards that wider enriched political, economic and cultural debate.

The opinion concludes by objecting that the Commission 'only refers to a wide range of transaction costs allegedly arising for traders, without considering any of the additional costs that may arise for consumers'. This is a general criticism of the Commission's work in this area. It is much quicker to quantify benefits of EU action than it is to count costs.

The German Bundestag submitted a nine-page opinion.[63] This is built on a careful argument, informed by contributions made by a number of named academic lawyers, that the scope of review in the name of subsidiarity should be interpreted widely, embracing also questions of competence and of proportionality. It then, in line with the Austrian opinion, it argues that it 'doubts that the different contract laws in the Member States noticeably impede economic activity in the European legal area'. It notes that 'it is above all linguistic barriers and geographical distance which act as obstacles to cross-

62 e.g. S. Vogenauer and S. Weatherill, 'The European Community's competence for a comprehensive harmonisation of contract law – an empirical analysis' (2005) 30 *European Law Review* 821; K. Thommes, M. Faure and K. Heine, 'The Internal Market and the Consumer: What Consumers Actually Choose' (2014) 21 *Columbia Journal of European Law* 47. See further Chapter 3.12.

63 For a note on that submitted by the Bundestag, see P. Sensburg, 'The Position of the German Bundestag on the Commission's Proposal for a Regulation on a Common European Sales Law' (2012) 8 *European Review of Contract Law* 188.

border economic activity', and this 'applies equally to consumers and to business, as proved by feedback from consumer and business groups.' So too, in line with the Austrian opinion, it finds that the proposed CESL would create a significant level of legal uncertainty which would prevent it from achieving its objectives.

The Belgian Senate's reasoned opinion runs to eight pages. It considers there are three dimensions to its power of review: the existence of a relevant competence, the pertinence of the proposed measure as a means to resolve the identified problem, and the capacity to find a solution through national initiatives. It shares with the Bundestag's contribution a readiness to cite academic comment. It expresses a mild concern that the proposed CESL may allow the evasion of mandatory rules under Belgian contract law, and it also considers that inadequate attention has been paid to showing just why an EU intervention is required. It is noticeably less strident in its criticism than the other reasoned opinions.

The threshold for a yellow card requires that at least one third of all the votes allocated to national parliaments are directed against the proposed measure. So the threshold was not crossed in this case. The CESL proposal has, however, subsequently been modified to take a much less ambitious shape[64] and it is at least plausible that the objections of national parliaments exerted some influence in prompting the Commission's self-adjustment. Whether or not this causal link exists, the opinions helpfully reveal the type of debates and objections which deserve to be conducted in connection with any measure associated with the development of the internal market. In particular the thematic linkage is scepticism that top-down rule-making can do much to improve the functioning of the internal market and that attention should be paid to other flaws and obstacles, such as, to borrow from the Austrian opinion, 'language barriers, fear of fraud, delays in delivery or problems encountered in the event of deficient products received'. The problem is that flaws of this nature are not readily addressed by the EU at all. Limits on its conferred competences must be taken seriously. Top-down rule-making is the EU's most buoyant *modus operandi*: Article 114 gives it a generous competence to intervene in this way. This is a tension in the internal market generally. The EU market is plainly less integrated than, say, that of the United States, because there is far less labour mobility, largely because of cultural and linguistic differences. The EU is a market but not a State. The EU tends to respond to this with ever more aggressive top-down rule-making. This is what its Treaty permits. But such rules may be aimed at things that really do not belong among the principal problems.

Other sources beyond the national parliaments commented on and criticised the CESL proposal. Beginning in 2012, the UK government pursued an inquiry under the title 'Review of the Balance of Competences'. The project

64 Above n. 60.

was concluded in 2014, by which time 32 reports on aspects of the EU's impact on and in the UK had been published.[65] The conclusion was that broadly the balance between the UK and EU was about right, though that finding appears to have been inconvenient for the government which appears promptly to have chosen to ignore it completely in the tortured debate about the UK's future relationship with the EU. Of present interest is the report on Subsidiarity and Proportionality. It takes CESL as a case study.[66] This reveals that the need for the CESL has been questioned, *inter alia* on subsidiarity grounds. The Law Society believed it 'to be a disproportionate policy response to an unclear problem and to infringe the subsidiarity principle'. The Society, it was reported, did not agree that it had been shown that lack of a common law of contract poses a significant barrier to cross-border trade. As the report put it, '[t]he overarching concern of UK stakeholders is that, as there is no robust evidence that a problem exists, then the Commission should not be legislating'. However, the report added that 'other groups support the CESL, for example, the Law Society of Scotland'. It considers that '[a] single system is preferable to a proliferation of national laws to cover the transactions envisaged'.

The case study concludes that '[t]his shows that assessments of subsidiarity can differ'. This is quite correct and it neatly underlines the problem. Subsidiarity is a useful basis to invoke as a starting point in the inquiry into the proper balance to be struck between EU action and State action – between centralisation and local autonomy, between homogeneity and diversity – but it has no power on its own to determine which outcome should be preferred. That requires a fiercely contested debate about the virtues and vices of uniformity and diversity, which demands too an appreciation of sector-specific context.

Academic reception of the CESL proposal was not warm. The Commission's insistence that the Regulation would promote choice was doubted by those who thought it more likely that it would permit the stronger and better informed party to the negotiation to induce the weaker party, typically the consumer, to make a poorly informed choice.[67] Choice might in truth be confusion. How worried one is about consumers choosing to opt in to the CESL without really understanding its scope depends in large part on an assessment of whether one believes it offers *less* protection than existing mandatory national laws, but part of the criticism holds that in any event one cannot know whether this is so until the CESL has come to life and been applied and interpreted over time by courts. The proposed CESL was also a wonderfully attractive adventure playground for

65 Available via https://www.gov.uk/guidance/review-of-the-balance-of-competences.

66 Para. 2.13.

67 e.g. J. Cartwright, 'Choice is good. Really?' (2011) 7 *European Review of Contract Law* 335; S. Whittaker, 'The Optional Instrument of European Contract Law and Freedom of Contract' (2011) 7 *European Review of Contract Law* 371; R. Sefton-Green, 'Choice, Certainty and Diversity: Why More is Less' (2011) 7 *European Review of Contract Law* 134.

comparative lawyers and it has attracted a large amount of criticism at the level of its detailed fit with existing understandings of contract law.[68]

There were constitutional questions too about the CESL. It was a stretch to advance it on the basis of Article 114 TFEU, as the Commission did. It was, as the Commission's documents declared, convincingly aimed at improving the functioning of the internal market, but, as Chapter 3.17 has made clear, reliance on Article 114 also demands that there be harmonisation of national laws. Where a new EU-level entity is being established which will co-exist with national systems which are left undisturbed, Article 352, not Article 114, must be used.[69] And the CESL seemed to be of this type. This constitutional objection is recorded in the reasoned opinions submitted by the Austrian Federal Council, the Bundestag, and the Belgian Senate.

The constitutional objections, the views of national parliaments, academic criticisms and objections of stakeholders such as the Law Society were not on their own decisive but they combined to create a political mood unfavourable to the Commission's proposal. In September 2013 the European Parliament's Committee on Legal Affairs agreed that the CESL could promote legal certainty for consumers and traders, but they expressed a wish to restrict its scope to distance contracts, that is, mainly those concluded online. This reduction in ambition has been carried through. The Commission's Work Programme for 2015 admitted that the CESL could not be maintained in the form proposed in 2011 and that instead a modified proposal should be prepared, which would be focused on promoting e-commerce in the development of a digital single market.[70]

5.10. IMPACT ASSESSMENT AND BETTER REGULATION

The Commission has a long-standing commitment to *Better Regulation*. The starting point was an Action Plan published in 2002, under the title 'Simplifying and improving the regulatory environment'.[71] This expressed a concern to attune legislation 'to the problems posed, to the challenge of enlargement and to technical and local conditions' in order to make it 'easier to implement for

---

68 e.g. S. Whittaker, 'The Proposed Common European Sales Law: Legal Framework and the Agreement of the Parties' (2012) 75 *Modern Law Review* 578; H. Eidenmüller et al., 'The Proposal for a Regulation on a Common European Sales Law: Deficits of the most Recent Textual Layer of European Contract Law' (2012) 16 *Edinburgh Law Review* 301; W. Doralt, 'The Optional European Contract Law and Why Success or Failure May Depend on Scope Rather than Substance' [2011] *Revue des Contrats* 1313.

69 Case C-436/03, *Parliament v Council* [2006] ECR I-3733.

70 Above n. 60.

71 COM (2002) 278. See S. Weatherill (ed.), *Better Regulation*, Hart/IECL, Oxford 2007.

the Member States and operators concerned and easier for everyone to read and understand'.[72] The aim, it was carefully noted, was 'to ensure a high level of legal certainty across the EU' and to 'enable economic and social operators to be more dynamic', not to deregulate the Union or limit its scope for action.[73]

Part of this campaign involves commitment to respect for the principles of subsidiarity and proportionality. Both principles are, broadly understood, dedicated to improving the quality of the regulatory environment in the EU. Indeed the annual reports which the Commission produces which provide statistical information and commentary on the practical application of the two principles are housed on the *Better Regulation* website.[74] Until 2011 they were entitled reports on 'Better Lawmaking'.

The Commission's own *Better Regulation* website captures the basic aim:

> 'Better regulation is about designing EU policies and laws so that they achieve their objectives at minimum cost. It ensures that policy is prepared, implemented and reviewed in an open, transparent manner, informed by the best available evidence and backed up by involving stakeholders. To ensure that EU action is effective, the Commission assesses the expected and actual impacts of policies, legislation and other important measures at every stage of the policy cycle – from planning to implementation, to review and subsequent revision'.[75]

This is splendid. But no one would disagree. It is temptingly easy to mock the Commission's pretensions. *Better Regulation* sounds heroic, yet no one would champion *Worse Regulation*. The 2002 launch document was entitled 'Simplifying and improving the regulatory environment', yet the Commission was not faced with the need to repel an aggressive campaign in favour of a more complicated and deteriorating regulatory environment. The problem, then, is not agreeing the aim, but rather the conversion of these fine words into practically useful action. A certain scepticism about how much truly useful content there is to the gloss of *Better Regulation* in general and its attachment to subsidiarity in particular would be fed by inspection of its May 2015 document entitled 'Better Regulation or Better Results – An EU Agenda' which in fact contains only two references to subsidiarity in its thirteen pages, both of them perfunctory.[76] The principal anxiety about the process of impact assessment is that it may lack the independence from the Commission's own preferences which is necessary to generate a genuinely impartial debate about choice of options. It may be no more

---

72 Page 3.

73 Page 3.

74 http://ec.europa.eu/smart-regulation/better_regulation/reports_en.htm. See also A. Meuwese and S. Gomtsian, 'Regulatory Scrutiny of Subsidiarity and Proportionality' (2015) 22 *Maastricht Journal* 483.

75 http://ec.europa.eu/smart-regulation/index_en.htm.

76 COM (2015) 215, both at p. 4.

than a means to impose a degree of rather spurious scientific respectability on a nakedly political decision based on preconception.

However, such scepticism should have its limits. The Commission is doing what it can in a dense regulatory environment which is not conducive to simple rule-making, given that it involves the replacement of often cherished national regulatory choices with a single EU rule that must somehow satisfy all affected interests to a degree that allows passage through the political process. EU rules have an in-built tendency to become cumulative and weighty. In 2002 the Commission launched two particular initiatives: the establishment of *minimum standards of consultation* and the definition of a *consolidated impact assessment method* for its key initiatives concerning policy and legislation. Both consultation and impact assessment are now addressed on dedicated and informative websites.[77] They are important parts of the project, which in 2015 was elaborated as a 'Better Regulation Package'.[78] Part of this package included the adoption of 'Better Regulation Guidelines',[79] which replaced the Commission's earlier 2009 Impact Assessment Guidelines.[80] The 2015 Guidelines accept that the determination of 'when and how EU action should be undertaken, reviewed or repealed is ultimately a political choice', but press the case for improving the 'quality of these choices … if better regulation principles and practices are followed when preparing, implementing and evaluating policies and measures'.[81] The Guidelines set out how this should be achieved at all stages of the law- and policymaking process. They are strikingly elaborate and stretch over 91 pages.

The animating ambition of *Better Regulation* is to open up the process of EU lawmaking and to instil a more questioning culture. In this it has something in common with the role mapped for national parliaments by the reforms instituted by the Lisbon Treaty, considered above (section 5.9), although the commitment to consultation and to impact assessment is largely to be carried through by and within the Commission in the preparatory stage of legislative activity. It is, however, deserving of support as an attempt to make EU practice more sensitive to its full consequences. The Commission, however, cannot do it all alone. In the 2002 launch document it astutely noted that the success of its strategy 'depends on the other institutions and Member States showing a strong political commitment to its formulation and implementation'.[82] This remains true.

---

77 http://ec.europa.eu/smart-regulation/stakeholder-consultation/index_en.htm; http://ec.europa.eu/smart-regulation/impact/index_en.htm.

78 http://ec.europa.eu/smart-regulation/better_regulation/key_docs_en.htm.

79 SWD (2015) 111, http://ec.europa.eu/smart-regulation/guidelines/toc_guide_en.htm.

80 SEC (2009) 92.

81 Page 4.

82 Page 5.

The commitment to consultation and to impact assessment is virtuous and holds promise. It is visible in contract law, as too is the drive to simplify rules.[83] In Chapter 3.10 it was noted that in 2001 the Commission initiated a process of review and consultation of the EU's role in contract law. The concern in Chapter 3 was with the constitutional dimension, and that is the most germane to the main themes of this book. It was there shown that the golden thread was the contribution to the internal market of an EU contract law, and that the attachment to Article 114 was the primary background constitutional concern animating the Commission's inquiry. However, the process was also driven by a genuine substantive concern to identify the scope and nature of the demand for (some kind of) EU contract law. There were – and there are – deficiencies in the pattern of EU lawmaking which, at the very least, could usefully be addressed by a more attentive approach to the drafting of measures and a more thorough articulation of their objectives.[84] The Commission consulted at length and was transparent about its findings.

The July 2001 Communication on European Contract Law was structured around four possible options for future EU action in the field of contract law.[85] These were: no action, based on the perception that markets have a capacity to achieve self-correction that should not be underestimated; the promotion of the development of common contract law principles leading to greater convergence of national laws; improving the quality of legislation already in place; or the adoption of new comprehensive legislation at EU level. The Commission invited comment on the preferred way forward. There was certainly a strategic disingenuousness lacing the Commission's apparent open-mindedness. It doubtless expected negligible support for the first and fourth options, and it doubtless expected the second and third would not readily be opposed. This was indeed the pattern of the feedback it received, so it managed to place a legitimate sheen on its own barely concealed preferences. But even so the process of the review since 2001 has been impressively transparent and fully explained, even if certain preconceptions may be spotted. The review took two distinct, though not unrelated, tracks: that which focused on the revision of the *acquis* and that which led circuitously via the Common Frame of Reference to the stalled proposal for a CESL which was considered above (section 5.9). Both were accompanied by a cascade of documentation designed to elicit consultation.

In 2006 the Commission published a Green Paper on the Review of the Consumer Acquis.[86] This was announced as the end of the 'diagnostic phase' of the review. The review of the consumer *acquis* was focused on a general review

---

83 E. Van Schagen, 'The Hidden Potential of Regulatory Impact Assessments (RIAs) in the Private Law Acquis' (2014) 22 *European Review of Private Law* 69.

84 E. Van Schagen, 'More Consistency and Legal Certainty in the Private Law Acquis: a Plea for Better Justification for the Harmonization of Private Law' (2012) 19 *Maastricht Journal* 37.

85 COM (2001) 398.

86 COM (2006) 744.

of eight particular consumer Directives, the so-called 'consumer *acquis*'.[87] Eight became four. In October 2008 the Commission adopted a proposal for a Directive on Consumer Rights.[88] This would have replaced four Directives with a single 'horizontal instrument'. The Directives were met in Chapters 3 and 4: they were the 'Doorstep Selling' Directive (85/577), Directive 97/7 on distance contracts, Directive 93/13 on unfair terms and Directive 99/44 on consumer sales. It was mentioned in Chapter 3.10, and will be explained more fully in Chapter 6.6, that four became two. In July 2010 the Commission published a Green Paper on policy options for progress towards a European Contract Law for consumers and businesses.[89] This paved the way for it to revise its proposal. In 2011 Directive 2011/83 on consumer rights was adopted.[90] It replaced and updated only two of the Directives previously under review, Directive 85/577 on doorstep selling and Directive 97/7 on distance contracts – which are certainly the less important pair among the batch of four. The explanation, provided more fully in Chapter 6.6 in connection with the debate about maximum or minimum harmonisation, is of stern political blockages to revision of the *acquis*, at least in the directions pressed by the Commission; however, taking account of the subject matter of this chapter, there was no lack of willingness on the part of the Commission to invite comment as part of the process of revision. Similar remarks can be directed at the Common Frame of Reference: its precise shape is not clear but the Commission's willingness to entertain debate about its possible functions was evident.[91] This is not to deny the Commission's persisting inclination for strategic disingenuousness. Its July 2010 Green Paper on policy options for progress towards a European Contract Law for consumers and businesses sought views on a range of several possible options, ranging from mere publication of the results of its 'expert group' at one extreme to, at the other, production of a civil code.[92] There was no serious support for a civil code, and the Commission could easily be accused of creating a 'straw man' as a target for criticism precisely in order to lure support towards its preferred and less radical option. In fact, the 2015 Guidelines on Better Regulation reveal precisely this concern: they counsel against use of 'straw man' options, that is those which are 'clearly more costly or less effective alternatives retained only to highlight the benefits of the preferred option'.[93] In the 2010 Green Paper it was in truth easy to identify the Commission's own preferred option, which was to propose an EU Regulation

---

87 http://ec.europa.eu/consumers/archive/rights/cons_acquis_en.htm.
88 COM (2008) 614.
89 COM (2010) 348.
90 [2011] OJ L304/64.
91 e.g. Commission's second Progress Report on the Common Frame of Reference, COM (2007) 447, 25 July 2007.
92 COM (2010) 348.
93 See p. 24 of the 2015 Guidelines, above n. 79. See also E. Van Schagen, 'The Guidelines and the Board before the Court' forthcoming.

creating a so-called 'optional instrument'. And this is exactly what emerged: the proposal for a CESL. As explained above (section 5.9), this did not succeed in winning adequate political support. It is wholly impossible to prove that a more open-minded process of consultation would have granted the proposal a happier fate, but the Commission would at least have been on firmer and frankly more honest ground had it prepared it by offering a more genuinely focused menu of options unadorned by the wildly implausible civil code.

The particular phenomenon of impact assessment has been part of this process. Directive 2011/83 on consumer rights was supported by an impact assessment document.[94] It is 42 pages long and contains detail on the pattern of consultation carried out and the views expressed about the problems to which the Directive is designed to act as a solution. The focus is on the incomplete nature of the internal market. The several possible policy options considered are explained and reasons are given, including with reference to the views of stakeholders, for the decision to discard all but one of them. Naturally one might not agree with the Commission's interpretation and its eventual choice of legislative model, but it has not emerged from a black box.

Equally an impact assessment accompanied the Commission Proposal for a Regulation on a Common European Sales Law, the CESL mentioned above (section 5.9).[95] This emphasises the intensity of the consultation pursued by the Commission, explains the Commission's view that the fragmented legal regime causes obstacles to the functioning of the internal market and sifts the available policy options. It gives reasons for discarding all but one – the proposal for a CESL as an optional instrument. This in turn was examined by the Parliament's own impact assessment unit, which in January 2013 reported its assessment of the Commission's assessment.[96] It praised it for the clarity of explanation and readiness to range over several possible policy options and their likely impacts, and noted too evidence of broad consultation with stakeholders. It notes that the Commission attempted to make a quantitative estimation of the transaction costs, though it also express some concern about the reliability of the available data.

The Court has on occasion inspected the impact assessment conducted by the Commission, usually to confirm that an adequate demonstration of the necessary impact on the internal market exists to justify reliance on Article 114. This is particularly evident in *Vodafone, O2 and Others v Secretary of State*.[97] As explained in Chapter 3.8, this was an unsuccessful attack on the validity of the so-called 'Roaming Regulation', Regulation 717/2007. The Court declared that the Regulation had been adopted in response to the likelihood that national

94 http://ec.europa.eu/consumers/consumer_rights/rights-contracts/directive/index_en.htm.
95 SEC (2011) 1166.
96 PE 496.736, www.europarl.europa.eu/thinktank/en/document.html?reference=IPOL-JOIN_ET%282013%29496736.
97 Case C-58/08 [2010] ECR I-4999.

price control measures of divergent type would be adopted aiming to address the problem of the high level of retail charges for EU-wide roaming services. So the Court was prepared to treat this as an instance of preventive harmonisation aimed at improving the conditions for the functioning of the internal market. In reaching this conclusion it rejected the submissions of the applicants and of its own Advocate General that there was no such likelihood. The Court drew on both the explanatory memorandum to the proposal and the impact assessment to substantiate the finding that there was a likelihood of divergent development of national laws. The recital stated there was pressure for Member States to take measures to address the problem of the high level of retail charges for roaming services, and the Court added that this was had been confirmed by the Commission at the hearing.[98] One can readily entertain a degree of concern about this approach: the Court places faith in documentation prepared by the legislative institutions, yet it is the constitutional validity of their choices that the Court is supposed to reviewing objectively in order to satisfy itself that the dictates of the principle of conferral have been met. This mild standard of review, however, seems to be the Court's preference.[99] The corollary of this approach is that an absence of supporting material in an impact assessment might be a factor apt to encourage the Court to invalidate a measure, in particular for want of adequate reasoning as mandated by Article 296 TFEU. This would reinforce the importance of impact assessment as an important procedural element within the EU legislative process, although it plainly would not impress those who suspect that impact assessment tends to be little more than a means to validate what has already been politically chosen as the preferred path.

98 Para. 44.
99 Cf. Case C-508/13 *Estonia v Council and Parliament* judgment of 18 June 2015.

CHAPTER 6
MODELS OF HARMONISATION: MAXIMUM OR MINIMUM

6.1. INTRODUCTION

The question which is addressed in this chapter is simply stated. It asks what is the scope for action at national level in a field in which the EU has adopted legislation. The most acute dimension of this question asks whether Member States may adopt stricter rules than those set as a harmonised norm by the EU. It is simple enough to ask these questions, but providing answers is not simple at all. The Treaty is evasive on the point. Legislative practice varies, policy preferences among the EU's political institutions have fluctuated (and continue to do so) and the Court of Justice has muddied the waters still further by delivering a spray of rulings, examined below, which seem irreconcilable.

The basic choice lies between a model of 'maximum harmonisation' and a model of 'minimum harmonisation'. This chapter is built on the argument that it is open to the EU, in adopting measures of harmonisation, to choose between setting rules that deny Member States room to choose stricter standards – this is the model of maximum harmonisation – and instead setting rules that allow scope for stricter national standards above the harmonised norm – this is minimum harmonisation. But it is admitted at the outset that this argument is made against a contested constitutional and policy background. The chapter begins by examining the governing Treaty superstructure (section 6.2). It then maps legislative practice in the field of harmonisation (section 6.3), before turning to exploration of the Court's unhelpfully ambiguous legacy in the field (section 6.4). It then tracks the Commission's policy-driven crusade against the technique of minimum harmonisation and in favour of maximum harmonisation, which has been animated by a belief that the maximum model is the superior means to deliver a well functioning internal market for the EU (section 6.5). This has clear resonance in the field of contract law. It then shows how politically contested this has – quite properly – become, and explains how the purity of the Commission's vision has met political resistance and how accordingly minimum harmonisation retains a place in the strategies for the construction of the internal market (section 6.6). It then moves to a more normative plane and insists that the cost/benefit analysis requires a nuanced appreciation of the choices and most of all an excavation of preconceptions and purposes underlying EU initiatives (section 6.7). Section 6.8 concludes, and insists that an unqualified embrace of either maximum or minimum harmonisation is an error. A sector-specific inquiry, attuned to the full range of influences and consequences, is needed.

6.2. THE DIRECTIONS CONTAINED IN THE TREATY SUPERSTRUCTURE

The basic question mentioned in this chapter's introduction, which is 'what is the scope for action at national level in a field in which the EU has adopted legislation?', is answered clearly and openly in some places in the Treaty on the Functioning of the European Union (TFEU). There is a batch of Treaty provisions which stipulate that legislative measures adopted at EU level pursuant to them do not exclude the competence of the Member States to adopt stricter rules within the scope allowed by the Treaty. This is minimum rule-making. A permissive formula of this type may be found in Article 153(4) TFEU, concerning social matters, and in Article 193 TFEU which deals with environmental protection. Article 169(4) governing consumer protection is another typical example. It provides that:

> 'Measures adopted pursuant to paragraph 3 shall not prevent any Member State from maintaining or introducing more stringent protective measures. Such measures must be compatible with the Treaties. The Commission shall be notified of them'.

The controlling proviso that measures must be compatible with the Treaties reminds that a Member State which prefers rules which are stricter than the EU's standard does not thereby escape the obligations by the Treaty provisions on free movement and non-discrimination, examined in Chapter 2. In this sense minimum rule-making by the EU sets a floor, but the ceiling is set by primary law. Maximum rule-making, by contrast, would contain both floor and ceiling within the same measure of secondary legislation.

The awkward twist is that Article 114 TFEU, by contrast, contains no such general concession to the competence of Member States to set stricter rules than the harmonised standard. It contains only one set of procedures which address the core issue of the impact of a measure of legislative harmonisation adopted pursuant to Article 114 on residual Member State competence. That is the complex derogations contained in Article 114(4)–(10) TFEU whereby States may be permitted to apply stricter standards than are envisaged by the agreed EU rule, but only under defined preconditions which are narrower than those available under Article 36 TFEU and which moreover are subject to supervision by and require the authorisation of the Commission. This procedure is in practice rarely invoked and it is still rarer that it leads to approval of national measures by the Commission.[1] Instances of its invocation have tended to concern disputes over matters of product safety: it is of peripheral significance to contract law.

Article 114 is therefore silent on the broader question whether it mandates the adoption of measures of maximum harmonisation or minimum harmonisation – or both. Article 4 TFEU lists both the internal market and consumer protection as areas of competence shared between the EU and the Member States, but this does not solve the particular question of the extent to which legislative action pursuant to Article 114 TFEU excludes residual Member State competence. The question which arises is therefore whether a measure of legislative harmonisation adopted under Article 114 may *itself* provide that stricter national measures are permitted. Put another way, the question is whether the derogation foreseen by Article 114(4)–(10) is the exclusive window through which Member States may skip free of the agreed harmonised standard or whether instead the EU legislative process may choose to grant such derogations by embedding them in the text of particular individual measures of secondary legislation.

The model of maximum harmonisation would seem more likely to promote an even regulatory environment in the internal market, by confining scope for States to fragment the common pattern of (re-)regulation to the limited circumstances foreseen by Article 114(4)–(10) TFEU. The model of minimum harmonisation would seem more likely to preserve local autonomy and expression of divergent regulatory preferences while also leaving room for 'bottom-up' regulatory experimentation, learning and emulation. There is a stark choice: it is one that is pervasive in the discussion of the proper intensity of EU regulation which was conducted in Chapter 5, and the thematic question about the tension between centralisation and diversity in the EU resurfaces in this chapter.

There are accordingly fiery debates about these competing models for the structure of the internal market, and there are varying legislative preferences too. At the heart of the debate, however, is a profound choice associated with the distribution of regulatory authority in the European Union.

6.3. LEGISLATIVE PRACTICE

Legislative practice is both rich and instructively varied.

It is common to find measures of legislative harmonisation which establish rules and procedures designed to ensure common standards of protection of

1 For the Court's control see e.g. Joined Cases C-439/05P and C-454/05P, *Land Oberösterreich and Austria v Commission* [2007] ECR I-7141.

animal and human health which are treated as a complete system, in the sense that they exclude any possibility for divergent national measures. On this model Member States are required to permit products that comply with the harmonised standards to be marketed on their territory without any restriction and, as the other side of the coin, they are also required to prohibit the marketing of products that do not so comply. Periodic decisions of the Court of Justice have emphasised the vitality of this structure. The dispute prompting litigation has typically arisen in circumstances where the question is whether a Member State may have recourse to Article 36 TFEU to justify measures that are stricter than those foreseen under the EU measure, usually a Directive. The Court, concerned to promote the integration of product markets, commonly finds that relevant measures exclude scope for Member States to have recourse to Article 36 TFEU in this way.[2] Conventional jargon holds that the EU measure of secondary legislation has 'occupied the field': it 'pre-empts' Member State action. This is, in short, maximum harmonisation and there is no room for the Member States to prefer a stricter standard. The regime can be altered only from within the EU legislative process. In fact, at a constitutional level, what has happened is that a matter, the regulation of the internal market, which is in principle a competence shared between the EU and its Member State,[3] has in the particular area covered by the relevant piece of secondary legislation been converted by legislative act into an area of exclusive EU competence.

However, practice reveals that much of the harmonised legislative *acquis* which addresses the protection of the economic interests of consumers is built on an assumption that minimum harmonisation is the norm. Several of the measures considered in Chapter 4 illustrate this trend.

Directive 93/13 on unfair terms in consumer contracts is explicitly minimum in character.[4] Its Article 8 provides that 'Member States may adopt or retain the most stringent provisions compatible with the Treaty in the area covered by this Directive, to ensure a maximum degree of protection for the consumer'. This therefore does not preclude the application of stricter control of unfair terms under national law. So, for example, a State could choose to prohibit all the clauses which are included in the Directive's Annex merely as 'terms which *may* be regarded as unfair'.[5] Article 8 of the Directive leaves room for the conversion of the 'grey list' into a 'black list', should a State so choose. Directive 99/44 on certain aspects of the sale of consumer goods and associated guarantees is of the same type.[6] This is minimum protection granted by the EU: its Article 8(2)

2 e.g. Case 35/76, *Simmenthal* [1976] ECR 1871; Case 190/87, *Oberkreisdirektor v Moormann* [1988] ECR 4689; Case 60/86, *Commission v United Kingdom* [1988] ECR 3921; Case 148/78, *Ratti* [1979] ECR 1629; Case C-374/05, *Gintec International* [2007] ECR I-9517.

3 Art. 4(2)(a) TFEU.

4 [1993] OJ L95/29. See Chapter 4.4.

5 Art. 3(3), emphasis added.

6 [1999] OJ L171/12. See Chapter 4.4.

provides that 'Member States may adopt or maintain in force more stringent provisions, compatible with the Treaty in the field covered by this Directive, to ensure a higher level of consumer protection'.

These measures set a floor but not a ceiling. The Member States must ensure the level of protection mandated by the Directives, but they may add further protection on top. Minimum harmonisation is therefore a model which promotes the integration of markets (by establishing a common rule) while also preserving regulatory diversity (by granting space for stricter national rules that supplement the common EU rule). It secures space for expression of cultural particularity.[7] In fact minimum harmonisation forms part of the political bargain that has characterised the growth of the harmonised legislative *acquis* affecting protection of the economic interests of consumers. On occasion Directives of this type have strained the outer limits of the principle of conferral, but political support for the development of a consumer policy for the EU muted constitutional disquiet. This story was told in Chapters 3.10 and 4.3.1: the 'Paris summit' of 1972 was crucial in promoting a vision of the EU as more than simply a liberalised market, but this was not accompanied at the time by any alteration of the Treaty superstructure. Part of the context within which the Member States acquiesced in this politically sanctioned 'competence creep' was the inclusion of the safety valve offered by the minimum formula: EU intervention did not foreclose national-level innovation.[8]

The model of minimum harmonisation shares with Article 114(4)–(10) an acceptance that harmonisation does not involve the unconditional subordination of national choices about the regulation of the market to the demands of the internal market. Minimum harmonisation is, however, noticeably broader and more flexible in the room for regulatory manoeuvre which it grants to States. In contrast to Article 114(4)–(10) it does not circumscribe the types of interests that may be invoked as a reason to prefer stricter rules. Nor is it subject to inspection and the requirement of approval by the Commission. In fact using the model of minimum harmonisation brings Article 114, as a basis for the harmonised protection of consumers' economic interests, into alignment with Article 169(4) TFEU, which makes explicit that minimum rule-making is the norm where supportive rules are adopted by the EU as measures of consumer protection pursuant to Article 169(2)(b). In this way, both the EU and the Member States retain competence to protect consumers even after the EU has intervened by way of secondary legislation. As Chapter 3.7 explains, in fact a great deal more such activity has been released by legislative reliance on Article 114 than on Article 169.

---

7 Cf. J. Stuyck, 'Patterns of Justice in the European Constitutional Charter: Minimum Harmonisation in the Field of Consumer Law' in L. Krämer, H. Micklitz and K. Tonner (eds.), *Law and Diffuse Interests in the European Legal Order*, Nomos, Baden-Baden 1997.

8 See S. Weatherill, *EU Consumer Law and Policy*, 2nd ed., Edward Elgar, Cheltenham 2012, Ch. 3.

6.4. THE SOURCES OF PRESSURE ON THE MODEL OF MINIMUM HARMONISATION: THE COURT OF JUSTICE

The model of minimum harmonisation leaves open space for national standards which extend above the harmonised EU rule. This treats the internal market as a site of regulatory diversity, the precise shape of which is determined by the extent to which Member States choose to add an extra layer of regulation. This will doubtless vary sector by sector, as States respond to competing pressures in favour of stronger protection and in favour of light regulation. However, there are two distinct sources of pressure on the preference for the model of minimum rule-making. The first is the Court; the second, considered in the next section, the Commission.

Some rulings of the Court are capable of being interpreted as forbidding minimum harmonisation pursuant to Article 114 TFEU. Others seem perfectly receptive to it. *Probably* the Court does not intend to adopt any general rule and *probably* the case law is best understood as expressing hostility to minimum harmonisation only in particular circumstances. But the supporter of minimum harmonisation must be at least aware that there is constitutional objection, albeit of an ambiguous nature, to its vitality.

The starting point is the first *Tobacco Advertising* case.[9] This, as explained carefully in Chapter 3.9, found that Directive 98/43 on the advertising of tobacco products was invalid because the harmonised rules it introduced made no adequate contribution to the functioning of the internal market. As part of its reasoning the Court criticised the Directive because it 'contains no provision ensuring the free movement of products which conform to its provisions, in contrast to other Directives allowing Member States to adopt stricter measures for the protection of a general interest'.[10] The challenged Directive permitted Member States to lay down such stricter requirements concerning the advertising or sponsorship of tobacco products as they deemed necessary to guarantee health protection. This, the Court observed, meant that 'the Directive does not ensure free movement of products which are in conformity with its provisions'.[11] This was not the ruling's only unfavourable finding about the validity of Directive 98/43, but it was one element in the conclusion that the Directive lacked a valid basis as a measure of harmonisation in the service of the internal market.

A short time afterwards the Court decided in *ex parte BAT* that Directive 2001/37, a different measure of harmonisation addressing the manufacture and

9 Case C-376/98, *Germany v Parliament and Council* [2000] ECR I-8419.
10 Para. 104 of the judgment.
11 Para. 101.

sale of tobacco products, was valid.[12] The Court decided that it, unlike Directive 98/43 on advertising, made an adequate contribution to the functioning of the internal market by eliminating divergence among national laws governing tobacco products. One element in the Court's reasoning which approved the validity of the Directive was the *presence* in it of a 'market access clause' or 'free movement clause' of the type that it had noted was missing from the Directive attacked in the first *Tobacco Advertising* case. It noted of Directive 2001/37 that:

> 'It must be added that, unlike the directive at issue in the case giving rise to the tobacco advertising judgment, the Directive contains a provision, Article 13(1), which guarantees the free movement of products which comply with its requirements. By forbidding the Member States to prevent, on grounds relating to the matters harmonised by the Directive, the import, sale or consumption of tobacco products which do comply, that provision gives the Directive its full effect in relation to its object of improving the conditions for the functioning of the internal market'.[13]

Furthermore, the measure annulled in the first *Tobacco Advertising* case was subsequently replaced by a more tightly drawn Directive, 2003/33. This included an explicit provision which required that that products and services complying with its provisions shall be entitled free movement throughout the EU. The validity of that Directive was confirmed in the second *Tobacco Advertising* case: as noted in Chapter 3.11 the Court concluded that it, in its revised and more carefully targeted form, it made an adequate contribution to the functioning of the internal market.[14] In this ruling the Court repeated the point it had made in *ex parte BAT* by inserting into the ruling express approval of the presence of a free movement clause.[15] The Directive provided that the Member States shall not prohibit or restrict the free movement of products which comply with the Directive. This is emphatically *not* minimum harmonisation.

A handful of other rulings, such as *Cindu Chemicals*[16] and *Gintec International*,[17] appear to be written in a way that expresses a similar hostility to the possibility of permitting the application of stricter national rules to imports once a measure of harmonisation has been adopted under what is today Article 114 TFEU. It seems that in these rulings the Court assumes that it is a condition of the validity of a measure of harmonisation that it excludes the possibility of States applying any stricter rules to the importation of goods and services than are envisaged by the Directive itself. 'Minimum harmonisation' is just not allowed, or at least it needs to be confined to circumstances where a State

12 Case C-491/01, *British American Tobacco (Investments) and Imperial Tobacco* [2002] ECR I-11453.
13 Para. 74.
14 Case C-380/03, *Germany v Parliament and Council* [2006] ECR I-11573.
15 Case C-380/03, *Germany v Parliament and Council* [2006] ECR I-11573, paras. 73–74.
16 Joined Cases C-281/03 and C-282/03, *Cindu Chemicals BV and Others* [2005] ECR I-8069.
17 Case C-374/05, *Gintec International Import-Export GmbH* [2007] ECR I-9517.

chooses to insist on compliance with stricter rules only in application to that State's own suppliers operating within the domestic market. It would mean too that a State's competence to make stricter demands of imports would be confined to the relatively narrow procedure envisaged by Article 114(4)–(10), over which the Commission stands watchful guard.

So far, so bad for the model of minimum harmonisation in the internal market. But the Court's case law in fact runs on two quite separate tracks. In other cases, especially those concerning the harmonisation of measures that protect the economic interests of consumers, the Court has not even hinted at the slightest objection to the model of 'minimum harmonisation'. *Buet* is the pioneering case in this vein.[18] The Court in that case ruled that although Directive 85/577 on 'doorstep selling', encountered in Chapter 4.3, required only that a consumer be allowed a right to cancel the contract concluded on the doorstep within a defined period of time, a complete ban imposed by France on doorstep selling was not excluded by the Directive. It, a minimum measure, provided explicitly in Article 8 that the Directive 'shall not prevent Member States from adopting or maintaining more favourable provisions to protect consumers'. An intolerance of minimum harmonisation analogous to that adopted by the Court in the first *Tobacco Advertising* case and those that followed it would have cast serious constitutional doubt on the validity of this proviso in so far as a State sought to rely on it as a basis for the application of stricter rules to imports. But in *Buet* the Court expressed no hint of objection in principle to the possibility that States may be able to justify rules above the harmonised norm, provided the Directive expressly authorises this possibility. And it decided that in the circumstances the stricter French rules were justified as measures designed to protect vulnerable consumers and so, even though they regulated the French market more strictly than the Directive mandated, they were lawful notwithstanding any damage they may do to the internal market.[19]

Moreover, in a clutch of rulings since the first *Tobacco Advertising* case, the Court has addressed measures of 'minimum harmonisation', commonly concerning the protection of the economic interests of consumers, and it has shown no suspicion of constitutional distaste for the chosen model.[20] The Court follows the logic of *Buet*: if the Directive permits stricter rules, then the only control which is exercised over the national choice is that of primary law, most prominently free movement law and non-discrimination. In *Rina Services*, for example, the Court, asked to provide an interpretation of Directive 2006/123,

---

[18] Case 382/87 [1989] ECR 1235.

[19] See Chapter 2.5 on the space left in EU law to justify national measures that restrict inter-State trade.

[20] e.g. Case C-322/01, *DocMorris* [2003] ECR I-14887; Case C-71/02, *Herbert Karner* [2004] ECR I-3025; Case C-441/04, *A-Punkt Schmuckhandels* [2006] ECR I-2093; Case C-212/11, *Jyske Bank* judgment of 25 April 2013; Case C-235/14 *Safe Interenvios* judgment of 10 March 2016.

the Services Directive,[21] explicitly contrasted the provisions of the Directive which do not permit Member States to justify stricter rules from those that do so permit, without even hinting that any constitutional objection may be raised to the validity of this particular instance of minimum harmonisation.[22] Indeed the enormity of the claim that minimum harmonisation is constitutionally impermissible can here be gauged. The Services Directive was adopted only after tortuous negotiation and part of the compromise involved agreement that in some defined circumstances a State could make sterner demands of a service provider operating on its territory than those laid down by the Directive's rules.[23] To rely on the first *Tobacco Advertising* case to insist that such a model is not permitted would be politically incendiary. It is scarcely conceivable that such an approach could be correct in the absence of clear direction provided by the Treaty – which is certainly lacking.

The case law lacks shape. In none of the group of cases beginning with the first *Tobacco Advertising* case did the Court attempt to explain how and why its ruling could fit with the long-established acceptance in *Buet* of stricter rules above the harmonised norm. And in the cases of the other type, which are wholly receptive to the validity of the model of minimum harmonisation, the Court does not mention the first *Tobacco Advertising* case at all, nor does it seem the issue was even addressed. Perhaps the most illuminating ruling is *María Victoria González Sánchez v Medicina Asturiana*.[24] This judgment deals with the pre-emptive effect of the Product Liability Directive, 85/374, which is a measure of harmonisation adopted pursuant to what is now Article 115 TFEU (section 3.5). The Court took the opportunity to include in its reasoning the observation that:

> '[U]nlike, for example, Council Directive 93/13 ... on unfair terms in consumer contracts ... the Product Liability Directive contains no provision expressly authorising the Member States to adopt or to maintain more stringent provisions in matters in respect of which it makes provision, in order to secure a higher level of consumer protection.'[25]

This seems to authorise the validity of Directive 93/13's minimum clause, and by analogy similar clauses found elsewhere in the *acquis*, while interpreting the Product Liability Directive itself as apt to exclude the possibility for the maintenance of stricter national rules within its scope. And this is probably the key to unlocking the case law: what matters is inspection of each individual EU measure. There is no general rule opposing (or requiring) either model,

21 [2006] OJ L376/36.
22 Case C-593/13 judgment of 16 June 2015.
23 See in particular Arts. 15(2) and 16(3).
24 Case C-183/00 [2002] ECR I-3901.
25 Para. 27.

maximum or minimum. It depends on the object and purpose pursued by the particular measure under review. So the first *Tobacco Advertising* judgment is best understood as a case in which the Court took the view that a market access clause was required to make constitutional sense of that particular Directive. It is an exaggeration – albeit one admittedly encouraged by the drafting of the ruling[26] – to regard it as a ruling which rejects in principle the model of 'minimum harmonisation'.

Similarly, *Cindu Chemicals* and *Gintec International* would be best understood as decisions inspired by the particular nature and purpose of the measures in question and not as a signal that the phenomenon of 'minimum harmonisation' is in general constitutionally suspect. In fact, in neither case did the Directive concerned contain a minimum harmonisation clause.[27] This then allows cases such as *Buet* and *Rina Services* to be read as rooted in the nature and purpose of the particular EU measures that formed the dispute's subject matter. As measures of minimum harmonisation they improved the regulatory environment of the internal market by setting a floor which replaced the previous completely unharmonised pattern, while also promoting regulatory objectives including consumer protection which are recognised by EU law both at EU level (in the form of the minimum harmonised standards) and at national level (in the form of scope for selected stricter rules). The dual function of harmonisation was emphasised in Chapters 3 and 4: this is the dual function of minimum harmonisation!

On this approach 'minimum harmonisation' is capable of being treated as valid even if the scope for stricter national rules which it assumes prevents it serving as a means to establish a perfectly even layer of regulation for the entire internal market. It is floor, but not ceiling – unlike maximum harmonisation, which is both. But both are harmonisation. It is for the legislature to choose which model is more suitable in particular circumstances.

A supplementary final point concerning the Charter must be added. The freedom to conduct a business is protected by Article 16 of the Charter. Might it be argued that this is violated where EU legislation permits stricter national provisions that will, on the territory of a State that adopts stricter rules, deprive a trader of the right to operate solely on the basis of the standards set by the EU measure? This is absurd: Article 16 cannot plausibly be read in such a concrete manner as a curtailment of legislative discretion to set a regulatory floor but no regulatory ceiling. But this feat of absurdity is what the Court pulled off in *Alemo-*

---

26 Case C-376/98, *Germany v Parliament and Council* [2000] ECR I-8419, especially paras. 101–105.

27 As AG Jacobs makes explicit in his Opinion in Joined Cases C-281/03 and C-282/03, *Cindu Chemicals BV and Others* [2005] ECR I-8069, para. 48. Admittedly in Case C-374/05, *Gintec International Import-Export GmbH* [2007] ECR I-9517, AG Ruiz-Jarabo Colomer's Opinion suggests more general hostility to minimum rule-making pursuant to Article 95 EC, now Article 114 TFEU.

Herron.[28] The case was encountered in Chapter 4.10.3, where it was criticised for reasoning that is far out of line with the Court's thematic interpretative concern to protect the employee as the weaker party to the contract. That same imbalanced interpretative stance arises in connection with the subject matter of this chapter too. Article 8 of Directive 2001/23, the harmonisation measure concerning transfer of undertakings,[29] provides that the Directive 'shall not affect the right of Member States to apply or introduce laws, regulations or administrative provisions which are more favourable to employees or to promote or permit collective agreements or agreements between social partners more favourable to employees'. So the requirements of the Directive serve as a floor and not as a ceiling of regulatory protection. Member States may prefer a more generous system of employee protection. But in *Alemo-Herron* the Court took the view that this proviso could not be interpreted 'as entitling the Member States to take measures which, while being more favourable to employees, are liable to adversely affect the very essence of the transferee's freedom to conduct a business'.[30] In principle this is correct: the Charter is constitutionally superior to secondary legislation. But it is truly extreme to find a violation of Article 16 where all that is at stake is room to offer protection of workers which reaches beyond the agreed EU minimum standard. The Court's only explanation for its extraordinary finding reveals how fragile is its reasoning. It claimed that it was deciding the matter by analogy with 'Case C-544/10 *Deutsches Weintor* [2012] ECR I-0000, paragraphs 54 and 58'.[31] But those paragraphs and indeed the judgment in *Deutsches Weintor* generally, which was met in Chapter 3.15, do not concern a 'minimum' provision of the type condemned by the Court in *Alemo-Herron*. The Court in *Alemo-Herron* was in truth doing something quite new. Use of Article 16 of the Charter to set aside a minimum rule contained in a Directive has the effect of promoting commercial freedom over regulatory protection. That, in fact, is the precise *opposite* of the conclusion which the Court reached in *Deutsches Weintor*! The aberrant and unreliable ruling in *Alemo-Herron* should not be relied on in future. It improperly re-distributes competences to intervene in the market in order to protect weaker parties away from the Member States.[32] Minimum rule-making by the EU should not be regarded as imperilled by Article 16 of the Charter.

In conclusion, it is for the EU legislative process to select between the models of maximum and minimum harmonisation. The choice should depend on the prevailing political and economic reasons. The Court's case law should not be read as expressing a clear *constitutional* antipathy to minimum harmonisation.

---

28 Case C-426/11 judgment of 18 July 2013.

29 [2001] OJ L82/16.

30 Para. 36.

31 Para. 36.

32 M. Bartl and C. Leone, 'Minimum Harmonisation after Alemo-Herron: The Janus Face of EU Fundamental Rights Review' (2015) 11 *European Constitutional Law Review* 140.

6.5. THE SOURCES OF PRESSURE ON THE MODEL OF MINIMUM HARMONISATION: THE COMMISSION

It was explained in Chapter 3.10 that in a communication released in July 2001 the Commission launched a programme of inquiry into the proper role of the EU in the field of contract law.[33] The impulse was largely *consumer* contract law, which Chapter 4 demonstrates has been the area of contract law in which the EU's harmonisation activity has been most prolific, and, as set out above (section 6.3), it is also an area where minimum harmonisation is evident as the long-standing preferred regulatory technique. The Commission's inquiry quickly turned towards a tone expressing a most sceptical assessment of the model of minimum harmonisation.

The theme of the inquiry was infused by a quest for 'a significantly higher degree of coherence in European contract law', to draw on the explanation of one of the principal architects of the review within the Commission.[34] As explained in Chapter 3.10 of this book, coherence was to be improved in part by ironing out detailed internal inconsistencies within the sector-specific measures as a means to improve the quality of the *acquis*. However, it quickly became apparent that 'coherence' as a leitmotif was also to be promoted by abandoning the minimum model of harmonisation in favour of maximum harmonisation. The maximum model would, by locating both the floor and the ceiling of regulatory protection within the uniform standard mandated by the EU measure, sharpen 'coherence' by excluding room for the fragmenting and uneven impact of stricter national measures.

The Commission's Consumer Policy Programme for 2002–2006 was emblematic. It advocated a 'move away from the present situation of different sets of rules in each Member State towards a more consistent environment for consumer protection across the EU'.[35] This, it was plain, entailed a policy preference for maximum rather than minimum harmonisation. The Commission's October 2004 document on contract law, the third in the series (section 3.10), referred critically to perceived failings of a minimum model of rule-making.[36] It portrayed the well-established pattern of minimum harmonisation of rules concerning protection of the economic interests of

---

33 COM (2001) 398.

34 D. Staudenmayer, 'The Place of Consumer Contract Law within the Process on European Contract Law' (2004) 27 *Journal of Consumer Policy* 269, 277. See also D. Staudenmayer, 'European Contract Law – What Does it Mean and What Does it not Mean?' in S. Vogenauer and S. Weatherill (eds.), *The Harmonisation of European Contract Law: Implications for European Private Law, Business and Legal Practice*, Hart/IECL, Oxford 2006, Ch. 13, pp. 235–244.

35 COM (2002) 208.

36 COM (2004) 651.

consumers in a relentlessly negative light. Minimum rules create unevenness in the overall pattern of legal regulation of the internal market in so far as Member States choose to apply stricter rules. The Commission bolstered its case with compelling evidence that Member States frequently take advantage of the competence to apply stricter rules which is the very essence of minimum harmonisation.[37] This is perfectly plausible and in fact academic investigation has confirmed this.[38]

Ruling out space for stricter national rules therefore became the Commission's driving policy concern as its review proceeded. Its Green Paper on the Review of the Consumer Acquis released in February 2007 concluded what the Commission described as the 'diagnostic phase' of the review of contract law, and, in forward-looking mode, it set out the main options for reform.[39] It was striking, though left largely unemphasised, that the orthodox pre-existing model of minimum harmonisation was not even listed as a possible option for the future.

Maximum, rather than minimum, harmonisation was on the march. The Commission's principal explanations for its policy preference were all devoted to the quest to improve the functioning of the internal market. A more 'coherent' regulatory landscape was the aim: a levelled regulatory playing field for the EU within which the eruption of stricter national rules would be constitutionally suppressed. Uniformity rather than diversity is the guiding vision of maximum harmonisation in the internal market.

The Commission has enjoyed successes in piloting its preferred design through the EU's legislative process. Directive 2002/65 on distant selling of financial services was the first measure in the orthodox heartland of EU harmonisation activity affecting consumer contract law to reflect the Commission's re-focused policy preference.[40] The Directive renounces the minimum formula and applies a model of maximum harmonisation to the field covered by the Directive. However, Directive 2005/29 concerning unfair commercial practices is the most remarkable measure which reflects the preference for maximum harmonisation.[41] The Directive was met and discussed in Chapter 4.5. It requires the suppression of unfair business-to-consumer practices in the internal market. It prohibits practices which, contrary to 'professional diligence', 'materially distort the economic behaviour' of an average consumer. Its Annex contains a 'black list' of practices considered unfair in all

---

37 e.g. Commission Report on implementation of Directive 97/7 on distance contracts, COM (2006) 514; Commission Communication on the implementation of Directive 99/44, COM (2007) 210.

38 See e.g. L. Miller, 'After the Unfair Contract Terms Directive: Recent European Directives and English Law' (2007) 3 *European Review of Contract Law* 88.

39 COM (2006) 744.

40 [2002] OJ L271/16.

41 [2005] OJ L149/22.

circumstances. It is, however, crucial that Directive 2005/29 leaves no scope for Member States to choose to establish stricter standards within the field occupied by the Directive.[42] If a practice falling within the Directive's material scope is not 'unfair' within the meaning of the Directive, a Member State may not treat it as unfair and may not apply any stricter control over it. The Directive's Article 4, crisply entitled 'Internal Market', states that 'Member States shall neither restrict the freedom to provide services nor restrict the free movement of goods for reasons falling within the field approximated by this Directive'. This exclusion of stricter national intervention motivates the stern message to this effect sounded by the Court of Justice in preliminary references in which it has been asked to interpret the Directive. So, for example, in *VTB-VAB NV* the Court found that a presumption of unlawfulness attached by Belgian law to a particular marketing strategy which entailed a stricter restraint on the commercial practice than was demanded pursuant to Directive 2005/29 could no longer be applied.[43] In *Plus Warenhandelsgesellschaft* the same approach was used to require the disapplication of a German rule prohibiting the combination of participation in a prize competition with the purchase of goods which failed to take account of the specific circumstances of individual cases.[44] This went beyond the standard dictated by Directive 2005/29: it was therefore not allowed. In effect, the whole field of market regulation which falls within the scope of Directive 2005/29 has been completely transferred to EU competence. The Directive's rules decide whether a practice is allowed or not: this means *inter alia* that the justifications for trade restrictions previously available under primary law to a regulating State pursuant to Articles 36, 52 and 62 TFEU are closed off. The values that might previously have animated a claim to justify a national measure have been transplanted to the Directive alone and the survival of a practice which falls within the material scope of the Directive depends exclusively on measuring its conformity with the benchmark standard of fairness set by the Directive. This, of course, is radically different from the Court's ruling in *Buet*, considered above.[45] *Buet*, however, addressed minimum harmonisation. Directive 2005/29 is based on the maximum model.

Maximum harmonisation disables Member State competence to do anything other than apply the EU's harmonised rules. The *evenness* of the resultant regulatory landscape is the point: this is a model driven hard by the desire to

42 Its Article 3(9) makes small exceptions: in relation to financial services and immovable property, Member States may impose requirements which are more restrictive or prescriptive than the Directive.

43 Case C-261/07, *VTB-VAB NV* [2009] ECR I-2949.

44 Case C-304/08, *Plus Warenhandelsgesellschaft* judgment of 14 January 2010. See also e.g. Case C-122/10, *Ving Sverige AB* [2011] ECR I-3903; Case C-421/12, *Commission v Belgium* judgment of 10 July 2014; and for discussion V. Colaert and M. Peeters, 'Combined Offers' in E. Terryn, G. Straetmnans and V. Colaert (eds.), *Landmark Cases of EU Consumer Law: In Honour of Jules Stuyck*, Intersentia, Cambridge 2013, Ch. 4.VI, pp. 427–446.

45 Case 382/87 [1989] ECR 1235.

release the economic benefits of the internal market. But there are costs. The principal anxiety is that the maximum model, in contrast to the more flexible consequences that apply in a case of minimum harmonisation, dictates that the nature and level of (re-)regulatory protection within the internal market is determined exclusively *by the EU*. Dissatisfaction with the EU standard – whether on paper or as interpreted from time to time by the Court of Justice, or both – must be addressed by seeking to provoke legislative reform *at EU level*. This is a model of the internal market which is not receptive to local regulatory variation at all.

The question was how far the Commission could push its policy preference in favour of maximum harmonisation.

6.6. REVIEW AND REFORM

Directive 2011/83 on consumer rights has already been met on several occasions in this book.[46] It is a measure of legislative harmonisation designed to improve the functioning of the internal market and its legal base is Article 114 TFEU. It is also, as already mentioned earlier with a promise of subsequent elaboration, a profoundly less ambitious measure than the Commission had initially hoped. This is now that promised elaboration. The Directive's mutation and its reduced scope are explicable largely with reference to the political turmoil which the Commission's uncompromising but ultimately unsuccessful adherence to the model of maximum harmonisation unleashed. In this sense the story of Directive 2011/83 shines a beam on the *politically* contested nature of the debate about which model of harmonisation to prefer.[47]

Directive 2011/83's Preamble asserts that it has been adopted in consequence on review 'in the light of experience with a view to simplifying and updating the applicable rules, removing inconsistencies and closing unwanted gaps in the rules'; moreover that it is 'moving away from the minimum harmonisation approach in the former Directives …'.[48] The cited 'former Directives' in question are Directive 85/577 on doorstep selling and Directive 97/7 on distance contracts, both of which are repealed and replaced by the updated and amplified harmonised rules contained in Directive 2011/83. Article 4 of Directive 2011/83 concerns 'Level of harmonisation'. It provides that 'Member States shall not maintain or introduce, in their national law, provisions diverging from those laid down in this Directive, including more or less stringent provisions to ensure

46 [2011] OJ L 304/64. See Chapters 3.10, 4.3, 5.9.

47 What follows is a compressed version of S. Weatherill, 'The Consumer Rights Directive: how and why a quest for "coherence" has (largely) failed' (2012) 49 *Common Market Law Review* 1279.

48 Recital 2.

a different level of consumer protection, unless otherwise provided for in this Directive'. This, then, is a measure of maximum harmonisation.

But this finally adopted text is the concluding chapter in a tale of diminished ambition. From the perspective of the Commission, Directive 2011/83 is no happy ending to the process of review which it initiated in 2001 and on which was constructed its quest to improve 'coherence' in EU contract law.

The story had begun with the Commission's review of the 'consumer *acquis*' which was focused on improving the coherence of eight Directives that had been adopted over time in the incremental evolution of EU consumer law: Directive 85/577 on doorstep selling, Directive 90/314 on package travel, Directive 93/13 on unfair terms in consumer contracts, Directive 94/47 on timeshare, Directive 97/7 on distance contracts, Directive 98/6 on price indications, Directive 98/27 on injunctions and Directive 99/44 on the sale of consumer goods and associated guarantees.[49] These, as noted above (section 6.3), had been adopted as measures of minimum harmonisation as part of the political bargain that governed this area of EU consumer policy and, in particular, consumer contract law. However, eight became four. In October 2008, as a result of its review of the consumer *acquis*, the Commission adopted a proposal for a Directive on Consumer Rights which, if adopted, would have replaced Directives 85/577, 97/7, 93/13 and 99/44 (only) with what it described as 'horizontal instrument'.[50] This would entail, according to the Commission, *full targeted harmonisation*.[51] This meant 'targeting' the most serious blockages to the functioning of the internal market and, in particular, the Commission's emphasis was on the virtue of the maximum model of harmonisation in delivering an improved legal infrastructure for the internal market. A basic shift in law and policy was therefore intended: from minimum to maximum. This would, in the Commission's painstakingly expressed view, create a more coherent regulatory environment within which to realise the full extent of the benefits on offer from the internal market. This would also eliminate scope for divergent choices expressed at national level, and in the particular matter of doorstep selling, distance selling, unfair terms and consumer sales, it would lock in the Member States to regulate in the way and at the level demanded by the EU's 'horizontal instrument', with no scope for locally determined divergence. The competence to apply stricter State rules within the material scope of the EU measure, the primary feature of the model of minimum harmonisation, would be switched off. This radically transformative dimension of the intended policy shift finds scant mention in the Commission's documentation.

---

49 See Chapter 4.3. 4.4.

50 COM (2008) 614.

51 COM (2008) 614, pp. 3–4. The phrase, with *targeted* and *full* inverted, also appears at p. 7 of *EU Consumer Policy Strategy 2007–2013: Empowering consumers, enhancing their welfare, effectively protecting them*, COM (2007) 99.

The Commission's 2008 proposal encountered a chilly reception in the academic literature. The pursuit of the maximum model of harmonisation was high on the list of perceived disadvantages. It was criticised both *per se*, as an undue suppression of national diversity, and also for the reluctance of the Commission to confess with candour to the costs as well as the benefits of its proposed model.[52] The Commission 'is not telling us the full story'.[53] It was in truth not easy to find any commentators willing to side *with* the Commission.[54] But the political climate was unwelcoming too, and this is why the 2008 proposal was ultimately cut off at the knees. The Report of the Parliament's Committee on the Internal Market and Consumer Protection, which was published in February 2011, is especially helpful in broadcasting the persisting political sensitivity which attaches to the choice of model of harmonisation.[55] Socialist and Green MEPs were largely hostile to maximum harmonisation on the basis that it risked upsetting established standards of protection at national level. It is, of course, not inevitable that maximum harmonisation will have this effect: it depends on the level at which the EU's maximum rules are pitched. But the *risk* of a lowering of standards – as a result of political negotiation in the EU and/or as a result of the Court's subsequent interpretation of the rules – is the point of friction. Representatives of the European People's Party and of the Alliance of Liberals and Democrats for Europe were more positive about the value of enhancing the applicability of the model of maximum harmonisation. They tended to embrace it as a means to simplify the regulatory environment within which commercial operators are situated, which, from this perspective, tends to enhance choice and competition in the internal market to the advantage of consumers. The sharply political context of choosing among models of harmonisation and divergent views about the nature of the internal market more generally is plainly visible in this disagreement.

In 2011 a political compromise was struck. Pursuant to the complex operation of the EU's ordinary legislative procedure, the Parliament adopted a set of amendments to the Commission's original 2008 draft. The Council

---

52 See e.g. H. Micklitz and N. Reich, 'Crónica de una Muerte Anunciada: the Commission Proposal for a Directive on Consumer Rights' (2009) 46 *Common Market Law Review* 471; M. Faure, 'Towards a Maximum Harmonization of Consumer Contract Law?!?' (2008) 15 *Maastricht Journal* 433; V. Mak, 'Review of the Consumer Acquis: Towards Maximum Harmonization?' (2009) 17 *European Review of Private Law* 55; M. Tamm, 'Das Grünbuch der Kommission zum Verbraucheracquis und das Modell der Vollharmonisierung – eine kritische Analyse' [2007] *EuZW* 756; G. Howells and R Schulze (eds.), *Modernising and Harmonising Consumer Contract Law*, Sellier, Munich 2009.

53 J. Rutgers and R. Sefton-Green, 'Revising the Consumer *Acquis*: (Half) Opening the Doors of the Trojan Horse' (2008) 16 *European Review of Private Law* 427.

54 But for one respected voice that was more positive, see E. Hondius, 'The Proposal for a European Directive on Consumer Rights: a Step Forward' (2010) 18 *European Review of Private Law* 103.

55 A7-0038/2011, www.europarl.europa.eu/sides/getDoc.do?type=REPORT&mode=XML&reference=A7-2011-0038&language=EN.

was satisfied, the formalities were duly completed in late 2011 and Directive 2011/83 on consumer rights was agreed.[56] It is, however, shorn of much of its original ambition. Eight had become four in 2008 – in 2011, four became two. Directive 2011/83 is a measure of maximum harmonisation which excludes stricter national initiatives in the area which it covers, but the area it covers is only slightly larger than that which was previously covered by Directive 85/577 on doorstep selling and Directive 97/7 on distance contracts, the two Directives which are overhauled and repealed by Directive 2011/83. This pair obviously has a much lower profile than the pair of Directives (93/13 on unfair terms, 99/44 on consumer sales) that were excluded from the Commission's planned regime of maximum harmonisation as a result of the political disquiet expressed in the EU's legislative institutions. The solitary adaptation of Directives 93/13 and 99/44 which the Commission was able to extract from the legislative process was a small amendment which imposes obligations on Member States to advise the Commission of rules they choose to introduce that are stricter than those mandated by the two EU Directives.[57] This doubtless improves transparency. But it leaves intact the core regime of both Directives 93/13 and 99/44: they have withstood the Commission's campaign to convert them from the model of minimum harmonisation to that of maximum harmonisation. They remain measures of minimum harmonisation.

In short, 'coherence' and the appeal to a better functioning internal market was not enough to win the day. Maximum harmonisation represents a vertical transfer of authority from Member States to the EU: it may well sustain a more competitive internal market but it does so at the expense of local autonomy, and the more politically sensitive and socially cherished the subject matter which is being fed into the mincer of harmonisation, the less likely is it that appeal to the economic benefits of the internal market will persuade Member States and the Parliament that the constitutional and regulatory adjustment demanded by the maximum model is worth it.

The Services Directive, 2006/123,[58] was mentioned briefly above (section 6.4) as a measure which pursues a particular form of minimum harmonisation. The story of its route from proposal to adoption offers further illumination of the political sensitivity attached to selecting among available models of harmonisation. The so-called 'Bolkestein Draft', the first iteration of the measure named for the responsible Commissioner of the time, was published in 2004.[59] It relied on a model of maximum harmonisation. This was intended to locate the exclusive source of regulation of the services sector at EU level, entirely pre-empting national competence. The promised prize was a much invigorated and

56 Above n. 46.
57 Arts. 32 and 33 Directive 2011/83 [2011] OJ L 304/64.
58 [2006] OJ L376/36.
59 COM (2004) 2.

competitive internal market for services. The plan quickly ran into vigorous political resistance. This adopted as its evildoer-in-chief the caricature 'Polish plumber' who would head West and undercut service providers in the Member States where he or she chose to operate, and in circumstances where the host Member State would be barred from imposing any qualification or quality requirements beyond those stipulated by the Directive itself.[60] To which one might respond: well, yes, this is the very essence of the internal market and why should consumers not be permitted to choose a Pole to fix their plumbing if they so wish? A problem, one might think, would arise only if the level of regulation and quality set by the measure of maximum harmonisation was so low as to allow incompetent plumbers (or drivers, or barbers, or dancers) access to the services market. Politics intruded. Concessions were made. The finally agreed version of the Services Directive, 2006/123, contains a model that lays down harmonised quality standards applicable to services that fall within its scope but it also leaves room for stricter national rules in some fields. In particular, its Article 16, concerning the freedom to provide services, declares in its first paragraph that Member States 'shall respect the right of providers to provide services in a Member State other than that in which they are established', but its third paragraph adds the restraining proviso that the host Member State may impose requirements which are justified for reasons of public policy, public security, public health or the protection of the environment. The scars of political compromise are plain on the face of the final version of the Directive and its true intent is in places troublingly ambiguous.[61] A 'pure' model of maximum harmonisation would have been more clean-cut. But there is more to patterns of regulatory protection in the internal market than simply crafting clean-cut rules. The Services Directive, which operates according to a form of managed minimum harmonisation in the sense that its concessions to stricter rules exist but are not open-ended, shows the political value that attaches to shielding a degree of regulatory autonomy at State level from the oppressively centralising influence of the maximum model of harmonisation. The quest for 'coherence' has its limits.

6.7. NORMATIVE PERSPECTIVES ON THE CHOICE BETWEEN MODELS OF HARMONISATION

The question is which model of harmonisation *should* prevail? The answer is – it depends. It depends on the objectives being pursued, and that in turn cautions

---

60 See e.g. J. Loder, 'The Lisbon Strategy and the politicization of EU policy-making: the case of the Services Directive' (2011) 18 *Journal of European Public Policy* 566.

61 Cf. e.g. C. Barnard, 'Unravelling the Services Directive' (2008) 45 *Common Market Law Review* 323; V. Hatzopoulos, 'Le Principe de Reconnaissance Mutuelle dans la Libre Prestation de Services' (2010) 46 *Cahiers de Droit Européen* 47.

that the inquiry must be sensitive to the context in which it arises. Some matters may be thought appropriate for a single meaning across the EU – safety, perhaps. Other matters, particularly of a more culturally or socially sensitive nature, may more readily resist the pull of maximum harmonisation on the basis that Europe should cherish and promote its historically determined diversity.[62] Contract law has a good claim to be assessed from this more cautious perspective.

The Commission is correct to connect the technique of minimum harmonisation with a persistently fragmented regulatory landscape in the EU. The question is, however, whether the *benefits* of moving instead to a maximum model of harmonisation outweigh the *costs*. This is the calculation which the Commission seems reticent to pursue in its review of contract law. It stands accused of a one-sided approach. The shift to maximum harmonisation involves a significant centralising and homogenising choice in favour of a priority for market-making to the exclusion of local regulatory autonomy. It causes a 'paralysis of state action', as Advocate General Villalón observed in an Opinion which is remote from contract law – it concerned air transport and environmental law – but which contains astute observations about the stifling peril of maximum harmonisation as a regulatory model.[63] Transplanting this sceptical attitude to matters of consumer protection, the objection to the maximum models holds that it asserts a single vision of consumer protection, delivered *exclusively* by the EU, in the face of ample evidence that consumer preferences, tastes and capabilities differ in Europe.[64] A critical perspective, which has been brought to bear on the debate about contract law, treats harmonisation as culturally and economically insensitive to local autonomy and diversity and a route to the imposition of a high level of centralisation within the EU.[65] Minimum harmonisation, by contrast, not only reflects but also champions diversity and differentiation as in themselves valuable within an EU dedicated to more than economic growth. Minimum harmonisation has the capacity to reflect the reality of legal and cultural heterogeneity between the Member States.[66] In addition one could stretch this normative perspective beyond the legislative process to argue that there should be a supporting *judicial*

---

62 Cf. A. De Vries, 'The Aim for Complete Uniformity in EU Private Law: An Obstacle to Further Harmonization' (2012) 20 *European Review of Private Law* 913.

63 Case C-120/10, *European Air Transport SA* judgment of 8 September 2011. The Court's ruling is much narrower in scope and ambition.

64 See especially (and influentially) T. Wilhelmsson, 'The abuse of the confident consumer as a justification for EC consumer law' (2004) 27 *Journal of Consumer Policy* 317.

65 e.g. with reference to contract law F. Gomez and J. Ganuza, 'An Economic Analysis of Harmonization Régimes: Full Harmonization, Minimum Harmonization or Optional Instrument?' (2011) 7 *European Review of Contract Law* 275; A. Wulf, 'Institutional competition of optional codes in European contract law' (2014) 38 *European Journal of Law and Economics* 139.

66 See e.g. V. Mak, 'Review of the Consumer Acquis: Towards Maximum Harmonisation?' (2009) 17 *European Review of Private Law* 55; S. Weatherill, 'Maximum or Minimum Harmonisation – What kind of "Europe" do we want?' in K. Boele-Woelki and

presumption against a finding that an EU legislative act which is ambiguous is apt to pre-empt national competence in the field which it covers.[67]

The more 'coherent' the EU regime, the less coherent national systems tend to become. Maximum harmonisation grants the EU rules a much 'cleaner' look, because their inter-relation with national law is no longer at all relevant – it is, in fact, excluded. However, by contrast, at national level significant dismantling of established rules that are found to fall within the material scope of the EU measure may be required in order to fulfil the stern demands of the model of maximum harmonisation to serve as not only floor but also ceiling of regulatory intervention. This is to the detriment of accumulated local preference and it is harmful to the integrity of national legal orders in so far as it carves out blocs that are exclusively governed by the EU's rule, fragmenting them from the wider sweep of national law. By the same token, minimum harmonisation preserves the coherence of national systems, by permitting the maintenance of existing rules that are more stringent than the EU rules, but it leaves a fragmented – incoherent – pattern at EU level. Whose coherence shall prevail? This is the choice – and it *is* a choice. Pursuit of coherence at EU level cannot possibly be cost-free. Nor can pursuit of coherence at national level.

This is not a purely technical matter. Emphasis on the intensification of competition through the internal market may subvert adjustments in national law which have been achieved only after bitter and extended struggle. The protection of groups such as consumers, workers and tenants under an assumption that such economically disadvantaged parties are deprived of a genuine right of self-determination in an unregulated market is a key feature of the development of contract law over the last century. No such regulatory protections were granted by benign fiat of the rich and powerful. They were fought for. Contract law's shaping is not apolitical.[68] Where the EU rules are maximum in character, they foreclose space for national variation, and the break with national autonomy is decisive. A maximum model means one must trust the EU – both through its political process and through the interpretative contribution of its Court – to secure an adequate level of regulatory protection within the internal market. A theme of this book has been that the EU's political and judicial institutions are sympathetic to the pursuit of a high level of protection in the development of the regulatory framework that underpins the internal market and that,

W. Grosheide (eds.), *The Future of European Contract Law: Essays in Honour of Ewoud Hondius*, Kluwer Law International, Alphen aan der Rijn 2007, pp. 133–146.

67 Cf. R. Schütze, 'Subsidiarity after Lisbon: Reinforcing the Safeguards of Federalism' (2009) 68 *Cambridge Law Journal* 525.

68 A thousand sources could be provided: prominent in the EU context are Study Group on Social Justice in European Private Law, 'Social Justice in European Contract Law: a Manifesto' (2004) 10 *European Law Journal* 653; M. Hesselink, 'European Contract Law: a Matter of Consumer Protection, Citizenship, or Justice?' (2007) 15 *European Review of Private Law* 323; M. Hesselink, 'Democratic Contract Law' (2015) 11 *European Review of Contract Law* 81. See further Chapter 7.

moreover, there are constitutional commitments in that direction contained in EU primary law, most prominently in Articles 12, 114(3), 168(1) and 169(1) TFEU and Articles 35, 37 and 38 of the Charter.[69] However, although this confirms the EU as a proper source of regulatory protection, it does not and should not follow that it should be the *exclusive* source. A model built *not only* on EU rule-making *but also* on national-level contributions above an EU minimum offers a compelling alternative. The story told above of Directive 2011/83 on consumer rights and Directive 2006/123 on services demonstrates political attachment to the worth of national-level regulatory choices within the internal market. This is the gift of minimum harmonisation. The Commission has not been able to secure a comprehensive shift away from that model because it was not able to persuade the key actors that what was at stake was a purely market-making process focused on the deceptive appeal of improved 'coherence'.

6.8. CONCLUSION

The 'maximum or minimum' debate is important in the development of EU contract law, but that is but one manifestation of a much deeper political and cultural inquiry into the proper relationship between the EU and its Member States. How much should be done in common, how much diversity should be tolerated, even encouraged?[70]

The shift from minimum to maximum harmonisation goes to the very heart of deciding which institution(s) are responsible for delivering regulation of the European market A maximum model radically shifts the pattern of European lawmaking away from a cooperative model towards a more hierarchical pattern. Maximum harmonisation is a centralising, homogenising approach. Moreover, it cleaves open national systems along lines of demarcation that may make some sort of sense at EU level, but frequently will not at national level. From this perspective there is a respectable case to be made *against* coherence at EU level – at least, one must appreciate that pursuit of coherence at EU level cannot possibly be cost-free. This leads to the appeal of minimum harmonisation. There is a strong case to be made for regarding maximum harmonisation as applicable

---

69 See Chapter 3.8.

70 See e.g. N. Boeger, 'Minimum harmonisation, free movement and proportionality' in P. Syrpis (ed.), *The Judiciary, the Legislature and the EU Internal Market*, CUP, Cambridge 2012, Ch. 4, pp. 62–91; S. Weatherill, 'Maximum versus Minimum Harmonization: Choosing between Unity and Diversity in the Search for the Soul of the Internal Market' in N. NicShuibhne and L. Gormley (eds.), *From Single Market to Economic Union: Essays in Memory of John A Usher*, OUP, Oxford 2012, Ch. 10, pp. 175–200; J. Stuyck, 'Patterns of Justice in the European Constitutional Charter: Minimum Harmonisation in the Field of Consumer Law' in L. Krämer, H. Micklitz and K. Tonner (eds.), *Law and Diffuse Interests in the European Legal Order*, Nomos, Baden-Baden 1997, pp. 279–289.

only exceptionally, where its use has been carefully justified in prevailing sector-specific conditions, taking full account of the costs and the benefits.

Ultimately the internal market as a legal concept cannot resolve this debate. It depends on one's conception of the contested character of the internal market. Pursuit of 'coherence' in Europe must be weighed against the virtue of local autonomy and the value of regulatory experimentation. It does not exaggerate to invoke the protection of national identity promised by Article 4(2) TEU as a reason for proceeding with the harmonisation of contract law – especially under an aspiration to adopt a maximum model – with supreme caution.[71]

71 See e.g. H. Micklitz, 'The EU as a Federal Order of Competences and the Private Law' in L. Azoulai, *The Question of Competence in the European Union*, OUP, Oxford 2014, Ch. 6, pp. 125–152.

CHAPTER 7

MEASURING THE EFFECTS OF THE CONTRACT LAW OF THE INTERNAL MARKET

7.1. THE CONTRACT LAW OF THE INTERNAL MARKET: A BRIEF SUMMARY

The EU is committed by Article 3(3) TEU to the creation of an internal market which, according to the definition provided by Article 26(2) TFEU, 'shall comprise an area without internal frontiers in which the free movement of goods, persons, services and capital is ensured'. The Court of Justice has had its moments of constitutional hyperbole: in 1971 it declared the 'essential purpose of the Treaty' to be 'to unite national markets into a single market'[1] and in 2011 it stated that completion of the internal market is 'the fundamental aim of the Treaty'.[2] That goes beyond what is in fact and in form contained in the Treaties, but there is no doubt that the project of economic integration has enjoyed enduring prominence as the EU's most visible transformative feat. The internal market is demonstrably central to the EU's activities.

The EU reaches contracts and contract law almost exclusively through the internal market. Chapter 2 shows how free movement law and competition law are not targeted at contracts or contract law but how nevertheless the impact that contracts and contract law exert on the functioning of the internal market brings them within the scope of the review exercised by free movement and competition law. It is especially 'regulatory contract law' that is affected. Chapter 2 also explains that there is a small, but potentially expanding, impact on contracts and contract law as a result of EU anti-discrimination law and the wider, albeit ambiguously shaped, 'constitutionalisation' of contract law – this is a glimpse of EU contract law beyond the internal market. Chapter 3 returns to the heartland of the internal market and shows how legislative harmonisation engages with contract law, especially 'regulatory contract law', on the basis that diverse national choices obstruct trade in goods and services or cause an appreciable

1 Case 78/70, *Deutsche Grammophon v Metro* [1971] ECR 487, para. 12.

2 Joined Cases C-403/08 and C-429/08, *FA Premier League and Others v QC Leisure and Others, Karen Murphy v Media Protection Services Ltd* judgment of 4 October 2011, para. 115.

distortion of competition within the internal market. Harmonisation improves the functioning of the internal market, and it has a 'dual function': both to put in place *common* EU rules which are the platform for an integrated trading space, and to put in place common EU *rules* which determine the intensity of market (re-)regulation within that space. The internal market is in principle a concept that *limits* the EU's legislative process when it relies on the competence to adopt measures of legislative harmonisation conferred by Article 114 TFEU, but the threshold to its invocation is so low that in practice it acts as a profoundly *empowering* concept. This means both that the EU is not easily shown to be constitutionally deficient when it is backed by political consensus in favour of harmonisation and also that it enjoys a rather wide scope to choose among available (re-)regulatory techniques and forms. That the *quality* of the (re-) regulated environment within the internal market is part of the constitutional narrative is mandated by Articles 35, 37 and 38 of the Charter of Fundamental Rights combined with Articles 9, 12, 114(3), 168(1) and 169(1) TFEU. This, then, is an instrumental contract law – contract law is used by the EU as means to make a more competitive internal market – but the story, which is certainly not confined to the particular case of contracts and contract law, is of the breaking down of the division between the EU as the place to secure market integration and the State as the place to secure market regulation.

Chapter 4 provides a store of detail which demonstrates the extraordinary range of EU legislative activity affecting contract law and contractual autonomy. It shows how the generous competence afforded by (most of all) Article 114 TFEU has been exploited in practice and how the (re-)regulatory patterns disclose a rather unsystematic structure, but one which nevertheless is built around certain guiding themes, such as pursuit of transparency and protection of the weaker party. Chapter 4 also examines the major contributions of the Court of Justice in elaborating still further the scope and meaning of the several sector-specific regimes of 'regulatory contract law'. It also aims to extract themes, principles and policy from the accumulated material – the most prominent idea is that contractual autonomy is regulated within the internal market. EU law places boundaries on its exercise: otherwise put, it channels its exercise. Chapter 5 reflects more broadly on the political context within which the EU's activities have developed and in particular on the need for a more questioning culture. This covers in particular the principle of subsidiarity and the involvement of national parliaments in its supervision; and the rise of impact assessment as part of the quest for *Better Regulation* in the EU. Chapter 6 addresses the – lately highly contested – question of whether the EU, once it has adopted a harmonised standard, does or should become exclusively competent in the field in question. This, the debate about maximum or minimum harmonisation, determines the shape of the internal market and, in particular, whether innovative regulatory practice developed 'from beneath', at State level, is to be allowed to challenge the centralising impact of 'top- down' regulatory homogeneity. The chapter pleads for use of maximum harmonisation only where it is shown to be justified, and rejects its claims to serve as the paradigm of EU legislative practice. In particular, the more socially, politically or culturally sensitive the matter which is subjected to the discipline of harmonisation, the stronger the case for liberating diversity and local autonomy through preference for a model of minimum harmonisation. Contract law deserves appreciation from this perspective.

7.2. THE MARKET-MAKING VOCATION OF EU CONTRACT LAW AS STRUCTURAL BIAS

The contract law of the internal market is neither systematic nor carefully planned and this flows from the constitutional foundations which have been the abiding concern of this book. Most of the EU's preoccupation with contracts and contract law is driven by the Treaty commitments to promote an integrated trading space across the territory of all 28 Member States – the internal market defined by Article 26 TFEU to mean 'an area without internal frontiers in which the free movement of goods, persons, services and capital is ensured in accordance with the provisions of the Treaties'. Removing obstacles to trade between Member States, either by finding them incompatible with the free movement or competition rules examined in Chapter 2 or by subjecting them to the discipline of legislative harmonisation explained in Chapter 3 and examined in detail in Chapter 4, promotes a more competitive market within which choice is maximised and in which, in short, contractual autonomy is enhanced. The Commission has frequently promoted its vision of the 'confident' or 'empowered' consumer who is enabled to take full advantage of the opportunities on offer as a result of the widening of the market in which he or she is able to choose from whom and from where to buy goods and services. The Commission's EU Consumer Policy Strategy 2007–2013, entitled 'Empowering consumers, enhancing their welfare, effectively protecting them', carries in Commissioner Kuneva's foreword the bugle call that '[c]onfident, informed and empowered consumers are the motor of economic evolution.'[3] The 2012 document entitled 'A European Consumer Agenda – Boosting confidence and growth' urges that 'empowered and confident consumers can drive forward the European economy' and 'can actively participate in the market and make it work for them by exercising their power of choice and by having their rights properly enforced'.[4]

This is asking a lot of the intrepid consumer. One of the most powerfully critical strains of analysis aimed at the EU as a project accuses it of structural bias in the building of its internal market. The core of this holds that the deregulatory

[3] COM (2007) 99, 13 March 2007; also at p. 5.
[4] COM (2012) 225, 22 May 2012, p. 1.

energy and vigour of EU internal market law outstrips that of the re-regulatory dynamic conferred by the Treaty. This complaint has three dimensions. First, it is a question of the scope of the rules: the free movement and competition rules have a much wider material scope than the more narrowly drawn legislative competences. Second it is a question of the nature of the rules: the free movement and competition rules require little elaboration beyond the Treaty, whereas the legislative competences require political support and legislative amplification which, even where the competence exists, may not be forthcoming. Third, it is a question of the enforcement of the rules: free movement and competition law are readily enforced not only by the Commission but also by private parties able to rely on their direct effect in proceedings before national courts, whereas by contrast legislative rules tend much less readily to create directly effective rights, particular where they promote the public interest in regulation generally rather than creating subjective rights for individuals. Moreover, where Directives are involved, their enforceability against private parties collides with the refusal of the Court to accept the horizontal direct effect of Directives.[5] The net result is to accuse the EU of a structural bias in favour of deregulation.

Some of this is true, but desirable. Chapter 2 has shown that many rules washed away by the deregulatory tide of free movement law had no defensible purpose. *Cassis de Dijon* is a high-profile ruling not only because it allowed the Court to develop a formula according to which to judge the permissibility of national technical standards that close off national product and service markets, but also because of its importance in exposing how in some circumstances the appeal to national autonomy is simply a cover for protectionism or, at best, retention of anachronistic rules that have no useful place in an integrating EU market.[6] Heaps of other narrowly detailed technical standards have been removed when exposed to the bonfire of red tape ignited by EU free movement, as explained in Chapter 2.5. The result is choice – a wider zone of contractual autonomy within the internal market – and what is lost is simply the accumulated deadwood of ancient regulatory history. In these instances it is no point of criticism to label the law of the internal market as 'deregulatory'.

Some of the criticism of the EU's structural deregulatory bias has force, but tends to neglect the room left to justify obstructions to free movement and to protect services of general economic interest from the breath of competition law. As explained in Chapter 2.5 and 2.7 the Court is actively receptive to sincere justification of rules that target particular problems – for consumers, for the environment, in sport, for rights of political protest and protection of

5 Case C-91/92, *Dori v Recreb* [1994] ECR I-3325; Case C-192/94, *El Corte Inglés v Cristina Blasquez Rivero* [1996] ECR I-1281; Case C-80/06, *Carp Snc v Ecorad* [2007] ECR I-4473; Case C-555/07, *Kücükdeveci* [2010] ECR I-365; Case C-508/14, *Česky telekomunikačni* judgment of 6 October 2015.

6 Case 120/78, *Rewe-Zentrale AG v Bundesmonopolverwaltung für Branntwein* [1979] ECR 649.

human dignity, and so on. Neither free movement nor competition law apply absolute prohibitions on national practices. So the internal market is and should be a site of diversity – mainly because of the scope allowed for justification and the sensitivity to local preference embedded in the margin of discretion or appreciation which the Court grants in landmark cases such as *Omega Spielhallen*.[7] Unquestionably the Court enjoys a hugely influential power to determine the shape of the internal market, which, in part because of the Treaty system but also because of its own interpretative choices, allows it to require the setting aside of national regulatory choices (the issue of the vertical distribution of competences) and sometimes in circumstances where its own rulings may not be displaced by political action at EU level (the issue of the horizontal distribution of powers), but the story of its adjudicative track record is far more complex and nuanced than relentless deregulation and disrespect for local social, moral and ethical choices that touch the market.[8]

But some of the lament is true and troubling. The allegation that the EU promotes deregulation which deprives its Member States of the competence to pursue socially progressive policies while failing to allow at EU level a sufficient possibility to adopt compensatory measures is a serious one. The work of Fritz Scharpf has been especially powerful and influential in this vein.[9] So, for example, in a recent inquiry Scharpf described a 'legitimate diversity' of socio-economic institutions and policies across the Member States, 'shaped by intense political conflicts and historical compromises'. They are, he demonstrated, highly politically contested and 'they need to be defended in public debates by governments facing the sanctions of political accountability'. But, he complained, EU law does not operate according to this model. Instead, he continued, 'the supremacy of European law allows for judicial interventions

---

7 Case C-36/02 [2004] ECR I-9609, Chapter 2.5.

8 Qualitative assessment certainly varies. Cf. e.g. D. Damjanovic, 'The EU Market Rules as Social Market Rules: Why the EU can be a social market economy' (2013) 50 *Common Market Law Review* 1685; J. Schwarze, 'Die Abwägung von Zielen der europäischen Integration und mitgliedstaatlichen Interessen in der Rechtsprechung des EuGH' [2013] *Europarecht* 253; F. De Witte, 'Sex, Drugs and EU Law: the Recognition of Moral and Ethical Diversity in EU Law' (2013) 50 *Common Market Law Review* 1545; O. Gerstenberg, The Justiciability of Socio-Economic Rights, European Solidarity and the Role of the Court of Justice of the EU' (2014) 33 *Yearbook of European Law* 245; N. NicShuibhne, 'Margins of appreciation: national values, fundamental rights and EC free movement law' (2009) 34 *European Law Review* 230; C. Semmelmann, 'The European Union's Economic Constitution under the Lisbon Treaty: soul-searching shifts the focus to procedure' (2010) 35 *European Law Review* 516; G. Davies, 'Democracy and Legitimacy in the Shadow of Purposive Competence' (2015) 21 *European Law Journal* 2; S. Weatherill, 'Economic Rights and Fundamental Rights' in S. De Vries, U. Bernitz and S. Weatherill (eds.), *The Protection of Fundamental Rights in the EU after Lisbon*, Hart Publishing, Oxford 2013.

9 See initially F. Scharpf, 'The Joint Decision Trap: Lessons from German Federalism and European Integration' (1988) 66 *Public Administration* 239; and subsequently in e.g. F. Scharpf, *Governing in Europe: Effective and Democratic?*, OUP, Oxford 1999.

that may short-circuit these political processes'.[10] There is unarguably something in this. For example, the Court, asked to review allocation of finite resources to health care in circumstances where a patient placed on a waiting list complained that refusal to authorise quicker treatment in another Member State violated the right to receive services guaranteed by EU law, observed that 'achievement of the fundamental freedoms guaranteed by the Treaty inevitably requires Member States to make some adjustments to their national systems of social security.'[11] This seems disdainfully insouciant to the risk of policy and budgetary implications for the provision of health care at national level which the Court cannot possibly foresee. The allegation is that the EU, and in particular its Court, is buoyed by its obsession with the economic project of completing the internal market and so becomes indifferent to, even contemptuous of, the particularities of the subject matter with which it comes into contact. EU free movement law puts national systems to the test, but, the criticism runs, the more sensitive the issues, the less likely that the test will be sufficiently sensitive to the breadth of issues affected. So, to recite a brief charge sheet, it undermines health care budgets,[12] it disturbs the specific character of sport,[13] it undermines initiatives to promote a healthy lifestyle[14] and, of especially fast-rising significance, it exposes national criminal law to claims based on mutual recognition of different traditions which deprive the State of one its most cherished and defining features, the monopoly on the use of force.[15] This road leads unerringly to the ruling in *Viking Line*, encountered in Chapter 2.5 and subjecting the actions of trade unions to free movement law exploited by migrant corporate entities according to an unsympathetically aggressive test of justification, as the most egregious example of how, in short, economic constitutionalism may imperil social constitutionalism.[16]

---

10 F. Scharpf, 'The asymmetry of European integration, or why the EU cannot be a social market economy' (2010) 8 *Socio-Economic Review* 211, 241.

11 Case C-385/99, *Müller-Fauré* 2003 ECR I-4509, para. 102; see also Case C-372/04, *ex parte Watts* [2006] ECR I-4325, para. 121.

12 Cf. C. Newdick, 'Citizenship, Free Movement and Health Care: Cementing Individual Rights by Corroding Social Solidarity' (2006) 43 *Common Market Law Review* 1645; J. Van de Gronden, E. Szyszczak, U. Neegaard and M. Krajewski (eds.), *Health Care and EU Law*, T.M.C. Asser Press, The Hague 2011.

13 See e.g. S. Weatherill, *European Sports Law: Collected Papers*, 2nd ed., T.M.C. Asser Press, The Hague 2014.

14 e.g. A. Alemanno and A. Garde, 'The Emergence of an EU Lifestyle Policy: The Case of Alcohol, Tobacco and Unhealthy Diets' (2013) 50 *Common Market Law Review* 1745.

15 e.g. V. Mitsilegas, *EU Criminal Law*, Hart Publishing, Oxford 2009; E. Herlin-Karnell, *The Constitutional Dimension of European Criminal Law*, Hart Publishing, Oxford 2012. Concerns of this nature are strongly expressed in the ruling of the *Bundesverfassungsgericht* which approved with caution the compatibility of Germany's ratification of the Lisbon Treaty with the *Grundgesetz*: 2 BvE 2/08, English version available at www.bverfg.de/e/es20090630_2bve000208en.html.

16 Case C-438/05 [2007] ECR I-10779. Cf. e.g. L. Azoulai, 'The Court of Justice and the Social Market Economy: the emergence of an ideal and the conditions for its realisation' (2008) 45

Some of these criticisms hold a great deal more water than others,[17] but all are important in revealing that there is a contested fault line where the beneficially deregulatory influence of EU law manifest in a case such as *Cassis de Dijon* is transformed into a potentially damaging suppression of local particularity. And, a further element of the critique, the EU is disabled from compensating for the subversion of national regulatory competence. In whole or in part, because of want of constitutional competence or because of absence of political consensus, the EU may simply not be able to act. Social policy is a good example. It has been explained in Chapters 2.9 and 4.10 that, aside from the equal pay rule embedded in (what is today) Article 157 TFEU, most matters concerning labour market regulation and social policy are unaffected by unconditional and precise rules set by primary EU law. Deepening of the EU's aspirations in the field depended on legislative amplification. This has occurred, and it is now framed by Title IV on Solidarity in the Charter of Fundamental Rights, but, as Chapter 4.10 shows, the *acquis* suffers from a relatively unsystematic and *ad hoc* manner of development. No Directive has the immediate transformative impact of a decision such as *Viking Line*, which at a stroke challenges attempts to construct and promote a 'European Social Model' from disparate legislative and other softer sources. There is in fact no crisper illustration of the relative vigour of free movement law in contrast to the EU's constrained legislative competence than *Viking Line*. Article 153(5) TFEU expressly excludes the right to strike from the legislative competence conferred by Article 153, but the Court ruled that this did not shield the trade unions from review in the name of free movement law. The reforms made by the Lisbon Treaty with effect from 2009 exhibit a high level of rhetorical flourish in their embrace of the values of a social dimension to EU law, in particular in Articles 2 and 3 TEU and the commitment to an (undefined) social market economy, and yet the failure to add any corresponding extended legislative competences suggests a careful rejection of concrete change. Dagmar Schiek has attempted nevertheless to find an EU constitution of social governance which will narrow, or even close, the gap between market liberalisation and the commitment to social integration.[18] This is bold and brilliant, but, as she fully recognises, it is a task made arduous by the Treaties' evasiveness.

Common Market Law Review 1335; C. Joerges and F. Rödl, 'Informal Politics, Formalised Law and the "Social Deficit" of European Integration: Reflections after the Judgments of the ECJ in *Viking* and *Laval*' (2009) 15 *European Law Journal* 1; D. Ashiagbor, 'Unravelling the Liberal Bargain: Labour and Social Welfare Law in the Context of EU market Integration' (2013) 19 *European Law Journal* 303; also D. Schiek, U. Liebert and H. Schneider (eds.), *European Economic and Social Constiutionalism after the Treaty of Lisbon*, CUP, Cambridge 2011.

17 e.g. S. Weatherill, *European Sports Law*, 2nd ed., T.M.C. Asser Press, The Hague 2014 is largely devoted to denying that EU law, and most of all the Court, is insensitive to the special features of sport.

18 D. Schiek, 'The EU Constitution of Social Governance in an Economic Crisis: In Defence of a Transnational Dimension to Social Europe' (2013) 20 *Maastricht Journal* 185.

Examination of the contract law of the internal market raises at least a suggestion of an intriguingly different story. Scharpf's work sought to focus on sectors 'where European solutions were ruled out by the heterogeneity and political salience of national interests and preferences while national solutions were impeded by the legal and economic constraints of European integration', and he picked out 'taxation of mobile capital and businesses, macro-economic employment policy, industrial relations and social policy'.[19] As Chapter 2 has explained, contracts and contract law narrowly understood are imperfectly but largely sheltered from review in the name of free movement law. They will not often affect inter-State trade and there are limits to the personal scope of the rules. So, following Scharpf, national solutions are not much 'impeded by the legal and economic constraints of European integration'. Broader rules of regulatory contract law are admittedly subjected to the disciplining effect of free movement but the Court is not insensitive to the need to offer room to justify legitimate social and political choices. The awkward cases, *Viking Line* most of all, in which the Court has arguably stretched the deregulatory infection of internal market law beyond its proper reach are not within the sphere of regulatory contract law. And, as Chapter 4 in particular shows, far from the EU presenting a picture of a deregulated or at least hard-to-regulate landscape, in fact there is a remarkably dense network of accumulated rules, many of which are dedicated to socially motivated regulation. So, again drawing on Scharpf, it seems European solutions are *not* 'ruled out by the heterogeneity and political salience of national interests and preferences'. The growth of the internal market generally shows how a programme which is presented as an exercise in securing market freedom inevitably involves a sustained commitment to rule-making.[20] In contract law that commitment has acquired deep roots. Themes such as protection of weaker parties abound. It is a story of multi-level rule-making, intersection and overlap.[21] It is not about building an internal market which is divorced from (re)regulatory choices. It is, as explored at length and in detail in Chapter 4, a process of instituting 'regulated autonomy' in the EU's internal market.[22]

---

19 F. Scharpf, 'The Joint Decision Trap Revisited' (2006) 44 *Journal of Common Market Studies* 845, 855–856.

20 Cf. e.g. M. Egan, *Constructing a European Market*, OUP, Oxford 2001.

21 See in particular L. Miller, *The Emergence of EU Contract Law: Exploring Europeanization*, OUP, Oxford 2011, especially Chs. 5, 6 and 7; J. Smits, 'Plurality of Sources in European Private Law, or: How to Live with Legal Diversity' in R. Brownsword, H. Micklitz, L. Niglia and S. Weatherill (eds.), *The Foundations of European Private Law*, Hart Publishing, Oxford 2011, Ch. 19, pp. 323–335.

22 G. Comparato and H. Micklitz, 'Regulated Autonomy between Market Freedoms and Fundamental Rights in the Case Law of the CJEU' in U. Bernitz, X. Groussot and F. Schulyok (eds.), *General Principles of EU Law and European Private Law*, Wolters Kluwer, Alphen aan den Rijn 2013, Ch. 4, pp. 121–154.

There is, then, a case for identifying a distinct strain to the inquiry in the field of contract and contract law from that traced by Scharpf as the sore point of European integration. The EU has achieved rather a lot in regulating contracts and contract law. But in fact the prevailing normative assessments are as unsystematic as the *acquis* itself. The judgement of the EU's influence on contract law is instructively varied. It has been attacked from both sides: as insensitive to the values of social justice that have animated the development of aspects of national contract law (section 7.3) and as insensitive to the virtues of personal autonomy and contractual freedom (section 7.4). Both sets of critics perceive the EU as force for transformation within national contract law (section 7.5) but they offer very different assessments of the consequences of those transformations.

7.3. THE EU'S INSENSITIVITY TO SOCIAL JUSTICE...

That contract law in the EU is in the main constitutionally driven by the pursuit of the internal market has generated the accusation that the EU *diminishes* a proper understanding of the place of contract law and strips away from national law its coherence and integrity.[23] This criticism is aimed not only at matters that are within the range of consequences intended by the EU rule but also at ripples that are unforeseen, including in areas that lie beyond the formal reach of the EU measure.[24] The most aggrieved strain of criticism focuses on the tendency of EU law, instrumentally driven by its concern for market-making, to weaken national contract law's social distributional concerns and, wider, the concern for justice which is neither tethered to nor limited by the concern to build a market.[25] The

23 The literature is vast and rich: the sources cited in this and the footnotes that follow are therefore simply examples of the range of distinct voices that are shaping this debate. See e.g. M. Hesselink, *The New European Legal Culture*, Kluwer, Deventer 2001; W.-H. Roth, 'Transposing Pointillist EC Guidelines into Systematic National Codes – Problems and Consequences' (2002) 10 *European Review of Private Law* 761; T. Wilhelmsson, E. Paunio and A. Pohjolainen (eds.), *Private Law and the Many Cultures of Europe*, Kluwer, Leiden 2007; L. Niglia, *The Struggle for European Private Law: A Critique of Codification*, Hart Publishing, Oxford 2015; R. Michaels, 'Of Islands and the Ocean: The Two Rationalities of European Private Law' in R. Brownsword, H. Micklitz, L. Niglia and S. Weatherill (eds.), *The Foundations of European Private Law*, Hart Publishing, Oxford 2011, Ch. 8, pp. 139–158.

24 Particularly influential in this vein is G. Teubner, 'Legal Irritants: Good Faith in British Law' (1998) 61 *Modern Law Review* 12; see also M.B.M. Loos, 'The Influence of European Consumer Law on General Contract Law and the Need for Spontaneous Harmonization' (2007) 15 *European Review of Private Law* 515.

25 e.g. Study Group on Social Justice in European Private Law, 'Social Justice in European Contract Law: a Manifesto' (2004) 10 *European Law Journal* 653; C. Schmid, 'The Instrumentalist Conception of the Acquis Communautaire in Consumer Law and its Implications on a European Contract Law Code' (2005) 1 *European Contract Law Review* 211; M. Hesselink, 'European Contract Law: a Matter of Consumer Protection, Citizenship,

influential Manifesto for Social Justice endorsed by a group of eminent jurists expressed the fear that '[t]he values and concepts of European law that are now replacing aspects of national private law tend to embrace a narrow conception of the principles of social justice applicable to a market order'.[26] Hans Micklitz fears that an emphasis on consumer law as a process of generating more competitive markets has erased the ambitions of consumer *protection* law. He expresses alarm about an EU which 'aggressively favours a consumer right which neglects the protection of the weaker market actor'.[27] Some consumers are doubtless empowered and made confident in and by the internal market (section 7.2), but many will not be.

It is a process, according to related anxieties, that is impervious to cultural particularity,[28] and it prejudices the cultural power of the nationalist (State-building) claim to private law.[29] Within this there is voiced warning of the peril of uncritically superficial excavation of 'common rules'.[30] National legal orders will resist harmonisation that pretends to converge on the exact same end point.[31]

These several lines of criticisms have their distinct points of emphasis but all share scepticism about the legitimacy of the EU's pretensions in advancing its contract law programme under a largely technocratic market-driven cover. It is the infection of the internal market bias – which leads to an *acquis* that is 'patchy, inconsistent, opaque and often poorly justified' – that prompted Hugh Collins to propose a European Civil Code that would comprise principles, not rules.[32] It would provide a common framework for the *development* of a European private law, not an imposition from the start, and it would help to promote a European civil society that would not be focused on the market alone.

---

or Justice?' (2007) 15 *European Review of Private Law* 323; M. Hesselink, 'Democratic Contract Law' (2015) 11 *European Review of Contract Law* 81; B. Lurger, 'Old and New Insights for the Protection of Consumers in European Private Law in the Wake of the Global Economic Crisis' in R. Brownsword, H. Micklitz, L. Niglia and S. Weatherill (eds.), *The Foundations of European Private Law*, Hart Publishing, Oxford 2011, Ch. 6, pp. 89–114; H. Micklitz, 'Do Consumers and Businesses Need a New Architecture of Consumer Law? A Thought Provoking Impulse' (2013) 32 *Yearbook of European Law* 266.

26 Study Group on Social Justice in European Private Law, 'Social Justice in European Contract Law: a Manifesto' (2004) 10 *European Law Journal* 653, 666–667.

27 H.-W. Micklitz, 'The expulsion of the concept of protection from the consumer law and the return of social elements in the civil law: a bittersweet polemic' (2012) 35 *Journal of Consumer Policy* 283, 285.

28 e.g. S. Sánchez Lorenzo, 'What do we mean when we say "Folklore"? Cultural and Axiological Diversities as a Limit for a European Private Law' (2006) 14 *European Review of Private Law* 197.

29 G. Comparato, *Nationalism and Private Law in Europe*, Hart Publishing, Oxford 2014.

30 L. Niglia, 'Beyond Enchantment – The Possibility of a New European Private Law' (2009) 28 *Yearbook of European Law* 61.

31 P. Legrand, 'European Legal Systems are not Converging' (1996) 45 *International and Comparative Law Quarterly* 52.

32 H. Collins, *The European Civil Code: The Way Forward*, CUP, Cambridge 2008, p. 62.

Whatever force these accusations possess is enhanced where the EU pursues maximum harmonisation. As shown in Chapter 6, this is far more disruptive of national diversity, including in use of contract law as an arena of social distributional concern, than is minimum harmonisation undertaken by the EU. Martijn Hesselink has described the abandonment of minimum rule-making as 'a totalitarian aspiration'.[33] The Study Group claimed that the 'harmonisation of law at European level involves both the demolition of national legal systems and the construction of a new legal order', which is no exaggeration if a maximum model were allowed to prevail.[34] It would 'serve the interests of business exclusively by pursuing uniform rules for the single market and excluding local measures, supported by democratic processes, which tend to give superior protection to those vulnerable to exploitation in the marketplace.'[35] The EU's legitimacy is strained still further where it purports not only to act as a contract lawmaker but to do so on an exclusive basis.

These types of anxieties should be understood as part of a wider unease about the 'marketising' effect of internal market law which connects to Scharpf and Schiek, mentioned above.[36] The EU promotes market integration but in doing so it both weakens State capacity to regulate markets and also it lacks the constitutional and material resources to act in its own right as a comprehensive and systematic regulator. This model of the EU has been described as a 'constitutionalized market-state, where the rapid forces of globalized trade meet the nation-state's heritage'.[37] The fear that market freedom becomes a constitutionalised value that elevates autonomy and a formal notion of freedom of contract above market regulation finds its sharpest expression in *Viking Line*[38] and *Alemo-Herron*.[39]

7.4. ... AND THE EU'S INSENSITIVITY TO PERSONAL AUTONOMY

But the EU is also attacked from the other direction – that it is too interventionist, that it shows inadequate respect for freedom of contract and for autonomy.

---

33 M. Hesselink, 'European Contract Law: a Matter of Consumer Protection, Citizenship, or Justice?' (2007) 15 *European Review of Private Law* 323, 331.

34 Study Group on Social Justice in European Private Law, 'Social Justice in European Contract Law: a Manifesto' (2004) 10 *European Law Journal* 653, 656.

35 Page 661.

36 Above nn. 18 and 19.

37 A. Afilalo, D. Patterson and K. Purnhagen, 'Statecraft, the Market State and the Development of European Legal Culture' in G. Helleringer and K. Purnhagen (eds.), *Towards a European Legal Culture*, Hart Publishing, Oxford 2014, pp. 277–302, at p. 299. See also M. Höpner and A. Schäfer, 'Embeddedness and Regional Integration: Waiting for Polanyi in a Hayekian Setting' (2012) 66 *International Organization* 429.

38 Case C-438/05 [2007] ECR I-10779.

39 Case C-426/11 judgment of 18 July 2013. See Chapter 4.10.3, 6.4.

Carsten Herresthal has complained bitterly that the EU legal order is structurally deficient in its protection of freedom of contract.[40] He finds 'a large set of rules included in EU law which interferes heavily with freedom of contract and the corresponding principle of personal autonomy'.[41] His claim that this disrespect for freedom of contract contradicts 'the economic foundations of the process of European integration'[42] is not supported by the process's constitutionalised foundation, as he is forced to admit subsequently in the same paper, as he confesses to the fragmented support for his claim to be found within the Treaties. He then moves to a lament for the absence of better and firmer protection for freedom of contract, *inter alia* criticising the harmonised contract law *acquis* as a site for the promotion of social justice at the expense of contractual and personal freedom. EU law, he finds, is too interventionist. To find a completely opposite normative perspective from that entertained by authors such as Hesselink and Collins is no surprise at all: it is simply to catch sight of the richly political debate about the function of private law in modern society. It is the completely opposite *descriptive* reading of the same legal material which is really intriguing.

Jürgen Basedow concedes that freedom of contract does not find explicit mention in EU primary law, but finds it safeguarded, albeit with limitations, by, in particular, free movement law, competition law and aspects of the Charter.[43] He is critical of the *acquis* on consumer contract law for its incoherence and absence of general principles, but although he combines this with a degree of more substantive criticism of its level of interference with freedom of contract, he carefully and in a balanced manner compares this with similar trends at national level. It is not the EU alone that is taking this path. The particular target for his venom is the attack on private autonomy which flows from the Directives forbidding discrimination on defined grounds[44] and in this vein he fears the rise of the Charter as a constraint of freedom to choose a contracting partner.[45]

Such perspectives would be fearful of rulings such as *Sky Österreich*, *Deutsches Weintor* and *McDonough v Ryanair* as instances of administrative intervention into contractual autonomy left untouched by a Court inattentive to the values of autonomy and commercial freedom.[46] Stefan Grundmann has expressed concern that regulatory intervention to protect a group of identifiably

40 C. Herresthal, 'Constitutionalisation of Freedom of Contract in European Private Law' in K. Ziegler and P. Huber (eds.), *Current Problems in the Protection of Human Rights*, Hart Publishing, Oxford 2013, Ch. 6, pp. 89–116.

41 Page 91.

42 Page 91.

43 J. Basedow, 'Freedom of Contract in the European Union' (2008) 16 *European Review of Private Law* 901, esp. 907–909.

44 Chapters 2.10, 3.16, especially Directives 2000/43, 2000/78 and 2004/113.

45 J. Basedow, 'Freedom of Contract in the European Union' (2008) 16 *European Review of Private Law* 901, esp. 919–921.

46 Case C-283/11 judgment of 22 January 2013; Case C-544/10 judgment of 6 September 2012; Case C-12/11 judgment of 31 January 2013. See Chapters 3.15, 4.6.3, 4.10.3.

vulnerable consumers may impose unappreciated costs on other groups of consumers.[47] Matthias Storme is considerably more savage. He criticises the EU's rules forbidding discrimination on the basis that they entitle a defined protected group of people to command certain categories of persons to enter into contracts with them, even in circumstances where there is no hint that the supplier has monopoly power. So the law decides whether choosing not to enter into a contract is unequal treatment or prohibited discrimination. And it may push those unwilling to be bound in this way to withdraw from the market, thereby reducing choice. So Storme concludes with a flourish: 'all prohibitions against discrimination by citizens without a monopoly have to be abolished'.[48]

7.5. THE TRANSFORMATIVE INFLUENCE OF THE EU ON CONTRACT LAW

So the EU is attacked for not being sensitive enough to the wider concerns of contract law beyond the market and it is also attacked for not being sensitive enough to the virtue of autonomy in the market. It would be trite indulgence to suggest that the EU is steering a savvy middle way. A subtler approach is to note that both accounts could be true: one might be frustrated by the complacent emphasis on information disclosure while inspired by the anti-discrimination *acquis*, or vice versa. But it is plain that it is not a neutral process. And when the Commission pretends it is, it runs into political trouble. This is why the story of the Consumer Rights Directive (2011/83) and the Services Directive (2006/123), told in Chapter 6.6, is so significant. It provides ample evidence that the pursuit of 'coherence' cannot be compressed into an apolitical and blandly technical packaging.[49] Quite right too! 'In many respects what happens to the law of contract will be a defining moment in the history of Europe'.[50] This *has* to be a process of addressing a contract law of the internal market which is not limited to the narrow pursuit of economic gain within the internal market.

My principal concern in writing this book is to expose the constitutional character of the contract law of the internal market, rather than to adopt an explicitly normative perspective on the matter. I do, however, believe that

[47] e.g. S. Grundmann, 'Targeted Consumer Protection' in D. Leczykiewicz and S. Weatherill (eds.), *The Images of the Consumer in EU Law*, Bloomsbury/Hart/IECL, Oxford 2016, Ch. 9, pp. 223–244.

[48] M. Storme, 'Freedom of Contract: Mandatory and Non-Mandatory Rules in European Contract Law' (2007) 15 *European Review of Private Law* 233, 250.

[49] Cf. T. Wilhelmsson, 'The Contract Law Acquis: Towards More Coherence through Generalisation' in *Proceedings of the 4th European Jurists' Forum*, Manzsche Verlag, Vienna 2008, pp. 111–154.

[50] Study Group on Social Justice in European Private Law, 'Social Justice in European Contract Law: a Manifesto' (2004) 10 *European Law Journal* 653, 653.

the EU promotes private autonomy by tackling substantive inequalities. In particular the protection of the weaker party has through legislative act and judicial interpretation become a principle of EU law.[51] Promoting a right of self-determination in the market demands not acquiescence in unregulated freedom of contact, which will deprive the weaker party of any true freedom, but rather a strong regulatory intervention into the way contracts are made and the terms on which they shall be enforced precisely in order to give a genuine substantive content to the freedom of weaker contracting parties. Broader still, where EU law reaches beyond the internal market as its motivation in touching contractual autonomy, anti-discrimination norms serve as a means to promote the freedom of the disadvantaged party.

Where the critics of the contract law of the internal market can join together, whether they treat it as damaging to social justice or antithetical to private autonomy, is in understanding it as a transformative force within national legal orders. The EU is a factor in the process that has long existed at national level whereby private autonomy is subjected to administrative regulation and in consequence cherished patterns within national legal orders are broken open. The *acquis* is characterised by a high level of fragmentation: each regulated sector has its own story to tell.[52] Albeit in an unsystematic way, the *acquis* erodes the coherence of categories kept separate under national law. The divide between public law and private law is well recognised in Europe: it carries implications at the abstract level associated with the legitimacy of the exercise of State power, on the one hand, and the value attached to private autonomy on the other, as well as more practical consequences associated with applicable procedures and competent courts. It has no *single* function or understanding in the several legal jurisdictions to be found across Europe, but versions of it are readily visible. Even EU law has its own glimpses of it: the rejection of the horizontal direct effect of Directives,[53] the refusal to allow the horizontal application of some but not all of the Treaty provisions on free movement[54] and the 'State' element to the State aid rules[55] are all moments when EU law makes a separation which is loosely of this type. An increasing number of influences challenge the vitality of the separation between public law and private law, and the field of contract law is a vivid example. The perception that parties need protection when contracting with more powerful partners has driven a wave of intervention, in areas such as consumer contracting, the employment relationship and rental of property. This is sometimes treated as paternalism: a more sophisticated understanding regards

51 See especially N. Reich, *General Principles of EU Civil Law*, Intersentia, Cambridge 2014, Ch. 2.
52 See especially H. Micklitz, 'The Consumer: Marketised, Fragmentised, Constiutionalised' in D. Leczykiewicz and S. Weatherill (eds.), *The Images of the Consumer in EU Law*, Bloomsbury/Hart/IECL, Oxford 2016, Ch. 2, pp. 21–41.
53 Case C-91/92 and other cases cited above n. 5.
54 See Chapter 2.3.
55 See Chapter 2.7.

it as a response to the absence of true contractual freedom in circumstances of economic asymmetry and so in fact intervention is a means to promote true expression of autonomy, not to confine it. So regulation has come to contract law. The erosion of the divide has prompted discourse such as 'regulating contracts',[56] 'the regulatory function of private law'[57] and 'private administrative law'.[58] Hans Micklitz has reached back to the work of Otto von Gierke in the late nineteenth century to show that this is a re-awakening of an old debate, but what is really new today is the scale and breadth of regulatory contract law, sweeping across much of the economy and operating in combination at both State and EU levels to open up markets and also to regulate them.[59] Several distinct phenomena are involved. There are processes of controlling private autonomy by resort to public law and of using private law to perform what might have been thought to be functions of public law. Such trends towards socially motivated regulation designed to protect particular categories of potentially disadvantaged or vulnerable groups at national level are important in provoking differentiation within the generalised patterns of private law, and they tear at the supposed divide between private and public law. In origin they certainly pre-date the EU, but the EU is a further transformative influence and, moreover, one which precludes unilateral reduction in protection at national level.[60]

EU law's tendency to attend to, but ultimately to disrespect, the division between contract law narrowly understood and the wider pattern of framing regulatory contract law is a concrete example of its functionally-driven disrupting effect. This, of course, does not mean that such trends are a good or a bad thing: it depends on where one stands in the debate about the virtue of a general contract law and in particular the interventionist trend that has caused adjustment at national level where particularly disadvantaged groups are concerned. This re-animates the debate mentioned above between those who regard the EU as a deregulatory threat and those who treat its intervention with

---

56 H. Collins, *Regulating Contracts*, OUP, Oxford 1999; and in an EU vein, H. Collins, *The European Civil Code: The Way Forward*, CUP, Cambridge 2008, esp. Ch. 4; H. Collins, 'The Hybrid Quality of European Private Law' in R. Brownsword, H. Micklitz, L. Niglia and S. Weatherill (eds.), *The Foundations of European Private Law*, Hart Publishing, Oxford 2011, Ch. 28, pp. 453–463.

57 F. Cafaggi and H. Muir-Watt (eds.), *The Regulatory Function of European Private Law*, Edward Elgar, Cheltenham 2009.

58 H. Micklitz, 'Rethinking the public/private divide' in M. Maduro, K. Tuori and S. Sankari (eds.), *Transnational Law: Rethinking European Law and Legal Thinking*, CUP, Cambridge 2014, Ch. 10, pp. 271–306.

59 e.g. H. Micklitz, 'The EU as a Federal Order of Competences and the Private Law' in L. Azoulai (ed.), *The Question of Competence in the European Union*, OUP, Oxford 2014, Ch. 6, pp. 125–153, at pp. 131–132; also H.-W. Micklitz, 'The expulsion of the concept of protection from the consumer law and the return of social elements in the civil law: a bittersweet polemic' (2012) 35 *Journal of Consumer Policy* 283. One could go back another century to Adam Smith for primordial scepticism about wholly unregulated markets.

60 For a helpful survey see L. Miller, *The Emergence of EU Contract Law: Exploring Europeanization*, OUP, Oxford 2011, Ch. 1.

disdain as an assault on autonomy. For EU law, the point is that its emphasis on the functional imperative of creating an internal market means its sight is not aimed at the character of a rule but rather its effect. It commonly blurs public/private divides without even drawing attention to this, because of its functional vocation of market-making. This market-making focus generates a form of 'hybrid regulation' which is unconcerned with respecting orthodox categories under national law.[61]

The contract law of the internal market therefore reveals itself as a political project reflected in legal rules that are based on constitutional underpinnings. Most of all, the threshold for invocation for Article 114 TFEU as a basis for legislative harmonisation affecting contracts and contract law is low and, once crossed, there is ample scope for choices to be made about the preferred model and intensity of (re-)regulation. The constitutional character of the contract law of the internal market is in this sense in principle limited and instrumental, but in its practical application it is broad and flexible, in consequence of the generously empowering scope of the internal market as a legal concept. Dependent for its substance on elaboration by the judicial and legislative institutions of the EU, it is a great deal more sophisticated than a project of deregulation alone. Put another way, the EU reaches contracts and contract law primarily because of their effects on the internal market, but its treatment of them is not confined to narrowly economic motivations. Contractual autonomy is regulated in the internal market.

---

61 H. Collins, 'The Hybrid Quality of European Private Law' in R. Brownsword, H. Micklitz, L. Niglia and S. Weatherill (eds.), *The Foundations of European Private Law*, Hart Publishing, Oxford 2011, p. 463.

INDEX